THE LAST WITCH
OF LANGENBURG

Langenberg.

THE LAST WITCH OF LANGENBURG

Murder in a German Village

Thomas Robisheaux

W. W. Norton & Company
New York London

Frontispiece: Illustration from Martin Ziller and Mathaeus Merian,
*Topographia Germaniae,*Vol. 8, *Franken* (Frankfurt A.M., 1656).
W. B. Yeats's "Lines Written in Dejection" is quoted with permission
of A P Watt Ltd. on behalf of Gráinne Yeats.

For information about permission to reproduce selections from this book,
write to Permissions, W. W. Norton & Company, Inc.,
500 Fifth Avenue, New York, NY 10110

For information about special discounts for bulk purchases, please contact
W. W. Norton Special Sales at specialsales@wwnorton.com or 800-233-4830

Manufacturing by Courier Westford
Book design by JAM Design
Production manager: Anna Oler

Library of Congress Cataloging-in-Publication Data

Robisheaux, Thomas Willard.
The last witch of Langenburg : murder in a German village / Thomas Robisheaux. —
1st ed.
p. cm.
Includes bibliographical references and index.
ISBN 978-0-393-06551-0 (hardcover)
1. Witchcraft—Germany—Langenburg—History. 2. Murder—Germany—Langenburg—
History. I. Title.
BF1583.R63 2009
133.10943'471—dc22   2008043052

W. W. Norton & Company, Inc.
500 Fifth Avenue, New York, N.Y. 10110
www.wwnorton.com
W. W. Norton & Company Ltd.
Castle House, 75/76 Wells Street, London W1T 3QT

1 2 3 4 5 6 7 8 9 0

For Léa Pierre Angélique,

my Luxembourgish rose

How much can we ever know about the love and pain in another's heart? How much can we hope to understand those who have suffered deeper anguish, greater deprivation, and more crushing disappointments than we ourselves have known? Even if the world's rich and powerful were to put themselves in the shoes of the rest, how much would they really understand the wretched millions suffering around them?

ORHAN PAMUK,
Snow

When have I last looked on
The round green eyes and the long wavering bodies
Of the dark leopards of the moon?
All the wild witches, those most noble ladies,
For all their broom-sticks and their tears,
Their angry tears, are gone.
The holy centaurs of the hills are vanished . . . .

W. B. YEATS,
Lines Written in Dejection

These days
the names of the dead
cast long shadows across our memories,
and the silence
of a lonely God
can be heard in the whispering of the wind.

GOTTLOB HAAG,
Liegt ein Dorf in Hohenlohe

Contents

Contents

Preface

first heard about the "witch of Hürden" in the summer of 1994. On a trip through the Hohenlohe region of Germany, my wife and I stopped at an old mill in that village, near the town of Langenburg. While we were looking at the building, a voice called out from across the street: "A witch used to live there!" After the current owner of the mill told us about the miller's wife who once lived there, she urged us to talk with the pastor's widow, who could tell us more. Later that afternoon, walking through a little gate and into her blooming cottage garden, Frau Ingaruth Schlauch of Bächlingen welcomed us to the parsonage, and, over cake and local cookies called *Wibele*, told us about how she had discovered the witch's story in the old parish register. She had been so taken by the account that she had written a play based on it. Urging me to read the account for myself, she then told us about other stories inspired by the witch of Hürden. Later that afternoon, as I looked out from the town walls of Langenburg toward Hürden, I wondered about the miller's wife whose life inspired stories three centuries after her death.

When I first read the records of her trial in 1672 for poisoning and witchcraft—in the castle archives in Neuenstein—I could scarcely believe the story. Those documents gave the miller's wife a name—Anna Elisabeth Schmieg—and an astonishingly detailed glimpse into the life of an ordinary woman that became the pivot of the last witch trials in the region. Anna Schmieg? Who was she? How had this everyday woman fashioned her life in such difficult times? Why was she suspected of witchcraft?

The story of the Langenburg witches—ten people accused of witchcraft between 1668 and 1672—had never been told before, let alone that of Schmieg's own trial. Knowing the records of the witch trials and the historical literature about witchcraft, I recognized that those on her and her trial were more vivid and voluminous than any I knew. When I then discovered that her daughter, Eva, husband, Hans, and son, Michel, had also been tried on suspicion of witchcraft and that their dossiers were as detailed as hers, I realized that Anna's story opened up a view onto a village world far richer and more complex than I had ever expected to discover. Here the personal and communal relationships that bred suspicions of witchcraft could be explored in a way rarely possible.

At first I envisioned a short book about Anna Schmieg, her family and village, and her trial. When I then discovered two eminent men of affairs associated with Anna's story, I realized that that story reached far beyond her home village and involved a historical drama larger and more complex than I had suspected. The first name piqued my curiosity: Moritz Hofmann, a highly regarded and innovative physician and anatomist. The second stunned me: Johann Wolfgang Textor, a prestigious jurist, an early proponent of natural-law theory, and grandfather of Germany's national poet, Johann Wolfgang von Goethe. Why would such prominent men become involved in a witch trial in Hürden? Answering that question took me to new archives and libraries and added several more years of research.

What seemed at first to have been events on a small village stage revealed themselves as scenes in a Baroque drama, complete with larger-than-life characters, tragic fates, unexpected interventions, family secrets and secret identities, violent passions, and life-shattering revelations. Anna's story changed completely. Her fate, I learned, was intimately connected to the world of the universities: fierce debates about evidence and proof, controversies about poisoning and the emerging science of forensic medicine, and arguments over the nature of politics, religion, and the state. Understanding how and why Anna's case touched raw nerves about so many issues turned upside down my understandings about witches and ordinary people, learned jurists, physicians, and rulers in early modern society.

At the same time, the way in which I imagined telling Anna Schmieg's tale changed as well. Seeking a fresh perspective, I decided to approach the material through microhistory, a method that explores events on the small scale in which people experience everyday life. While the technique has its limits, it afforded me the opportunity to approach certain problems about witchcraft—and the late witch trials in particular—that have proved elusive to understanding. In particular, I wanted to use the narrative potential in microhistory to explore the multiple layers of experience and meaning important to understanding witchcraft.

On its surface the story I have written might seem like a modern-day detective story. But it more closely resembles a "social drama," anthropologist Victor Turner's notion of the "spontaneous social process" that a small society undergoes when a crisis suddenly breaks out. This idea, it seemed to me, offered the potential to explore the social and political dynamics that were at work in Anna Schmieg's society. Later, still deeper layers of meaning were revealed when I took into account the nature of village gossip, the way that the inquisition and the law shaped experience, and how certain religious sensibilities at the time enabled contemporaries to see in the events a cosmic drama that we cannot today.

While we cannot share the experience that is the subject of this history, it is my hope that I can help general readers and specialists better understand a society and culture that took witchcraft as a given. Since this book also addresses general readers, I have placed my references to scholarly and technical issues in the endnotes. While this decision might remove from view the craft that informs this historical account, the results should not be mistaken for a work of fiction. Where I have found it necessary to bridge gaps of understanding, I let the reader know.

I believe that the meaning and experience of witchcraft is best understood at the level where real life was lived. Abstractions based on the fine regional studies already written have taken the understanding of witchcraft only so far. If readers wonder whether this account shows them something that is "typical" regarding witchcraft, they should know that the meaning of witchcraft lies in its atypicality. If general readers and specialists can set aside some comfortable assumptions and explanations and take from it a better understanding of witches and witchcraft, then I will have succeeded.

For myself, I realized that for Anna Schmieg's contemporaries the experience and meaning of witchcraft was tied up in stories. Even the jurists, men known to think in the abstract terms of the law, were driven to come to terms with the events through narratives. Physicians also couched their explanations of the case in the form of medical stories.

One afternoon ten years ago I asked a seemingly simple question: what professors reviewed and ruled on Anna Schmieg's case? In seeking the answer to that question I began to pull back the curtain on a drama with a much larger cast of actors than I had at first imagined. Instead of pushing these figures, most of them unknown to me at the time, to the wings, I decided to track them down and find out what I could about them. Their accounts not only transformed the way that I understood the life and fate of Anna Schmieg; they also changed the way that I understand my craft as a historian. The tragic parts of Anna Schmieg's story would haunt my imagination for ten more years. The time has come to let these specters have their say, and free me from the burden of their tales.

———

I DOUBT THAT I can fairly acknowledge the debts, scholarly and personal, to all who have had a hand in helping me write Anna Schmieg's tale. I started this work with the generous support of an Alexander von Humboldt Fellowship and have benefited at many turns from their legendary support for scientific and humanistic projects that span the Atlantic. Only now, many years later, do I feel that I understand the spirit of that enterprise carried out in Humboldt's name and embodied in scholars like Winfried Schulze, my own Humboldt sponsor and mentor. To the German Academic Exchange Service, I owe a debt of gratitude for short-term research support with which I learned the scholarly pleasures of the Herzog August Bibliothek in Wolfenbüttel. Through the years I also benefited from the steady support of Duke University, especially William Chafe and Karla Holloway, who granted me a Dean's Leave to work on substantial parts of the project. I thank the unique Josiah Charles Trent Memorial Foundation not only for its support of my modest foray into the history of medicine, but also for the spirit of international cooperation that animates many of its projects. I hope that all my sponsors' faith in this project will be rewarded and that they recognize their generous support in the pages of this book.

Every historian recognizes his dependence on archivists and librarians for manuscripts and books, and also for invaluable tips to read a document that would otherwise be overlooked. The advice of many such colleagues made their way in countless ways into this book. Pride of place must go to the staff at the Hohenlohe-Zentralarchiv in the Hohenlohe Castle at Neuenstein. Those who have worked in the archive tower in the Neuenstein Castle know what treasures from the early modern era are preserved there. Over the years *Oberarchivrat* Winfried Beuter steadfastly responded to all my requests, made many of his own, and patiently guided this American into the ways of a German archive. *Archivdirektor* Peter Schiffer fully supported this work as well. Through his work and advice years ago Dr. Gerhard Thaddey, former director of the archive, quite simply made this project possible. I can only hope that the extraordinary treasures whose stewards they are remain available for other scholars in the years to come. In addition, I thank the staffs at the Stadtarchiv in Schwäbisch Hall, Hertha Beuter in particular; the Hauptstaatsarchiv Stuttgart; the Staatsarchiv Ludwigsburg; the Württembergische Landesbibliothek Stuttgart; the Manuscript Collection of the Universitäts-Bibliothek at the University of Erlangen; Jill Bepler and the staff of the Herzog August Bibliothek in Wolfenbüttel; and the Bodleian Library, Oxford. Close to home, week in and week out, the help I received from librarians at Duke University was indispensable, including the staff of Lilly Library and Bob Byrd's splendid staff and resources at the Rare Book, Manuscript, and Special Collections Library. The librarians of Duke's Interlibrary Loan Office worked more than one miracle on my behalf.

To the people and land of Hohenlohe, a corner of Europe that long ago earned this foreigner's lifelong affection, I owe a particular debt. For advice of a very special kind about Hohenlohe, I am grateful to Ingaruth Schlauch, formerly of Bächlingen; Dieter Klapschuweit, former mayor of Langenburg; and Pastor Ruopp of the town's Lutheran parish church. To them I owe the realization that the past is more than intellectual knowledge. The past as everyday experience lives on in the people in and around Langenburg. For hospitality and advice about the town, in many ways still Agnes Günther's land, I am especially grateful to the Bühlers of Langenburg, Frau Lisa Ziegler of the Moses Mill in Bächlingen, and from Hürden itself Peter Baumann, Hedwig and Hermann Schell, the Kastners, and the Stallmanns, current owners and stewards of the mills at Hürden.

The advice and tips from scholars and colleagues are so numerous that I cannot number them, let alone do them the honor that they deserve. In Germany, I owe a great personal and intellectual debt to Winfried Schulze (Munich), Hans-Christoph Rublack, Heide Wunder, Peter and Renate Blickle, Johannes Dillinger, Herbert Eiden, Dirk Hoerder, Frank Kleinehagenbrock, Peter Oestmann, Robert von Friedeburg, Franz Irsigler and his research group at the University of Trier, Luise Schorn-Schütte, Markus Friedrich and Alexander Schunka, and especially to Claudia Ulbrich and her students at the Free University (Berlin) who helped make Anna Schmieg flesh and blood. In Great Britain the list may be shorter, but the advice has been cogent from Stuart Clark, Robin Briggs, Alison Rowlands, and Diane Purkiss. Tom Scott has been an inspiration in too many ways to detail here. In this country I never cease to be amazed at the generosity of scholars and friends who took time out of their busy academic lives to take an interest in Anna Schmieg and parts of her story, including Amy Burnett, David Steinmetz, Gerhild Scholz Williams, Constantin Fasolt, Mitch Hammond, Ed Bever, Ann Tlusty, and Randolph Head, to name just a few. To Tom Brady and the early modern seminar at the University of California, Berkeley, and James Van Horn Melton and the Vann Seminar at Emory University, I am grateful for the opportunity to discuss some of the work in progress. For poetic and scholarly inspiration I owe a most special debt to Max Reinhart.

Colleagues and friends at Duke University and the University of North Carolina at Chapel Hill have had the largest impact on my thinking about this project. They good-naturedly entered the world of witchcraft with me and nudged me to see things in wider perspectives. Among them are the members of the Triangle Medieval and Early Modern German Studies Seminar. To Anne Marie Rasmussen and Terry McIntosh, I owe particular debts for their steady collegial interest in the project. When Anna Schmieg's story grew too complex, when I lost my way, John Headley, Lance Lazar, Ron Witt, and John Thompson bucked me up. Sy Mauskopf and Michael McVaugh advised me about early modern medicine. For insightful suggestions about some of the concepts at the heart of this book, I would like to thank Ed Balleisen, Malachi Hacohen, William Reddy, Peter Burian, and Kristen Neuschel. To Carolyn Nuhn, I am grateful for research assistance. And my gratitude goes to the legions of Duke students who have endured lectures and workshops based on Anna Schmieg for helping me realize that the story might have a larger audience than I first imagined.

When I became uncertain about the way I wanted to write this story, two colleagues and friends kept me from returning to a less risky and more conventional approach. David Luebke offered invaluable advice and criticism. To Erik Midelfort the debts are so many that they can hardly be named. I never thought I would follow in his footsteps in writing on witchcraft, and realize, knowing now the paths and byways better that he has walked these years, how much we owe his erudition and insightful scholarship. He read a penultimate version of the manuscript and offered the kind of support that was critical.

This book is dedicated to Angélique Droessaert for inspiring me to picture Anna Schmieg's life as part of the larger canvas of her time. She encouraged me to abandon a small and cramped project, to let the drama of Anna Schmieg's story come through, and to take the risk of thinking new, and thinking big. She has worked on the maps and illustrations and brought countless insights into this tale almost every step of the way. With love I dedicate this book to her.

THE LAST WITCH
OF LANGENBURG

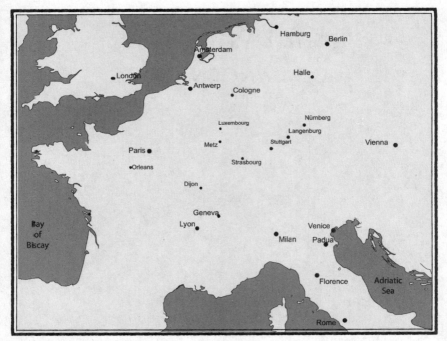

Europe and Langenburg.

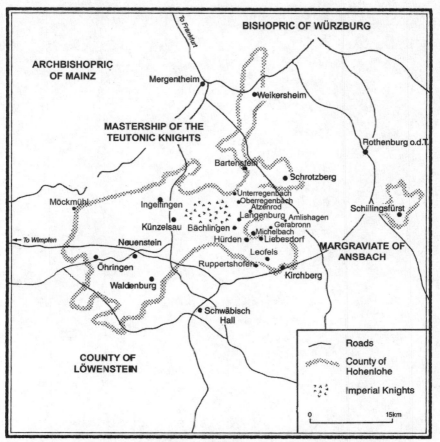

LANGENBURG AND THE SWABIAN-FRANCONIAN BORDERLANDS. *Towns and villages of the Swabian-Franconian borderlands affected by the Langenburg witch scare of 1668–72.*

CHAPTER I

Death on Shrove Tuesday

Hürden, February 20, 1672

n the afternoon of Shrove Tuesday, Eva Küstner, the miller's daughter, gathered up freshly baked Shrovetide cakes from the basket in her mother's kitchen and, tucking them into her apron, hurried out the door of the old mill and down the lane to her neighbor's house. Like other village women from this region, Eva was celebrating the festive last eve before Ash Wednesday by giving the neighboring women and their families the customary gifts of little buns. She first made her way to the door of Hans Barthel Walther, the village wagon driver, known locally as the *Kutscher* (teamster), and his wife, the *Kutscherin* (teamster's wife). A few weeks earlier Eva, distressed by her mother's habit of cursing under her breath, had sought solace in the company of Walther's wife. Now she wanted to offer the *Kutscherin* and her family a gift in return.[1]

Normally an offering of Shrove cakes was met with warm words of welcome. The gift-giver might then be accorded the courtesy of the neighbor accepting the cakes and enjoying a bite or two before she left or be invited into the house for a visit. On this occasion, however, Eva met a chilly welcome. The *Kutscherin* thought that the cake had fallen in and was not at all pretty. Eva asked the couple three times to eat her mother's cake. The Walthers took the gift, but pointedly refused to eat it in Eva's presence. Insulted, the miller's daughter hurried away.[2]

Once Eva was out of sight, the Walthers broke off a piece of the cake and threw it to the dog. In some regions, dogs were thought to sense the future, sniff out danger, or indicate to their masters the presence of spirits and demons.[3] Significantly, the Walthers' mutt refused the cake. Even when their youngest daughter came in and beat the poor animal, trying to force him to eat Eva's cake, the dog refused to have anything to do with it. When the older daughter then offered him a bite of her own Shrovetide cake and he devoured it, the Walthers' suspicions were confirmed. "Gladly, the oldest of the daughters then grabbed the little cake, took it out [of the house] and threw it into the bushes."[4]

Eva was visiting the houses of her own friends, not her mother's. She passed by the little cottage of Appolonia Huebmann, the woman who often visited the mill and shared a drink with her mother: the miller's daughter hurried on to her next and last stop, the household across the lane from the mill, the cottage of Oxherd Michel and his wife, Anna Fessler.

By the time she arrived at the Fesslers' door, the bells of the church in the neighboring village of Bächlingen were about to sound Ave Maria, signaling twilight and prayer. Since midday the Fessler household had been caught up in the Shrovetide spirit. Although Michel Fessler was away at the time—he had business in the nearby town of Langenburg—his wife, Anna, was enjoying the company of her younger sister Barbara Truckenmüller. Barbara had come for a visit from the family home in Nesselbach, the village on the heights across the river valley. Around midday Anna Heinckelin, Anna Fessler's good friend and neighbor, had joined the sisters.[5] Naturally, Heinckelin had brought her own Shrovetide cakes. She had an additional present for Anna Fessler as well: a measure of barley.

The barley helps explain why spirits seemed to be running unusually high in the Fessler household. It was a traditional gift to a new mother. After the ordeal of childbirth, a hearty barley soup was thought to help restore the mother's strength. Anna had given birth to her second child about a month before. By all accounts she seemed to be in good health, as was the child. The most vulnerable phase of the ordeal was nearly over. Although still physically separated from the rest of the community—Anna stayed at home and had not been going to Langenburg, where she worked as a servant—she was no longer confined to the childbed. While gathering her physical strength, she enjoyed the special protection of her female relatives and friends. In a few weeks Fessler could look forward to the public ritual that would formally bring her lying-in to an end: she would be churched in the Lutheran parish church in Bächlingen. Still, she was not yet in the clear, and the dangers were not just to her physical health and well-being. Spiritual ordeals and magical dangers might threaten a woman during the lying-in. Fessler's sister, Barbara, and Anna Heinckelin were not simply guests but guardians.

When Eva arrived at the door to the Fessler cottage, she received a warm greeting. Anna Fessler was, after all, a friend of Eva's, a confidante who had often counseled the young miller's daughter in recent months. Still, the three women seemed surprised that Eva had come to offer Shrove cakes. Was it the hour? Twilight brought unseen dangers that could threaten a village and a peasant household, especially one at the edge of the woods like the Fesslers. Thieves and rogues, of course, but spirits, demons, and witches were known to come out of hiding and be more active at that time.[6] Or were the women troubled to receive a gift from Eva, and, by extension, her mother? An air of anxiety and concern hung over the conversation and the offer of the gift.

Eva first presented the women six little cakes. She then pulled out another—no one at the time seemed to notice whether she drew it from a secret fold in her apron or not—and urged Anna Fessler to eat it. "She [Eva] said that she should eat it, that it would not hurt her, that it was baked with butter." Truckenmüller and Heinckelin noticed that this particular cake looked different from the others. "It was a beautiful little yellow cake," Truckenmüller noted; "it was taller than the other ones and also much heavier." In accepting the cake Fessler honored Eva and their friendship. When Eva then urged Fessler one more time to eat the pretty yellow cake, telling her once again "that it would not hurt her," Fessler broke off a piece and did so.[7]

VILLAGE AT NIGHT. *At twilight villagers retreat to the safety of their homes seeking protection from the dangers of the night.*

As she watched her friend, Heinckelin thought that the new mother seemed strangely drawn to Eva's cake. She seemed unable to stop herself from eating the delicacy. When she had finished, Fessler ate a bite from a different cake—apparently one that Heinckelin had brought earlier that day—and mentioned to her sister that this second one tasted much better than Eva's. Perhaps sensing by this time that something was odd about the food, Fessler's sister gave the rest of Eva's cake to the two Fessler cats.[8] For a second time that afternoon Eva's cakes were being put to the test. In observing how a cat ate its food, a shrewd village woman might see portents of the future: good times yet to come or, more ominously, signs of an approaching evil.[9] The problem with reading cat behavior, Barbara Truckenmüller later said, was that cats could also safely eat noxious things that might put off or even harm a dog.[10] Some even thought that cats were immune to the effects of eating rat poison. Barbara's test proved inconclusive.

By this time Eva had returned to the mill and did not have to bear the humiliation of seeing her cake tossed to the cats. Of the seven cakes that Eva Küstner had presented to the women, only one had been eaten. The women took inside the remaining cakes and placed them on the kitchen table. Now that Eva was out of earshot, the women began to talk freely. All three expressed misgivings about the Shrovetide cakes they had just received. "Who knows whether I should eat such a cake?" Fessler asked them. Rationalizing the haste with which she had eaten the one urged on her, and comparing Shrove cakes in general to the bread of the Eucharist, she said, "You cannot put anything into Holy Bread." But Anna Heinckelin was not so certain. "Why not?" she said. "When a cake is no longer needed, you can do whatever you want to it." She then reminded her friends of Turk Anna, the notorious witch from the nearby village of Unterregenbach.[11] Only four years earlier the elderly cow maid had been discovered lacing her bread and cakes with poison. Before she was caught, however, she had murdered a number of children. By mixing her poisoned bread and cakes into animal feed, she had also slaughtered cattle from the lord's estate at Lindenbronn and from many neighboring villages as well.[12] Stories about the fear, trial, and public execution of Turk Anna were still told. In referring to the tale, Heinckelin did not have to say what everyone also knew: The old witch had done her work with the help of her daughter. Both of them were in Satan's grip. Leaving the sisters with this unsettling memory, Heinckelin took her leave from the Fessler house, and went home to husband and bed.

———

Why were the women of this hamlet so anxious about Eva Küstner and her gifts of Shrove cakes? The answer lies in understanding who these women were, the concerns about motherhood and childbirth at the time, and how an alarm among the women of this remote German hamlet might ripple through the villages and towns around them, triggering events with unforeseen consequences for everyone.[13]

The women drawn together by Eva's gifts that day were most alert to the sanctity and perils that attended pregnancy and child-

birth. Of these five women, three—Eva Küstner, Anna Fessler, and
Anna Heinckelin—had recently given birth. About twenty-five
years old at the time, Anna Fessler already had one small child, a
boy two or three years old, and, after the birth of her second child
at the end of January, was in her lying-in period. Anna Heinckelin,
another young mother, not only had special responsibilities for her
neighbor but was acutely sensitive to the harm that might come to
mothers and their babies. Only a couple of years before, her child
had wandered down to the river, not far from the mill, fallen into
the water or the millrace, and drowned. The loss still haunted her.
At eighteen Barbara Truckenmüller, Anna Fessler's sister, may have
been the youngest woman in the group and still unmarried and
childless, but she had gained firsthand experience through tending
her sister during her first pregnancy and was once again at her side
during her second. In December, Eva Küstner, twenty years old at
the time, had given birth to her first daughter, Margaretha.[14] While
she may not have been among the women officially caring for
Anna during her lying-in, she had cared enough for her friend and
her new baby to come to the baby's christening and place a customary gift of a few coppers in the baby's crib.[15] The *Kutscherin's*
children were a bit older—one daughter was eleven and her second daughter a few years younger—but she, like all the other village women, knew about Anna Fessler's condition and the
precautions that were being taken by Anna's kin and neighbors to
keep her safe from harm.

The Fessler party was therefore more watchful and alert than
usual. From the moment a woman became pregnant to six weeks
after childbirth, she might experience trying physical, medical,
even religious and spiritual ordeals.[16] For this reason villages sometimes accorded special legal rights to a woman during this period,
including the right to special foods and protection from shocks or
violence to her body. Beyond physical trauma, violent images or
frights might harm or deform her fetus. Pamphlets and books
about pregnancy and childbirth displayed gruesome pictures of the
monsters born from such shocks. Some German village ordinances
even forbade husbands from beating their wives during pregnancy.[17] Naturally, Fessler's guardians would also have been alert to

dangers from other sources: ill-willed neighbors, evil spirits, demons, and especially witches.[18] Visits from neighbors, casual conversations, gifts of food, meats, and other mundane activities therefore took on heightened significance.

Up to this time no one who knew Anna Fessler had registered serious concern about her health. During her pregnancy she had continued to work as a domestic servant to the Langenburg court barber-surgeon, Hans Albrecht Unfug, and his wife. Even though they must have seen her often, the couple remarked that, far from suffering from any ailments associated with her condition, "she had only a healthy and lively color the entire time. She had a cheerful and happy disposition, and liked to go out dancing."[19] Fessler's other employer, the Langenburg baker Michel Bauer, supported their view. Even though Fessler had worked for him and his household a year, "she had never been sick for even a quarter of an hour."[20] After the childbirth Fessler suffered considerable pain, her husband noted, and sometimes hurt so badly that she could not sit up in bed. Her feet had swollen painfully and a sore on one foot had festered and broken open. Her husband Michel worried that she might have jaundice. On the Saturday before Shrove Tuesday (February 17), she had finally gotten up from bed and warmed herself by the oven for three hours, but she still had a difficult time catching her breath.[21]

These recent setbacks aside, Anna showed none of the worrisome signs of serious complications that sometimes afflicted new mothers. She ate heartily and never reported feeling the sharp pinpricks in her body that could signal corruptions or poisons in her blood. There were no lasting signs of jaundice. The women who took care of Fessler—her sister, Barbara, her mother, Amelia, who came over several times from Nesselbach to look after her, and Anna Heinckelin—all confirmed her husband's reports about her general good health. Heinckelin summed up Fessler's pregnancy in a matter-of-fact way: "Before her lying-in she didn't complain of anything that a pregnant woman doesn't normally complain about."[22]

The women of Hürden were accustomed to having female kin and neighbors provide the care that midwives normally provided

NEW MOTHER IN THE LYING-IN. *Women care for a new mother, her children, and her household.*

elsewhere. The lying-in party took care of the young mother, knew the signs of illness, as well as the medicines, herbs, and even magical charms that could cure their charge were she to fall ill. They helped out with the domestic duties: cooking, cleaning, taking care of the children and domestic animals, and provided companionship and emotional support through the recovery. Other women not formally charged with lying-in duties kept an eye out, too. From time to time, the Bächlingen pastor's wife, Anna Maria Wibel, looked in on Anna Fessler.[23]

The women kept a close eye on Fessler, and with good reason. On Shrove Tuesday women expected extraordinary social and even cosmic forces to come into play. The day marked the festive days before the beginning of spring and the season of Lent, a time of penance leading up to Easter. For a brief time the "sour weeks" of winter, as the poet Johann Wolfgang von Goethe later called this time, gave way to "happy feasts," that is, the often bitterly cold winter days of February work were broken by holidays with eating, sociability, and high spirits.[24] On and around this day peasants invoked the ritual observances of the season not just to honor this time but to help protect the fields, shield domestic animals from illness and harm, and keep their own households free of unwanted or malevolent spirits and influences. Despite the well-ordered customs governing the holiday, there was always the chance that divine, preternatural, or even demonic forces might unleash the unexpected.

For communities completely dependent on agriculture no other season of the year was charged with quite the same life-giving hopes or life-threatening dangers. It started at Christmas when, shortly after the winter solstice, the days lengthened, epitomizing the coming of the light of Christ into the world, followed by Three Kings Day or Epiphany (January 6) and Lichtmess (February 2), or the Feast of the Purification of the Virgin. Protestant villagers like those from Hürden closely associated this sequence of feast days—even if shorn of their Catholic associations—with the anticipated renewal of the land and the fertility of their domestic animals. Protective rites were practiced in the fields to guarantee their fertility during the spring sowing. Blessings were said over the cattle to protect them from illness.[25] In some parts of Germany, Shrove Tuesday itself was a propitious day associated with weddings and popular rites aimed at guaranteeing the fertility of women.[26]

At the same time, the church warned Christians of the special dangers of sin and the need for repentance. Throughout the forty days of Lent ministers spoke of the need to honor Christ's suffering with prayer and penance. The season would ultimately end with the joyous celebration of Christ's passion and resurrection at Easter. For early modern Christians there was no more powerful stirring of Providential forces than those that began on Shrove Tuesday.

In this part of Germany, known as Franconia, the Reformation had long since put an end to the raucous public celebrations of the season typically known as Carnival, which reached its climax on Shrove Tuesday. Despite zealous Protestant reformers who repeatedly tried to abolish the "pagan" or "popish" elements still associated with the feast day, many customs were simply too deeply embedded for the clergy to ever quash completely. In some villages it was still considered good luck to plow the fields on Shrove Tuesday. Fruit trees pruned on the holiday were believed to bear more fruit. Peasant women avoided going out into the fields, and were to take particular care in cleaning the cattle stalls and closing the stall doors so that no harm would come to the animals. There were also fears that witches were more active than usual and that wild hordes cf phantoms were about at night.

In Hürden the exchange of Shrove cakes marked the central event of the holiday, a gesture that reinforced family and neighborly ties. Some village women even looked upon the cakes as possessing extraordinary powers. The practice of baking and giving Shrove cakes can be traced back to the early Middle Ages. The Venerable Bede, a sharp-eyed early-medieval chronicler, wrote that February was "the baking month" among the Germans, and that around Shrove Tuesday they honored the deity of Frigga with their offerings of cakes. Some villagers baked the cakes in the hearth— not in the oven—in order to keep witches from dancing there at night. In Austria peasants buried Shrove cakes in the fields to guarantee the land's fertility. In the Rhineland Palatinate villagers fed them to their chickens so that the hens would not lay their eggs in odd places.[27] When Anna Fessler called her neighbor's little cake "Holy Bread," she associated it with the salvific powers of the Eucharist.

Protestant pastors, on the other hand, often saw Shrove Tuesday customs as worrying signs of paganism or, worse, as the work of the devil. The Protestant authorities from nearby Ansbach denounced the peasant feasting as a "pagan custom," with one Lutheran clergyman blasting it as a "feast of Bacchus." Other pastors, dismayed at the persistence of these customs, saw the celebration as a "sign of godless living," and at worst, as a seduction by the devil.[28] A Shrove cake was not just any ordinary gift of food. It symbolized all that was hopeful and dangerous about the season.

———

*I*F THE circle of women around Anna Fessler was unusually alert at the time, their dense network of ties to other villages, the town of Langenburg, and even to important people high up the social hierarchy at its princely court, made it likely that a dispute among them might ripple outward quickly.

Would their rank and property have made them stand out in the territory? Hardly. None of them came from the top end of the region's rural hierarchy, the proud peasant households with big compact farms. Not one of them even came from the middling ranks of peasant households. In fact, as a group—with the possible exception of Eva Küstner—the women of Hürden came from households with only the most tenuous ties to landed property; they were members of the region's poor laboring families. Anna Heinckelin's husband, Georg, earned his living working as a day laborer. The Walthers may have had a steadier income—he was a teamster who hauled grain, flour, and other goods around the area—but they were hardly better off. Anna Fessler's people were the Truckenmüllers, a family of poor cottagers from Nesselbach. Once a cow maid, Anna continued to work as a domestic servant in Langenburg. Her husband, *Benzen* (Oxherd) Michel, the son of the Billingsbach smith, made his living mostly as a stable hand, cattle herder, and day laborer at the lord's estate in Lindenbronn.[29] When they had married and moved to Hürden in 1669 or 1670, his mother, a poor widow, had reluctantly agreed to the match but endowed her son with no resources of any kind, pleading at the time that "she had but barely enough to support herself."[30] Eva Küstner may have been the daughter of the Hürden miller, but she and her husband still lived at her parents' mill, and had no independent means of their own.

The importance of these women actually lay in their rich social networks, and the possibilities these connections offered them for mobilizing help and support when needed. Collectively their networks might be imagined as a set of three overlapping circles, each containing a myriad of different kinds of relationships. Naturally the first of the circles involved Hürden itself. The women saw each other almost daily as they went about their regular activities. The village cow maids, the girls from the Walther, Heinckelin, and Huebman families, routinely drove the cows out past their neighbors' cottages, past the mill, and across the Jagst River, where they pastured the animals in the meadows along the river.

The lane along which all of the Hürdeners lived led north through the woods to the village of Bächlingen about a mile away. The road then branched off to the west, crossed a bridge over the river, and wound up the valley slopes to the village of Nesselbach on the western heights overlooking the river. These three villages—Bächlingen, Nesselbach, and Hürden—formed the parish of Bächlingen, and here the networks of Hürden's women widened out considerably. Walking the lane, which skirted the Jagst, the women often stopped to talk with one another or called out to friends and neighbors on the side paths branching up the hill and into the vineyards that surrounded Bächlingen. Every week the women might see one another at the Lutheran church in Bächlingen, sitting next to one another in assigned seats in the women's pews, the seating order reminding them of their rank, marital status, and age. If they skipped church on Sunday, as Eva's mother, Anna Schmieg, sometimes did, they might be found gossiping in the home of a friend or sharing a glass of wine at one of Bächlingen's small taverns. Perhaps the most important woman was Pastor Wibel's wife. It is difficult to say whether the pastor's wife had the confidence of the Hürden women. Pastors and pastor's wives tended to come from educated small-town families, and the social gap between them and their parishioners could be difficult to overcome. The pastor's wife sat alone in the first row of the church on Sundays, and the rest of the women sat in the pews behind her.[31] Still, it is clear that Frau Wibel not only knew all about Anna Fessler's pregnancy and health but kept tabs on which women visited the young mother and what they brought her to eat.

Of greatest significance was the network of ties that bound the Hürden women directly to Langenburg, the district market town

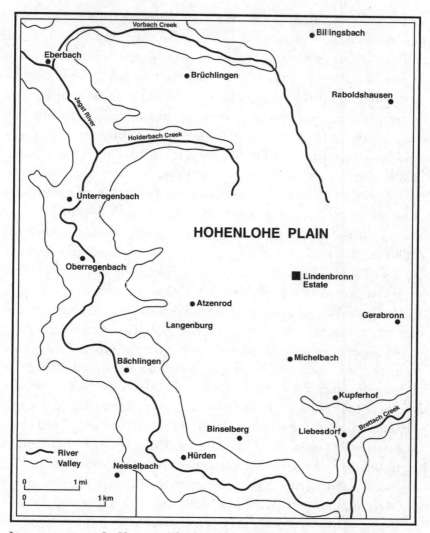

LANGENBURG AND ITS VILLAGES. *The close proximity of Hürden to Langenburg fostered intimate everyday contacts between villagers, nearby communities, and the court at Langenburg.*

and the residence of the territory's prince and his court. Located on a spur jutting out over the Jagst River valley, the town was hardly a quarter mile up the steep, winding road from Bächlingen. In Langenburg the Hürdeners frequented the weekly markets or visited shops. Occasionally they were summoned for disciplinary purposes to the district office house, located close by the palace, at the far western end of the town. Both Eva Küstner and Anna Fessler had been summoned before the Langenburg court preacher and the Lutheran marriage court on at least one occasion.

Anna Fessler was fortunate to work for two prominent Langenburg men. The barber-surgeon tended to the medical needs of the entire Langenburg court, including the prince and his family. The baker came from a prominent Langenburg family. Both of them held their servant, Anna Fessler, in high regard. Given that Michel Fessler also worked at the prince's personal estate in Lindenbronn, a couple of miles to the east, the humble Fesslers were rather well connected in the lower rungs of the court. Add to this the fact that Eva Küstner's father was well known too, since he was the personal miller to the prince and the court and occasional government headman in Bächlingen, one must set aside the assumption that these village working women were obscure people living in a remote little German hamlet. News about them could light up the gossip networks that reached right into the prince's court.

On Shrove Tuesday the women of Hürden had more immediate concerns: the unexpected gifts of food from the miller's daughter and her mother. Ever since Hürden had been established in the Middle Ages, the mill and its family dominated the hamlet, the village land, its sparse resources, and even the families who lived close by. The miller's household was the most imposing in the hamlet, more than twice the size of the other cottagers' households.[32] So when Eva offered gifts to the neighbors, the normal order of things reversed itself, even if symbolically and only for a moment.

The women knew that gifts of food normally went out from the mill only at the command of Eva's mother, Anna Schmieg, commonly referred to as the *Müllerin*, the miller's wife. Schmieg was not known for her generosity. Years before, Anna Heinckelin had had a bitter falling out with Schmieg over cherries. When the stingy woman had had her cherry tree shaken, she had refused to give Heinckelin—who had no fruit trees of her own—any cherries.[33] While the miller's wife had once let Eva bring a few pears over to Anna Fessler, neither Schmieg nor her daughter had ever visited or offered a gift to the Fesslers before.[34] From time to time, Schmieg's one friend in the village, Appolonia Huebmann, came over to the mill and Schmieg offered her food and a glass of wine. Still, even this one friend would concede, "She is an angry woman. Everyone knows that."[35]

———————

*M*ICHEL FESSLER returned home after Anna Heinckelin had left. It was about an hour after the church bells announced Ave Maria. When he entered the main room of the house, two different sets of Shrove cakes—Anna Heinckelin's and Eva's—were sitting next to each other on the table. When he heard that the miller's daughter had given them the cakes, he immediately made clear to his wife and sister-in-law that no one was to touch them. Throwing them under the table, he said something about "not knowing what was in them" and "those people have a bad reputation."[36]

For a little while the cakes seem to have been forgotten, and Anna, Michel, and Barbara enjoyed one another's company and the few remaining hours of the holiday. A little after seven Anna did something that her husband had never seen her do before: she paced around the room several times.[37] Was she feeling so good that she simply wanted to walk off the excitement or was something troubling her?

Anna calmed down and retired to bed. Michel stayed up a little longer, but around eight or nine o'clock he went to lie down next to his wife. She must have woken up when he came into the bedroom because Michel noted that she seemed fine. Later "she woke up suddenly and sat up and said that she was hurting so badly that she could not stay in bed." She got up and went into the other room, Michel following her. Anna felt that "her body would explode on her." Losing some of her personal decorum, she "acted like she does when she is dressed and needs to pass some gas but she had on nothing but a shirt." She then threw back her head in pain, bending over as if she had to throw up. Michel thought that something was forcing its way up into her throat, but nothing came out.[38]

Then the crisis gained hold of the poor woman's body. Her torso began to swell. Waves of heat broke over her. An unquenchable thirst seized her. She got up, and, her bowels suddenly loosened, passed "brick red blood." By then word of her sudden illness had somehow reached the Heinckelins. While the wife raced over to her friend's house, Georg went next door to the Walthers, woke them up, and asked them to hurry over to the Fesslers.[39] When Anna Heinckelin got to the house, she found her friend in such terrible condition that she could no longer talk. Georg and Michel picked up Anna and carried her to bed.

Tormented by acute pain, Anna Fessler may have lingered for a little while, but around ten or eleven o'clock the end approached. Her husband, sister, and Anna Heinckelin knelt at the sick woman's bedside and recited the Lord's Prayer. By then Michel thought that the strain would literally tear his wife's body apart. Afraid of dying, Anna turned to her faith for comfort. Repeatedly she called out: "Oh God! I must die!" "Oh Jesus! Come to me in your hour!" For about three-quarters of an hour she remained still. Anna Heinckelin noticed that nothing more than a little foam dribbled from her mouth and that the poor woman seemed to fall asleep. Anna Fessler was dead.[40]

CHAPTER II

The Autopsy

Hürden, February 21–22, 1672

hen reports about the strange death of Anna Fessler reached the Langenburg town steward, Georg Friedrich Assum, the morning after she had died, he lost no time in launching a government investigation. Michel Fessler, his wife's sister, and Anna Fessler's friends thought they recognized the hand of a poisoner and witch in the events of the night before, with their suspicions centered on the miller's daughter and especially her mother, Anna Schmieg. While their passions were aroused, Steward Assum and his colleagues approached the events in their role as detached, objective government administrators.

Assum exercised overall responsibility for the routine administration of Langenburg District, which included Langenburg and the eleven villages and hamlets around the town. Villagers in the district quarreled almost constantly with one another, and the quarterly docket of cases before the local village courts of discipline (*Ruggericht*) were often full. Slanders, attacks on a neighbor's honor, and even violent assaults routinely came to his attention. Calling someone a thief, a murderer, or worse, a witch, was common.[1] In all such cases the first step involved hearing out the complainants, summarizing their depositions, and perhaps asking a question or two. If the situation warranted it, Assum or one of his men would go to the village to gain a firsthand sense of the situation. Assum followed this routine procedure, but given a suspicious death, he also called to the initial meeting two medical experts: the court barber-surgeon and employer of Anna Fessler, Hans Albrecht Unfug, and the master of the Langenburg Bath, Johann Georg Waldman. The town was too small to support a physician.

In the February 21 meeting Michel Fessler spoke first and at greater length than the women who accompanied him. Twice Assum brought Fessler before him, prodding Michel with questions about any quarrels he or his wife had with the Schmiegs. By prioritizing Fessler's testimony Assum was recognizing the fact that Fessler, as a man, had legal standing to bring formal accusations. But even if custom did not accord women the same standing before the law as men, the testimony of Barbara Truckenmüller and Anna Heinckelin proved more decisive than Michel's. Not only were they eyewitnesses to the exchange with Eva Küstner and knew details about Anna Schmieg's activities and reputation of which Michel may have been unaware, they were responsible for the new mother's care, giving their words special weight. While Fessler and his wife's relatives cagily avoided directly accusing Anna Schmieg of poisoning and witchcraft, their insinuations were inflammatory. Assum took no sides, simply calling his account "the reported death of Anna, Michel Fessler's housewife from Hürden," and then sent it on to his superiors in the chancellery.[2]

The exercise of restraint and the instinctual use of administrative procedure probably came easily to Assum and his associates. One cannot know for certain—Assum left behind no personal reflections about the case—but one clue may lie in the fact that the trained instincts of any good district officer at this time was to meet contentious matters from their villages with the routine practice of government administration. By refusing to endorse the inflammatory language of witchcraft, Assum and his superiors stayed above the alarm, preserving vital maneuvering room for the government as it gathered information and deliberated about appropriate action.

All of the important government civil servants were townspeople closely associated with the Langenburg court. They lived their lives at arm's length from the villages below the town and down in the Jagst River valley. In Assum's case, loyalty to his prince, Count Heinrich Friedrich, and to the territorial government and its administrative routines had been reinforced by his upbringing and training. A descendant of a long line of civil servants, Georg Friedrich Assum had taken in the ethos of government service and administration from his father, a much-respected chancellor of the government of Hohenlohe-Langenburg at the time of the Thirty Years' War. Assum's associate, the court barber-surgeon, Johann Unfug, is an even more interesting illustration of the civil servant distancing himself from the passions and fears that were stirring in Hürden. He knew Anna Fessler personally. In his medical report handed in on February 21, he showed no partisanship or hint of supporting Michel Fessler's provocative insinuation that his wife had died of poisoning and witchcraft.

The barber-surgeon and the bath master that Assum engaged to help him represented the best medical advice available to the Langenburg government at the time. Typically a barber-surgeon in southwestern Germany met high professional qualifications: a Latin education, a three-year training as an apprentice, a period as a wandering journeyman, and then validation by the guild, which would include, in addition to proof of his honorable birth, a demonstration of skill and an inventory of his instruments. Many even collected a small library of medical books that, in addition to handbooks on surgery, frequently contained a surprising number of books on internal medicine and pharmacy.[3] First among Unfug's duties was to care for the count and his family and to acquire and administer medicines when necessary. He also provided additional medical support for physicians when they were called to tend the count or his family. Unfug also tended patients in the town and countryside.[4] In his leisure time he cultivated a life of letters, composing occasional poetry for the Langenburg court.[5]

The master of Langenburg's bathhouse, Johann Georg Waldman, complemented Unfug's medical expertise. Bathhouse patrons might engage him to undertake bleeding, treat wounds, set broken bones, pull teeth, or treat skin diseases. In Langenburg he also had special responsibilities for cleaning dead bodies and preparing them for burial.[6] Waldman's intimate knowledge of the human body made him a valuable expert in determining the cause of a suspicious death.

Despite their skills, Unfug and Waldman would soon discover that Fessler's suspicious death was an unusually complicated problem that demanded skills, experience, and knowledge beyond their own medical expertise. Even a literate and cultured surgeon like Unfug had no formal university training in anatomy, pathology, and internal medicine. Although he and Waldman had probably seen many strange causes of death, his medical knowledge, like a surgeon's, was limited to the surface of the body. Skilled and experienced though they might have been in observing and describing the outside of the body, how could they judge the cause of death in a case where the most important signs might only appear on the *inside* of the body?[7]

The law required only a visual inspection of the *outside* of the body, however. This fact might explain the difficulties that the court barber and bath master would soon run into, but, at the same time, the fact that Steward Assum sent them to Fessler's house for a visual inspection of the corpse also indicated just how modern and up-to-date administrative practice had become in this tiny German territory. While not citing the law in his documents, Assum was following the guidelines for a forensic medical investigation of suspicious deaths written in the *Carolina*, the criminal law code of the Holy Roman Empire. One of the most advanced Renaissance law codes in Europe when it had been adopted by the Imperial Diet in 1532, the *Carolina* was applied by the 1640s and 1650s even in small principalities.[8]

The *Carolina* laid the foundations for modern forensic medicine outside of Renaissance Italy. In this regard the routine administrative practice of a civil servant like Assum from a tiny German principality was a century or more in advance of his peers in France or England. In cases of suspicious deaths Article 147 prescribed a careful visual inspection of the body or corpse:

When someone is attacked, and afterwards dies after a period of time, that is, in cases when it is doubtful whether or not he had died from the blow delivered by the person accused [of the crime], then both parties, as the wise saying goes, should present knowledge about the affair before the authorities, and a Surgeon should be made familiar with the affair and other witnesses should be brought in who, according to the rumors, knew how the victim had acted after the blow.[9]

Not merely relying on the eyewitnesses, the law prescribed that the investigating government officer should on his own inspect the victim's body and" . . . all of the wounds, blows and throws, how each of them were found; [he should] measure them, diligently note them down and describe them." During this personal inspection of the corpse the magistrate should also be accompanied by two local judges (*Schöffen*), a scribe, and one or more surgeons.[10]

In the Fessler affair, which involved suspicion of poisoning, the *Carolina* pointed Assum and his medical experts to pay attention to any indirect evidence of foul play, the possession of poisons by a suspect, for example. Better yet was a suspect's confession.[11]

─────

*E*XACTLY WHERE and how these two Langenburg medical officers examined the corpse on February 21 is unclear. Custom suggests that the investigating team went to the Fessler cottage and laid the corpse out for inspection on the kitchen table.[12] It is not known if Anna's husband and female kin were actually present.

From the start of their inspection these two officials seem to have known that they would be unable to solve the mystery of Anna Fessler's death. While they dutifully noted that they were meeting their obligation to inspect the "pale and white" corpse, they explained equally clearly that "reporting the actual causes [of her death], in whatever hopeless and swollen condition she died . . . would be extremely difficult to do." The body, they noted, "looked horrible." "The body was swollen up like a drum from the stomach down to the thigh and then on up to the neck and head." On the left side of the corpse they discovered "a blue streak running right up to the breast."[13] Considering Fessler's previous general good health and her painful death, the puzzle only deepened. The complexities of the case surpassed Unfug's and Waldman's expertise.

"Nothing can be said about this [case] without cutting open the body," Unfug wrote, and, pressing the need for additional expertise, he urged Assum to call in a doctor of medicine.[14] Fessler's body might yet reveal evidence, but getting at it required an autopsy.

———

*I*N RECOMMENDING that a physician be summoned to Hürden to conduct an autopsy, Unfug and the Langenburg government sided with reformers in the Holy Roman Empire who sought to have forensic medical examinations meet a new and higher legal standard for evidence. Only around the turn of the seventeenth century had the idea gained momentum that forensic investigations required the professional expertise of a physician trained in anatomy.[15] As they had throughout the history of Renaissance medicine, the Italians had led the way. The turning point in the debate in the Holy Roman Empire had come about as jurists, physicians, and government authorities were won over by the arguments of the Italian physician Fortunatus Fidelis (1550–1630). Whatever resistance lingered concerning the carrying out of autopsies in cases of suspicious deaths withered away under the professional medical and legal arguments of Fidelis's followers. In his *De Relationibus Medicorum Libri Quatuor* (1602), Fortunatus argued forcefully that legal investigations and autopsies required specialized knowledge and should therefore be carried out by a university-trained physician.[16] By the 1660s several Saxon universities, led by Leipzig and Jena, added that consulting physicians should also have direct experience with dissections. One of the leaders of this movement, the Leipzig physician Gottfried Welsch, concluded that only physicians could meet the rigorous legal standards demanded by magistrates and jurists. In difficult cases physicians' expert testimony provided a sure understanding of complicated medical evidence.[17]

Accepting Unfug's recommendation, Assum summoned Dr.

Andreas Thym, who worked for the nearby city of Schwäbisch Hall as the municipal physician and provided his services to nobles, princes, and local governments. In his letter Assum voiced for the first time his suspicions, asking Thym to carry out "the dissection of a woman who has suddenly died and to consider whether she was given poison." Assum described the case as involving "a woman who had given birth four weeks ago, and who had been given a Shrovetide cake by a neighbor which she had then eaten without warming up, and soon thereafter she felt terrible pains in her body."[18] Assum had begun to put together a story.

⎯⎯

DR. ANDREAS THYM was one of a new breed of physicians. Born in Waltershausen in Thuringia in 1631, he attended the Latin school at Gotha before moving on to the University of Jena, one of the best-known and most progressive schools for the study of medicine in the German lands. From the start of his studies in 1653 he impressed his professors as gifted not only in Latin—it was said that he spoke Latin as well as he spoke his native tongue—but in medicine "for which he had a special gift ever since he was a boy."[19] By the time Thym took up his medical studies, many of the leading German medical faculties, especially in the Saxon universities, had broken with a strictly classical Galenic and Arabic education. The works of the revered ancient Greek physician, Galen, had been revived in the early sixteenth century and formed the basis of university medicine. To the standard instruction in Galenic teachings about human physiology, illnesses and diseases, and their treatments was added the study of the Arabic commentators on Galen, especially Avicenna and Rhazes.[20] But Jena had also begun to train its students in the newer disciplines of anatomy, surgery, chemistry, and botany. There was no clean "revolution" in medicine, however, even though the reformed curriculum at Jena indicated that the old-style Galenic medicine grounded in an Aristotelian view of nature was clearly on the wane. While students might still embrace the "way of the anatomists"—the primacy of firsthand observation—over ancient authority, Galen, Hippocrates, Avicenna, and Rhazes were not only still taught but were in fact reconciled with the new anatomical and chemical approaches to medicine.

Thym was a perfect example of this blend of the old and the new. He entered the University of Jena after the reforms in the medical curriculum had come about under Werner Rolfinck (1599–1673). Rolfinck had studied at the University of Wittenberg with one of the most illustrious Lutheran physicians of the day, Daniel Sennert (1572–1637). When Rolfinck took up his professorship at Jena in 1629, after having studied in Leiden and Padua, he greatly expanded the instruction in anatomy and introduced students to surgery. Following the University of Padua's example, Rolfinck opened an anatomical theater at the university in 1630 and through public dissections demonstrated the wonders of human anatomy. Rolfinck also supported the views of William Harvey, the English physician who discovered the circulation of the blood and publicized his findings in his famous work *De Motu Cordis* (1628).[21] In 1641 he became the first professor of chemistry at Jena. The virtuoso Rolfinck also added botany to the curriculum. He made Jena one of the most innovative centers of medicine at the time.[22] Through his teacher, Thym had therefore received one of the most advanced medical educations available.

Thym's own training embodied Rolfinck's dictum *Anatome medicinnae oculus* (Anatomy is the eye of medicine). While at Jena, he attended Rolfinck's lectures on internal medicine, the lectures of Gottfried Möbius (1611–64) on Galenic physiology and other lectures emphasizing the importance of relying on firsthand experience and observation. Added to these courses was instruction under Johann Theodor Schenck, professor of anatomy and surgery, from whom Thym acquired a particular expertise. After receiving the licentiate in 1659, he wrote the "Inaugural Medical Disputation on Wounds."[23] To cap his studies he went on a grand tour, as many medical students in his day did, taking particular care to visit the advanced Dutch universities at Leiden and Utrecht, where he furthered his knowledge in anatomy and surgery.[24] Before being tapped as a municipal physician and moving south to Schwäbisch Hall, Thym had even given lectures at his home university in Jena and become a professor of medicine.

Thym's appointment as the city physician of Schwäbisch Hall in 1665 meant that he spent his career diagnosing and treating patients. Among his clients were noble and princely families from the surrounding territories, including the counts of Hohenlohe. In his personal demeanor he was crisp and efficient and known not to abide formalities.[25]

———

*W*HEN THE courier caught up with him in Kirchberg, a small Hohenlohe town and seat of one of the counts of Hohenlohe, Thym must have considered the request an urgent one—the longer he waited, the faster the body would decay—for he mounted the horse that Assum provided to attend to the autopsy immediately. Most likely it took place at the Fessler house itself. With Fessler's corpse laid out on a table, Court Barber-Surgeon Unfug, under the direction of Thym, made an incision down the woman's chest and laid open her stomach cavity.

Late-Renaissance autopsies resembled modern forensic autopsies in some ways, but in key respects the procedure remained very much under the influence of a different culture of medicine. Physicians respected their patients' own knowledge about their bodies and relied heavily on them for understanding their symptoms and the conditions associated with them, as well as the progress of their illness. Diagnosis and treatment involved a great deal of give-and-take between physician and patient.[26]

But what was a physician to do when the patient was already dead? Thym had no firsthand knowledge of the course of Fessler's illness, nor had he had the opportunity to hear her describe her symptoms and ailments. So instead of immediately plunging his knife in, he took careful stock of the next-best source of information before beginning: the reports of her husband and the women who had cared for Fessler during the lying-in. From their accounts Thym already knew what he was supposed to be looking for: evidence of poisoning.[27]

Thym and Unfug worked together closely. Before they started, Unfug noticed that the body of the young woman appeared to be

A CORPSE UNVEILS ITS SECRETS. *Turning for guidance to anatomy, toxicology, and forensic medicine, physicians conducting an autopsy looked for signs of the hidden "lethal wounds" left behind by poison and resulting in illness and death.*

"greatly swollen from the feet right up to the head" and that foam had formed around her mouth. After Unfug made the long incisions cutting open the torso, exposing the rib cage and the internal organs, Thym then had him open up the abdomen. The appearance of the stomach and the surrounding cavity told him that something had gone seriously wrong. He noted first of all that the intestines and the gastric plexus around it were torn into two parts "as if someone had forcibly ripped them apart." The intestines themselves, he observed, were blown up "as if someone had exploded them with great violence." Looking closer at the intestines, he noticed that they looked bluish yellow and that "a great deal of yellow water surrounded them." He found disturbing signs on the liver as well, which was "very nicely red but greatly enlarged." As for the other organs—the kidneys, the gall bladder, and the spleen—there were fewer disturbing signs. Her womb looked "as it should" for a woman who had borne a child only a few weeks ago. The stomach, however, looked distressingly abnormal, with a "large black mass about half a hand thick" located near the spleen. In the stomach itself, he observed, there was still an undigested piece of Shrove cake. In the lower intestines a foam had formed.[28]

Then Thym turned his attention to the upper torso. When Unfug cut into the area around the neck, a large quantity of blood flooded out. Because of a later review of these results, Thym's comments about the condition of Fessler's heart bear particular attention. Thym saw little that was unusual or alarming: "In the heart there was otherwise no sign except that the usual amount of blood was on hand." That he did not notice "corrupted" blood pooling around the heart was significant. He would have known that poison often attacked the heart directly, leaving behind signs of corruption in the blood. Still, Thym noted the cavities around the heart and lung were pressed together in an abnormal way.[29]

Looking over the condition of the rest of the body, he quietly noted that "she otherwise looked fresh and healthy." He had been informed about the brief periods of illness and bodily swellings during the pregnancy and afterward, as well as a brief bout of jaundice. But he did not see any evidence of them from the time of her death.[30]

As Thym drew together his thoughts about what he had seen, he faced a dilemma. He thought that Fessler's internal organs showed clear signs of poisoning, but he would not leap to the conclusion that the Shrove cake was the culprit. So he asked a key question: if Fessler had been poisoned, where had the poison come from? With this seemingly simple question Thym arrived at a particularly delicate and controversial issue, one that would turn the suspicious death of Anna Fessler into a medical mystery.

Seventeenth-century physicians frequently debated with one another about poison and poisonings. Thym's puzzlement might be best grasped by understanding this debate as it was reflected in one of the most balanced and widely respected physicians of the day, Daniel Sennert (1572–1637).[31] When Thym's professor, Werner Rolfinck, studied at Wittenberg, Sennert's works were standard reference manuals. His medical textbook, widely read and consulted in Thym's day, drew together the best opinions about all kinds of issues in medicine.[32] Drawing on Galen and others, Sennert summed up the conventional view that everything in nature worked through primary properties or qualities, which were either visible to the eye, or not—that is, they could be "occult."[33] Sennert thought that poisons often worked through occult properties, since they were hard to detect and worked on the body in complex and mysterious ways. Even Galen mentioned some substances—he had poisons in mind—that might seize upon the whole body and work powerfully throughout "the whole substance" of the body.[34] Sennert noted that poisons had natural origins, coming from insects, scorpions, poisonous snakes, animals, plants, and minerals. Sennert preferred material and physical explanations of poisons, and his work gave little voice to the view that poisons originated through the incantations of a witch or sorcerer. A materialist in general, Sennert classified poisons that affected the human body according to two origins: either external or internal to the body.[35]

In his report Thym, like Sennert, followed conventional thinking in classifying poisons as either being introduced into the body from some external source—food, for example—or being produced naturally within the body itself. The idea that the human body generated its own poisons was a very difficult subject, as Sennert understood it, but Galen himself thought it likely, and Sennert, echoing this view, offered explanations as to how and why this might occur. "Malignancies" within the body, he argued, might manifest themselves and generate fevers and poison.[36] Another possibility was that the body's humors, normally in balance with one another, might become corrupted and in this way generate poisons. Sennert's own view was that food might not be wholly or properly digested, and when it mixed with corrupted humors, poisons might be generated. The body might have the capacity to vacate itself of poisons, but sometimes poisons accumulated, even to fatal proportions, on their own and could, in extreme cases, cause death. [37]

Within this debate many physicians, and Sennert was certainly one of them, considered women to be particularly vulnerable to generating poisons within their bodies. Menstrual blood, Sennert thought, might be a tainted fluid but it also purged poisons regularly. But what happened when a woman became pregnant and the menses stopped? Under these circumstances women suffered the risk of foods mixing in harmful ways with their blood and milk and creating poisons. These toxins then circulated around the body, contaminating and poisoning the organs.[38] Pregnant women might even generate toxins through overly active imaginations or sudden shocks. Women who at childbirth only partially expelled the placenta or who did not bleed sufficiently might also retain poisons, sicken, and die.

Could Fessler who had recently given birth, Thym wondered, have simply built up a pool of poisons within herself which had reached such toxic levels that they had killed her? Some of the signs of her earlier ill health such as the evidence of jaundice might point precisely in this direction.[39]

Thym was not hasty. He carefully considered the second possibility: that the poison had been introduced into her body from an external source. Such an explanation could explain the abnormalities he found in Fessler's stomach and intestines. Here the likely object of Thym's concern was the partially digested Shrove cake in her stomach. He did not mention other possible sources of poison, and he did not mention the other Shrove cake from Anna Heinckelin that Fessler had eaten.[40]

At the end of his report Thym drew back and offered no firm opinion. Poisoning, he concluded, likely caused her death, but he refused to venture a guess about the source of the poison.[41]

The case was not yet two days old, and already two different views of the events had emerged. To the villagers' suspicions that poisoning and witchcraft had killed the young mother came a more complicated view from the medical expert of Schwäbisch Hall. Andreas Thym, too, tended to see poisoning as the root cause of Anna Fessler's death. Yet his view of poisoning presumed not only a more anatomical understanding of how toxins could infect the body, it included the possibility that Fessler might have generated the poisons herself, that she may have died a sudden and tragic death but an altogether natural one. One should be cautious against assuming that Thym's more naturalistic view excluded the possibility of witchcraft as the *ultimate* source of the poison. A long tradition closely linked poisoning with witchcraft precisely because it was understood that the devil and witches worked their evil through natural processes and substances.

Not long after Thym turned in his report, Assum bundled it together with the other reports and the depositions of the eyewitnesses from Hürden and sent the whole package to the Langenburg chancellery. He offered no opinions about what had happened, but his administrative efficiency represented decisiveness in the face of confusion. It also suggested urgency. Higher authorities and more discerning minds than those in the Langenburg district office would have to be brought in, and brought in immediately.

CHAPTER III

A Confusing and
Suspicious Affair

Langenburg Chancellery, February 22–29, 1672

round nine o'clock in the evening on February 22, the bundle of reports from the district office arrived at the door of Assum's superior, Dr. Tobias Ulrich von Gülchen. As chief counselor to Count Heinrich Friedrich of Langenburg and the court and director of the chancellery, von Gülchen lived directly across the street from the district office. His residence was also right next to the castle. In five to ten minutes Court Adviser von Gülchen could walk out his front door, cross the spacious plaza in front of the castle and the bridge spanning the moat, and, entering the courtyard, climb the winding stairs to the second-floor gallery of rooms where he presided over the day-to-day operations of the chancellery. In 1672, however, he often worked at home late into the night, not just because his discipline demanded it, but because he suffered from a painful illness. From his bed von Gülchen pored over papers and sent out orders to subordinates even though "he was so wracked by pain that even a cow could hardly stand it."[1] Despite the hour, it was therefore not unusual that von Gülchen began immediately to grapple with the facts of the "very difficult, confusing and suspicious affair" in the little hamlet of Hürden.[2]

The court adviser had received three sets of reports. Together they gave him very different types of information. From Steward Assum and his district officials he had the raw, emotion-laden stories of Michel Fessler and his wife's sister and neighbors about the events on Shrove Tuesday. From the medical experts—Andreas Thym and Court Barber Unfug—he had carefully written descriptions about the condition of the corpse. Both of these first two sets of reports pointed to suspicious signs of poisoning but neither explicitly mentioned witchcraft.

The third report painted a more alarming picture. Shortly after hearing about the shocking death of one of his parishioners, Johann David Wibel, the Lutheran pastor of Bächlingen, wrote to his superior, Ludwig Casimir Dietzel, the Langenburg court preacher, alerting him to the fact that "the woman who died during the lying-in had been given poison." He added "that a week ago my wife and I had been [in Hürden] with her, that she suffered somewhat from swellings, but [at the time] we did not know where it came from." Fessler's sudden death now made him see the swellings in a different light. "Perhaps she was worried, that she had gotten a soup from the old witch and that the witch had given [Fessler] the rest [of the poison] in the little Shrove cake." He went on to write that he had heard from Hub Friedrich—Anna Heinckelin's husband—and that he was amazed by how quickly she had died. Could the authorities, he wondered, use their powers to "eradicate the evil" quickly?[3]

While Wibel had come to the position of pastor only in 1670, his word may have carried added weight because of his connections. In 1662 he had married Anna Maria Hohenbuch, daughter of the much-respected former Langenburg chamber secretary, whose family had long and close ties to the Langenburg court.[4] Through Wibel came the first mention that the terrible affair may actually have involved sorcery and witchcraft.

Von Gülchen did not leap to conclusions. Instead he outlined the beginnings of a plan to get to the bottom of the affair, which revealed his instinctual respect for the ordinary procedures of the law. Not once did he consider suspending the "ordinary law" and its rules and treat the case as an "exceptional crime" (*crimen excep-*

tum). This fact alone distinguished von Gülchen from magistrates earlier in the seventeenth century, who, when facing possible cases of witchcraft, shortened the legal procedures and suspended normal rules of evidence. In these cases the law had been a crude instrument of persecution of suspected witches, which was far from the practice of jurists like von Gülchen. Not once this night did von Gülchen use the word "witchcraft" or "sorcery" as descriptions of what might have happened to Anna Fessler.

At this point the court adviser viewed the case simply as a "suspected case of poisoning." In doing so he would have to defer to the authority of the medical experts in determining whether poison had killed Anna Fessler, and, if so, then what kind of poison it had been. Yet he also realized the medical authorities themselves had a very hard time "determining what had administered the poison, and the pros and the cons [of each of the explanations]." Anticipating the possibility of medical controversy—with all of the attendant difficulties this might occasion—von Gülchen made clear that no physician had the legal standing to make the final ruling on the evidence, that this responsibility belonged squarely with the chief magistrate. In short, he reserved for himself the legal power to determine whether a crime had occurred and what the final truth in the matter might be.

On the one hand, von Gülchen proposed: "I certainly want to believe or take the position, that because so many different immediate signs of poisoning from both external and internal sources present themselves after the autopsy, that in light of this and the great swiftness of death (*vel maxime celeritatis mortis*), the alleged cake must have been poisoned (*venenirt*) and certainly the poison that was present was either quite lethal (*veneno praesentaneo maxime exitiali*) or otherwise given in great quantity (*vel aliis in magna quantitate dato inficirt*), and that the lying-in woman died from it." On the other, he acknowledged the ambiguous nature of the evidence. If the toxins from the poor woman's own body had built up and then suddenly killed her, he would not even have a crime to investigate.[5]

He would have to consult the opinion of the medical faculty of a university, since only learned professors of medicine could establish the legal status of the evidence with any certainty. Once again he was showing respect for the ordinary procedures of the law. The *Carolina* itself prescribed consultations with learned authorities when local magistrates ran into difficulties with the procedures. The evidence had to meet a high standard—that is, it had to be certain, even if consultations would delay the case. The court adviser signaled that he aimed to focus strictly on the evidence. He concluded that night that for jurists "*the evidence of a crime must be certain.*"[6]

In the legal terminology of the day, von Gülchen ordered his officials to begin a "general inquisition" to determine whether a crime had been committed. Once the fact of a crime had been established, he could proceed to the next step: a "special inquisition."

Not knowing whether the Hürden affair involved a crime or not, von Gülchen proceeded carefully and methodically, ordering witnesses to appear before him. Orders also went out to arrest Eva Küstner and her mother, Anna Schmieg, and hold them in the castle tower for interrogation. The hearings would take place in the chancellery. Once he had gathered initial information and evidence about the events, he would then send for an opinion about the autopsy from a college of medicine. Two different instincts came into play for von Gülchen thinking about the perplexing events. The dominant one, the ideal, that first guided his thinking was the product of a lifetime of experience with the law.

———

*U*LRICH HAD been born into a family of jurists with a proud tradition of service to the legal institutions of the Holy Roman Empire. His father, Marcus Hubinus von Gülchen, had been an advocate and procurator at the Imperial Chamber Court at Speyer, one of the chief appellate courts of the land. The elder von Gülchen groomed all three of his sons for careers in the law. Instructed by tutors and then schooled in the humanist curriculum at the academy in Speyer with the sons of other jurists and jurisconsults, the young Ulrich had developed a love for Latin letters, philology, philosophy, ethics, history, and politics. These disciplines provided him with the basic intellectual tools he later relied on in his reasoning about the law.[7]

In addition von Gülchen drew on particular lessons about the law he had learned during the Thirty Years' War. In 1636 he had been sent off with his two older brothers to Nuremberg, where they had begun their legal studies together at Altdorf University, the city's university located in the nearby town of Altdorf. The seventeen-year-old traveled across southern Germany and arrived in Nuremberg precisely when the war had spilled over into the region, and destruction and civil strife had begun to seem unending. Some of the towns and lands he had to pass through had been scourged by soldiers and depopulated by the plague. The grim experiences of the war drove home the bitter lesson that only a thin veil separated an orderly and stable society from chaos, strife, and utter lawlessness. Only just authority and firm applications of the law could keep such horrors at bay.[8]

His Altdorf education underscored the point. While hard times had also come to Altdorf University—the numbers of students had declined and its most illustrious professors had passed from the scene—there was lively interest in current events and how the law and public institutions could once again be made into the guarantors of everyday order. By the middle of the seventeenth century, Altdorf was one of a handful of German Protestant universities—along with Strasbourg, Jena, Marburg, Giessen, Basel, and Heidelberg—that had led the way in creating public law, the kind of law that put the early modern state on a new legal footing.[9] Turning away from the abstract theorizing about Roman law that had bedazzled Renaissance jurists, these Altdorf professors taught the law as an instrument that could remedy the conflict, confusion, and disorder in real-life circumstances. The new emphasis fell on the Holy Roman Empire and its institutions and the circumstances that the jurists actually encountered.[10] The Altdorf professors naturally trained their students in Roman law, but they tended to emphasize the use of these legal concepts to reform local institutions and laws, and to grasp murky and confusing legal circumstances. Von Gülchen credited his teachers, Wilhelm Ludwell,

Georg König, and Nicolaus Rittershausen, for these early lessons
in the law.[11] Later these pragmatic approaches would be recognized as "the modern use movement" of the law (usus modernus).
Von Gülchen was one of its students.[12]

In his Altdorf education one can therefore see the signature
qualities of von Gülchen's initial approach to the Hürden affair:
deference to the Holy Roman Empire and its laws, clear lines of
jurisdictional responsibility, high regard for procedural correctness,
and careful attention to the messy facts and details.

Von Gülchen's other instinct, to leap ahead of the evidence and
rely on his intuitions or beliefs, came from another source: his religious and moral thinking. As a devout and orthodox Lutheran, he
believed that moral and religious truths were not at odds with the
law. They underpinned the law and completed it, providing those
quick flashes of truth that evidence was slow to illuminate. Both
therefore served not just the temporary expediencies of morality
and the worldly order, but divine ends.

In viewing the law as an instrument of moral, even metaphysical, discernment, von Gülchen revealed a turn of mind that had
been given fresh impetus and a modern Lutheran outlook at Strasbourg, where he had completed his legal education. Like Altdorf,
the University of Strasbourg was one of the new centers of public
law and the pragmatic approaches to the law associated with the
"modern use movement." As the war between Catholics and
Protestants dragged on, however, Strasbourg had also become a
bastion of the Lutheran political cause and militant supporter of
Lutheran religious orthodoxy. When he arrived in Strasbourg in
1641, von Gülchen was therefore exposed to the drumbeat of the
city's preachers and churches. The most famous and charismatic
preacher, Johann Schmidt, set the tone. True Christianity, the only
firm bastion of truth, he intoned, was besieged on all sides. Lutherans must therefore not only remain outwardly faithful to the teachings of Christ, but they must also learn inward spiritual discernment
instead of being deceived by outward circumstances and appearances. Turn the heart inwardly away from Satan and convert it
wholeheartedly to Christ.[13] Von Gülchen also completed his legal
studies under the guidance of Johann Rebhan and Johann Tabor,

professors known for their interest in the religious and ethical aspects of the law. The mature von Gülchen's interest in theology and orthodox religious devotion would have been formed during his Strasbourg days.

If the court adviser was guided by a single saying, it was likely the one (Psalms 25:21) that he would later choose to have read aloud at his own funeral: "Let integrity and uprightness preserve me; for I wait on Thee."[14] To him the words of this prayer were best understood in the light of another Old Testament passage: "Let us praise famous men. . . . Such as did bear rule in their kingdoms, men renowned for their power, giving counsel by their understanding . . . and by their knowledge of learning meet for the people, wise and eloquent in their instructions." (*Sirach, Apocrypha*, 44: 1, 3–4).[15]

Von Gülchen's thinking in the Hürden affair was also tempered by experience. He was a tough-minded administrator working in small Protestant lands, which had suffered some of the most dire consequences of the long and ruinous war. When he left Strasbourg in 1642, he had distinguished himself as an administrator in the service of the counts of Limpurg, followed by other appointments, including posts at the Imperial Chamber Court in Speyer, where his father had worked. Then in 1651 he had come to Langenburg, where he assumed the demanding job of court adviser and chancellery director in the war-ravaged little land of Hohenlohe-Langenburg.[16] His highest priorities were to restore the functioning of the government and to return order to a people who for years had to fend for themselves while soldiers and armies came and went. Whether negotiating with the Holy Roman Empire over his prince's rights, privileges, and lands, pressing his master's claims in long and wearisome family disputes over land and money, restoring distrustful and undisciplined villagers to obedience, or working to instill a new sense of moral order and religious piety, the court adviser had become a local legend.[17]

By the time the Hürden affair came to his attention, von Gülchen could therefore draw on twenty years of experience with almost every aspect of Langenburg's domestic affairs and its people. His duties included advising the count on domestic and foreign matters, writing up reports about ongoing concerns of the government, directing the daily operations of the chancellery and its personnel, registering the records and contracts recorded in the territory, even dealing with the petitions from individual villagers about their problems and then executing the decisions of his prince.[18] When a popular disturbance broke out, von Gülchen assumed the mantle of the Langenburg chief magistrate. The "Langenburg twelve," the judges who staffed the court, and the other government officers answered to him.[19]

In all of these affairs von Gülchen's instincts were always to see wider issues of imperial law and the moral order. It was not a question of *whether* flashes of moral or religious insight would enter into his legal reasoning about the affair, but when, under what circumstances, and the weight he would give to them.

I N THE time between von Gülchen's first reflections and the first depositions that he took in the chancellery on February 27, what he learned about the affair became more alarming, sinister, and threatening. A real crisis began to brew in the villages around Langenburg. Anna Fessler's death had stirred up the people in the surrounding countryside with talk that "evil" lay behind the events. Von Gülchen had also studied Pastor Wibel's report. He made notes to find out whether the miller's wife had given Fessler soup on other occasions and to ask the *Kutscher*, Hans Barthel Walther, whether he, too, had received cakes from her. Was Fessler's death part of a wider pattern? It was at this point that the court adviser wrote openly not only about legal procedures and following them, but about the powers of the law to discern evil hidden in mundane events. On the morning of February 27, at the start of the day's interrogations, he prayed for strength and wisdom, "that through God the Law might proceed and the truth brought out into the light so that the evil might be eradicated."[20]

Properly executed, an inquisition was intended to give a presiding magistrate a clear and unambiguous view of the events in question. The greatest contemporary commentator on criminal law,

Benedict Carpzov (1595–1666), considered the procedures to have the power to place the magistrate at the scene of the events as if he himself were observing them. The "true signs" about the events were distinguished from the less reliable "probable signs" on the basis of the credibility of the witness and how close that witness had been to "seeing" firsthand the events in question.[21] From the mass of testimonies collected and dutifully written down, those that would then be considered "legally relevant" would be selected. In theory, this process was not guided by the arbitrary and subjective judgment of a magistrate. Inquisitorial procedure itself, jurists thought, weeded out personal passions and partisan interests, binding a judge so thoroughly to the rules and procedures that the magistrate simply acted as an instrument of the law. "Every jurist should keep his eye not on the person but on the thing itself," the Langenburg court preacher said about von Gülchen. "If the deed is bad and the person good then he should repudiate him. If the thing is good and the person bad then he should accept him." Good judges also knew the warning that went with this process: "Christ also says that the eye is nothing and a deceiver."[22]

A chief magistrate worked out these procedures in secret, his critical decisions of subsuming the facts into the law occurring completely out of view. How then did people know that extralegal concerns did not impinge on his judgment? How was anyone to know whether his findings, rulings, and judgments were right? How, in fact, was anyone else to judge if the truth had indeed been discovered? These doubts naturally concerned magistrates and jurists, and von Gülchen had doubted himself and his judgments in cases in the past. All he wanted to do now was gather as much information as possible from all the relevant witnesses before confronting the two chief suspects.

Von Gülchen planned in advance every aspect of the interrogations that took place in the Langenburg chancellery between February 27 and 29. He drew up a master list of carefully numbered questions for each witness. He made sure that key questions were standardized so he could compare answers. Regarding critically important questions, he made a note to observe and record not just the answers but the overall demeanor, emotions, and facial expressions of the witness. His scribe followed the practice of sum-marizing testimony, translating phrases from the local dialect into German. Reading the protocols today, one can be overwhelmed by the mass of details they reveal about the events and the people in question. The smallest details mattered. The canons of evidence demanded empirically verifiable facts, and to establish "full proof" of a fact one needed two supporting eyewitness accounts.

In short, the court adviser carefully scripted each and every one of the interrogations. It was as if he were writing out the scenes of a play, the parts of the leading characters already roughed in, and space for the dialogue blocked out. Only their statements were unknown. But the actors retained the power to reveal or conceal their own characters, to add and subtract from the script, to sur-prise and even to thwart the playwright. The dictum *Quod non est in actis, non est in mundo* (Things not recorded in the protocol do not exist) reminded a judge that he could note nothing not writ-ten down in the protocols.[23] He might confirm facts, cross-reference and compare testimonies, and check that the procedures had been properly followed. Villagers might tell their own stories, and sometimes broke out into long-winded tales, but von Gülchen had to make sure that the presentation of the facts conformed strictly with the forms and rules of evidence.

The court adviser began with witnesses who were more remote from the events of Shrove Tuesday, and then moved methodically, witness by witness, to those closer to the scene of the crime. Over the last three days of February he interrogated fifteen witnesses, a handful of residents from Langenburg and Bächlingen, some Nes-selbachers, and almost every single person from Hürden.

In the first session, on February 27, he began with the two respected men well known to the Langenburg court: Hans Albrecht Unfug, the court barber, and Michel Bauer, the Langen-burg baker—Anna Fessler's employers. From both of them he wanted to know exactly how Anna Fessler looked and felt in the weeks before her illness and death. The court barber said, "She had only always shown a healthy and vivacious color."[24] Bauer was even more categorical.[25] While these responses may have indicated that Fessler's illness had come on only after she had eaten Anna

Schmieg's Shrove cake, neither cast suspicions directly on Anna Schmieg. The most that von Gülchen could get from them was an admission from Unfug that he had recently heard the story from Michel Fessler about Anna Schmieg trying to poison the cattle.[26]

Once he had imposed silence on the two Langenburgers regarding their testimony, the court adviser had Michel Fessler brought in. Fessler could not provide firsthand evidence about what had actually happened when Eva Küstner had appeared at his home's doorstep or what the women had said to each other. But he could provide detailed testimony about his wife's pregnancy and lying-in, and something perhaps even more important: the history of enmity between himself and his wife and the Schmiegs. On the one hand, Fessler confirmed that his wife had indeed had health problems during her pregnancy and lying-in, saying that she complained the whole time, and that she had suffered from swellings in her legs and feet. What really interested von Gülchen, however, was the evidence of bad blood between the Fesslers and the Schmiegs. Here he grilled Fessler sharply, knowing, of course, that villagers often bore grudges against one another and that these could fester and lead to false accusations. Fessler denied any ill feelings on his or his wife's part toward the Schmieg family, insisting that he had never even been in their house. He then went on to recount the story of how, the previous summer, Anna Schmieg had cursed the pasture where his cow had been grazing, that she "wanted to poison the pasture so that his cow would die from it." Von Gülchen did not question Fessler about why he had failed to accuse his irascible neighbor before the Langenburg disciplinary court. Perhaps von Gülchen recalled that the Langenburg courts had suspended hearing complaints in 1670 and 1671 and that this would have made it difficult for Fessler to put the matter to rest. Schmieg's curses rankled still. The court then heard Fessler's painful account of his wife's death, confirming the first hurried and emotional accounts that something alarming had happened to Anna after she had eaten the cake, and that she had died full of anxiety and fear for her soul.[27]

The key witnesses, who could make the most direct connection between Eva and Anna Schmieg and Anna Fessler's death, then came before the court adviser. They were the women who had cared for Anna during her pregnancy and lying-in: her younger sister, Barbara Truckenmüller; her mother, Amelia Truckenmüller; and Anna Heinckelin, the neighbor. Because they had either stood at Fessler's side when Eva had arrived at the door or witnessed firsthand Anna's health over the last several months, they became the most critical eyewitnesses as von Gülchen began to build a case that pointed suspiciously at the Schmieg women.

———

WHAT STANDS out about these women's accounts is that all of them accorded with one another almost exactly. All of the women agreed: except for some minor episodes of illness Anna Fessler had been healthy and normal throughout her pregnancy and lying-in. As her sister put it: "She was not particularly ill in her second pregnancy except that she had a cough and then for eight days or so some swellings."[28] The court adviser tried to elicit more specific details from Amelia, Anna's mother: Had her daughter experienced any burnings, heart palpitations, or jaundice? Amelia's answers confirmed that the young mother had enjoyed normal good health up to the moment she ate the Shrove cake. Barbara Truckenmüller and Anna Heinckelin then provided telling and vivid details about how Eva arrived at the house, bearing cakes, and urged an especially large and golden one on Anna. Anna's sister then told essentially the same story she had told Assum the morning after her sister had died.[29] This time she recalled the exact number of cakes Eva had brought and emphasized how she had urged one of them in particular on her sister. Anna Heinckelin added to this account a more anxious and fearful tone, emphasizing once again Anna Schmieg's bad reputation and recalling her own fears of Schmieg and misfortunes since moving to the village.

Court Adviser von Gülchen then probed the women carefully regarding their relationships with Anna Schmieg. What did they know about her? What had they heard? These were not frivolous questions or unrelated to the events that interested him. The law required a chief magistrate to inquire carefully into a suspect's

reputation—a bad reputation would count legally against her—
and to assess the relationships between her and those who
denounced her. Given the alarms the women had already sounded
about Anna Schmieg, and the fear of witchcraft that now animated
the local gossip, they were not likely to back off their first stories.
With almost a week to think about the events and talk among
themselves, the women could now embellish their original
accounts with more details about Anna Schmieg's reputation for
witchcraft. Yet all of them carefully avoided denouncing Schmieg
outright for witchcraft. Instead they insinuated the accusation into
their stories and let the court adviser draw his own conclusions.

In these interrogations Anna Heinckelin comes across as the
most frightened of the eyewitnesses and also the one with the most
firsthand experience of old Schmieg. When von Gülchen queried
her about Schmieg's reputation, a bitter story of resentment poured
out of the young woman:

> The miller's wife has a bad reputation. Since she [Anna Heinckelin]
> came to Hürden she has been afraid of her. She can't blame her [for
> anything], however. She [Anna Heinckelin] has had a lot go wrong
> in her house in Hürden. A child of hers drowned and this made her
> feel extremely anxious about whether there was a gruesome mon-
> ster in her house, but since she did not sense anything otherwise
> before or after, [the loss] had made her sleep a lot and made her sad.
> She has even pleaded earnestly to God for protection. A while ago
> she went into her barn and she saw a gross and repulsively large
> toad, and since she was pregnant at the time it shocked her in her
> heart, and she committed herself and her unborn child to the pro-
> tection of God.[30]

This episode struck the court adviser as especially significant. He
went on to elicit from Anna Heinckelin the fact that she never
went to the mill and had no relations with the miller's family. In
fact, when pressed, she said that she had had a falling out with the
miller's wife years ago, that she was mean-spirited and stingy with
the cherries from her orchard, cursed a great deal and often drank.
Later von Gülchen returned to these passages, put brackets around

them, and noted in the margin that similar stories circulated four years ago about Turk Anna, the notorious witch.[31] One of his intuitions alerted him to a possible pattern: buried in this woman's story were not just the ordinary signs of friction between neighbors but sinister signs that could tie Anna Schmieg to other known witches.

The other witnesses that day, Hans Barthel Walther and his wife, rounded out this worrisome portrait of the miller's wife. As residents of Hürden and neighbors of the Schmiegs for more than fifteen years, they testified to the fact that the fears and suspicions about Anna Schmieg went back several years. They also told how Eva Küstner, Schmieg's daughter, had come to their doorstep offering them a single Shrove cake from her mother, how she had urged them to eat it, and how they had wisely refused. The details about this exchange and their dog's odd behavior around the cakes caught von Gülchen's particular attention.[32] Two times he marked an *NB* (*nota bene*) in the margin next to their story. If Schmieg had sent them a poisoned cake, then the beast's instincts now made perfect sense.

———

$\mathcal{A}$T THE end of this round of interrogations the court adviser withdrew, read over the protocols from the first day's sessions, and then crafted a new set of questions for the next witnesses. What struck him was the appearance of a pattern of behavior on the part of the miller's wife stretching back to the previous summer. Was Anna Schmieg staging a series of malicious attacks on the Fesslers, beginning with their cows and culminating in the poisoning of the young mother? At two in the afternoon the next day he brought Michel Fessler back to see what he knew of other attacks. He replied that "because he was working at the count's estate at Lindenbronn at the time he had seen absolutely nothing, but he can say that his wife's brother told him that his [wife's wedding] calf had suddenly fallen over in the meadow, and that the Master [the executioner, Endris Fuchs] said that the calf had been killed by the evil people, that its flesh had turned completely black."[33]

The court adviser sharply pressed Eva's husband, Philip Küstner from Nesselbach, to tell all he knew about his wife's part in the suspicious death of Fessler, and her behavior since then. Küstner insisted that Eva had acted on her mother's directions and, while she showed sadness over Anna Fessler's death—the two women had been friends—she revealed no signs of a guilty conscience.[34] Hans Barthel Walther's wife and Appolonia Huebmann were then called, but neither of them provided any new evidence. Their daughters, however, provided disturbing new evidence about Anna Schmieg and the Fesslers' cows. As cow maids, they shepherded the cows past the mill, across the bridge and out to the meadows along the river, and knew the full and terrifying fury of Anna Schmieg. Elisabeth Barbara, the teamster's daughter, said she herself had not been there that day, but "she heard from Heinckelin's little maid [Ursula Maria] that the miller's wife had thrown out a terrible curse, saying she wished that poison were sown in the meadow so that the cows would die from it and wished that the devil—God protect her—would take all of the cows away."[35] The other girl confirmed the story: "Ursula Maria [Huebmann] said she was leading the cow across the upper water and heard the miller's wife say she wanted thunder and hail to blast the cows, and that they should all eat death, poison and plague, and afterwards she told everything to her mother."[36]

All these interrogations tended to raise many more questions about Anna Schmieg and her reputation for malice and cursing than about her daughter. And yet Eva might have played a pivotal role in the Shrove Tuesday events when she delivered cakes to the Walthers and Fesslers. Had she done this on her own? Or was she acting, as most villagers assumed, on her mother's orders? If she had merely carried out her mother's instructions—the code of conduct assumed that daughters did their mothers' bidding—then Eva might not be a suspect at all. In fact, she might be an eyewitness to a crime, indeed the pivotal key, because she could testify to what her mother had put into the cakes and perhaps to the other secrets that daughters know about their mothers. The questioning of Eva would therefore be the most important of the early interrogations.

———

O<small>N THE</small> morning of February 29 when the court adviser had Eva Küstner brought before him, he lectured her sternly on the seriousness of the situation. He warned her that she must tell everything she had done either on her own or at her mother's behest, "right down to the smallest detail." If she did so, then God and the authorities were willing to show her mercy. Then he said to her several times "that there is more behind this [matter] than appears, that she must not be silent and play around with words and the truth."[37]

His lecture had an effect on the young woman. A freewheeling confession spilled out of Eva about what had happened when she went to the Fessler house on Shrove Tuesday:

> Her mother ordered her to take a number of little cakes—she didn't know if it was 5 or 6—and to bring them to Fessler. When she came in Anna Fessler was sitting on the big mixing bench. She gave one [cake] to her and set the others on the table. She ate none of the cakes from her mother herself. They then chatted [or gossiped] with each other. She neither baked the little cakes herself or helped to bake them. Whether her mother has done something wrong she doesn't know. She can't swear about her mother just as she wouldn't swear about anybody. Her mother might be a witch or she might not be, she can't swear an oath on it.[38]

Though Eva revealed a number of new details, she was still concealing more than she told. The questions that followed elicited more facts, but the core story did not change. Eva showed deference to von Gülchen, deflected suspicion away from herself, while implying that her mother might in fact be a witch. But her language was equivocal, and she could not supply any certain evidence.

The court adviser grouped his questions around four themes. Each set of questions built on the ones before and led to two emotionally charged confrontations, crescendos in which von Gülchen harshly bored in on Eva about the cakes.

The first set of sixteen questions focused on Eva's background and reputation. Had she gone to school? Did she learn to pray, read, and write properly? Had she learned about the evils of immorality from sermons in the church? To all of these questions Eva responded with simple affirmative answers. When the court adviser explored more directly whether Eva had picked up her mother's notorious vices of cursing and drinking, Eva turned defensive, admitting some indiscretions but also distancing herself from her mother: "No one can say that she curses like her mother except that sometimes she swore a little. She's never been involved in immoral sexual behavior, except with her husband before they promised each other marriage. She had never in her life gotten completely drunk nor had she hurt anyone physically or harmed their property." When pressed about the cursing and drinking, Eva distanced herself even further from her mother. "At times her mother stayed home all day and got drunk and when she drank she cursed awfully," she admitted. When her mother tried to get her to take up these foul habits, Eva refused to do so and was beaten for it. She went on to admit that she often heard her mother muttering under her breath—jabbering that might smack of secret conversations with the devil—but she could not recall her mother saying these things in the week or so before she took the Shrove cakes to Fessler. Moreover, she said she knew nothing of her mother wanting to kill the Fesslers' cows or any open animus between them.[39]

Eva then warded off aggressive suggestions that both she and her mother had tried to kill themselves. Von Gülchen did not know if these rumors were true—he had heard them from Friedrich Huebmann. If they were true, then he would have presumptive evidence of their guilt, since the law made it clear that suspects who attempted suicide were struggling with a guilty conscience. Did she still trust her mother? he asked her. Did she know that her mother had tried to hang herself? She said that "she does not want to repeat anything wrong about her mother or that she was burdened with sorcery and witchcraft. She was not worried about her mother. She does not know anything about her wanting to hang herself." Did Eva know that people who try to take their own lives are damned and belong to the devil? To this she replied that "she does not know. She is not as clever as all that." But she did admit that "for her part whoever wants to take their own life belongs to the evil enemy." Von Gülchen then confronted the young woman with the story that she herself had once tried to drown herself in the Jagst River. But she admitted none of it. "Yes," she confessed, "she went to the water and said that it would be no real loss if she jumped in. She thought this several times and asks God again for forgiveness."[40] This story would come back later to haunt Eva, but for now she had successfully fended off its implications.

With Eva on the defensive regarding her own reputation, von Gülchen focused in on the Shrove cakes. Closely watching her facial expressions, he asked her: "Why then did you murder Anna Fessler with a poisoned cake?" Eva immediately denied altogether that she had knowingly given Fessler a poisoned cake, but she also evaded the real implications of the question. "Her mother gave her the cakes and, as she had given them to her, so she gave them to Anna. Her mother may have put something into the cake [and] she readily admits that she said to Anna she should eat the little cake, that it is made with butter." Under repeated questioning she told him there were five or six cakes, that her mother alone had baked them, that she had brought them around the suspicious hour of Ave Maria because her mother's baking was running late that day, that she had put the cakes into her apron, and that she was unaware that her mother baked different batches of cakes. In responding to the critical twenty-ninth question—why Eva had delivered the cakes to her neighbor and whether she had done it on her own or at her mother's command—she denied that her mother told her to tell Anna to eat the cake.[41]

Von Gülchen then pressed Eva for information about her actions, thoughts, and feelings after Anna Fessler had died. Legal manuals made it clear that because the memory of a crime was imprinted on the conscience, criminals could not hide guilt. And because the conscience could not be manipulated at will, it would struggle to reveal the truth in indirect ways through what could be viewed as suspicious behavior. The next morning she seemed sad but not guilty to hear about her neighbor's death. In fact, her answers to the court adviser's questions suggested that she had been friends with Anna Fessler, that she had offered the young mother a customary gift of coins on the occasion of the birth of her first child and visited Fessler during her second pregnancy and lying-in. Eva said that she regretted her death.

The next morning she had gone over to the Fessler house "and gave the little child a bath." She might even have brought another one of her mother's cakes to give to the little Fessler boy, but could not remember whether she had actually given it to him.[42]

The court adviser turned, unrelentingly, to the central question. "What did she or her mother put into the cakes?" "What harm did she or her mother mean the [Fessler] child?" In marginal comments in Latin he noted that he questioned this repeatedly. Eva did not break. She admitted that her mother had taken the cake for the little boy out of the oven and given it to her, but she herself, she said, had eaten half of it and given the other half to the child.[43] She described bringing cakes to the *Kutscherin*, whom her mother hated, but that Eva had done so of her own accord. She admitted that the teamster's wife did not eat the little bun in her presence.

Now the court adviser threatened Eva, marking in his written notes, that if she did not come out with the truth, "the executioner will teach her to sweat." His threat triggered a long and emotional outburst:

> No one told her a thing about the *Kutscher's* dog not eating any of the cake. She doesn't know what her mother put into the cake or even if she baked something into it. Her mother did not talk to her, her mother thought she was no good because she [Eva] wanted to leave Hürden. . . . She has nothing to confess even if in the end she is honorably threatened with torture. On Shrovetide she ate none of the little cakes herself. Her mother had shamed her, and banished her because she wanted to get away from home, but the day after, however, she finally ate a bit of one of her cakes.[44]

It became clear that Eva and her mother were themselves at odds. Why Eva wanted to move away from her mother, and leave

Hürden, was not explored. For the moment the court adviser left any contradictions aside.

Instead von Gülchen pressed Eva to answer one last question: "Who then bears the most guilt in the death of Anna Fessler, herself or her mother?" The protocol reflects that at the same time he went beyond mere questioning: "Threaten her with torture and if she refuses (*sic veritatem edando*) [to tell the truth about the food] then let her sit in the executioner's prison and she will be denied all mercy." Eva professed that "her entire life she loved Anna who had just died." About her mother, she was equivocal: "she does not know whether or not she [her mother] put something terrible into the dough, because she was not there at the time. [Her mother] will know better than she does."[45] If Eva knew what her mother had put into the cakes, or what her mother had intended, she was not telling.

———

AT THE end of the day, the court adviser had a great deal of information about the Schmieg women and their relationships with their neighbors. None of it, however, proved that mother and daughter had conspired to murder Anna Fessler with a poisoned Shrove cake, let alone that witchcraft had been involved. Eva may not have led a blameless life, but she inspired no fear among villagers.

Her mother's reputation was an entirely different matter. The court adviser might read into the reports of her drinking and cursing the signs of a dissolute and immoral life, something not entirely out of the ordinary in Hohenlohe villages. More ominous were the signs that she harbored malice toward the Fesslers, that harm had befallen them and their cattle, and that this pattern of harm was associated with the kind of harm that "evil people" were known to do. The evidence hardly amounted to certain proof that she had committed a crime.

After two days of interrogations von Gülchen had only an incomplete and puzzling picture. But as his marginal notes in the protocol suggest, here and there flashes of insight had come to him.

Too good a jurist to confuse his beliefs with proof, he nonetheless was trying to see hidden patterns as yet unproved in the evidence. His tendency to blend reasoning with flashes of moral insight were in play, and aimed at a lofty ideal: objectivity. We would misunderstand him if we were to associate his turns of mind with irrationality or flawed reasoning as we might use these terms today. One need only turn to the sermon preached over von Gülchen's casket just a few years later to recognize how law and religion were two aspects of true justice. Like two horses straining in the same direction, law and religion worked in tandem. Together they might help keep the magistrate's eye trained not on individuals and their moral circumstances but "on the thing itself."[46] Above all else, passion was the enemy of true justice, and "evil jurists" could fall victim to this folly. As Luther had taught his followers, the just jurist relies on both his eyes and his ears "so that he hears the Law, that he hears both sides."[47]

That was the ideal. The truth was that no one really knew what lay behind Anna Fessler's death and the other strange events in Hürden. The more the court adviser probed into the affair, the more questions arose. Had Anna Fessler really died of poisoning? If so, where had the poison come from? What part, if any, did Eva and her mother actually have in Fessler's death? What lay behind all of the strained relationships with Anna Schmieg, not just those between the miller's wife and her neighbors, but even between her and her daughter? Why was she so feared in the village? Was a wider plot at work? When von Gülchen finished interrogating Eva, he noted in the protocol that "nothing more was to be brought out of her" and ordered her back to prison.[48]

CHAPTER IV

Warding Off Evil

Langenburg Palace, Winter 1671–72

ourt Adviser von Gülchen's late-night orders to open an inquisition into the Hürden affair came to the attention of his ruler, Count Heinrich Friedrich, almost as soon as the ink dried on his report. All such reports were meant for the eyes of the prince and lord of Langenburg. Serious disturbances in the little county drew his attention quickly. In an era dominated by emperors and kings with aspirations to absolute power, a lord of a small Franconian principality might easily be overlooked as an anachronism from an era of petty princes, blocs of Protestant and Catholic powers arrayed against one another, and endemic religious warfare. Small princes and noblemen still governed the largest parts of the Holy Roman Empire, however, ruling most of the lands running along the western borders of the empire from Switzerland down the Rhine, right through Westphalia and on to the borders with the Netherlands. Like many small German princes after the Thirty Years' War, Heinrich Friedrich may have ruled his domain with diminished stature and resources, but he still governed with a keen sense of dynastic duty and pride, faith and a sense of responsibility before God, and remarkable familiarity with his lands and people. When reports came to him from the chancellery, he sent back his commands in his own hand at the end of the report. Only a sentence or two were necessary to communicate his wishes. So intimately did his court adviser know his intentions that even the prince's silence could set the wheels of government turning. If the investigation of the Hürden affair and Anna Schmieg unfolded like a Baroque play, with the court adviser as scriptwriter and stage manager, then Heinrich Friedrich was the impresario or the director of the drama. When the curtain went up, he was seated in the royal box.

That Heinrich Friedrich left no written responses to this first chancellery report can be taken as a sign that the investigation under way expressed his will perfectly. It could be run as a routine matter. The count's seeming aloofness from the affair may have had other causes as well. Papers—imperial dispatches, correspondence, legal briefs, financial reports, chamber accounts, church documents, petitions, and more—converged on the prince in a steady stream, all of them demanding his attention and action.[1]

This flow of paper tied the Langenburg prince and his government into a vast and intricate web of communications spanning Europe, the Holy Roman Empire, and his native land of Hohenlohe-Langenburg. Von Gülchen's chancellery report must be seen within this wider world of pressing princely concerns. From Prague, Vienna, and other foreign outposts came news about Louis XIV and his aims to conquer the Netherlands and occupy the western provinces of the empire, or alarming reports about the advance of the Ottoman armies on Austria and the empire's eastern borders. These were often accompanied with urgent requests for money, troops, advice, and other forms of support. From other seats of power closer to home, such as Mainz, residence of the archbishop and imperial chancellor, the Franconian Circle, and the Franconian College of Counts, came urgent requests for help in organizing the defenses of the empire, news about lawsuits, requests from neighboring lords for help in hunting fugitives, or disputes over borders and tolls. These often contained even more urgent requests for money. From his fellow counts of Hohenlohe and relatives came legal briefs, correspondence, and financial reports. His relatives' repeated claims represented the most serious drain of money. The suits and countersuits dogging him on the eve of the Hürden affair cost Heinrich Friedrich many working days, and often his peace of mind.

In spite of the array of daily reports from afar, the count made time to pore over the routine local documents informing him about the minutiae of his government's everyday operations and the conditions of his people. There were district officers' reports from the three districts of Langenburg, Kirchberg, and Schrotzberg; a daily flow of chancellery reports; dreary financial news; reports from his court preacher and the Lutheran Church involving everything from the qualifications of a candidate for the pastorate to plans for new public days of penance and prayer, visitation reports about the state of affairs in the parishes, even protocols of the latest trials and punishments of violators of the marriage laws; and, finally, perhaps most important, stacks of reports from Steward Assum concerning his seigniorial incomes, fines and punishments, and conditions at the manor at Lindenbronn; bad news about uncollected peasant debts; schemes for agricultural improvements; reports on tolls; and a large number of pleas addressed to the count by his subjects. To every one of the hundreds upon hundreds of petitions, he wrote a personal response.

To grasp this princely outlook during the winter of 1671–72, one might start with Heinrich Friedrich's palace at Langenburg, one of many small castles nestled across the countryside. If one listened to the praises of Mathaeus Merian, the great cartographer, and Martin Zeiller, coauthors of the *Topographia Germaniae*, no land of the Holy Roman Empire could match the reputation of Langenburg for its tradition of "nobility and freedom."[2] From his palace Heinrich Friedrich looked out onto affairs in Europe, the empire, and Franconia from a family seat intimately tied to the little towns and villages around him.

The Langenburg palace—built on a rocky cliff jutting out into the Jagst River valley—dominated the landscape, the town, and the villages around it. From the north it looked over the hills of the Sulberg and Kaiserberg toward the village of Brüchlingen and down into the valley onto the villages of Ober- and Unterregenbach. From the western and southern sides of the palace—where the chancellery and government offices were located—one looked down onto the Jagst River, the bridge spanning it, and the large village of Bächlingen. From the western side, peasants and travelers could be seen coming down the steep road from the village of Nesselbach and the Hohenlohe Plain on the other side of the valley or heading along the river road to the *Herrenmühle*, the "lord's mill," outside the village of Bächlingen, where Hans and Anna Schmieg once lived. Winegrowers could be seen trudging out to the vineyards lining the south-facing slopes of the hill below.

The eastern façade of the palace towered over the town's market square. Designed in the Renaissance style by Count Philip Ernst, Heinrich Friedrich's father, it served as a backdrop for public ceremonies, processions, and spectacles. From the windows on this side one could look out over the moat and drawbridge separating the palace from the town, the princely granaries and storehouses nearby, and over the long narrow street lined with government buildings, shops, and houses. At the far end of town one could see the spire of the Lutheran church, a church closely associated with the Langenburg counts and Heinrich Friedrich in particular. Out beyond the town gate one might even catch a distant glimpse of riders or carts coming in on the road from Atzenrod and the princely estate at Lindenbronn, the market town of Gerabronn or other Franconian towns to the east.

The skillful Renaissance cartographer Heinrich Schwencker drew the Langenburg palace as the center point of the whole countryside. The map portrayed not just people and villages, but forests, meadows, and fields. All the roads from the surrounding countryside and all perspectives converged on the Langenburg Palace as their central point and Heinrich Friedrich, its noble owner and resident.

In fact, as all of nature seemed to defer to the palace, so all of the territory revolved around Langenburg and its count. The count was no mere prince. Even French and Spanish barons did not enjoy the same political status, powers, and privileges of a German prince like the count of Langenburg. Heinrich Friedrich was an imperial count, a patriarch among the patriarchs of the Hohenlohe-Neuenstein family, lord of high justice, head of the territory's Lutheran Church, and sole landlord over all of the peasants of his land.

The palace layout reflected how all these powers came together. Behind the ornate Renaissance façade lay not only the princely residence, but the chancellery and central government offices, a clearinghouse of information of all kinds, a place of scholarly study and reflection, and a place of worship.[3] Corridors connected the family residence and rooms to the large central courtyard around which were located the chancellery, the chamber, and the archive tower. After the Thirty Years' War, Heinrich Friedrich, chronically in debt, had been able to make only a few repairs. He added one new structure, however. In a corner of the palace, just off the central courtyard and easily accessible from the chancellery, he built a chapel—a symbol not just of his personal devotion, but of the importance he attached to the Lutheran Church as a pillar of his government.

Even Heinrich Friedrich's one other change to the palace, a splendid Baroque library, served the government. The library plunged Heinrich Friedrich and his officials deeper into the practical worlds of power and action, instructing them in ways of reading the signs of a turbulent and sinful world and how a devout Christian ruler could bring order and stability to his corner of it. Heinrich Friedrich intended his studies to be a means of making himself into a better ruler and his court officers and pastors better educated and more devout administrators.[4]

The largest collection of books focused on statecraft, war, history, and contemporary politics. The political works ran the gamut from contemporary histories of the Thirty Years' War, such as the *Theatrum Europaeum*, the Bohemian Chronicles, and accounts of Protestant leaders like King Gustavus Adolphus of Sweden. He indulged a German nobleman's passion for Roman history with the works of Tacitus, Ovid, Cicero, Xenophon, and Seneca. The books of the Dutch political writer Justus Lipsius, whose neo-Stoicism appealed to many philosophically minded nobles and civil servants, complemented the historical-political volumes. Rounding out the collection came the works of Machiavelli, manuals on government and estate management, guidebooks on contemporary law, even university disputations on law and theology.[5]

The count also had a passion for Baroque literature, such as

Daniel Casper von Lohenstein's play *The Magnanimous Field Marshal Arminius* or the poetry of Andreas Gryphius.[6] In blood-curdling tragedies he might read stories about how terrible sins remained hidden from view until their sudden revelation brought poisonous enmities to the surface and condemned the parties to horrible fates. Through his collection of books of emblems, he might learn how knowledge of the symbols embedded everywhere in the political and social world, aided a nobleman in ruling and maintaining order. Even books about distant and exotic places—the Ottoman lands, Persia, India, Arabia, Palestine, and the Orient—showed him the moral superiority of the Holy Roman Empire and the virtues of just, Christian rule.[7]

Pride of place however went to his large collection of religious works, especially the practical works that helped him renew the territory's church, so badly shaken by the Thirty Years' War. These included German and Latin Bibles, the works of Martin Luther and Philipp Melanchthon, Luther's close associate and chief architect of Lutheran orthodox theology. To these were added a huge collection of church ordinances, catechisms, hymnals, and devotional tracts. Works associated with the Lutheran devotional writer Johann Arndt were especially well represented. Arndt's massively popular work, *Vier Bücher vom wahren Christenthum* or *The Four Books of True Christianity* (1604), warned against the deceptions of those who conformed outwardly to Protestantism but who remained untouched by Christ in their hearts.[8] With an emphasis on living the Christian life and cultivating an interior life of the heart, Arndt called upon Christians to convert themselves and others wholly to Christ. Devotional works of Arndtian popularizers, including Christian Hohebruck's guide to Arndt and sermons by Christian Scriver, completed the collection of the prince's library.[9]

Cultivating an interior style of piety, the Langenburg prince shared a religious worldview with his closest advisers, Court Preacher Dietzel and Court Adviser von Gülchen. In the 1640s all three had lived and studied in Strasbourg, where this piety had been intensively cultivated and broadcast to Lutherans in southern Germany. At the Langenburg court they shared in a style of reading devotional works that involved reading a selected passage alcud, commenting on its meanings, then using it to interpret other passages or works of literature. Maxims and epigrams became sharp intellectual tools for discovering the hidden meanings of literature or obscure circumstances.[10]

When Heinrich Friedrich dealt with the Hürden affair, he therefore drew on a way of reading events and people that distinguished between the deceptive, misleading appearances of things and the truths hidden within them. Search the meaning of events and the moral message might be one of divine punishment; turn over the meaning of someone's words carefully and they might reveal sinister motives; read emotions, facial expressions, and gestures and one might discover deception, moral corruption, and evil in the heart.

══

*T*HE INCLINATION of the bookish Heinrich Friedrich to read events for hidden meanings and signs of danger was not just an intellectual exercise, but had been nurtured through the formative experience of the overwhelming calamities in his early life: "the helplessness and bitterness of war."[11]

Heinrich Friedrich was born into a noble family threatened on all sides by war and political chaos. As a fervent supporter of the Protestant cause in Europe and against the Holy Roman emperor, Heinrich Friedrich's father, Count Philip Ernst, and uncle, Count Georg Friedrich, had thrown the family's support behind the rebels who had begun the war in 1618. By the time Heinrich Friedrich was born in Langenburg in 1625, the war was going badly. By 1628 the dangers of the family's open stand against the Catholic emperor had become apparent. Emperor Ferdinand II declared Count Georg Friedrich a traitor. His lands were forfeit: the entire County of Weikersheim, the valuable land adjacent to Langenburg, part of Heinrich Friedrich's patrimony. The emperor then declared that many lands "unlawfully" secularized during the Protestant Reformation, including some of the Lutheran lands in Hohenlohe, were to be returned to the Catholic Church.[12] Schäftersheim, a Hohenlohe possession, was confiscated and given

Abbildung des vnbarmhertzigen/ abschewlichen/ grausam- vnd grewlichen Thiers/

WElches in wenig Jahren/ den grösten Theil Teutsch-

landes erbärm- vnd jämmerlichen verheeret/ außgezehret vnd verderbet. Beneben einem Bericht/ woher dasselbe seinen Vrsprung/ wer solches erzogen/ ernehret/ ꝛc. Endlich durch was Mittel seiner wieder loß zu werden. Männiglich an Tag gegeben.

THE MERCILESS AND GRUESOME MONSTER OF WAR. *By the 1630s the Thirty Years' War had devastated large parts of the German lands. Here a warning and lament about the Beast of War run amok: villages and towns go up in flames, churches are destroyed, soldiers rape women, stores of treasure are destroyed, and villagers are driven from their homes.*

over to a Catholic religious order. To make matters worse Count Philip Ernst died and left Heinrich Friedrich's mother, Countess Anna Maria, as regent of a vulnerable little land. At one blow the counts of Hohenlohe were threatened not only with the loss of some of their lands, but with the prospect of towns and villages being forcibly returned to Catholicism as well. The Lutheran Church itself was now imperiled.[13]

Disaster followed. In 1634 the plague swept the land. War taxes soared and agricultural production began to collapse. Government revenues fell to a trickle. Then in August a hostile imperial Catholic army marched into Hohenlohe.[14] "Everywhere they robbed, plundered, destroyed, scorched, and burned the County," the chancelleries in Langenburg and Weikersheim reported.[15]

Fearful for her and her family's safety, and against the advice of her advisers, Countess Anna Maria gathered up her children and fled. Hardened imperial veterans moved in, besieging and plundering Langenburg and the villages around it. The horrors of the flight and the foreign occupation of the land came to symbolize the terrors and humiliations of the war for an entire generation of Hohenlohe counts, including Heinrich Friedrich, who was only nine years old.[16] Preachers portrayed the calamity as God's judgment and punishment of Christians for their sins. From the pulpits came emotional appeals to do personal penance, to root out Satan from the heart, and to accept a living faith in God. These messages saturated the religious culture in which Heinrich Friedrich had grown up.[17]

His mother died during the flight from Langenburg, and his uncle, Georg Friedrich, brought the boy and the family to safety in Strasbourg. Heinrich Friedrich's lifelong admiration of the city, its university, and its piety originated during his exile there from 1634 to 1638. The orthodox Lutheran city exercised a powerful influence on him. Only short-lived and fleeting moments of peace and serenity marked these years. The orphan prince, it was said, considered Strasbourg to be a father to him.[18] Strasbourg provided the boy with refuge, education, and religious instruction. His other more vividly described memories were of the time he had left Strasbourg and a devastated southern Germany to go on a grand tour. The trip began in 1640 with a brief visit to war-ravaged Langenburg and then Augsburg before he continued on to Geneva, and then to Lyons, Provence, Gascony, and Saumur, the city on the Loire River. By this time a lover of the classics and history, the boy paid homage to Petrarch in the Vaucluse, where the great Renaissance poet experienced his own fleeting moments of peace in a world full of suffering and loss. By this time France had entered the war on the side of German Protestants. Furthering a new interest in French culture, Heinrich Friedrich completed his education in Paris, taking up "knightly exercises" and perfecting his mastery of the French language.[19]

This peaceful interlude ended abruptly when the young prince returned to Langenburg in 1644, becoming ruler with his brother.

Twenty years old, he later recalled his first experiences of princely rule as full of suffering, the uncertainty of war, and the difficulties of governing. Wresting order out of the chaos was beyond his powers. Bands of French, Bavarian, Swedish, and German soldiers occupied towns and villages at will, extorting food and taxes from peasants, and leaving violence and plague in their wake. By the 1640s, Langenburg and many of the surrounding villages had lost between 40 and 60 percent of their populations, agricultural production had plummeted, and food shortages were so severe that at times even Heinrich Friedrich could barely put food on his table. With no army or police to enforce his orders, the beleaguered prince often endured the humiliation of being unable to protect his land and people. "During these years and up to the time of conclusion of the peace," he wrote, "there was enough to do with the soldiers, and a couple of times I was in danger of my own life."[20]

Unforeseen events repeatedly upended his early efforts to restore authority and public order. After the Peace of Westphalia declared an end to the war in 1648, raising hopes for peace, the crops failed around Langenburg, threatening food supplies and the public order. In December 1649, Swedish troops returned, occupied the land, and demanded their "peace monies." Not until the summer of 1650 did the last of the soldiers finally pull out of Langenburg. That same year Heinrich Friedrich settled one more source of aggravation: the divided rule with his brother came to an end, and he assumed complete lordship over Langenburg. His subjects were gathered on the marketplace at Langenburg to take formal oaths of loyalty and obedience to him. The recruitment of Dr. Tobias Ulrich von Gülchen in 1651 signaled the real start of his restoring the rule of law. The young prince recognized in von Gülchen's legal education and his experience the qualities he needed in a chief minister who would help him to rebuild his land.[21]

⸺

*T*HE RESTORATION of princely authority extended the count's powers to meet new threats to public order. Like other princes shaken by the long civil and religious war, Heinrich Friedrich regarded the Peace of Westphalia not simply as a peace treaty, but as a constitutional document that put princely government on a sure political and legal foundation. In recognizing its three hundred or more territories as small states sharing sovereignty with the Holy Roman Empire itself, the treaty guaranteed German princes cooperative rights in the affairs of imperial government. The treaty also extended full legal and political protections to the Protestant and Catholic parties in the Imperial Diet.[22] When the last troops had withdrawn and the peace finally took hold in the summer of 1650, Heinrich Friedrich proclaimed a joyous annual "Feast of Peace" in Langenburg.[23]

In 1653, Heinrich Friedrich traveled to Vienna for a personal audience with Emperor Ferdinand III, an event unimaginable ten years before. The next year he signed the imperial order making the Westphalian Peace into articles of government. The Hohenlohe family's confiscated lands were returned. Strict regard for imperial law and institutions became state policy. Relying on imperial law in the Hürden affair was not just sound legal practice but good politics, too.

At the local level the count used his authority to meet challenges to public order. His powers soon became wider, more intensive, and more effective than any that his father had enjoyed before the war. One of his first steps was to renew the land's basic laws, including the general police ordinance and the marriage laws of the Lutheran Church. These measures were then enforced through an expanded system of three types of courts. Couching a radical innovation in terms of respect for custom and "ancient institutions," Heinrich Friedrich instituted new village discipline courts (*Ruggericht*) aimed at punishing everyday infractions and bringing "all the evil and cursing" under control.[24] These courts also channeled local disputes and acts of revenge into the legal system, punishing villagers for slander, violence, and ordinary injuries to honor. The courts obliged ordinary villagers to cite their neighbors for violating the laws while local dignitaries heard the cases.[25] The count's seigniorial court (*Vogteigericht*) complemented their work. Above them and policing the general territorial laws came the courts of the chamber of accounts, the chancellery and the Lutheran Church. In policing violations of the Lutheran Marriage Ordinance, Heinrich Friedrich's marriage court intruded deeply and routinely into the lives of his subjects.[26]

When the reports of the Hürden affair first came to his attention, Heinrich Friedrich therefore saw in them the signs of disorder that had consumed so much of his attention over the last twenty-five years. It confirmed once more his view, expressed on other occasions, "that many people have fallen into immoral and dissolute lives."[27]

Crowning this legal system were Heinrich Friedrich's powers to try cases involving murder arson, rape, theft, and other "high crimes." These cases came before specially convened sessions of the Langenburg *Blutgericht*, or blood court, so named for its right to impose capital punishment on criminals. In the early years of Heinrich Friedrich's reign, the number of trials for "high crimes" seems to have increased significantly. These trials and the resulting punishments of criminals were "rituals of retribution," spectacles that displayed to his subjects his powers to punish miscreants and restore the rule of law.[28] In staging these public displays the count's government blended law and morality with religion. Following a short ceremonial trial, the miscreant, branded "a poor sinner," was marched out of Langenburg in a procession to Gallows Hill, where the punishment was carried out. The executioner, under orders from the count's chief magistrate, calibrated the punishment to fit the crime. For serious crimes, hangings or beheadings were common.

Not long after his efforts to restore princely power were underway, Heinrich Friedrich suffered a setback. In 1657 his wife, Countess Eleonora Magdalena, died. After withdrawing into his books for consolation, the grief-stricken prince left Langenburg and went on a tour of Thuringia. At the court of the Duke of Saxony-Weimar he was inducted into the *Fruchtbringende Gesellschaft* (Fruit-Bearing Society), a literary society, and given a

SAFE HARBOR. *Funeral engraving commissioned by Count Heinrich Friedrich shortly before his death in 1699. To the end of his life the count saw his world threatened by hidden dangers, violent storms, and chaos. Only death and salvation offered a prospect of lasting security and peace.*

name evoking the virtues of a judge and princely protector: *Der Ablenkende*. The honorific evoked the virtues of a ruler who "shielded against" or "deflected" dangers or, stronger yet, "protected" against harm or even "parried" the blows of evil. One poet referred to Heinrich Friedrich's reputation for skillfully deflecting danger in unsettled and difficult times:

> Indeed, this Solomon of the *Fruchtbringende Gesellschaft*
> Is rightly known as the Deflector:
> So beautiful is the name, as he seeks only
> To ward off Evil, and be the Avenger of Virtue.[29]

$\mathcal{B}$ETWEEN 1657 and 1668 the slow efforts to rebuild the little county of Langenburg continued. Routine government began to replace crisis management. But in 1668 signs of a new crisis, the most serious test of Heinrich Friedrich and his government since the end of the war, began to build.

Among the most worrying reports reaching his ears were rumors of a new war. In the early 1660s the Ottoman Turks had renewed their westward march against the Austrian Habsburgs and the eastern dominions of the empire. As their armies converged on Vienna, urgent appeals for money and support came to the Langenburg court. That was bad enough. But the more alarming reports concerned the looming threat from Louis XIV, who had designs on the Netherlands—long considered allies in the Protestant cause—and the western provinces of the Holy Roman Empire. About a year after Louis's first lightning strikes against the Spanish Netherlands in 1667–68, Heinrich Friedrich renewed his family's old ties to the Netherlands and visited Holland.

The new threat from France pointed out the failure of the counts' policy to shore up the security of the vulnerable lands of Hohenlohe through friendly ties with Paris. A new war would draw foreign armies into the western territories of the empire, once again exposing Hohenlohe and Langenburg to troop quarterings, war taxes, and worse. The counts turned for help to the chancellor of the Holy Roman Empire, the Archbishop of Mainz, Philipp Schönborn, to mobilize the fractious forces of the western empire and meet the threat.[30] By spring 1672, French troops would be on the move.

While war threatened, two of his relatives, Counts Christian and Gustav of Waldenburg-Schillingsfürst, converted unexpectedly to Catholicism. The conversions sent shockwaves rippling through Langenburg and Neuenstein.[31]

To make matters more uncertain, no one understood the implications of such conversions under the terms of the Westphalian Peace.[32] The treaty guaranteed the right of any prince to convert as an individual to another religion, but in defiance of the law, the Waldenburg counts provoked their Lutheran cousins and neighbors by bringing Jesuits to their courts, promoting the work of Franciscan and Capuchin missionaries, and recruiting Catholic artisans to settle in their lands. The controversy, unresolved at the time of the Hürden affair, raised the specter of a renewed assault on Lutheranism.

At the same time, a long and costly dispute over Heinrich Friedrich's own lands was coming to a climax. In the wake of the imperial occupation of Langenburg, the emperor had finally seized the lands of Heinrich Friedrich's uncle at Weikersheim. The family was threatened with the loss of one of its most glittering symbols of power and prestige. When his uncle had died in 1645, Heinrich Friedrich and his relatives in Neuenstein began a wearisome series of suits and countersuits. The Langenburg count fiercely resisted the claims of his brother and other relatives to what he considered his rightful patrimony. The dispute was so bitter that Heinrich Friedrich allegedly had a wall built down the middle of the hall of the palace at Weikersheim, keeping his relatives out of his portion. The empire had intervened and helped settle the family dispute. But the terms of the settlement, announced only a couple of months before the Hürden affair broke, were costly for Heinrich Friedrich. As part of the accord the hard-pressed prince had to relinquish incomes that affected the Langenburg treasury for years to come.[33]

While these disputes intensified in the late 1660s, day-to-day administration from Langenburg was sometimes disrupted. Services to the surrounding districts lapsed and the prince seemed to lose a little of his grip on domestic affairs. Rumors about bands of arsonists, vagabonds, and witches swept the region in 1668 and again in 1670. In March 1670, Heinrich Friedrich raised the alarm among his people about "the growing number of beggars and poor highwaymen who wander around the land and neighboring communities with false papers or other fake appearances" and who then "steal bread, money and eggs or threaten people with their godless blasphemies, cursing and swearing."[34] In the summer the government alarms grew more frequent and more ominous, but by the winter of 1670–71 they had subsided.[35] Fears remained, however. To make matters worse, Heinrich Friedrich received accounts reporting that his debts remained high and incomes from his seigniorial privileges had stagnated.

The crisis even disrupted the work of the courts. Quarterly sessions of the Langenburg disciplinary courts were suspended altogether in 1670 and again in 1671. Routine complaints—mostly slander and verbal insults—were left unheard.

Since the 1630s a deep and persistent depression in grain prices had plunged the agricultural economies of the region into crisis. Because grain production was the mainstay of the economy, seigniorial revenues had fallen steeply. Lords like Heinrich Friedrich, already overwhelmed by the costs of the war, were driven into deeper debt. To replace lost income the count and his peasants had begun to develop a cattle-farming economy. Always on the lookout for schemes to boost his lord's revenues, Steward Assum had begun to increase the number of cattle, moving away from traditional stall-feeding and converting abandoned grainfields to pastures. Assum had the manor at Lindenbronn experiment with a system of letting out cattle to tenant farmers, cottagers, and wage laborers. By the 1660s the livestock herds had grown considerably.[36] One reason why Michel Fessler became so alarmed over the sudden sickness of his cattle grazing on the Hürden common in the summer of 1671 was that the cows were not his own. They belonged to the prince.

The new reliance on cattle bound everyone in the social hierarchy. Cow maids like the Heinckelin girls earned small wages by taking the cows out to pasture. Laborers like Michel Fessler supplemented their meager incomes by tending Heinrich Friedrich's cows. Tenant farmers or whole villages either raised their own cows or leased pastures to their lord. Langenburg court officers like Assum, Unfug, and even the executioner, Master Endris Fuchs, bought and sold a few cows. They had the privilege of having them tended at Lindenbronn alongside the count's own cattle. The prince also profited from the income that the cattle trade generated through tolls and taxes, and around the time of the Hürden affair he was even beginning to have the cattle trade publicly regulated, in accordance with new market ordinances.

The rumors of threats to the cattle came at a sensitive time. A few years earlier a cattle murrain had swept the region. Villagers had sent disturbing reports to Steward Assum of cows suddenly taking ill, languishing miserably in pastures, and then dying. As part of her deposition, Amelia Truckenmüller, Anna Fessler's mother, recounted how her daughter's wedding calf had sickened and then mysteriously died. It was no accident that the first accusation of witchcraft took place in the spring of 1668 against the village woman who tended cattle in Unterregenbach, the notorious Turk Anna.

Thus rumors about a poisoner from a little hamlet along the Jagst River might threaten the prince's own economic interests. When Steward Assum first heard from Michel Fessler about his wife's death, he jumped on one part of his story in particular: the rumor that Anna Schmieg had poisoned the lush meadows of Hürden and harmed the cows who grazed there. That was also why von Gülchen had summoned the Heinckelin and Walther girls to testify about the cows of Hürden and curses they may have heard. Everyone knew that Lindenbronn's and Heinrich Friedrich's interests were at stake. An alarming menace might be imminent behind these events. The tip of the dagger pointed not just at some poor villagers, but directly at Count Heinrich Friedrich and the Langenburg court.

CHAPTER V

A Secret Crime?

*Hürden and the Langenburg Chancellery,
February 21–March 8, 1672*

y the morning of February 21, Eva had heard about Fessler's death. "She cried bitterly, saying 'Oh, good little Anna, only yesterday you ate the little cake so heartily and today I find out you are dead.'"[1] Then Eva went to her mother's kitchen, got another freshly baked cake, left the mill and headed across the lane with this new gift. Eva felt especially badly for her friend's little boy, and she wanted to comfort the poor lad now that he had lost his mother. She found him playing outside the Fessler house. Approaching him, she broke her Shrove cake into two parts, and offered him a piece. On her way back to the mill, she ate the remaining portion herself.[2] When they heard about this latest gesture from the miller's daughter, Michel Fessler and Anna's sister became still more alarmed, quickly seeing it as evidence that the plot against them was even more sinister than they had first imagined: the Schmiegs aimed to eradicate the entire family. As suspicion gave way to conviction, the Fessler party now knew exactly who was behind the plot.

As the rumors spread, Anna Schmieg fell into a panic, fearing for her life. She and her husband Hans knew the danger that she now faced. Sometime that day Hans went to Jörg Morwart's tavern in Bächlingen to settle scores with Fessler, or so the gossip had it. Wanting "to get justice against Fessler," Hans was willing "to put up all his property to show that his wife was completely innocent."[3] A brave display in a moment of peril, this was the first sign of the depth of his commitment to his wife. All too often husbands in similar circumstances distanced themselves from their wives and failed to show them the protection that custom and honor demanded.

Alone at the mill Anna Schmieg sank into despair. Her only friend in Hürden, Appolonia, wife of Fritz Huebmann, the village brickmaker, serves as the best witness for what happened next. On February 28 she told the authorities:

> The next evening [the day after Fessler's death] the miller's wife was completely alone in her house and sent a boy over to her, [asking] that she [Appolonia] come to see her. When she went to her, the miller's wife came down [from the mill] to meet her, and said "she's suffering under such a terrible cross: out there she's been called a witch 20 times; everyone is saying that she is a witch."
>
> She carried a rope in her hand and wanted to hang herself. She [Appolonia] then led her up the steps and into the [mill's] sitting room, and she sat down on the spindle on the kneading trough. She [Appolonia] then took the spindle away from her and took it home and left it there. She talked to her and said she shouldn't do it, [hang herself] pleading with her, and saw that she had a clean conscience. At this she [Anna Schmieg] quieted down and once again became happy. And she explained that she had ordered [Eva] to bring the deceased Anna [Fessler] only 3 little cakes, but her daughter had taken more than that from the basket, and that she had chastised her, and said "You fool, don't take them all."
>
> At the time the miller's wife was also drunk. She wailed and complained and said that her son was about to get married, but that now everything was going to pieces. She acted as if she would still hang herself unless someone helped her out of it. She wanted to take the rope out to the barn, into the stable because there was always straw there and she didn't want to hang herself in the house—that she had already chosen a little corner to do it.[4]

Had her friend, in the only gesture of sympathy recorded toward her that day, comforted Anna, or was she not ready to take such a drastic step as suicide? Through her despair the miller's wife saw lucidly that the crisis was not simply a personal one. Not only did she lament her daughter's foolishness over the Shrove cakes, but she realized now that her son's marriage plans would unravel. The family's future, and all that she and her husband had done to secure it, was about to come undone.

When the Langenburg officers finally came to arrest Schmieg a few days later, a fatalism seemed to have settled over the distressed woman. No evidence suggests that she considered resisting arrest or abandoning her house and fleeing Hürden. She had no living relatives outside the territory who might offer her refuge. If she left the village and took to the roads as a vagabond, as some desperate women had done when a formal accusation of witchcraft seemed imminent, she would suffer what amounted to social death, since vagabonds suffered worst of all in this society. Besides, she would have to leave her husband.

When she was led away from the mill, Hans and Anna exchanged the last words they would ever freely say to each other. Anna later recalled old Hans saying to her, "Go on up to the castle with them, if they want to take your life, they'll take it."[5] With equal fatalism she was heard to reply to Hans, "Good night, you will never see me again in this life."[6] Someone else recalled hearing her say that once she left for Langenburg she would never return home alive, that they would burn her as a witch. As the officers led her down the river road to Bächlingen, she came upon Hans Hofmann, the village shoemaker whose wife had befriended her. "The miller's wife said to him," Hofmann later testified, "that he should say 'good evening' to his wife for her, that he has seen her and nothing else." Even though he and his wife had recently had a falling out with Anna, he gave her perhaps the only words of comfort she heard that day. "Ach," he said, "it won't be so bad."[7]

Von Gülchen carefully noted Anna Schmieg's parting words to Hans in his protocol. When he confronted her a week later and asked her if she had really made these statements, she denied it. Touching and poignant though they might seem to us today, her interrogators, she knew, took them as evidence that she could peer into the future and discern the shape of things to come. Still, von Gülchen marked the words with bold brackets.

———

MEANWHILE, WITH Anna Schmieg bound in chains in the prison tower of the Langenburg Palace, von Gülchen thought through the evidence and the testimonies he had gathered. His mounting suspicion that poisoning and witchcraft were at work did not change the way he conducted the general inquisition that he had set into motion. One must bear this point in mind in order to understand the picture that von Gülchen began shaping of the crime and his chief suspect. His education and experience had trained him to select from the complex mass of facts only those issues that were "legally relevant." Only when certainty had been established would he then make a judgment.[8] The court adviser was filtering those facts and testimonies through the principles of the law as he understood it.

This was why the strategy of his first interrogation of Anna Schmieg aimed at bringing to light a hidden and secret crime: Anna's pact with the devil. He was also guided by the legal imperative to acquire a confession. It was the compelling reason why he crafted this interrogation, and those that followed, with such care to every minute detail in the case—a hallmark of the *usus modernus*, the "modern school" of German jurisprudence. The legal manual that he most likely drew guidance from, the popular "little Struve," in wide use in the 1670s, instructed magistrates that they must establish with certainty that a crime had been committed.[9] In a case of murder the certain evidence would be the body, a weapon, and eyewitnesses. But what evidence could establish the fact of a poisoning, let alone witchcraft, since they took place in secret? Witnesses rarely saw a poisoner or witch directly at work. Moreover, material evidence either did not exist or remained hidden from view. The only sure evidence was a suspect's confession. While von Gülchen exercised overwhelming power over Anna during these interrogations, she nonetheless retained a certain amount of room to maneuver: Ultimately, he needed her cooperation.

Because he suspected that a secret crime had been committed, he decided not to question Schmieg in a "political way." Instead he proceeded "more theologically and addressed her out of the law of the Gospel—*ex lege ex Evangelio.*"[10] In doing so von Gülchen was applying theology as a practical science closely allied to the law— one that provided crucial guidance in ferreting out a person's hidden life and making sense out of it.[11] Theological inquiries might reveal a dark pattern in the details of Anna's childhood, moral behavior, and reputation for drinking, cursing, and blessing strange objects. They might therefore reveal the source of the enmity she was alleged to have for her neighbors and might even unearth the secrets about how she had baked her Shrove cakes. By opening the interrogation this way, the magistrate also assumed a quasi-pastoral role vis-à-vis his suspect, turning the answers over not only for their legal weight but also for signs of secret sins. One goal of the interrogation was to guide the suspect back to the mercy of the state and Christ through confession, contrition, and forgiveness. Another was to establish whether Anna was no simple murderer but a poisoner, a witch, and an apostate.

For these reasons von Gülchen asked that his close colleague, the highest Lutheran official of the land, Court Pastor Ludwig Casimir Dietzel, appear with him for the first part of Schmieg's interrogation on the afternoon of March 7. While the court adviser himself carried out the questioning, Dietzel would listen and advise von Gülchen privately. Dietzel's presence in a criminal inquisition would have been unusual, not only communicating the seriousness of the charges to Schmieg, but proving invaluable in helping von Gülchen later to review the record of her responses for clues as to the real nature of her life and activities. Witchcraft's horror lay in its apostasy, its rejection not just of the sovereignty of the state but of God himself. It would help to have two seasoned court officers who were alert to the cosmic world hidden in the mundane events they were about to explore.

Right at the start of the session von Gülchen made it clear that he was searching for a confession to the crime, and that the full power of the state would be brought to bear on Schmieg to bring it out. "The crime is not a light one, but a serious one," he said to her. He added gravely "that she is standing under the punishment of death." Still, were she to confess her crimes freely "she can move God and the authorities to mercy and appeal to the Lordship's counselor von Gülchen himself for compassion. But if she does not, if she wants to cover up her misdeeds, then she will receive no mercy and will be questioned under torture."[12] This was a commonplace warning, yet it pointed directly at the understanding that in this small territory the magistrate represented both the divine and the secular orders.[13] He was offering an exchange. If she confessed the crime truthfully, he would invoke the power of the state to protect her and seek mercy on her behalf.

After the court adviser admonished Anna Schmieg to tell the truth, he gave her—for the first and last time—the opportunity to speak freely on her own about the matter. The scribe was instructed to listen carefully and record every part of this first voluntary confession.[14] However, Schmieg insisted on her innocence in Fessler's death.

> In the past she sent little Shrove buns to her mother-in-law, the *Kutscherin*, Oxen Jorg in Binzelberg as well as to the Fessler woman who died, wishing that they and other members of their households eat them. She and her own people ate them. Despite what has happened to Fessler's wife her cakes have never hurt anyone before. She baked only one kind of cake. May God punish her body and soul if she has done something wrong, and she insists that she has not.[15]

Anna Schmieg was showing that she was following village traditions and had always done so. As if to anticipate von Gülchen's later questions about how the cakes were baked, she explained, without prompting, that she had baked only one kind of cake. This unsolicited comment may have been one of the unwitting mistakes that she made that afternoon; von Gülchen noted in Latin in the protocol that she sounded nervous and suspicious when she told the story. Her response also implied that she saw the process of justice as a kind of ordeal, much the way it had been viewed in the Middle Ages. It was not just von Gülchen and Dietzel who saw this confrontation as having a cosmic dimension. Anna assumed it as well: she was putting her soul in peril before the court.

Unconvinced by her story, von Gülchen warned Schmieg that to earn the mercy of the state she would have to tell the truth. However, these opening queries seem like an effort to establish who she was—how old she was, where she was born, and her parents' circumstances. Schmieg's responses to von Gülchen's questions seemed almost perfunctory, the kind of short autobiographical stories any illiterate villager might tell, but von Gülchen heard her stories with an ear for any clues that Schmieg had renounced Christ and turned to the devil.

That he was trying to fit these facts into a pattern of criminal rebellion and apostasy became evident in his next questions: "Have you been baptized?" "Where?" "What kind of a godmother did you have?" Then he pressed her with an explicitly theological question: "Does the Evil Spirit also have baptism and does he baptize his own?" Any irregularities in her baptism or Christian education might suggest that she had entered into a pact with the devil at an early age. But she answered these questions about baptism clearly and confidently. She denied having renounced her baptismal vows.[16]

Then von Gülchen approached the issue from a different angle. He turned first to Anna's reputation for cursing, swearing, and blasphemous outbursts. He followed up with the wide reports of her drunkenness, to which Schmieg admitted "that she cannot deny that she had drunk immoderately." Turning to a more serious sign of witchcraft—the fact that she might be consumed with envy, anger, and a desire for revenge—von Gülchen asked her pointedly whether it was not true that "she wanted revenge against those who had done harm to her?"

Anna knew that she could not deny the report of her previous summer's conflict with the Fesslers. Stories about that disturbing episode were common knowledge in Hürden and Bächlingen. So she admitted that "when a cow of Fessler's had gone into her pasture that she wished it to eat death and the plague, that she wanted to poison her own pasture." Downplaying any hint of inordinate anger or lasting enmity in the episode—Hohenlohe peasants often got into disputes over grazing rights and practices—she insisted, however, that "she has no envy or revenge in her heart, that she did not want to kill any person, that she would thereby also poison her own cow and suffer the great expense by doing so."[17]

Court Adviser von Gülchen had evidence of other, more serious episodes, however. His next series of questions suggested that Schmieg was not just a neighbor who lost her temper on occasion, but someone consumed by fury. Anger as deep and powerful as hers could only be explained as driven by a secret diabolical power. He pressed her to explain why, when the bailiff had come to arrest her, she had considered attempting suicide. While physicians may have considered her impulse a sign of melancholy, a medical condition thought to arise from an imbalance of humors in the body, von Gülchen had the more orthodox Lutheran view in mind: suicide was a sinful impulse planted in the heart by Satan.[18] He dismissed her explanation that she "had so much anxiety that she did not know what to do."[19]

Schmieg's explanation made von Gülchen even more suspicious. Her desperate pangs suggested a guilty conscience. Moreover, her failure to confront the Hürdeners spreading the rumor that she was a witch also pointed to her guilt. Had she *really* been innocent, her husband would have brought suit against her enemies before the court of discipline.

Schmieg's language was ambiguous and evasive. She may have considered von Gülchen's accusations ridiculous. In other circumstances Anna confronted her enemies with coarse sarcasm. But the scribe did not consistently record the tone of her words or her demeanor when she spoke, those critical nonverbal clues that give meaning to speech.

When von Gülchen challenged her to say openly that the evil spirit had helped her, she turned defiant. She insisted "she was not a witch. May God punish her in body and soul if she did not freely admit that she is a witch and if it were true, then she should be burned." She may have thought that she was denying any possibility of being a witch, or that by showing revulsion about witchcraft she might indicate to von Gülchen that she shared his feelings, but that final conditional, "if it were true," caught von Gülchen's attention, and he marked her response for review later on. Perhaps even more difficult were the occasions when von Gülchen confronted her with her own words but drew a different and sinister meaning from them. A witness, he said, heard her cursing and saying "The devil take her!" Who but a witch or a serf of the devil would say such a thing? At first she denied it, then she equivocated. Finally, she admitted that she didn't really know if it happened. "If she said it then may God forgive her." Excusing her cursing as raw impiety, the kind that peasants often engaged in, she then related how the *Kutscherin* once told her that her husband does not pray. "She hasn't heard him pray the Our Father in two years," Schmieg said.[20]

Being confronted with stories that Schmieg knew were true enough in general but that were given a different and diabolical connotation could be a confounding experience. The inverted logic of witch beliefs could be so baffling when someone encountered them directly that even a hard-boiled old miller's wife might be confused.

Von Gülchen then pushed ahead with new and tough questions about the rumors that she was a witch. If von Gülchen could establish that Schmieg had a wicked reputation materially relevant to this particular set of circumstances, then, combined with additional evidence, it could provide justification for questioning the old woman under torture.[21] More than this, however, the rumors might also serve as additional signs that pointed to her secret identity. So he confronted her with the testimonies he had gathered about her reputation as a witch.

Schmieg dismissed them brusquely. She had heard them before, and her experience may have hardened her to the possibility of ever countering such malicious gossip effectively. "You can't sit on everyone's mouth," she said. "People will say whatever they want."[22]

Her daughter's testimony, however, she could not dismiss so easily. Not only did von Gülchen consider Eva's testimony valuable because of the close relationship between a mother and daughter—who would know a mother better?—but he was also deliberately exploiting an emotional fault line that ran between the two. "If her daughter says that she is a witch then she's one too, since she [her daughter] would have learned it [witchcraft] from her."23 Schmieg may have been outraged simply to have been confronted with her daughter's testimony against her, but the remark might be read as tantamount to a confession of witchcraft.

Her intemperate response may have indicated strain and frustration under questioning. Maybe Schmieg was trying to dismiss Eva's comment as ridiculous and spoke with sarcasm and spite. The mere mention of her daughter may also have triggered her anger, and she may have responded with the kind of insult that only a mother can make about her own daughter. In any event, the exchange revealed that ill will ran deep between them.

Schmieg's angry response may also have revealed how closely her own identity was bound up with those closest to her. In the villages of southwestern Germany at this time, people did not have an internalized sense of self as we would understand it. They saw an individual through a matrix of relationships established externally by lordship, public authorities, the family and community.24 No identity was fixed and immutable. Over time gossip could remake a person's reputation. This may be the reason why, as time went on, Anna Schmieg would at times seem uncertain about herself and her activities. To outsiders family members held the surest clues to other family members' activities and any secret identities they might harbor. In any event, von Gülchen, alert to hidden meanings in almost every answer, found Schmieg's answers about her relationship with her daughter particularly suspicious. After the session was over, a neat chancellery hand noted her responses and marked them for review later on.

In the last set of "theological" questions, numbered eleven through fourteen, von Gülchen turned to the ominous, even shocking and terrifying way that Schmieg talked. He had already noted the rumors of her curses and blasphemous outbursts. Was it not true, he asked her, that her mutterings to herself were really conversations with the evil one?

Schmieg denied these stories at first. Then she burst out: "What her daughter says is not true, her daughter is not worth the bread that she eats." As if to discredit Eva further, Schmieg then recounted how her daughter had quarreled constantly with her father throughout the winter. "She has no shame."[25] Then von Gülchen asked her, "If she is not involved in witchcraft or magic why [when she was arrested] did she say to her husband: 'Good night, you will not see me again in your life'?"

> If she were a witch she would want to say so for [the sake of] her soul and the oath [she has sworn]. The parting words that were mentioned she doesn't actually remember anymore. She doesn't know if she said them or not; even if God commanded it she could not help him [with this question]. She can't say anything . . . If the master [the torturer] comes over her he will see whether she is a witch or not, he can certainly see it."[26]

As far as von Gülchen was concerned, this was a curious response. Schmieg was not simply contradictory about whether she was protecting her husband with a magical spell—such a blessing when uttered in anticipation of one's death was thought to have binding magical power—she was openly inviting torture. Was she so convinced of her own innocence, or was she simply becoming unsure of herself, or were the questions making her wonder whether she might actually be a witch and that she was simply not yet aware of it? An executioner was thought to have supernatural powers, and if he could "see" the truth, then maybe she, too, wondered what terrible truths he might reveal.

Von Gülchen then confronted her with a story that the *Kutscherin* had heard her say that "she did not care if the devil took her, if she was to be burned then she should be cut up, that there were certainly others involved." The protocol continued:

> If she were a witch she would want to say so openly and reveal it along with all those who come [to the Sabbath]. Two years ago the *Kutscherin* said there were two witches in Hürden and she knew that she and her daughter must be them. If she were a witch she wishes that God would sink her.[27]

Schmieg seemed to admit that she and her daughter must be Hürden's witches. Moreover, she associated herself closely with her daughter once again. This admission, more than almost anything else in the session, caught von Gülchen's eye. In the margins he noted it with two *NB*s and had it underlined. Were her neighbors right? Was she a witch after all? Were they both witches?

This "theological" line of questioning took up most of the afternoon session. When von Gülchen turned to the events of Shrove Tuesday, however, he was still seeking responses that might confirm his suspicions about her identity as a witch. The point has sometimes been made that the careful attention to evidence in trials like this foreshadowed a more modern jurisprudence focused on establishing empirical evidence. Yet to everyone involved in this case the exchanges between people were not signs pointing to material facts but pointers to invisible realities. They might simply be the state of the heart or emblems of goodwill or enmity. When von Gülchen interrogated Schmieg about her Shrove cakes and their distribution, he knew that the gifts might seem benign and mundane. The challenging part was discovering in these customary transactions the hidden signs that pointed to a conspiracy of evil.

The cakes interested him, of course, but he was after Anna Schmieg's real motives in making them and offering them to the people that she did. Had she added secret ingredients to the dough? Had she set aside a secret batch for her enemies?

Schmieg readily admitted to having baked the cakes. She then went on to describe the mixing and pouring and baking as completely normal. "When she made the dough her daughter poured in something, two eggs that had been beaten before, and to this she added some milk and water. Her daughter watched her."[28] She also added cream and oats to the dough. When he asked about the ingredients, von Gülchen was trying to find out whether Schmieg had kept some dough back secretly and mixed in suspicious ingredients. Witches worked this way. But Schmieg insisted not only that she had prepared them herself—hence she knew that they were made wholesomely—but that there was only one kind of dough.

In the last set of questions of the day, von Gülchen wanted to find out whether she would admit to having introduced poison into the cakes, especially the cake meant for Anna Fessler. In a

THE WITCH'S KITCHEN. *In the dark secrecy of a vaulted kitchen, attended by their familiars, three witches prepare a gruesome concoction for their victims.*

hamlet like Hürden one critical clue to the tenor of relationships between women turned on the exchanges of food. Had she baked a first batch of cakes for her husband and daughter and then baked a second for the neighbors? "She baked everything at the same time." The *Kutscher* and his wife, she went on to say, were the first neighbors to receive cakes, but this was her daughter's initiative, not hers. When asked about the cakes that went to Anna Fessler, she denied any intention of sending them to her at all. "No, she [her daughter] was supposed instead to bring the cakes to Benzen Michel [Fessler]. She did not want to send her [Anna Fessler] any because she was still in the lying-in period."[29] Schmieg showed her respect for Anna Fessler's special condition while demonstrating neighborly goodwill toward the Fesslers by offering one bun to the husband. Still, von Gülchen considered the fact that she had sent any cakes at all to be suspicious. Was there not enmity between them? Schmieg denied it. "She never sent Anna anything except last St. Martin's Eve [November 11] when she had slaughtered a little cow," she replied, "and had sent her a soup from it."[30]

The court adviser pressed her as to "whether she put the cakes in her daughter's hand herself which she brought to Anna or whether the daughter did it herself? And where or from what did she take it out?"[31] Schmieg seized the opportunity to express misgivings about how her daughter had presented the gifts. "She had heard from people that her daughter took a little cake in a bag into Anna's house and gave it to her." But Schmieg knew that drawing cakes out of a bag was a suspicious thing to do. "This is not a good sign," Schmieg said. This was an undisguised effort to cast suspicion on her daughter, and von Gülchen was no doubt aware of it. If Schmieg's account was true, it suggested that Eva may have secretly slipped a poison cake to Anna Fessler on her own. Yet to von Gülchen's way of thinking, shaped by the law's presumptions about someone with Schmieg's reputation, the gesture merely deepened his suspicions. Once again he noted in the margins of the protocol that it was Schmieg herself who had given these particular cakes to her daughter.[32] When asked whether one cake looked different from the others—von Gülchen was drawing here on eyewitness testimonies—Schmieg denied any knowledge of it.[33]

That the court adviser doubted her professions of innocence was evident in the last exchange between them that afternoon. He bluntly accused her of baking a batch of poisoned cakes for her enemies and using her daughter as her messenger of death. In his notes he made a special comment that her demeanor was to be carefully watched in response to this last question: "What poison did you put in the dough of the cakes sent to Anna, her child, and the teamster's wife?" But unlike in her earlier confused testimony, Schmieg was adamant. The protocol states, "As God is her witness, if she has ever seen poison in her life then she should be struck dead."[34]

Unconvinced, von Gülchen ended the session. Admonishing her to think carefully on this point, he had Schmieg returned to her cell.

⸺

ANNA SCHMIEG was in a stronger position than it might seem. It remains striking how dependent von Gülchen and the Langenburg court were on her cooperation to solve the case. Given the political necessity driving the counts of Hohenlohe to identify their lands loyally with the empire, the instincts of von Gülchen were to administer the law in a way that made that political loyalty a day-to-day reality. The magistrate was required to proceed with certainty about the guilt or innocence of someone accused of a capital crime. To expose the depths of the conspiracy arrayed against the government and its people, von Gülchen needed to get this recalcitrant, wavering, occasionally confused, but very tenacious woman to cooperate.

When Schmieg was brought back before the court at two-thirty the next afternoon, the questions were harder, and the court adviser pressed for answers more forcefully. The threat of torture also loomed larger the longer she refused to confess. And it is possible that the pressures of the previous day's questioning had weakened Schmieg. Her response, in fact, came close to a confession of poisoning:

> Q28: Was it not certain (because Anna [Fessler] went back into her house sick from the cake, complaining loudly that her body felt like it would explode, and died three hours later) that she had died from eating the cakes?
>
> A: Anna may have died from this little cake, she does not know. God help her. If no one else ate from it then she has to believe that it is certain.[35]

To von Gülchen, Schmieg's ambiguous answer pointed to the need for more clarity. She was admitting that the cake may indeed have killed Fessler, yet this was phrased as a possibility, not a certainty. She did not have direct personal knowledge that Fessler had actually died from the cake. How could she?

More frustrating yet for von Gülchen was that Schmieg quickly followed this tantalizing admission with new and vehement denials. She not only professed her innocence, she taunted the court to turn her over to the executioner for torture:

> Q29: Did she not give herself to the evil spirit about 14 days earlier, that she would get revenge with the cake on Anna since she is an enemy? (*NB*: this was just the time that she was muttering under

her breath a lot and her daughter says she was talking with the devil.) A: She has had nothing to do with the evil spirit. She also does not admit to the muttering. She does not know anything. You should let Master Enderle go over her and see. You won't find anything on me. (*NB*)[36]

On the previous day Schmieg had admitted to the muttering, and even that she had recklessly called out to the devil on occasion. But now she had taken these admissions back. Was Schmieg so certain of her innocence that she thought she had nothing to lose by calling in the executioner? If it were true that Master Endris had the powers of a seer, that he could detect witches supernaturally, then he might just pronounce her innocent of the crime. Still, the court adviser considered Schmieg's answer in a completely different light. Might this not be the defiant cry of a guilty conscience pleading to be liberated by the executioner? Either way, the progress of the day before seemed to be completely undone.

At the end of the session von Gülchen exploited, one more time, the strained relations between mother and daughter, trying to get Schmieg to confess that she had sent yet more poisoned cakes to the Fessler's household the next day, this time to the Fessler's son. Schmieg denied the accusation and cast suspicion once again on her daughter. Her response suggests that Eva had secrets of her own to hide:

> She [Schmieg] did not give her daughter any other cakes that she was to bring to Anna [Fessler's] child the morning after. Rather when she heard that Anna [the child's mother] had died her daughter went over to the house without her telling her to. She, the deponent, did not give her daughter any cakes, as she mentioned above. She wanted to give her daughter a small cake that she was not supposed to take [over and give to the Fesslers]. She did not want to do it. If she is right then her daughter took the cakes out of the sack.[37]

Von Gülchen's marginal comments make clear his own conviction that the daughter was innocent in the affair. The legal norms guiding him would have him dismiss Eva as the primary suspect since she seemed to have a good reputation. But was Eva entirely innocent?

Von Gülchen was aware that the evidence was complicated, and that the signs might point to the mother and daughter in league with each other, a reading of the affair that would not have been surprising given the persistence of stories about mother-daughter conspiracies that reached back to before the twelfth century. Yet von Gülchen thought this less likely at the moment. In his mind it was enmity that drove someone to murder and sorcery, and he had not uncovered any enmity between Eva and Anna Fessler. Instead the evidence pointed to a history of bad blood between Schmieg and the Fesslers.

The court adviser knew that he would have to decide whether the mother or the daughter was speaking the truth. This was why the last questions of the afternoon hammered at the issue of who was really guilty in Fessler's death: Anna or Eva? He proceeded to ask Anna, as he had asked her daughter the week before, who had decided that cakes were to be sent to her enemies in the village. Schmieg again deflected the suspicions onto her daughter, insisting that if cakes went to the *Kutscherin*—another enemy of Schmieg's—then it was Eva who had decided to take them over on her own. Schmieg was still maddeningly ambiguous about crucial details, however. She did not actually accuse her daughter of lacing the cakes with poison. She now contradicted her account of the day before and admitted that her daughter had not been there when the ingredients were mixed and the cakes baked.

Then von Gülchen threatened her. Did she not know that the *Kutscherin*'s dog had refused to eat her cake? "Come out with the truth, or the executioner will teach you to sweat." When she still denied her guilt, he wheeled on her one last time and asked her who murdered Fessler.

> She doesn't know. If she is guilty, well, she will just have to tough it out. She does not want to confess to anything regardless of whether she is asked harder or even if she is threatened with torture.[38]

After this last maddeningly ambiguous answer Anna Schmieg was bound away to her cell.

———

THOUGH SCHMIEG'S stories about her childhood and upbring-ing, her hesitant admissions about her drinking, blasphemy, and cursing, her history of conflict with the Fesslers, and her frustrating denials of witchcraft provided more than sufficient grounds to hold her and press the inquisition further, von Gülchen still did not have his clinching evidence. He had begun the long and painstak-ing process of reinterpreting Schmieg's life and activities. In the end, theology and the law, as practical sciences, would eventually provide the guidelines to grasp the shadowy reality that still eluded him. The signs may have pointed to Schmieg having a conspiracy with the devil, but signs were not the same as legal evidence.

In responding to these tough questions, Anna Schmieg devel-oped no common threads in her answers, let alone a compelling explanation for all of the facts, accusations, rumors, and testimonies that she had been forced to face during the interrogations. She had had to respond to questions—disturbing ones at that—and had lit-tle opportunity to draw her responses together into a cohesive and compelling testimony. The questions also exposed raw wounds, painful losses and regrets, quarrels with members of her own fam-ily, and conflicts with neighbors, and, so it would seem, perhaps even doubts about her own identity as well: her answers show both a moral revulsion for witchcraft and, at the same time, a curious uncertainty about her actions and motives. Who was Anna Schmieg after all?

CHAPTER VI

The Outsider

Amlishagen, Unterregenbach, Bächlingen,
and Hürden, ca. 1611–72

hile Court Adviser von Gülchen tried to get a fix on Schmieg's identity through her activities and motives on Shrove Tuesday, then sifted them for clues as to her role in the cosmic struggle between God and the devil, Anna tended to see herself and her relations through a different lens. She knew the basic Lutheran vocabulary about the heart and conscience, how the emotions and the influences that stirred her heart were reflected in her reputation and deeds. Using this moral register, Lutherans saw the most significant clues to a person's life in what lay within—grace or sin? Christ or Satan?—and how those stirrings propelled the moral drama of the Christian life. Anna admitted her sins, her drinking and cursing being too well known to deny. But she insisted that she had a pure heart and that her relations with others remained unblemished by anger, malice, and envy that would have driven her into Satan's grip.

While Schmieg also responded to questions about different periods of her life, she had never strung together those events as episodes in a moral drama unfolding in the logic of God's time. She tended instead to ground them along a second moral axis: the universe defined by family, honor, and household resources. It was within this little moral universe that one finds the most telling clues about her relations with neighbors and what lay behind the accusations of poisoning and witchcraft she now faced.

Schmieg spoke spontaneously about her early life. She felt that her childhood and adolescence had set her decisively on a certain course. Her early years left her, she suggested, with losses so large that she saw her life shaped more by what was missing or lost than by what had supported her:

[1] She is 57 years old and was born in Amlishagen. [A marginal note said she was actually 61]. She lived there 8 or 9 years and because her parents died early in her life she went from there to the tavern keeper at Unterregenbach, . . . as he was called, [and] stayed there 13 or 14 years until she got married. Her current husband's name is Schmieg. . . .

[2] Her father was called Sebastian Lampert and his craft was that of a carpenter. He died through God's power. After her father died her mother went with the children to Crispach [and] married the schoolmaster Georg Kefer. She stayed in his house 3 years because she [her mother] then died, too. She had a brother who joined up with the nobleman from Amlishagen during the war and never returned. She also has a sister who married and lived in Amlishagen Hernbach with a cobbler and died 3 years ago.[1]

What is striking in these two stories is how she saw misfortune and loss tossing her about from household to household, the primal event being the death of her father. The subsequent losses of her mother, brother, and sister further diminished her family. When peasants related parts of their lives to state officials—to justify petitions or explain their circumstances before a court—they almost always situated themselves among their kin, whether burdensome or quarrelsome, well or sick, needy or hardworking. Anna's stories revolved around family members who died or went missing when she was young. The close family and kin that anchored her in life, providing support, opportunities, and property, were gone. Over the years only her husband, Hans, remained by her. Her stories

were incomplete and only half true, since they glossed over the significant help she had received from unexpected quarters. Old,
alone, and in prison, Schmieg saw herself as an orphan and an
outsider.

———

ANNA ELISABETH Schmieg began life in Amlishagen, a tiny village in an exceptionally poor community located in an exposed
region of the gently rolling Hohenlohe plain and very different
from the Hohenlohe landscape she would know as an adult. Since
1463, Amlishagen had belonged to a noble but impoverished family of imperial knights, the lords of Wolmershausen, who made it
their family seat. From their castle they controlled a handful of villages and jealously guarded their liberties, rights, and jurisdictions.[2]
The tenor of village life was different, too. Amlishagen consisted of
impoverished artisans, most of them, one surmises, serving the von
Wolmershausens, some supplementing their living with tiny
parcels of land.

Her father's sudden death in 1620 cast Anna out of Amlishagen
and marked her as an outsider and dependent on others at a young
age. Sebastian Lampert was a carpenter and his family lived on the
razor's edge of survival. Without resources, his wife and children
fell on hard times. Soon thereafter, with the outbreak of the Thirty
Years' War, imperial Catholic troops, triumphant after their defeat
of the Protestants in Bohemia, moved through the region on their
way to the Rhineland. Making life more uncertain for the rural
poor, a ruinous inflation called the *Kipper- und Wipperzeit* came in
1622–23, the result of the debasing of the coinages of the Holy
Roman Empire. Food of all kinds became even more scarce, driving many into hunger. Since the new and burdensome war taxes
had to be paid in cash, scraping coppers together during a time of
inflation and famine could push even the most resilient peasant
households into a desperate struggle for survival.[3]

Anna Schmieg mentions none of these larger events, but they
exacerbated the circumstances in which her mother found herself
as she sought to take care of her children. It would have been dif-

ficult for a poor carpenter's widow to survive on her own. In a
larger principality like Hohenlohe or near a town, charity and
assistance for the poor might have provided her and her children
with a small measure of help, but tiny lordships like Amlishagen
never developed such public institutions. She may have survived
for a short while a domestic servant or a laborer, but the records
do not mention it. Such setbacks drove many women into
vagabondage, and the roads of southern Germany at this time
swelled with large numbers of men and women displaced by the
war and driven into ruin.

Given the circumstances, Anna's mother's marriage to a schoolmaster can be considered a stroke of good fortune. Anna did not
remember it that way, however. When she told the story of her
mother's marriage to the Hohenlohe schoolmaster, she stressed the
loss of her father and the move to a new village. Even though
Crispach was only fifteen to twenty miles from her home, the
young Anna entered a foreign land and became a stepchild in a
stranger's household. Stepchildren were often vulnerable; the
region's ledgers are full of conflicts involving children who felt
cheated out of a legacy when their mother or father married for a
second time.[4] Around this same time her brother, having marched
off to war in the service of the lord of Wolmershausen, disappeared.
More likely he died, either in battle or from the plague, dysentery,
or some other disease. If he was fortunate, he might have made a
new life for himself in some other land. In any event, the loss of her
last male kinsman left Anna more vulnerable than ever. Her mother
died soon after they moved to Crispach—around 1623 or 1624—
leaving Anna and her sister alone in Georg Kefer's household. Anna
would have been eleven or twelve years old.

A short time later Kefer arranged for Anna to become a domestic servant and sent her off to Hans Haffner, a tavernkeeper in the
village of Unterregenbach, not far from Langenburg.

In the seventeenth century most peasant girls and those from
solid burgher families became domestic servants as part of the life
cycle. If the funeral sermons of Lutheran pastors near Hohenlohe
are any guide to common views at the time, many people saw this
step as a misfortune that made it impossible for a family to support

a child.[5] In the words of a maid called Regina, the pastor of the parish of St. Michael's in Schwäbisch Hall saw domestic service this way: "Yes, many of us servants can still clothe ourselves as if we were the daughters of craftsmen, because we are, but we no longer have our parents, or our parents have lost everything due to misfortune, so that they have had to put their daughters out among other people."[6] This common view of domestic service as a step down the social ladder or as a period of uncertainty helps us to understand why Anna Schmieg explained this same transition in her life as another disruption and loss. Even though the Haffner household was a relatively prosperous one, Anna was once again an outsider in a new village.

In fact, fortune favored her when she moved to the village of Unterregenbach, which enjoyed more advantages than Amlishagen. Unterregenbach was wealthier, and it nestled where the Jagst River cut a deep and wide valley into the plain. Steeply winding roads led down to the valley, almost out of sight of travelers' or soldiers' eyes, thus making it a protected world. High above and jutting out on the rock promontory above the village were the town and castle of the counts of Hohenlohe-Langenburg, who on the whole offered more protection than the von Wolmershausens of Amlishagen. The houses of Unterregenbach were densely packed together, with fields, pastures, and woods spreading out around them. But the village was not closed in on itself. The road connected it with villages up and down the river and with the town above. Unterregenbach's companion village, Oberregenbach, lay close by, and ties between the two villages were deep, drawing a steady stream of peasants, millers, travelers, and peddlers.

These two villages along the Jagst were also shielded from the worst depredations of the war. While soldiers and the plague ravaged Langenburg and Bächlingen between 1630 and 1636, Anna worked at the Unterregenbach tavern, and the Regenbach communities were sheltered. Anna never suffered the fate of a war refugee. She not only survived the war but even made a fresh start as a young woman, thanks to her luck in moving in with the Haffners.

Haffner's wife was actually Anna's aunt, her dead mother's sister.

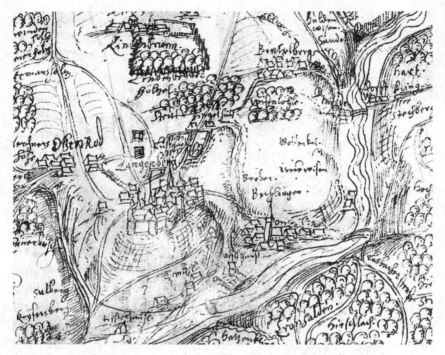

ANNA SCHMIEG'S WORLD. *Anna's little world revolved around the mill at Hürden—marked on this drawing by a tiny mill and bridge—and the nearby communities along the Jagst River. Dominating every part of it was the palace at Langenburg.*

In honoring the kinship, the Haffners offered Anna a new home, support, and extensive family connections. The 1630 tax assessment listed sixty-five households in the two communities—forty-two in Unterregenbach and twenty-three in Oberregenbach—and the Haffners had properties in both. His combined assets—a tavern, fields, and pastures in Unterregenbach, and a large farm and several parcels of land in Oberregenbach—made him one of the wealthiest, if not the wealthiest peasant householder in the entire district.[7] At the Haffners', Anna found her first secure footing in life.

When she recalled these early years as abrupt movements from one household to another, Schmieg expressed herself in rich language about household and kin. Lutheran reformers and state officials grasped the social order as a collection of households—a hierarchy of values shared by society as a whole. For pastors the well-regulated household reflected the harmony of God's order.

Sermons and pamphlets extended the idea to politics. Lords and princes were fashioned as "*Landesvatter*," or "fathers of the land," governing their subjects like well-loved children and servants. In drawing up taxes and drafting ordinances, state officials treated the household as the basic social unit of the community. Anna's move to Unterregenbach therefore brought her into one of the better-regarded households in the village, but, as a domestic servant and female relative, she assumed a place at the bottom of the household's hierarchy. One government ordinance admonished the lands' housefathers to raise girls "with the fear of God, piety and good manners, . . . Daughters were to be raised with discipline, to keep a good house industriously and to be kept from disagreeable or any other disobedient behavior."[8]

Anna's association with the Haffners also brought certain advantages and opportunities. For one, the Haffners honored their obligations as kin. For another, the tavern was a well-frequented gathering place where men met to drink, swap information, tell stories, make alliances and deals.[9] As a prominent man, Haffner enjoyed ties to families all up and down the Jagst River valley and even across the entire district.

Haffner was also a rebel. During the harsh winter of 1630–31 peasants gathered at his tavern to petition the government for relief from oppressive taxes, economic hardship, and the war. The plan of the so-called Oberregenbach Assembly was to force the government to provide protection and justice and shield them from the war taxes and troop quarterings that were driving them to ruin. In February 1632 they met once again at Haffner's tavern, drawing up yet another petition of protest. Haffner and the other ringleaders were rounded up "so that their punishment would be an example to the others, forcing them to recognize their wrong and crushing them into respect and obedience."[10]

Rough talking, a taste for wine, a fierce defensiveness shading over into defiance—Anna may have begun to pick up these behaviors during her formative years at Haffner's tavern. At the time of the peasant rebellion Anna was between fifteen and twenty years old. She would have served for seven or eight years in a peasant house better positioned than most to survive the hardships but nonetheless still struggling to find coping strategies. She witnessed firsthand the brutal hardships of famine, plague, perhaps even waited on the angry and desperate men meeting at the tavern, and then witnessed the fall and occupation at Langenburg by Catholic troops. Anna spent her formative years among villagers thrown on their own wits and meager resources to survive.

———

ONE STROKE of good luck did come her way. Through the Haffners she met her future husband, Hans Schmieg, whom she married in late 1636 or early in 1637. Anna was twenty-five or twenty-six, the average age at which Hohenlohe women married for the first time.[11] The Schmiegs owned a mill at Berndshofen, a village downriver from Oberregenbach, and their business seems to have brought them to Oberregenbach to drink, socialize, and make deals. The records also hint that the Schmiegs were related to Haffner, a fact that, if true, made Anna's marriage to Hans Schmieg part of an alliance between two families in the alimentary trades— tavernkeeping and milling—during a time of shortages of grain, food, and cash. Haffner backed the young couple when they set up at a new mill; he and other Haffners sometimes appear as partners of Hans Schmieg in his dealings. When the Haffners arranged Anna's marriage, they may also have felt that, as guardians, they were obligated to treat their ward with honor, to teach her Christian virtues, and to repay Anna's loyal and faithful service with additional help.[12] The Langenburg Marriage Court—which kept excellent records on its punishments—lists no scandal or even a hint of a violation of the moral laws in Anna's courtship and marriage.[13] Baptismal registers later record Georg Haffner—probably one of Haffner's sons—and his wife becoming godparents to the Schmieg children, thereby deepening the Schmieg-Haffner alliance. Anna was richer in kin and connections than she let on, and one cannot imagine any other way that the orphaned daughter of a carpenter could move into a clan of millers.

Luck also had a hand in Anna's move up the social ladder. As the Thirty Years' War intensified, the Langenburg government collapsed, and villagers died, fled, or were reduced to ruin, new positions opened up in what was once a rigid social order. In 1633 and 1634 plague swept through the region and the deaths in Bächlingen and other villages mounted swiftly. Then the crops failed. As panic and chaos spread, many peasants were reduced to eating field stubble or tree bark, or any stray cats and dogs they might find. Bodies littered the village streets. In September and October 1634 victorious Catholic troops, hard on the heels of the Swedes after their triumph at Nördlingen, marched into the region and besieged and took the castle and town at Langenburg. While Count Heinrich Friedrich and his family fled into exile in Strasbourg, their subjects had to survive as best they could.[14]

But agrarian crises also opened up positions for young people, emigrants, and outsiders. With some support, luck, and shrewdness one might marry, acquire an abandoned or ruined property, and enter the ranks of village property-holders—which was exactly what Anna and Hans did. In 1636, Kilian and Moses Preuninger— the old lord's miller and his son—could not keep the *Herrenmühle,* or lord's mill, at Bächlingen, gave up the lease, and abandoned the mill. *Corruptio unius sei generatio alterius,* went a Latin proverb sometimes cited during the Renaissance: "The ruin of one produces opportunity for another."[15] In 1637, at the edge of the half-deserted village of Bächlingen, just below the castle, Anna and Hans established their household in the rundown mill.

———

*W*HEN ANNA married Schmieg and moved to the *Herrenmühle,* it was only a short distance from the Haffners' tavern. While she may have beaten the odds and set up her new household, she did so at the cost of assuming the role of a different kind of outsider in the village: the miller's wife. The position brought with it suspicion, disrespect, and even dishonor. With an essential place in the agricultural economy, however, millers might also become big men in the village, and, in the right circumstances, accumulate a fortune. While these prospects may not have been important at the time— the village hardly functioned as a normal community in 1637—the match still made Anna into a local woman to reckon with when the village began to rebuild.

No records suggest that in the first years at the lord's mill Anna was unduly at odds with her neighbors. Central European villages were agonistic societies known for a high level of daily conflict between neighbors and family members. In part, such verbal and physical conflict over honor could be linked to the underlying competition for limited resources. The honor of a woman, for example, did not depend solely on her marital status and reputation involving sexual conduct. Birth, home village, legal standing before village and state institutions, and her reputation associated with her husband's or her own occupation or craft figured into considerations of her honor as well. Cases of slander before the local courts of discipline were one of the most important barometers of this daily give-and-take, and Hohenlohe peasant women appeared regularly before these courts. One would expect a miller's wife like Anna Schmieg to have attracted a fair amount of slander and other types of conflict simply because of her husband's occupation. Village communities, dependent on millers, also deeply distrusted them. They were suspected of stealing grain, charging unfair prices, or violating the market ordinances during hard times and selling scarce food supplies out of the district at night. Moreover, as the lord's personal miller, Hans Schmieg assumed the notoriety associated with holding a low-level government office. Despite the prominence of her position and for whatever reasons— the court did not meet regularly during the remainder of the Thirty Years' War, and when it did, records were spotty—Anna's name did not appear in disputes over her honor.

One aspect of Anna's early married life did stand out, however: a string of tragic deaths among her children. In the wake of a sudden and sharp loss of population, villages often experienced a surge in marriages, births, and baptisms. The response was part of a self-regulating demographic system that helped villages to overcome a population crisis and restore an equilibrium between resources and people.[16] Between 1638 and 1652, Schmieg bore nine children, seven boys and two girls. Nothing in the sequencing of these births suggests that she practiced contraception. The evidence points instead to a desperate effort to battle the long odds against children surviving into adulthood and provide her and Hans with heirs. Seven of her children died at young ages: Michel (6 years) in 1643; Hans Martin (5½ years), and Eva (2 months) in 1645; Jörg (4½ years) in 1646; Hans Martin (1½ years) in 1648; Johannes (1¾ years) in 1649; and another Johannes (3 months) in 1650. Only the second Michel (b. 1644), the Schmiegs' intended heir, and Eva, her last daughter (b. 1652) survived into adulthood.[17]

In some ways these deaths, heartbreaking though they must have been, were not that unusual. Infant mortality remained high in the seventeenth century and rose higher still during the last two decades of the Thirty Years' War. But two of these deaths attracted public attention. The pastor of Bächlingen normally recorded the funerals in the parish with short entries with the name, the date, and perhaps the age of the deceased. But when two Schmieg boys died in accidents at the mill, he made longer entries that described the tragedies. The first Hans Martin "fell over the dike and into the millrace and drowned in the water."[18] In 1646 poor Jörg suffered a similar fate: "Hans Schmieg, the lord's miller buried here a little son with the name of Georg [Jörg] who was 4 years and 33 weeks [old] who on the day before towards evening fell off the path and into the water, flowed under the wheel and was crushed to death."[19] It was true that Pastor Martin Hirsch knew the Schmiegs well—he was godfather to Hans Martin—and so he was perhaps moved by the deaths of the two Schmieg boys. Mills often were the site of terrible accidents. The machinery was loud and a child's call for help could not be easily heard if he fell into the millrace and got swept up in the swiftly turning wheels.

The two tragic deaths were wrenching for the Schmiegs. Knowing personal loss and suffering firsthand himself, their new lord, Count Heinrich Friedrich, showed understanding and sympathy to his servants for their losses. In expressing his gratitude for this gesture, Hans explained: "It is heart-breaking. Two times one of our children lost their lives in the water, and because of this I thank His Grace for understanding. No one can understand this sorrow unless they have unexpectedly lost their children."[20]

The deaths also engendered malicious rumors about the

Schmiegs. In the gossip that inevitably went around one might easily suggest that uncanny or dangerous forces were at work. It is possible that the malicious story that Anna had a hand in killing her children began to circulate at the time that these accidents happened. Her husband alluded to his neighbors' hateful stories in a petition to Count Heinrich Friedrich in 1651 and credited the count's personal faith in his story in damping down the unfavorable gossip surrounding the deaths.[21] The stories probably circulated for years, and when Anna Schmieg later stood accused of witchcraft and the court began listing all her crimes, they came up again.

———

ANNA'S REPUTATION was affected by a series of crises that broke over her and her household between 1647 and 1654. The troubles began at the end of the war, when troops occupied Langenburg once again, this time plundering villages and wreaking havoc. As Europe's great powers maneuvered for advantage before the signing of the Peace of Westphalia, contingent after contingent of soldiers from both sides occupied the Hohenlohe, located strategically along one of the main east-west roads in the empire. Between 1647 and 1650, German Protestant mercenaries under Duke Bernhard of Weimar, French soldiers under General Turenne, and then Swedish troops occupied Hohenlohe's villages and towns; on their heals came Catholic imperial and Bavarian units.[22] The depredations were ruinous. Hearing that more troops were to winter in the region at the end of 1647, a distressed district official wrote to Heinrich Friedrich that the peasants were ruined as it was, few had any money left, and many had, in fact, abandoned their homes.[23] The official Peace of 1648 made no difference. Indeed, the exploitation intensified.

The Schmiegs suffered as well. Lamenting his losses from these years, Hans Schmieg remembered "that I was ruined and plundered by the troops that came through."[24] On top of this, Anna's husband suffered two humiliations that put the Schmiegs at odds with their neighbors and tarnished their reputations for years to come. The first incident began to unfold in 1646 and 1647 when, while troops occupied the country, the harvests failed and prices for grain and bread shot up. Famine spread. When hungry villagers and townsfolk blamed the calamity on the millers, tavernkeepers, bakers, and butchers, the government stepped in and levied harsh fines. Among those singled out for hoarding food and selling it illegally out of the territory—for harming the public good—was Hans Schmieg.[25]

Shortly afterward, Hans got involved in a far more serious scandal. In 1649 he got into a scuffle with Count Heinrich Friedrich, whose mercy spared the Schmiegs from ruin, but when the villagers from Bächlingen heard about the assault on their lord and prince, they ostracized the Schmiegs.[26]

In facing these bitter setbacks at the *Herrenmühle*, Anna responded with tenacity, fiercely and aggressively defending her husband and her household's honor. She became involved in a string of quarrels and brawls with neighbors, responding defensively to the sharp verbal taunts. When Endris Schaffert's wife, who was pregnant at the time, insulted her with "heavy words," Anna responded with physical blows. Both women were fined by the court.[27] A year later Georg Hepper accused Anna of stealing flax from Adam Thon's wife.[28] He was found in the wrong and fined. As the count instituted judicial reforms, many such complaints came before the courts of discipline. The noteworthy aspect about the encounter with Schaffert's wife, however, was that Anna had struck the woman. While women often fought each other with words, returning an insult with physical blows suggests that, when Anna fought for her household's reputation, she escalated the violence.

The situation was somewhat offset when the count pardoned Hans and the couple left the *Herrenmühle* and bought their own mill in Hürden. In addition to the pardon, Heinrich Friedrich may also have allowed Hans to buy the mill at Hürden, assuming a higher than average burden of debt in doing so, in order to help his old servant out of his difficulties. Even though the Hürden mill was run down, requiring investment and repairs, the move meant that the Schmiegs improved their social standing: Hans Schmieg became a "freeholding" miller, a property-holder in his own right, and Anna, as his wife, improved her status as well. They also acquired a second smallholder's property in Bächlingen, thus putting the Schmieg household in the solid upper ranks of the smallholders of the river valley.

Still, the conflict followed Anna to Hürden. When she returned to the Bächlingen court of discipline in 1654, her disputes were in fact more violent than the last ones. The improvement in the Schmiegs' fortunes stirred up gossip and resentment. Rumors circulated about how Hans had put together the money to buy the mill by stealing money over the years at the *Herrenmühle*. One day while Anna was in a Bächlingen tavern, she was publicly confronted with these suspicions and called a thief. Anna exploded. Court protocols state:

> [Fine] for the woman miller of Hürden who was drinking wine in Hans Ebert's house in Bächlingen and who slandered and punished Claus Wihrt as it was said that her husband had stolen so much at the lord's mill that he could buy his mill with it, and then threw a goat's head in his face. The honorable judge, however, fines Wihrt because he insulted her by calling her a tall witchy whore 1 *fl.* 2 *fl.* 30 *kr.* [fine for Schmieg][29]

Anna defended her husband's honor. Only after she had bested Wihrt with the goat's head had he called her a name in response. While his name-calling did not amount to an accusation of witchcraft—calling a woman a "witch" was like calling a man a "rogue" or a "filthy black dog"—calling her a "witchy whore" was a particularly outrageous insult. Still, the slander was not unusual. In the constant bickering over honor, insults were one way to harm or test someone or perhaps drive home an attack and taint an enemy in the eyes of the community. The public arena of the tavern made the incident especially provocative. Had Anna let it pass, she might have invited even more damaging attacks at some later time. Once again she faced down an enemy by escalating the violence. Anna had become a brawler.

Another dispute in 1654, this one with a neighbor from Hürden,

Beſchreibung vnd Figur der zukünfftigen böſen vnd Manntheuren Zeit:
Nemlich / daß ſich
Sieben Weiber vmb ein par Mannshoſen ſchla-
gen werden.
Vermahne derowegen alle böſe Weiber / vnd Jungfrawen die jhre Männer vnd Schöſſe / ſo wenig / vnd nicht
weßet achten / daß ſie from werden / dieſelbige jhre Männer vnd Freyer lieben vnd ehren / ehe denn ſie ſolche
böſe Zeit betreffe.

SEVEN WOMEN FIGHT FOR A MAN'S PANTS. *When village women fell into disputes with one another, their antagonisms were seen as threats to public authority and order— symbolized here as an unseemly fight for a man's pants.*

escalated as well. When neighbors could not resolve a dispute on their own, one of them might turn to the village court of discipline. Doling out justice to one or both parties was thought to have an almost magical power to correct the injustice, to reconcile the parties, and restore someone's battered honor.[30] In especially troubling feuds the authorities intervened on their own, however. This is what seems to have happened when Anna fell into a dispute with a new neighbor's wife, over a goose. Describing the case in sparse language, the court scribe noted that "the miller's wife and Hans Wallhofer's wife of Hürden came at each other with words over a slaughtered goose, reconciled themselves together at the Pastor's, and then went together to communion, therefore each is to pay 15 *kr.*"[31] Later when Court Adviser von Gülchen, Court Preacher Dietzel, and other officials visited the parish, the pastor even called their attention to the dispute, noting it as one whose resolution came about only through pastoral intervention and the parties reconciling over the sacrament of Holy Communion. Later the pastor described the incident this way: "Two times he met her [Wallholfer's wife] on the path along the hedge and he heard the screaming. The pastor went to her and she was so overcome with enmity that she could not talk any more and then he went to meet with the miller's wife in Hürden."[32]

The court fined Anna, but a smaller amount than the one she had paid on Claus Wihrt's account. Harsh words were common among peasant women. Occurring soon after the Wallhofers had moved to Hürden, the dispute suggests that the two women were feeling out the terms on which they would relate to each other.

But the intervention of the Bächlingen pastor also suggests a breach in the peace serious enough to require both arms of the state to resolve. In the view of the Church an unrepentant heart threatened the entire community. Neighbors who lived in enmity, who left their disputes unresolved, should confess them as sins to the pastor and then be reconciled to God and the parish through the sacrament of communion. Few cases brought before the court of discipline at this time mentioned the necessity of the church intervening in village disputes. Since the time of the Reformation, however, Lutheran authorities had often worked hand in hand with the state to force villagers to overcome enmity with one another through forced attendance at confession and Holy Communion.[33] This coordination of power had broken down during the Thirty Years' War, and so one might view the intervention in 1654 as a sign that Langenburg was becoming more responsive to local breaches of the peace.

The incident was also one of the rare reported occasions when two women went alone before the pastor to overcome their enmity through confession and communion. In this region most villagers only confessed four times a year, and, when they did so, they insisted on confessing as a group so that others could hear what they said.[34] The rite did not lend itself to deep individual introspection, discouraging Lutherans from listing their individual sins—one's memory could hardly recount all of them—and emphasized instead the general sinfulness of sinners.

But the reconciliation worked for only a short while. In the spring of 1656, Anna was once again before the court of discipline, this time with Hans Wallhofer himself. The court scribe wrote that the court fined the two of them for insulting each other while having a drink:

> In the indecent exchange between Hans Walhofer and the miller's wife [who were] drinking together, trading insulting words, in a completely drunken stupor she called him a wild sow, he then [called] her a duck, she then insulted him in response by calling him a black cowardly dog. [Schmieg] also said that she had been called out by Walhofer's wife, [saying] that she drank so much wine that she would scream out at her neighbor, but she would not admit to anything, saying instead about it, this is all Devil's gossip as is well known.[35]

Once again Schmieg outdid her opponent, this time with her insults. It is hardly surprising that Schmieg gave more than she got in this exchange. It was not just that she called Wallhofer "a wild sow." Slander often involved animal name-calling. Anna went further and unmanned him with her insults, calling him a *female* pig and not just a dog, but a *cowering, cowardly* dog. This was probably why the judges fined him 40 kreutzer, but her more, a full gulden. The record also refers for the first time to Anna's reputation for drinking, an unfavorable attribute normally attaching more to men than to women in this period, and one that distinguished her from other village women in the protocols.

Four years later Schmieg found herself in a more serious quarrel with Johann Conrad Hohenbuch, the Langenburg steward. Trading insults and getting into fights with peasant neighbors was one thing; lashing out at the count's steward was another. Hohenbuch came from a family of civil servants that had served the counts for a generation or more. As steward, he represented the count's interests as a landlord, collecting rents and dues and other levies on the land and individuals. He kept the district account books, meticulously entering and sorting every income according to type. To help him carry out these duties, he employed a number of petty servants: messengers, foresters, shepherds, and assistants, among them on occasion, Anna's own husband. So when Hohenbuch fined Hans 5 gulden at Pentecost in 1658 for illegally selling a cow, he did so in the usual course of his duties. The fine was a heavy one. Schmieg, he pointed out to the court in his long report, had flaunted a decree against selling cattle without first offering them to the Langenburg court.

Peasants often balked at paying such fines. Some quietly refused to pay, forcing a confrontation at a later point, or some formally protested the levy and petitioned directly to the count. In difficult times, as we saw in the 1630s, peasants might even recruit their neighbors and organize a collective protest, but such actions were unusual. Open defiance of authority in this region was rare after 1648.

What was even more unusual was the disturbing response of the miller's wife to the fine. Hohenbuch deferred collecting it immediately after Pentecost. Either Schmieg did not have the cash or he hoped, as Hohenbuch implied in his report, that the government would simply drop the matter or settle it off the books. When instead in the fall Hohenbuch assessed the unpaid balance of the fine against the Schmieg's wine harvest, Anna flew into a rage. She confronted Hohenbuch personally, threatening him, thus creating an incident more disturbing than the original infraction. As the steward reported the matter, Anna came all the way from Hürden to his cellar in Bächlingen. She was drunk, he wrote, and then, ritually blessing himself with a "*salvie venie*" to keep her foul language from polluting him, reported that she flew at him with "utterly foul lies":

> The miller woman then acted in such a way as she is want to do when she is completely soused, she came to the district office, making a bloody nuisance of herself, [asking] why he was seizing her new wine? When I explained the reasons to her, she answered back: "in God's name, if I have the right to it then I should take her new wine." The mill is there, as well, and it has long been for sale, I might take that as well, then she could say that I have taken her things by force. . . .

I said nothing in response or I would have her locked up in the madhouse. Then I asked her why her husband had not respectfully petitioned the government to reduce the fine. . . .

She then answered me with a string of abusive words . . . , frivolously implying that in my duties I have been prejudiced against her: when she has petitioned it has long been known that she gets nothing in return and that it is useless, that she has petitioned a lot of times, but never gotten a thing out of it, when I do not reduce [the fine] it is all for nothing and pointless.[36]

The matter was not left there. Still needing to collect the fine, Hohenbuch sent one of his messengers to the Schmiegs. Hans and Anna stood by while they heard what Hohenbuch's lackey had to say. Before her husband could speak, Anna, acting insolently, or so the boy reported later, said that "she refuses to do it with either this or that person, that the new wine should be left alone, that they will have to take what is hers with force."[37] Meanwhile, her husband softened and showed a willingness to compromise.

What is interesting about this confrontation was Anna's reckless defiance of public authority. She showed disdain for the steward, questioning his honor by challenging the justice and the legality of his actions. A fine line separated legitimate fines from illegitimate ones, and she claimed the steward had not only crossed it, but that one could never expect justice from him and his office. She was virtually calling him a thief to his face. The relationship between peasants and their lords rested on a delicate sense of reciprocity, the lords' officials providing protection and justice in exchange for a subject honoring his right to tax his resources. To question the steward's fairness was to insult the honor and integrity of the government. A steward might punish insubordination like Anna's with an additional heavy fine. But Hohenbuch backed away from Schmieg—he had clearly been shocked by the unexpected ferocity of her insults—and appealed to Count Heinrich Friedrich for help.[38]

As one would expect, Count Heinrich Friedrich upheld the original fine. On the other hand, he decided not to punish Anna for her insubordination. He did not explain his mercy to her or his officers. In his decree, he wrote only that, should a similar incident happen again, Hohenbuch should fine the Schmiegs stiffly. The count reviewed hundreds of such cases every year. While he rarely justified his decisions—scribbling them on the back of the petition or report—he also calibrated the justice he exercised in each case carefully. Acts of justice were personal matters between him and his subjects. This had been one of the secrets to his success in rebuilding his shattered principality after the war; the thousands of individual petitions he judged represented thousands of personal acts of justice to assert his authority and win the loyalty of his subjects. It is quite possible that the old personal bond with Hans as his own miller played a part in his showing mercy. Many others were never granted such leniency, and there was not a single other case from this time of a woman showing such shocking disrespect for a public official. Hohenbuch never expressed any misgivings about the prince's decision—his position made that difficult, after all—yet one could not begrudge him feeling that he had been slighted in letting Anna off so mildly.

The incident sealed Anna's reputation in the eyes of some government officers as a menace to the community. While she may have been defending her household and expecting justice, thus linking her protest to the widely respected norms about the common good, Hohenbuch labeled her a menace:[39]

> . . . this well known good-for-nothing woman, who is given to wine and to the quarrels, brawls, shocking curses, swearing and blasphemous insults of all kinds that stem from this drunkenness, as is shown by the established court protocols and by others who have fallen into recalcitrance with her. This is testified to not only by Herr Dr. Gülchen, but also here and there around town where she has called me names. [She says] to the loss of her soul and spiritual welfare that she no longer wants her share in the Kingdom of Heaven.[40]

In his diatribe Hohenbuch used the legal and moral terms of the government's police and church ordinances to denounce Anna. While his rant was not surprising for an insulted government official who expected women to show him deference, still it was harsh. Already some were inclined to see her a reckless disturber of the peace, a blasphemer.

The incident passed without further action. By this date—Anna was around forty-seven years old—there was little she could do to remove the stain on her reputation. Besides, she continued to respond with volatility to what she considered affronts to her, her husband, or her household. In 1662, for example, she was back again before the court of discipline, this time accused of having stolen a piece of leather from the wife of the Bächlingen tanner and then for insulting the tanner, Hans Ebert, at his house. Anna admitted to having taken two pieces of leather, but she insisted she did so by mistake. She explained that she had assumed that she had paid for both of them when actually she had paid for only one. She also admitted that, in response to his calling her a "thief," she shot back a "hateful" insult. Recognizing that this was a mistake on her part, Schmieg described the incident this way:

> When after [buying the leather] I went over to Hans Ebert's house and the tanner was there as well, he insulted me by calling me a thief, and I did not want to be [called] one, but out of the weakness of being a woman the rage so overcame me that I shot back an insult at him in return and I otherwise did not behave in a seemly manner. (. . .) If I did it, I acted out of ignorance, and the other happened out of haste for which my heart is deeply sorry.[41]

In this rare account in her own voice, Anna explains that she lost her composure in the heat of a confrontation, that rage overcame her quickly and got out of control. If her anger was set on such a hair trigger, then it is likely that in her many quarrels with neighbors she was not acting out of some cleverly thought out strategy for advancing her interests or defending herself and her honor. She reacted spontaneously and emotionally—especially when she was drinking—and that then in a full rage set upon her opponent with blows or furious curses and insults.

One should also realize that she was capable of presenting herself in a calculated way. In this petition, for example, she shrewdly invoked a rhetorical style preferred by women pleading for mercy from the count. The secret was to address Heinrich Friedrich in all humility, admit guilt, show heartfelt remorse and piety, and, if at all possible, show how one's household had suffered from the error and could be brought back to order and harmony through an act of grace. Schmieg pleaded for mercy "because this punishment has not only given trouble to my husband, but has in fact turned our marriage into a completely evil one."[42] She knew how hearts were moved.

Anna's appeal worked. Once again Heinrich Friedrich showed her mercy, reducing her fine by half but taking the opportunity to admonish her to change her life. In approving her request, he advised her "in the future to refrain from provocative cursing, blaspheming and other unseemly behavior, and to commit herself diligently to an honorable Christian life and transformation."[43] Only on rare occasions did petitioners receive such a personal sermon from Heinrich Friedrich. The count seems to have adopted the opinion of his advisers that she was an ungodly nuisance. But he still struck a chord of Christian optimism. For breaching the peace she should pay the fine, but she also deserved mercy and some pastoral care. She might yet reform her life.

<hr>

*L*OOKING BACK over the arc of her life, the traits that angered Anna's neighbors and, on occasion, alarmed the authorities were the same ones that enabled her to survive and, despite all the odds, even rise above her station. Feeling the loss of her parents and family and being sent off to relations as a servant—while seeing others suffer, flee, and starve to death—armed her with an unusual tenacity and aggressiveness to defend what was hers. As a young miller's wife, she had learned to defend her and her husband's honor, even violently. When the crisis broke over her and her husband at the end of the Thirty Years' War, and she and her husband faced a harsh and uncertain fate, again she fiercely defended what was hers. From this time on, battling her neighbors' envy and ostracism became a way of life. Hohenlohe women were distrustful and quarrelsome in the best of times, and perhaps the dire circumstances of the Thirty Years' War made them more so. But Anna Schmieg fought differently from other women. Where her neighbors might fight their enemies to a standstill, Anna stunned and overwhelmed them, if not with physical blows then with words so shocking that even seasoned state officers were stung by their violence.

When Court Adviser von Gülchen questioned Anna Schmieg in that first interrogation of March 1672, he therefore confronted a woman whom he knew and whose reputation had long ago set her apart. In some ways her notoriety fit contemporary stereotypes of a witch as a quarrelsome and aggressive older woman beyond her childbearing years.[44] But when the young women of the village adopted these views, they were expressing a generation gap that separated them from Anna. Not only were these women much younger and in the prime of their childbearing years, but they had also settled more recently in Hürden than she had. As poor domestics and the wives of wage laborers, the Hürden women also envied Anna her and her household's resources. Moreover, they escaped the horrors of the 1630s and 1640s. Hardship and poverty they knew, but they had never battled for survival as she had. Besides, these younger women had been brought up under the influence of Heinrich Friedrich's campaign to instill religious, moral, and social discipline after the war. When Anna's neighbors called her a quarreler, a "no-good woman," a drunk, a tight-fisted hoarder, even an "evil woman," they were articulating the moral values that saturated public life after 1650. Many kept their distance from her. Anna's fierce reputation served as a cloak of protection she threw around herself, her husband, and her family.

Say what one will about her reputation—and she knew what the gossipers said about her—Anna Schmieg had also used her few breaks in life to make her way in a violent and hostile country. Her luck in surviving the war, her connections to the Haffners, her marriage to Hans Schmieg, her position as a miller's wife, their income and resources at the mill, her combative streak and her rich vocabulary of abuse, the ties of patronage that connected her to Count Heinrich Friedrich himself, perhaps even her notorious reputation—all of these helped her to survive, advance herself, build a household, and move into a dominant position in the village. Instead of meeting threats with deference, piety, or silence, she gave in to her rages, threatening vengeance on neighbors and their property, uttering blasphemies, muttering curses under her breath, dissembling, even defying public officials. She did so with a moral compass set firmly toward the stars that guided other Hohenlohe women as well: honor, blood, and household.

Once arrested, however, and sitting alone in her prison cell, all she had left to meet her interrogators was her fierce temper, her tenacity, her sarcasm, and a bit of wiliness. Would these instincts be enough to save her one more time?

CHAPTER VII

Sorcery at the Mill

The Mill at Hürden,
February 20–April 30, 1672

hile Anna and Eva languished in prison and the inquisition's work ground on, a few Langenburgers began to wonder whether other diabolical conspiracies were at work. To their credit the high Langenburg authorities who were conducting the investigation were not behind the effort to widen the circle of suspects. Regardless of how von Gülchen and Court Preacher Dietzel drew upon the law or used witch theory in conducting the trials, neither of these learned men showed any eagerness to extend the scope of the investigations, the pressure coming instead from a government official lower down the hierarchy: the executioner, Endris Fuchs, and other common people. The arrest of Anna Schmieg seems to have been the catalyst for suspicious folk to reconsider other uncanny and disturbing events.

From the moment his wife was arrested, Hans Schmieg faced one problem after another. The absence of his wife and daughter from the mill made the day-to-day operation of the household difficult if not impossible. While men worked the fields and tended the equipment, women took care of the animals—the cattle, goats, sheep, and chickens—ran the kitchen and prepared the meals, made and mended clothes, tended the vegetable garden, and even worked in the vineyards or brought in side livings as laborers. Hans

Schmieg and his son, Michel, simply could not maintain the household. Besides, Hans was over sixty and no longer up to the heavy physical labor that running a mill required. Over the last year, he and Anna had been planning to have Michel marry, turn the mill over to him, and then retire.

Within a short time of the arrests Hans became so overwhelmed that he drew up a plea for relief to Count Heinrich Friedrich. In his petition of March 18 he struggled to find the right words to describe the calamity breaking over him:

> As the scribe takes his quill in hand . . . I don't have the right words
> . . . to describe my wretched circumstances after the arrest of my
> wife and daughter or even how I should accurately explain it, since
> there is only a measly little bit of bread left at the mill. . . . How to
> keep up the household and the essential things, how to heat the
> main room, how to take care of our few cows, or whatever else has
> to be done, must be considered, as well as how to carry on with the
> millworks which is like a stone around my neck. And going on like
> this for long is much too hard: in fact, it is impossible.[1]

The work of the mill, difficult though it was for an old man, could somehow be managed with the help of his son. What overwhelmed him was the women's work. The gist of his petition was that the loss of the women's labor made the household unmanageable, so that he now had to consider leasing out the mill. More to the point: he asked the count to release his daughter from prison. Instead of pleading his daughter's innocence or praising her character, he made a very pragmatic argument, by pointing out that his household and the mill stood under princely protection, that their functioning was now impaired, and that only an act of mercy could rescue them. Hans created a curious emotional distance from his daughter.

In declining the request Heinrich Friedrich showed nevertheless sympathy for Hans and his difficulties. His tone was conciliatory, even caring, but the lord of Langenburg wrote to Hans that he could not yet release his daughter. The count's habit was to uphold the normal course of the law: Only at the right time, when the truth had finally come to light, might princely mercy be shown. Heinrich Friedrich was known for his sternness in matters of justice, so his note of personal reassurance to Hans and his promise to have the trial hurried along is noteworthy. "In addition, as to the matter of his wife and daughter, as best as time allows, it will be handled as quickly as possible."[2]

Meanwhile, the troubles at the mill deepened. In April, Hans turned to the only people who might yet help him: his relatives. Peasants counted on male kinsmen when legal problems arose—only men had standing before the law—and drastic measures were now called for to help Hans halt the mill's decline. Joined by Hans Hag, a relative from Pfedelbach, three Schmieg brothers—Georg from Pfedelbach, and Adam and Peter from Berndshofen—traveled to Langenburg to plead for help for their beleaguered brother:

> Unfortunately, it is common knowledge that these last several weeks the wife and daughter of Hans Schmieg, the miller at Hürden, have been clamped in iron chains, and that the millworks and the upkeep of the little household have fallen to him and his son, and that it is going sour for him. In these circumstances . . . care should be taken to provide them with food.[3]

Signing a petition to Count Heinrich Friedrich "on their own behalf and that of other kinsmen," they renewed the plea to free Eva so that she could come to the aid of her desperate father. They were met with silence.

Hans also faced new tensions with his neighbors. Feuds that involved formal accusations of witchcraft often turned rancor and discord into a life-and-death struggle.[4] When the Fesslers and their partisans denounced Anna for poisoning and witchcraft, they did not simply destroy what was left of Hans's wife's reputation, they also attacked his welfare and the operation of his mill and farm. Worse yet, a conviction might mean the confiscation and sale of the mill itself. So when Hans learned of Michel Fessler's accusations and went looking for him in Bächlingen, he was in the fight of his life.[5] His defense of Anna looked different to the Schmiegs' enemies, however. To Michel Fessler, who was warned by Rainer Melcher's wife of Bächlingen and by the *Kutscher*, Hans's threats looked like acts of vengeance.

Under the circumstances, Hans's bravado made sense. Anna was his wife after all—he needed her, and any new blow to her honor diminished him and his standing in the community. They were firm allies and partners, and Anna's cursing and insulting neighbors went back to her fierce defense of Hans and his honor. Although her insubordinate attack on Hohenbuch may have strained relations between them, Hans had no record of mistreating his wife, let alone abandoning her when she was in trouble. The unspoken code of honor demanded that Hans protect his wife by countering damaging slander and accusations. Rumors were rife that Hans threatened to ruin Georg Heinckelin and burn down his house, that if his wife did not come home safely he would make sure that Heinckelin paid for his treachery with his life.[6] In the peril created by an accusation of witchcraft, cautious or cowardly husbands might establish their distance from their embattled wives. Hans did not. Besides, giving in invited further attacks.

---

*U*NBEKNOWNST TO Hans, a new and even more dangerous attack had already been leveled at him. On February 28, less than a week after Anna's arrest, Master Fuchs secretly went to the Langenburg court and accused Hans of sorcery. The law allowed for secret denunciations, because in cases of heinous crimes like witchcraft or sorcery the authorities wanted to make it possible for someone to come forward without fear. Fuchs's denunciation would not be acted on for five weeks—it would require further investigation—but the implications of the executioner's story did not escape Steward Assum, the court officer who received it. Even though the executioner never used the word "sorcery," the conclusion was inescapable if Fuchs's story was true.

On Good Friday of the previous year (1671), having finished clipping the ears of his lordship's English hunting hounds, Fuchs was walking back to Langenburg accompanied by his dog,

Melcher. The way took him by Hürden, where he stopped to rest near the pond that fed the millstream. Suddenly his dog saw a cat and chased it up a tree. When the cat ran off toward the mill, followed by the dog, Hans Schmieg appeared, saying that if the cat was a black one he would have a good use for it. Catching Schmieg's meaning, Fuchs put his professional expertise with animals at the miller's service, replying "that he could get him just such a black cat." Fuchs went on to explain that "Hans wanted to take the head and bury it under his door, God protect me, in the name of the devil." Custom had it that if you put a cat's head in the earth beneath a door and then invoke God or the Devil, the charm would protect a house or barn from harm. After this meeting, Schmieg asked Fuchs "two more times for [black cats], each time on a Wednesday, one time about an hour after the hour of prayer and another time at the market in Künzelsau from Fuchs's brother Michel." Fuchs even mentioned that Hans's son, Michel, and a millworker knew of Hans's interests in black cats and could corroborate his story.[7]

What made this story even more credible, and Steward Assum intimated as much in his comment when he sent the report to Court Adviser von Gülchen, was that Fuchs had implicated himself and his brother. If the story was true, then one of Langenburg's own government officials, an agent critical to the exercise of criminal justice, was involved in the underground traffic in the paraphernalia of sorcery. Noteworthy, too, was that Fuchs's brother was reported to be Schmieg's godfather.

———

*E*ven in the best of times, millers enjoyed ambiguous and conflicted relations with their neighbors. On the one hand, they performed a vital economic service. Every village and lordship relied upon mills and millers to grind grain into flour. Already by the end of the thirteenth century a dense network of mills lined every river and stream in Franconia. Along the banks of the Jagst River in the Langenburg lordship alone, for example, were mills at Eberbach, Oberregenbach, Bächlingen, and Hürden. Lords and princes either

WATER MILL AT FOREST'S EDGE. *For practical reasons mills were often located on the outskirts of a village or town. This drawing highlights the separate and isolated world of the mill by locating it at the edge of a wild wood far from the town.*

established and operated the mills outright as quasi-feudal properties or regulated the "free" mills in the interest of serving the common good. Mills like the *Herrenmühle* in Bächlingen belonged to the count of Langenburg and were burdened with a variety of rents, dues, and servile obligations that other "free" millers did not have to endure. Other mills had become "freeholds" and, while still subject to tight government regulation, could be inherited and passed on within the family. Both types of mills were subject to the conflicting pressures of state controls and unpredictable economic ups and downs. Millers profited so long as the population grew, the economy expanded, and prices for grain and bread continued to increase. During the long economic expansion of the sixteenth century, millers often became rich, their properties the envy of their less well-to-do neighbors.

Villagers and the government authorities distrusted millers, however. Even in Franconia, known for its many wealthy millers, townspeople and villagers treated them with the suspicion and distrust reserved for dishonorable folk or those living on the margins of society.[8] Stories, ballads, and songs about millers described them as rogues and thieves. The Franconian proverb "*Neben jeder Mühle steht ein Sandberg*" (Next to every mill stands a pile of sand) referred to the suspicion that millers routinely dilute the flour with sand or chaff.[9] And a typical refrain from the song "The Thieving Miller" went like this:

> Miller, grinder, rye robber,
>> how do you feed your pig?
> Grain you buy for less than a copper,
>> like you they get fat and big.
> Others must for themselves make do
>> while all of their goods come to you.
> Just like a thieving hawk you prey,
>> circling 'round and stealing where you may.[10]

Mill ordinances forbade millers from forestalling, exporting grain out of the land, and profiteering during times of dearth.

So deep ran the distrust of millers that popular culture associated them with magic, sorcery, and dark supernatural powers. "*Es spukt auf der Mühle*" was a common saying—"Uncanny things happen at the mill." They were rogues and thieves. Living at the edge of respectable society, along the river or stream at the edge of the village, millers acted in clannish ways and kept apart from honorable folk. The notion of mills as safe havens and sanctuaries, a holdover from medieval customary law, also fed suspicions that they were dens of criminals, heretics, and gathering places for strangers and other unsavory characters. The secrets of their craft they kept to themselves.[11] At night the devil and demons hid out in the mills.[12] Masking their activities behind the loud clattering and unnerving pounding of the wheels and gears, millers practiced the dark arts of sorcery. Why else did so many accidents occur around mills or along the swift-moving waters of the millrace? In 1605, Hans Albrecht, the miller at Bächlingen, was overheard through the clatter of the wheels talking with Satan, plotting the ruin of his enemies.[13] A fellow miller from Oberregenbach, Caspar Steigleder, was fined 30 *kreuzer* in 1645 for curing a cow of an illness with "witch's work." The record is silent about why he was let off so lightly.[14]

Well into the eighteenth century many German communities maintained sharp boundaries between honorable craftsmen and those who practiced trades considered dishonorable, disreputable, and even unclean. While the authorities may have tried to discourage such prejudices, they still ran deep and spilled over into communal conflicts or incidents that reinforced the isolation and stigma of certain individuals and groups.

There were three such categories of dishonorable people. All of the *fahrende Leute*, or traveling folk, those who belonged to no town or village or had no fixed residence, were disparaged as social outcasts, including Jews, Gypsies, beggars, peddlers, entertainers, prostitutes, cardplayers, charlatan healers, actors, singers, and musicians. Almost all of the lowest-level state functionaries—those who "dirtied" themselves with the vital but distasteful work of the state and the criminal justice system—were considered dishonorable: executioners, gravediggers, street-cleaners, court lackeys, police flunkeys, and skinners or those who removed dead animals. Even the touch of one of these polluted individuals could tarnish the reputation of an honorable person. And finally there were occupations slightly polluted or tainted with ill repute: shepherds, tanners, weavers, potters, bath masters, barbers, and, finally, the millers.[15]

When Hans Schmieg took over the *Herrenmühle* in 1637, he therefore also inherited the suspicion and ill will directed at millers. Adding to these prejudices and setting him up for chronic problems and strife were the rundown state of the mill and the harsh terms of his lease. When the medieval lords of Hohenlohe had first had the mill built, they chose a site at the bend of the Jagst River close to the castle but beyond the compact settlement of houses and farm buildings that made up the village of Bächlingen. Even today the mill sits off on its own, lonely and isolated, as if to emphasize the separate life that the miller and his family lived in Schmieg's time.

To get the mill running properly Hans had to make considerable repairs and invest a sizable sum of money. Two of the three large millwheels had to be replaced completely, along with the two large geared companion wheels, two huge shafts to hold these four wheels, and sturdy new settings that attached the massive shafts to the foundations of the building itself. In addition, new grain and flour troughs were needed and repairs had to be made to the grate governing the flow of water through the weir. However, the mill came equipped with iron rods, rings, mallets, chisels (for sharpening the millstones), buckets, troughs, sieves, and storage bins. The holding pond and canal that diverted and controlled the flow of water under the millwheels seemed in good repair. The Schmiegs could move into the living quarters upstairs and sleep on an old bed, bedding, and pillows, although they were shoddy and "of little value." Anna could grow vegetables and herbs in the two summer gardens next to the barn and tend any cows or goats they acquired in the pasture along the canal. While the Langenburg government promised wood from the count's private forests for repairs and help in paying the carpenters, the burden of the costly repairs fell to Hans.[16]

Operating the *Herrenmühle* proved to be a touch-and-go struggle for the Schmiegs. When the former tenants, the Preuningers, gave up the mill, they had complained that the steep rents so burdened the mill that they could no longer make a living from it.[17] For years Hans did no better. Not only paying the same high rents, he also struggled to pay off loans to take over the lease and make the costly repairs. Hans borrowed 300 reichsthalers, a princely sum for a peasant, from Anna's uncle Hans Haffner, Adam Thon, the smith from Oberregenbach, and Catharina Bauer, a widow from Unterregenbach. Hans signed the lease on the mill together with his three backers.[18] In addition, as a "lord's miller," Hans had to perform extra duties. As well as provisioning the court with flour, he and Anna had to take care of the count's prized flock of twenty-four geese, the feathers and eggs to be delivered to the court. Responsibility for the lord's dovecote also fell to the miller and his wife. In going back and forth to the castle, Hans won the personal favor of Heinrich Friedrich, but compared with the territory's other "free" millers, Hans was still poor, heavily in debt, and exploited.

The downturn in the agricultural economy beginning in the 1630s only exacerbated these problems. Hans had the misfortune of taking over the *Herrenmühle* precisely when the production of grain—and all of the income derived from it—had begun to fall steeply, making a turning point when population declined precipitously, the demand for agricultural products fell off sharply, and grain prices tumbled to their lowest point in the entire early modern period. With many villagers having died or fled, the economy was experiencing a wrenching contraction. As a young miller Schmieg was caught in a crushing vise. His income was greatly reduced, but the rents remained high.

Through resourcefulness, cunning, and sheer tenacity, however, Schmieg repaired the mill and found new ways to make a living. The trick, he learned, lay in bargaining almost constantly with his lord and the steward, offsetting declining income from grain with lower rent and relief from some of the burdens. In 1640, for example, Schmieg found that he could pay only 100 of the 125-reichstaler rent; he petitioned the government for relief and won it. Schmieg took advantage of the government's weakness and a general shortage of millers. The steward noted that the government had no choice but to accept the new terms, because he was unlikely "to find another miller somewhere else who would have the money as I have asked throughout the land and can learn of no one."[19] Hans then pressed his advantage and successfully had the burdensome cash rent converted to 220 measures of grain per year.[20] By the time Heinrich Friedrich returned to Langenburg and took over the government in 1645, Hans had managed to keep the mill working, becoming a valued and seemingly irreplaceable servant. He appears to have struck up a personal bond with the young count.

At the end of the 1640s, however, one scandal after another set Hans against the authorities and his neighbors. The affairs stained his honor, perhaps irretrievably, and set him and his wife at odds with the community for years to come. It was at this time that Anna became known as an aggressive defender of her husband's honor.

In 1647, Swedish and French troops occupied the land, triggering an avalanche of crises. By the spring of 1648 grain production collapsed, prices spiked, and supplies began to disappear even from mills and marketplaces. One district official described how the soldiers

> stripped away all of the grain from the subjects, even the grain set aside for eating and sowing next year's crops, and took away most of the essential cattle, in addition to household goods and even clothes. The subjects were oppressed to such a degree that even the well-to-do were stripped of all food and provisions and consequently faced hunger. . . . All of this burdened them daily, and the soldiers demanded the impossible from them, pressing them, executing them, threatening them to within an inch of their lives, martyring them, torturing them, inflicting pain, beating them at the slightest [provocation], setting upon them with sharp knives and cocked pistols . . . so that the frightened and exhausted people, bled to the bone, run away and flee.[21]

Famine began to spread. Millers came in for harsh treatment. The government tried to regulate the marketing of grain and cattle in the service of the "common good," demanding that millers and bakers observe posted prices, that they make their precious reserves of grain available to local buyers, especially that they not export grain outside the territory.[22] Bakers and millers were vilified for their "unchristian" behavior.[23] So often did grain and bread run short between 1646 and 1651 that the steward kept a separate protocol to document all the fines and punishments.[24]

From his first years at the *Herrenmühle*, Hans had fallen into disputes with some of his neighbors and the authorities over his activities at the mill. Within just a couple years of beginning his trade, he was fined on at least one occasion for slipping into the fields at night and stealing someone's wine.[25] Veit Planck of Bächlingen accused him of shorting him on grain, although the charge was not proven.[26] In the spring of 1649, however, tensions pitted him and the other millers against the villagers over the high grain prices and unfair or other marketing practices at the mills. On May 23, the millers appealed to the government for mediation. Responding to

. DN. 🐐 . H .
DIE SPRICH SALOMO DAS XI CAPITEL
WER KORN INHELT DEM FLVCHEN DIE LEIT
ABER SEGEN KOMPT VBER DEN SO ES VERKAFFT
M D XXXIIII

THE GRAIN HOARDER. *Laws regulating the sale and distribution of grain, bread, and foodstuffs rested in part on the moral condemnation of unscrupulous traders who hoarded grain or sold it unfairly. Citing the Book of Proverbs, this broadside lambasts the fat, immoral, and demon-inspired grain hoarder: cursed is he who hoards grain (left) but blessed is he who sells it (right).*

the insistence that the millers abide by the tariffs posted on the church door, Schmieg and his allies explained that "because of our sins and those of everyone else [the prices of] grain have risen quickly recently . . . 2 Reichthalers more." Moreover, "the heavy ice during the last winter has ruined our millwheels," and Hans and the others had to rig up their horses to turn the millworks. Worse yet, the millers had to sell grain below their own costs. Were they forced to continue, they would all be ruined and driven out of business.[27]

The government showed little sympathy for the plight of the millers, however, currying public favor instead. With the end of the war in sight and Count Heinrich Friedrich reestablishing his authority, a harsh stand against the millers allowed him to stand for social justice, punishing greed and unchristian behavior, and protecting the hard pressed and impoverished Langenburgers from exploitation. The young count not only dismissed the millers' complaint, he levied a stiff fine of 20 reichsthalers on them for "showing themselves wholly obstinate and recalcitrant for refusing for two days to cart the required 24 measures of grain."[28] Right through the lean year of 1650 the government kept its hard line against Schmieg and the other millers, branding them as greedy privateers.[29]

On the heels of the bruising communal battle over his marketing practices, a troop of soldiers seized and plundered the *Herrenmühle*. Shortly afterward, Hans recalled "that his heart fell for a second time into deep suffering when two of his beloved children fell into the water and were robbed of their lives." Then one night in September came the ruinous scuffle. Strolling through the vineyards along the Langenburg church lane, Hans was startled by a stranger. Without thinking, he accosted the man—who turned out to be his lord, Count Heinrich Friedrich himself.

Assaulting a prince was a grave offense. The attack could be seen as tantamount to attempted regicide, treason, rebellion, or *lèse-majesté*.[30] Hans later described the struggle as an accident and a misunderstanding on his part, that he had been startled and in the dark had not recognized his lord.[31] That the inquisition did not make an example of him and confiscate his property, mutilate him on the gallows, and banish him from the territory, but instead settled upon a steep fine and six months in prison, can be seen as an exceptional act of mercy. Perhaps the count felt sympathy for his miller and the plight of his family—Hans lamented that his wife and children had suffered terribly on account of his crime—and wanted to show his gratitude for twelve years of loyal service under extraordinarily difficult circumstances. Or perhaps the government valued Schmieg as a miller. Still, his crime and the punishment branded Hans a rogue and a malcontent.[32]

The incident shattered Hans's honor. The village ostracized him, Anna, and their son, Michel. He became vulnerable to attacks. Some shunned him and vilified him as a thief and cheat, while others picked fights over petty dealings and property. After months of this abuse Hans turned for help to Heinrich Friedrich, describing the pain he felt "as piercing my heart and going right into the marrow of my bones." He begged his lord to help him out, "pleading to God the Almighty to forgive me my sins and throw me into the depths of the sea."[33] In a decree issued on Christmas Eve of 1651, Heinrich Friedrich announced that he was extending mercy and forgiveness to Hans and called for the attacks on him and his family to cease, promising the maligned miller that he would personally intervene to counter any unjust accusations leveled at him. Hans Schmieg was encouraged to stand up for himself, to counter unjust injuries to his honor by citing his enemies for slander before the court of discipline. The count even officially absolved Hans and Anna and their family from the communal ostracism.[34]

The count's favor and support was probably the main reason that Hans's affairs suddenly brightened in 1650–51. For one, Hans began to bring in extra money as a petty government forester and *Schultheiss* (headman) in Bächlingen.[35] When Veit Albrecht, the old and heavily indebted miller of Hürden died, Hans stepped in and purchased his mill.[36] Where the money came from is unclear. What is clear is that in purchasing the mill, Hans assumed a larger than average debt with the government and the Albrecht heirs, a fact that points to laxness or the keenness of the government to find a new miller for Hürden, or even a new princely favor to help Hans out of his predicament at the *Herrenmühle*.

Located on the far side of Bächlingen but still part of the commune, the Hürden mill dominated the hamlet. In 1663 the complex included the mill and house, a barn, three fields, two pastures, a small vineyard, four small gardens for Anna, and a cellar at Hans Barthel Walther's house. When he and his family moved to Hürden, he did not have oxen to plough his fields, but they did have cows and sheep, and donkeys to help with the carting work at the mill.[37] Even though it needed considerable repairs, the mill was a sizable property. Hans and Anna were now the biggest people in their new community.

But he held his position through a curious balancing act. While the miller associated himself with the government and sought its protection and favors, he also skirted the laws and engaged in shady dealings that put him repeatedly at odds with the authorities and his neighbors. For years he operated on the edge of survival, the financial squeeze driving him to cut corners with customers and to skirt the law concerning milling and marketing practices. Soon after moving to Hürden he described his household as "meager because I can only earn so much that next to the cost of the house and clothes, not to mention dealing with the yearly taxes of 20 reichsthalers that I have no other solution" than to beg for tax relief.[38] Villagers usually curried favor by describing their situation in desperate terms, but Hans's description of his plight in 1655 has a ring of truth about it. The squeeze made him fight a little harder for his share of the local resources, even taking petty government jobs that his neighbors despised, tainting him even more in their eyes. But the count repeatedly came to his aid. Early in his years at Hürden, Heinrich Friedrich intervened on behalf of his former miller to return a disputed field to the Hürden mill's assets, helped Hans out when robbers ransacked the mill, granted relief when he fell ill and could not work, and eased the burden on his debts.[39]

Conflict followed him and Anna to Hürden. The Bächlingen court of discipline records him being involved in one dispute after another to defend his honor and resources from his neighbors. Most of the cases involved spontaneous outbursts against him, although some suggest calculated malice to hurt him. In 1654, Schmieg got into a tavern brawl with Hans Bernhard Wirth, and the court fined each of them 1 gulden for breaking the peace and injuring each other's honor.[40] When the village headman called Hans "the filthy snout of a dog" at a communal meeting, Schmieg cited the man for slander. Siding with the injured miller, the court fined the headman.[41] Around the same time, a feud broke out between Veit Arnold and Hans when Arnold "came by Hans Schmieg's house in the night and attacked him with a knife." Schmieg testified "that he reached for a spear and, cursing him, chased him away."[42] On another occasion Arnold tried to tarnish Hans's name by accusing him of indecent philandering with someone's wife in Unterregenbach.[43] Behind this and many other disputes were conflicts over resources. Arnold probably bore Schmieg a grudge since Schmieg had benefited from his close ties to Heinrich Friedrich to have a parcel of land claimed by Arnold restored to him and the mill.[44] Others accused Hans of cheating neighbors out of grain, stealing their hay, or pinching their pears.

Many of his enemies were neighbors from Hürden, villagers with whom Schmieg was in almost daily contact. Arnold lived next to the Schmiegs, Walther lived just across the way, and the Schmiegs had the right to store their goods in Walther's cellar. Over in Bächlingen, Hans fought with the petty government officials like himself, sometimes the headman, sometimes the *Bürgermeister*. Several of the disputes with communal and seigniorial officers occurred in 1665 and 1666 when Schmieg was once again seeking the post of village headman. Once he became headman, insults flew at him simply because the office and its duties attracted resentment.[45]

While in some cases the court protocols make it difficult to determine who initiated these disputes, more often than not Hans was on the defensive, either fighting back, or citing his attackers before the court. Toward his superiors in the government Hans was always deferential, however. When Steward Hohenbuch fined him in 1658 for violating marketing restrictions by selling a cow to Weikersheim, Schmieg accepted the fine without protest. It was Anna who exploded at Hohenbuch.

———

*G*IVEN HANS's long history of exploiting opportunities while fending off attacks, currying favor with the government while occasionally skirting its laws, the allegation that he also practiced "sorcery" at the mill begins to make sense. Fuchs's denunciation was nothing more than a new and shrewdly timed attack to destroy the miller at a moment of unusual vulnerability. Or was it?

First of all, the reputation of millers as sorcerers worked against Hans. True, he had no record of turning to the black arts in his battles with neighbors, but other millers from the region had been known to do so. More important was the expertise of the accuser himself. As an executioner, Fuchs spoke with authority about the magic arts and folk medicine.[46]

Even with a credible witness, securing a conviction was no sure thing. And even if it could be proved that Hans performed secret rites with cats, these activities might be dismissed as mere folk magic and superstition. If he were engaging in nothing more than common folk magic, the authorities might simply sanction the miller and his activities as deplorable. The problem was that the lines between the diabolical, the magical, and the merely superstitious were fluid and confusing. Determining whether an activity was one or the other depended on the intentions of the practitioner, the perceptions of the authorities, and the precise circumstances of the allegations. Police ordinances only added to the confusion. Many lumped together a wide variety of different practices, condemning them all as illegal. The Hohenlohe Police Ordinance of 1588 punished any practices hinting at sorcery and the black arts, imposing harsh fines on anyone "who swears by the devil or seeks through him prophecies, also demon fiends, sorcerers, and sorceresses who give themselves over to the devil, and mix with him." Even someone who used protective magic was to be disciplined. The ordinance evoked Exodus 22:18: "The sorcerer and the sorceress shall not be suffered to live."[47]

The Thirty Years' War disrupted church administration, making moral supervision sporadic at best. Church authorities did not always treat reports about magic uniformly, and churches lacked trained pastors and the administrative infrastructure to carry out a sustained campaign. But magical practices were deeply rooted in village culture.

Even when the Lutheran state churches began to rebuild and reintroduce moral discipline after the war, they lacked either the means or the will to launch serious investigations into reports of popular magic. Mild rebukes were common. When in 1648 the pastor of Ingelfingen learned that a woman practiced sorcery and witchcraft, he merely admonished her on his own and had her promise not to do it again.[48] In 1654 the Langenburg authorities mounted their first church visitation since before the war, and Pastor Hirsch of Bächlingen told how he had handled just such a case:

He [Pastor Hirsch] knows about no witches other than the tavern keeper's wife in Nesselbach who practices as an herb lady. This tavern keeper's wife cut into the bone of a neighbor woman from Nesselbach with a sickle, blessing the blood with a strange spell: "in the name of the Holy Trinity let the Holy 5 Wounds stop the bleeding right now." She's promised me to stop doing it, however.[49]

In this case, witchcraft was clearly confused with folk medicine. When a boy from Crispenhofen wanted to learn witchcraft, he was treated with fatherly admonishment and discipline.[50] There were other reports around Hohenlohe as well.

The most famous case involved one of the Hohenlohe countesses just before the Thirty Years' War. Peasants from all across the region flocked to the castle kitchen of Countess Magdalena, where she treated them for a variety of ailments. Her medical practice struck one religiously minded officer as witchcraft, yet she was never charged. Still on the shelf of the count's library, and probably consulted long after her death, was her *Arzneibuch*, or Medical Book, of 1619, a practical compendium of her own medical recipes.[51]

Besides, the allegation that Schmieg was involved with certain strange activities would hardly have been surprising. Before the Thirty Years' War government officials often noted that "for a variety of reasons many common people seek out soothsayers, asking their advice, and look to prophecies and other kinds of blessings and superstitious practices . . . , [including the use of] herbs, salt, water, candles and the like which are blessed to protect themselves, their children, cattle and other animals from the Devil, illness, storms, wolves and other misfortunes."[52] If everyday folk turned to magic and charms to cope with the risks and dangers in everyday life, then millers had equally good reason to use magic to counter the unruly forces haunting mills.[53]

Moreover, the story about Hans referred to specific acts that anyone familiar with the magical lore surrounding cats might find plausible. Earlier, when the authorities paid attention to whether the Fesslers' cat ate Anna Schmieg's cake or not, they were interested to see whether the cat discerned the presence of danger or malicious spirits at work in the house. Folk healers also relied on cats for medicine: their fat against burns or frostbite, the blood against epilepsy, the liver against gallstones, or the skin against toothaches, to name only a few such uses. The cat heads that interested Hans might have been used to treat eye diseases or perhaps counter the effects of a mental disorder.[54] Peasants also used cats to protect a household not only against vermin, but from other enemies, which might be called magical but not necessarily diabolical.

At first professing ignorance about what Schmieg did with the cats, Fuchs eventually admitted that he thought that Hans had buried the heads under the door to the mill to protect the premises from harm.[55] But if it was true that he had heard the miller invoke the name of the devil, then Hans would have crossed a line.[56] In his widely read work, *Daemonolatria; or, All About Demon Fiends and Magical Spirits* (1595), Nicolas Remy warned that once evil spirits had recruited their human helpers, they then cleverly changed themselves into the form of different animals. By turning into a cat, a demon could squeeze through the tight spots.[57] If Hans was bringing black cats to the mill, he might either be practicing Satanic rites against his enemies or secreting a horde of demons or witches in the mill. Given that Anna had just been arrested on suspicion of poisoning and witchcraft, Fuchs's allegation therefore seemed credible.

⸻

*O*N APRIL 11, about five weeks after Fuchs's denunciation, the authorities summoned Hans to the chancellery to answer the charges. The story about Hans's alleged activities represented a part of the fact-finding investigation into Anna's reputation, her activities, and anything else that might help the court decide the case against her. Even though the court did not charge him with sorcery, that possibility hung in the air as he was questioned about Fuchs's allegations.

Hans denied that any sorcery was involved, but he launched into a long story about his activities and why he had had such a pressing need for the heads of black cats lately:

About two years ago his mill was damaged when the gear teeth kept springing loose from the cogwheels. No sooner had he repaired them than they popped out again. This distressed him deeply and he told himself . . . that they must have been—*Salve Venie*—cursed. One day a miller's apprentice approached the mill, . . . and suggested that he should take the head of a black cat and place it under the crosstie, then no one would be able to do any harm to the mill. He [Hans] admits that he did say to Enderle [Fuchs] that he should shoot a black cat for him and give him the head. But he never did it (God protect him!) in the name of the Devil. With his godfather, Hanns Jörg, Enderlein's brother, he had done the same thing one time, but he had told him that he couldn't get one. He does not admit that he wanted more. He didn't receive any and he hadn't wished for more.[58]

As a master miller, Schmieg knew how his machinery worked and how to fix it when it broke down, but the mischievous cogwheels raised the suspicion that an evil spirit or perhaps one of his enemies wished him harm and had cursed the gears so they could not mesh properly. The only way to counter such ill will was to use protective magic.

Unconvinced at first by his testimony, his interrogators then summoned Fuchs and had him confront the old miller directly. At first Hans held to his original story that he had procured a cat only once. Then, feeling the strain of the questioning, he blurted out "that it wouldn't be a wonder if he died from his suffering." Finally, Schmieg reluctantly admitted that the executioner was right in saying that he had often procured cats for him and that in working his rituals he had also invoked the name of the devil.[59]

Later in the afternoon, when the court brought Hans and Fuchs back for further questioning, the executioner embellished his story, saying that Hans had also threatened him. Warning Fuchs that he had a big strapping lad who did his bidding, and then using some coarse language, Hans suggested that he would come after him since "he is the kind of man who gets even with anyone who messes with his shit."[60] Hans confessed that all this was true. But he justified it by saying "Only a sorry man wouldn't give as much as he got." But there was more. His questioners did not believe him when he said that he had gotten a cat only once or twice. Then the court brought out the testimony of Fuchs's brother—Hans's godfather—who asserted that Schmieg had repeatedly asked him for cat heads. The insinuation was clear and devastating: Hans was routinely using sorcery at the mill.[61]

That his kinsman testified against him was too much for the old miller. When told that he had gravely sinned and deserved to be punished, Hans broke down. "He would suffer for it all," the scribe reported him saying, "if someone would only let him have his little piece of bread for as long as he lives. He cried bitterly and asked for forgiveness." The court did not press further. The authorities allowed Hans to return to Hürden, but he had to live under the virtual certainty of further investigation and the possibility of punishment. For now the court turned its attention back to his wife and daughter.

The miller's juggling act—skirting the law and then currying favor when he was caught—may have worked one more time. The prince may have felt sorry for his old miller and shielded him yet again. Hans had no reputation as a sorcerer. It may also have counted in Hans's favor that no one, not even the executioner, had been harmed by his little rituals with the cats. The court may simply have considered his actions as reckless and reprehensible but hardly criminal. One final possibility was that Count Heinrich Friedrich and the authorities were afraid that sanctioning a rumor that there was a nest of sorcerers and witches in Hürden might touch off a wider panic.

When Hans returned to Hürden, help had arrived. One of his brothers and a sister-in-law had moved in to help him keep the household and the mill running. Together with his relatives from Berndshofen and Pfedelbach and his son, Michel, Hans would ride out the storm that now began to sweep through the villages around them.

CHAPTER VIII

Wider Conspiracies

The Swabian-Franconian Borderlands, Fall 1668-June 1672

aster Endris Fuchs, the Langenburg executioner, came from a family of professionals known for their service to the law and confidence in their rare skill in ferreting out malefactors. While the government respected Fuchs's special talents—the criminal justice system depended on him—most people looked on him and his kind with loathing, fear, and even a little awe. From what Fuchs knew and heard, the dangers that threatened Langenburg were wider and deeper than the court may have suspected.

As an executioner, Fuchs had special knowledge of all manner of crimes, including sorcery and witchcraft. The most visible and gruesome service he performed for the criminal justice system—publicly mutilating and then hanging, beheading, or burning his victims—made him the criminal's most intimate companion in the moments before he met his Divine Maker. But his knowledge about criminals' doings also rested on his relationship with them as their torturer. From the moment that he first showed the accused his tools of torture, right through his putting on the thumbscrews or hoisting his victim up with the strappado, he heard all the secrets and wild imaginings that a tortured mind was capable of telling. Visits to the prisoner gave him other occasions to know his victim. To this were added the stories he heard as he went about his rounds in the countryside. People so loathed the executioner that merely touching him, his clothes, his tools, or the gallows where he worked dishonored or polluted a person.[1]

He was also an expert on the magical arts. Like executioners elsewhere, Fuchs had a reputation as a folk healer whose brand of medicine relied on his unique access to highly prized charms, magical substances, and medicines.[2] His responsibility to clean up after suicides and to cart off animal carcasses meant that he had a steady supply of material for his special medicines. These human and animal substances were thought to have fantastic healing properties, and executioners could also sell them to apothecaries and through them become part of the mainstream traffic in medicines. After he carried out public mutilations and executions, he cleaned up the gallows and had the right to collect the by-products of his gruesome work. The human blood, bones, hair, and body parts he then either used in his own cures or sold them as powerful medicines to apothecaries, physicians, and other healers. He did the same with animals and their body parts. Loathsome and dishonorable work that it was, the craft gave executioners like Fuchs an aura of authority about magic and the black arts.

Though Fuchs's reputation rested in part on his general knowledge of the magical arts, he also had experience in ferreting out the secret crimes of witches. During earlier witch trials he had fingered at least four women. When Barbara Reinhart was accused of witchcraft in 1668, the Langenburg court relied on his knowledge of occult matters to detect her activities. When Anna Schmieg challenged the court to have Fuchs examine her, she was invoking the executioner's reputation as a seer who could look through a person and tell if she was a witch or not.

When Fuchs suggested to the authorities that Hans Schmieg may have been involved in sorcery, he was acting out of a complicated set of motives. While it is possible that he had an ax to grind against Schmieg, he was also using his special information to help out the authorities. As a broker of information about magic and witches, Fuchs was alerting the government to the potential of harm from a new quarter. Even though the community may have shunned him and his kind, Fuchs heard from many quarters stories about witches and other demon fiends. Moreover, as a member of the very tight caste of executioner families—often related by blood to one another—he picked up stories from other executioners in Franconia. All these ties provided him with stories, rumors, and information about the criminal underworld. His greater perspective allowed him to detect in local events a wider and more sinister aspect: the Schmiegs might be the tip of the iceberg.

As the spring of 1672 wore on, reports and rumors about witches swept across southwestern Germany. Attitudes toward the Schmiegs could not but be influenced by this contagion. The theological principle that witches worked through a hidden underground, bound by secret pacts with the devil, seemed to receive empirical affirmation. To the court Anna Schmieg began to take on the aspect of a secret fiend, one of many, perhaps hundreds.

The epicenter for these rumors lay to the west and south of Langenburg, in the villages and small towns of the neighboring Duchy of Württemberg, and in the nearby imperial cities and small territories of the Swabian-Franconian borderlands. Up to the end of the Thirty Years' War, Württemberg itself had a reputation of discouraging prosecutions of witchcraft. The law professors at the University of Tübingen, the duchy's own university, employed caution when consulted about witchcraft, a restraint shared by Württemberg's Lutheran theologians. After the height of witch hunting in the late 1620s and early 1630s, the number of trials had fallen sharply. Yet after the war, in the 1650s, the prosecutions in the duchy quietly increased.[3]

A larger wave of intense suspicions and accusations swept the region after 1660, stirring towns and villages reduced by up to 50 percent by the end of the Thirty Years' War.[4] The per capita rate of prosecution was twice as high as any other time in Württemberg's history.

In the mid-1660s, witch trials roiled two imperial cities on the northeastern borders of Württemberg. The first trials began in Esslingen in 1662 with a young man whose father, it was said, taught him how to fly and whisked him off in the night to witches' Sabbaths. Further revelations prompted the city fathers to appoint a zealous witch finder, Daniel Hauff, who turned up evidence of a monstrous conspiracy involving mass poisonings. When children began to tell fantastic tales about the horrors taking place right under their parents' noses, the panic widened. Witches, they said, poisoned soups with black flies, murdered babies with the touch of a finger, stole the penis from the smith, and dried up the milk from lactating mothers. By the time the panic had run its course, 214 people had been brought under suspicion, 79 people were arrested, and 37 executed. Only when Hauff died in 1666 did the reign of terror end.[5]

Just as tensions eased in Esslingen, trials started up elsewhere. In 1665 and 1666 the magistrate from nearby Reutlingen, Johann Philipp Laubenberger, oversaw twenty-two witch trials. Fourteen people were executed. News about the witches of Esslingen and Reutlingen spread throughout Swabia and up into the Swabian-Franconian borderlands. A pamphlet critical of the trials, "A Shocking but True and Pitiful New Report About the Witch Masters of 1665," circulated widely in the region.[6] The prosecutions ended only when the authorities doubted their abilities to find witches and hunt them down successfully. Among the townspeople—who had pressed for the trials in the first place—pressures to prosecute suspected witches continued well into the 1670s.[7]

More important, and more ominous for the Schmiegs, was the way that these stories of witchcraft traveled out along the roads into nearby regions, creating a climate of apprehension. In the 1650s most of the Württemberg cases were in the central and southern parts of the duchy. By the late 1650s they had spread into villages and towns in the north and even into the Odenwald Forest. One might see the suspicions about Eva Kleinbach in Kupferzell, just south and west of Langenburg, in 1652, within this context. Word about the events spread to Unterregenbach, Ober-regenbach, Buchenbach, and Sonnhofen—all villages near Langenburg and Hürden.[8] Around this same time, Anna Schmieg's reputation for drinking, brawling, cursing, and blaspheming took shape. In the meantime, court cases continued to take place in the region around Hohenlohe and Langenburg.[9]

Pamphlets sensationalized some of the accounts. Out of Reutlingen came a ballad sung in taverns and other places where musicians, travelers, and local folk gathered and shared the news of the day. Couriers spread the word, too. To pinpoint rumors, find witnesses, and make arrests, governments sent out their functionaries armed with warrants to track down suspects. Other couriers carrying thick dossiers about the trials crisscrossed the region on trips to Tübingen, Strasbourg, and Nuremberg seeking legal opinions from university professors. Notices went out to be on the alert for signs of suspicious activities. Merchants, peddlers, and wandering craftsmen passed on gossip and stories. Preachers warned their congregations of the dangers of witchcraft, enlivening their sermons with references to local events. People in nearby areas were deeply affected when interrogated for additional information or called upon as witnesses.[10]

Lying near the two major highways that ran through the region, one a major east-west thoroughfare and the other a north-south axis, news and rumors from Swabian and Franconian cities readily reached Langenburg and its villages. By the late 1660s the news that witches were sowing mischief in nearby communities heightened concerns. Even the normally skeptical authorities of nearby Rothenburg ob der Tauber were concerned, and they arrested a mother and her seventeen-year-old daughter in 1668 for witchcraft and made another arrest in 1671.[11] Rumors about vagabonds and arsonists heightened the impression that a crime wave was sweeping the region.

Real misfortune contributed to the alarm. The murrain that decimated Langenburg's cattle and sheep struck at this time. Outbreaks recurred for several years thereafter, including the summer of 1671, when Michel Fessler's cow "ate pestilence and death" in the meadow beyond Anna Schmieg's house. Large numbers of cattle, sheep, and even horses perished. At Lindenbronn livestock belonging to the Count and other members of his court fell ill and died. Palpable fear, rumors, and suspicions centered on the estate at Lindenbronn, encompassing almost all of the nearby villages. As far away as Ingelfingen, officials reported cattle and sheep wasting away and dying mysteriously.

———

CONNECTING THE rumors about witches and the cattle murrain was Endris Fuchs. Not only did he learn stories about witches from other executioners, but, given his duties to tend the animals at Lindenbronn and dispose of the carcasses that piled up, he was better placed than anyone else to grasp the scope of the calamity. Not surprisingly, blame for the cattle illness settled on two women tending the cattle at the Lindenbronn estate: Turk Anna, a local legend, and her daughter. Their trials might have settled the affair had it not been for the manner in which they were conducted. Instead of calming fears, the investigations tended to spread rumors throughout Langenburg's villages and raise worries that witches might be behind still more mysterious deaths. When at the end of her trial Turk Anna and her daughter denounced two other "cattle women" who worked at Lindenbronn, Barbara Reinhart of Ruppertshofen and Barbara Schleicher of Atzenrod, dozens of villagers between Langenburg, Kirchberg, and Gerabronn were brought in and deposed. The panic had spread.

On October 24, Reinhart was arrested and brought to Langenburg for questioning. When led to her first interrogation before von Gülchen, a battle of wits and wills unfolded. Not wanting to reveal his information too quickly, and perhaps hoping that Reinhart would confess to witchcraft, von Gülchen initially asked her why she thought she had been brought before him and urged her to "speak with one heart." He asked her, "Why did you do it?" She said that "she did not know what she has done, that she has done nothing wrong." Feigning ignorance about the accusations against her—she had heard the rumors that they were coming for her— she said "she should go and hear what they wanted to talk with her about." In the meantime, Court Preacher Dietzel had set the tone for her interrogation by delivering a sermon in Langenburg about the dangers of witchcraft. When Reinhart met Dietzel that morning, "she knew very well what they wanted to make out of her." Using the same Lutheran religious language, von Gülchen insisted that Reinhart confess her secret identity. Turk Anna had masked her real identity at first, he said. Such evil folk always do. But she resisted. She was, she said, "as pure as God in heaven."[12] The real crime, it was clear, was apostasy.

The interesting thing about the exchange between the learned magistrate and Reinhart was that both of them talked about witchcraft in the same terms. This is striking in that earlier in the seventeenth century, in many other trials in the region, villagers tended to understand witchcraft not as a spiritual crime—this was a notion of theologians—but as a material crime against people and property. Here, in the Langenburg courtroom, a lowly cattle maid debated witchcraft as a spiritual crime, a crime against God. Later, material crimes would be brought up and then, very late in the proceedings, the more fantastic elements of witchcraft. But even then the focus was on the more theological aspects of witchcraft: Satan, the pact, and attendance at witches' dances. Fantasies played only a minor role in this and the other Langenburg trials.

Over the course of the interrogation von Gülchen confronted Reinhart with her accusers and then with her alleged accomplice, Barbara Schleicher from Atzenrod. No one budged. When Turk Anna was brought in and confronted her "right to her face" that she had aided her in killing cattle at Lindenbronn, Reinhart responded derisively. "She then laughed a full throated laugh several times," and proclaimed her innocence. Similarly she refuted Turk Anna's daughter, Barbara Schüler, when she, too, was led before her and denounced her as the witch who had helped her kill a horse at Lindenbronn. Von Gülchen then turned to the expert testimony of one of Fuchs's colleagues, the executioner from Möckmühl. The man testified "that there were so many witches around here that he had already accused a lot of households, the same people, and they all say that the Cattle Woman [Reinhart] was involved."[13] By citing the scary stories from Möckmühl's witch finder and executioner, the court gave credence to the rumors that a conspiracy of "evil people" was festering throughout the entire region. The executioner's tale sealed Reinhart's fate.

The stories about witchcraft also fed on long-simmering conflicts in Langenburg's villages. When Barbara Schleicher, also known as the *Spätzin*, or Little Sparrow, was brought before the court and Reinhart accused her of killing a horse at Lindenbronn, she immediately shook off the accusation as jealousy. Schleicher testified, "that her husband had once worked at the Cattle Woman's [Reinhart's] farm in Ruppertshofen and when she [Schleicher] celebrated her wedding, the Cattle Woman appeared as others were offering their blessings at her wedding, and slandered her by calling her a witch." Reinhart insulted her, Schleicher explained, "because the Cattle Woman would have gladly taken her man."[14] A year later, she went on, when she and her husband had gone to the church festival at Liebesdorf, they met Reinhart again. When the Cattle Woman drew up alongside them, the couple suddenly found themselves bewildered and lost, walking along the wrong path. They shook off Reinhart's uncanny spell by spending the night with a relative. Schleicher's contempt of Turk Anna ran equally deep. When von Gülchen brought Turk Anna into the courtroom to confront Schleicher, the enraged Schleicher would have assaulted her had the bewildered Turk Anna not defended herself. So agitated was Schleicher, it seems, that when Turk Anna's daughter was brought in for a second confrontation, Schleicher fell to the floor, senseless. The court resumed its session when she came to her senses.[15]

While they were meant to end fears of witchcraft, these investigations awakened dread in new quarters. In fact, von Gülchen's thoroughness in investigating the cases lent an official stamp of authority to some of the rumors, though this seems not to have been the court adviser's intention. Carrying out his first witch trials, von Gülchen expressed doubts about how to proceed. He knew that, absent a confession, nothing could be proved. He was shaken by Reinhart's tenacious refusal to confess to any crimes, a pattern that reminded him of Turk Anna's resistance to confession and the likelihood that the evil one protected her. If Reinhart repeatedly refused to confess, he asked, what should he do?[16]

If Langenburg's prince harbored any doubts about the case, he did not reveal them to his court adviser. Telling his minister that the dangers facing Langenburg transcended the normal considerations of the law, he ordered von Gülchen to press on. In this case, it was "God's merciful will that Satan living in this evil woman be called out, that she finally tell the truth, renounce him and that her soul be brought once again to the divine truth." Tellingly, Heinrich Friedrich linked the witchcraft affair to the other dangers threatening his land's stability: the French menace against Protestantism and the Netherlands and his dynasty's particular interests there, and the uncertainties coming to a head with a looming imperial decision over Weikersheim and his disputed legacy within the House of Hohenlohe. True religion and political stability hung in the balance.[17] Not since the Thirty Years' War had the prince sensed so much chaos looming on the horizon.

Reinforcing this pressure from the count were mounting pressures from villagers, to carry the hunt for witches in new directions. The network of ties binding the Langenburg court to its peasant households, so carefully restored and extended at the end of the war, buzzed with government reports, rumors, and unfounded gossip. Officials used these networks, putting about their inquiries for evidence and witnesses, the stewards playing a particularly important role in this process. When the steward from Kirchberg investigated Barbara Reinhart, he inflamed the fears of witchcraft back in Langenburg. The village elders from Ruppertshofen sounded a cautionary note, however, agreeing that Reinhart was "widely considered a disreputable wench," but they refused to tie her to witchcraft. The Kirchberg steward also passed on unverified and malicious slander, such as the inflammatory account of Michel Schenckh, who "claimed that he knew her for well on 40 years and says she is called a whore."[18]

Endris Fuchs was particularly important in providing information of this kind to the court. During Reinhart's trial he testified to conversations he had had with her in the barn at Lindenbronn. He also made sure that von Gülchen knew of a conversation he had had with her at a wedding in Bächlingen where the merrymakers taunted her that she was a witch and she had remained suspiciously silent in response.

Neighboring governments registered alarm over Langenburg's witch fever. When the Ansbach Margraviate was asked whether it had information about Reinhart, an official wrote back to say that his government was very concerned.[19] "It makes one seriously wonder why the lord [of Langenburg] is dragging in witches, hotly pursuing them and how he intends to continue on this course. One should make sure that no one is done an injustice."[20] Another Ansbach official cautioned "that one should not be so quick to admonish people, that God stands by his own, and helps one to get out of this witchcraft business." If nothing more could be found, one was better off dropping the prosecutions.[21]

Yet rumors of witchcraft continued to sweep the countryside. Some of the stories were vague, alarming accounts about unnamed witches. From Gerabronn and Michelbach came the story about a cow who was dying and nothing seemed to stop her mysterious wasting away. Witches were known to be at work now, a villager said, without naming names.[22] General rumors like these were often followed by someone connecting the vague rumor with a known suspect, as when two men and a woman from a village near Michelbach came forward to say that Barbara Reinhart was "openly talked about for witchcraft."[23]

Villagers gossiped constantly about family members and neighbors, of course, sifting their memories about past events and weighing them against the new accounts. Within a context of heightened suspicions either old stories were brought forward or new, harsher evaluations made. When Reinhart fell under suspicion, the stories ran the entire gamut: To the men of Ruppertshofen, Reinhart was simply a "bad woman," a "disreputable woman." To others she was a "slut" or even "an evil woman." But some went further, branding her "a longtime witch" or "a known witch." These stories tended to come not from people who knew the suspect personally or who recalled any specific events, but from those who took it upon themselves to pass judgment on their neighbors' reputation in general.

As rumors intensified about Reinhart, the tales were embroidered with new details. In late-seventeenth-century trials, adults seemed fascinated with children's tales of witchcraft.[24] Only nine years old, Rosina Magdalena Niethin worked for her grandmother Reinhart as a maid. Filtered through the perceptions and imaginings of a child, she wove into her tales intimate details of the woman's life. "The evil spirit," Rosina said, often came and went from her granny's house. Sometimes he appeared before her "dressed handsomely." One time the devil spoke directly to her, scolding her like an angry adult, telling her "not to make herself useless."[25] When she and her parents were brought before the Kirchberg steward for questioning, she related how the devil walked about her grandmother's village, that she had sometimes seen "a black man" come for her mistress, whisking her away into the night, to some unknown house on the edge of the village. Her grandmother called him Hans, Rosina said, but the little girl was not fooled. She knew he was really the evil one. At home she saw them drinking wine and eating bread. On another occasion her grandmother went off to a dance—obviously a rustic Hohenlohe dance and not one of the wild and fantastic orgies reported by demonologists. On one occasion, Rosina noticed that the man was teaching her grandmother something, the key to his instructions being "a hateful word." At night when the black man visited, the little girl said, she was in bed, but peeked out and saw him all the same: he wore a black coat and a hat. On another occasion her grandmother left the house riding an old horse. She especially remembered when her grandmother "sat for a while on an open pitchfork, took some green-looking fat out of a broken pot, and had then smeared the pitchfork with it. Her mistress sat in front, she sat on the back, but the evil one alone had actually ridden it." On two different occasions Hans Ebert's maid had witnessed this with her, and Rosina had sworn her friend to secrecy over it. When the evil one approached the girl on his own, asking her if she would love him, she just laughed, blessed herself, and offered a prayer. Naturally she was afraid to tell everything to her mother and father, but here, before the court, with her mother and father present, she swore she was telling the whole truth.[26]

When Reinhart appeared before the Langenburg court, Rosina's tales became the basis for interrogations and even for testimony against her. Copied down, and an oath taken on their veracity, this young child's stories were transformed from fantasy into sworn legal evidence. When Reinhart faced renewed questioning on January 5, 1669, and she denied her granddaughter's testimony, von Gülchen solemnly prepared the poor woman for questioning under torture. In von Gülchen's view, imperial criminal law justified this ominous step since Turk Anna and her daughter had affirmed their accounts of Reinhart's crimes, the last time just before they were executed. Despite the horrors that lay in store for her, Reinhart resolutely denied everything.

On February 3, Reinhart finally broke down. Following her torture, she confessed to having lived the life of a wanton woman led astray by the evil one. Her account of meeting with the devil sounded like a secret courtship that turned into a nightmare. Dressed as a handsome young man, the dark lord came to her in the fields, showed his desire for her, and gave her some money. He renewed his suit until she gave in. Once she had given herself to him, he told her that she could never get free of him again. Reinhart refused to admit that her demon lover had branded her body with the witch's mark, but when Master Fuchs exposed her shoulder, revealing a mark to the court officers, she could hardly deny it. Solemnly, the court adviser asked everyone to pray, whereupon she revealed that the evil one had asked her to renounce the Holy Trinity.[27]

She admitted to a staggering ninety-four crimes altogether, a spree that went back between fifteen and thirty years. She concentrated her crimes in her home village, but from there her malefice reached out into the surrounding villages and hamlets, then striking the estate at Lindenbronn, and finally touching low-level government officials and villagers living near Langenburg in Bächlingen. The mayhem ranged as far as Ingelfingen on the western side of the Jagst River valley. While Reinhart denied having murdered men and women, she did confess to laming her enemies, giving them "witches' shots" to the arms, legs, feet, hands, breasts, and sides. Sixty-two people had been injured in this way. Her victims ranged up and down the social hierarchy: lowly maids, farmhands, winegrowers, farmers, but also an alarming number of attacks on state officers, including the stewards and Endris Fuchs.[28] She claimed to have killed twenty cows and calves, fifteen sheep, three horses, eight pigs, and two oxen. Most alarming of all—from the state's vantage point—was that this grandmother from Ruppertshofen struck Heinrich Friedrich's own estate and barns and people close to the court.

As a secret tribunal, the Langenburg inquisition was to keep the details of its proceedings to itself, but the sensational stories about the old Cattle Woman's campaign of terror spread far and wide. The secrecy surrounding the court's proceedings lent the stories an aura of truth that commonplace rumors might never have had on their own. Despite the fact that district officers followed up Reinhart's confession and tried to document every single one of her ninety-four "secret" crimes, the investigation so taxed the resources of the government that Town Steward Landbeck admitted that the undertaking was hopeless.[29] Still, the diligent inquiries spread new fears far and wide, an ominous development that later made the locals receptive to fresh rumors of witchcraft associated with Anna Schmieg.

The trials became mills turning out terrifying tales inflected through local experiences, then legitimized and spread by the government. They made sense out of the cattle murrain that had swept the land, strange illnesses that afflicted villagers, and misfortunes that no one living could even testify to any longer. As elements of ancient stories about witches circulated widely, they gained fresh credibility. It would take only the shock of Shrove Tuesday to stir memories of these events and weave Anna, Hans, and Eva Schmieg into the stories.

The cases of Turk Anna and Barbara Reinhart touched the Hürden affair and the Schmiegs in other ways, too. While tending cattle at Lindenbronn, Michel Fessler either saw livestock wasting away or heard his coworkers tell stories about the mysterious murrain. He no doubt heard stories about how Turk Anna and her daughter, Reinhart, Schleicher, and perhaps other witches had infiltrated the barns, stables, and meadows where he worked and put poison about. Others who worked at Lindenbronn would later come forward to testify against Anna Schmieg or Barbara Schleicher, including Endris Fuchs. Reinhart, he said, killed at least two horses and a cow belonging to him. Emboldened by Anna's arrest, Fuchs suddenly remembered his conversations about black cats with Hans Schmieg. Since three convicted witches had sworn that others were involved in their crimes, and had gone publicly to their deaths, it is not surprising that fears of a wider conspiracy lingered.

In other words, the witches' confessions did not bring peace and a release from fears, but instead spread the contagion further, giving new impetus to the gossip mills.

Furthermore, when the court resumed its interrogation of Reinhart on March 6, a sharper pattern emerged. While admitting that she had exaggerated some of her claims and made false confessions in February, the old Cattle Woman focused on the way she had poisoned the prince's cattle and horses not only at Lindenbronn, but also in Bächlingen, Atzenrod, and Unterregenbach. Witchcraft breached the palace gate itself. Reinhart confessed to "having placed a charm on [the gatekeeper's maid] in the name of the devil, [and] anyone who picked it up was harmed." Then she admitted to giving poisoned eggs to the wife of the Langenburg chamber secretary. In short, the court had to wonder about the audacity of a witch willing to strike at its sources of food, its cattle, horses, and even the servants who waited on the count and his family. She also confessed to deceiving her daughter and to poisoning her first husband with a bitter soup. In one session, she told the horrifying tale of the evil one himself stealing right into the tower prison night after night, disguised as a farmhand, counseling her how to handle questions.[30] Her stubborn resistance to confessing early in the trial had been because of the devil himself.

Her confession of March 6 also cast suspicions on others, who allegedly attended witch's dances with her: Schleicher, the shepherd, the carpenter, Thomas Kinn's wife and her daughter, and Philip Schöll's wife.[31] In a follow-up interrogation of March 8 she named more witches, living right next to Langenburg, in Atzenrod. About all of them save one she was vague: Barbara Schleicher. Reinhart said that Schleicher had given her the powder with which she had killed livestock in the lord's stable.[32] Knowing that she had lied before, and following the law requiring at least two eyewitnesses to a crime, von Gülchen concentrated his attention on Schleicher. Besides, Turk Anna had herself fingered the *Spätzin*, as Schleicher was also called, before she had been executed.

———

THE INTERROGATION of Schleicher in March marked the closest yet that witchcraft had come to the court at Langenburg. As a poor widow, Schleicher lived in Atzenrod, less than a thirty-minute walk from Langenburg. After her husband died, she had had a difficult time keeping her little household together, raising much-needed cash by selling a parcel of land to Georg Abel. Other parcels she placed under the guardianship of Peter Balduff, the tavernkeeper in the village. While it is unclear whether she also worked at Lindenbronn, villagers frequently spied her there. Suspicions first surfaced on October 24, 1669, when both Turk Anna and her daughter accused her of helping them kill cattle at Lindenbronn. When the court had the terrible witch matriarch and her daughter confront Schleicher, the old woman vehemently denied any wrongdoing.[33] But the suspicions surfaced again in Reinhart's testimony.

Some of her activities resembled those of a witch out to lace the food of cattle and people with poison. Carl Lang, a baker and brewer who lived just beyond the walls of Langenburg, reported that Schleicher had attempted to put something into his sauerkraut when they sat down to eat together. He admitted that they had sometimes fought—much as Schleicher had with Turk Anna—and they obviously did not get along well as neighbors. Peter Balduff, the ward over her property, reported seeing strange lights coming on in her little hut at sunset. Even von Gülchen thought he detected a revealing slip of the tongue when, under interrogation, she began to pray nervously, saying "that she relied upon God the Father, God the Son and the Lord Jesus Christ." Such a slip—she had omitted the Holy Spirit—von Gülchen saw as a possible sign that the evil one had turned her against God.[34] In the absence of additional evidence von Gülchen concluded for the moment that she might simply be feeble-minded. He had her placed under observation in the Fools' House, which housed and watched over the area's mad people and melancholics.

=====

THE SUSPICIONS and fears about witches spread throughout Atzenrod, nearby Bächlingen and Oberregenbach, and right into Langenburg, where many families served Count Heinrich Friedrich and the court. Some people rejected the rumors, but on closer reflection others, usually low-level court servants, reported that they had recently suffered strange injuries, confirming Reinhart's stories about her attacks on court personnel. Anna Maria, the chancellery secretary's maid, recalled suffering puzzling pains in her limbs that required medical attention. Court Barber Unfug— who would later conduct the autopsy on Anna Fessler— remembered that two of his calves had inexplicably died two years ago. The gatekeeper's maid remembered being afflicted by strange pains.[35] Witnesses in nearby Bächlingen and Regenbach confirmed the strange illnesses and deaths of livestock.

These rumors were nothing new, but what was once rumor and gossip was transformed into substantiated legal evidence. The stories would therefore prove Reinhart's crimes. Even more stories were put into circulation when twenty-nine men were deposed about Barbara Schleicher and her alleged crimes. Their accounts varied considerably, and not one of them pointed to firm empirical evidence of her having engaged in witchcraft. They had been asked to recall their encounters with her and to account for her reputation in the village, which set in motion a public reassessment of her reputation. Here they largely agreed: Schleicher was a "useless woman," "a wicked woman," "a godless woman," "a bad wench," "she has a foul mouth," "a whore." These accusations were the stuff of everyday slander, but there was even more. Several men repeated Balduff's tale about seeing strange lights in her hut at night. "One day after the pastor had visited Schleicher, he saw the old woman cut off a lock of hair from her father and, after making a hole in an egg, put the hair into it. Suddenly, a terrifying wind rushed out of the egg."[36]

The final evidence was her own confession, on March 8. When von Gülchen tried to get her to confirm her testimony without torture, Reinhart refused. Maddeningly, Reinhart would confess to witchcraft before the court and then turn around and in a private confession to Court Preacher Dietzel deny that she was a witch.[37] Such inconsistencies and recalcitrance took a heavy toll on von Gülchen. In a letter to the prince on May 28 he wrote that "an accursed bit of flesh makes me anxious and worried and torments me with anger and gives me no peace."[38] The possibility that he might fail to convict her or commit an injustice weighed on him.[39] Daily he turned to God to calm his troubled heart and relieve the burden on his conscience.[40] After further wearisome and troubling interrogations, several interventions by Count Heinrich Friedrich, and two consultations with the law faculty at Altdorf, a legally valid confession was secured.

Court Adviser von Gülchen drew up Reinhart's final confession himself, and when it was read aloud to the court and the assembled onlookers, the words sounded as if they were Reinhart's own. Gone were the hearsay and gossip. Here was an official account, sanctioned by the court, that made sense of all of the rumors surrounding her accusation and inquisition. While her *Urgicht*, or confession, was a legal document, it nevertheless closely resembled the stories about witches and witchcraft that circulated in pamphlets, broadsides, and song.

Reinhart's confession listed twelve separate crimes, strung together like a master narrative of her life.[41] The story began when, as a maid at Hasfelden, she made a pact with the devil. Coming to the maid in the guise of a handsome peasant lad, the devil offered her money and then enticed her into sex with him. Her seduction and obedience assured, the evil one then forced her into renouncing God and binding herself over to him. She described going off to the witches' Sabbath, which resembled rustic dances. She then started the next phase of her life by secretly harming people and damaging property, beginning with the murders of those closest to her: the child of a houseguest; the smith, who was lamed and then killed with a witch's shot to the leg; a man called Albrecht who was poisoned; two vulnerable little children who depended on public

charity; and then her two husbands. Then she sought victims farther from home, first at Lindenbronn then in nearby villages where
she committed so many crimes against people and livestock that
no one could tally them all. Finally, Reinhart confessed to fifty
years of immorality and godlessness as a witch, secretly teaching
witchcraft to two girls, one of them her own granddaughter, and
engaging in adultery with her brother-in-law.[42] The judgment
having been read against her, Barbara Reinhart was publicly executed on Gallows Hill on July 30, 1669.

In THE meantime, the court suspended its investigation of Barbara Schleicher. When interrogated in June and July, she refused to
confess to witchcraft. The strain of her ordeal nearly broke her.
When brought before the judges, she often prayed in odd ways, fell
to the floor, crawled around, and wept loudly.[43] Jurists at the University of Altdorf reviewed the case and wrote to Langenburg that
"they were concerned that she was not in her right mind." Lacking sufficient evidence to question her further under torture, the
case was at an impasse. Unless she was frightened into confessing—
by bringing in Master Fuchs and letting him show her his instruments of torture, the *territio*—the court had no case and was
advised to let her go. She was released on August 4, 1669.[44]

Rumors about witches continued to circulate for the next two
years. In June 1670 the steward from Morstein and Steward Landbeck of Langenburg heard suspicious reports about a woman from
Raboldshausen, Michel Weltz's wife, who was allegedly teaching
village girls witchcraft.[45] Philipp Marx told the authorities that
Weltz's wife had taken his nine-year-old daughter, who worked for
her, into the woods behind the barn one night and taught her to
pray in an odd way. The girl told her father that the woman would
wake her up at night, take her into the loft over the barn, and show
her "a little golden man, like a painting in the church, his head
turned on its side. The girl said she had not become anxious and
she never reported anything about the strange statue to anyone."[46]
The authorities dragged out the investigation through the sum-

mer, debating whether to believe the child's stories and whether
Weltz's wife should be brought to Langenburg for questioning or
not.[47]

––––

W HEN ANNA Schmieg's arrest put villagers on edge once again,
fears from 1668–69 revived. Never put to rest, the old suspicions
about Barbara Schleicher flared up again. All it took was a fresh
incident for neighbors to denounce her. On May 4, while the
court waited to resume its interrogation of Anna Schmieg and her
daughter, four alarmed villagers from Atzenrod approached district
officers from Langenburg to tell how Barbara Schleicher had very
nearly poisoned Paul Treher, a butcher from Gerabronn. The four
accounts converged on the fact that Treher had stopped by Peter
Balduff's tavern to talk with him about buying some wine. While
Treher and Balduff talked, Schleicher and other women entered
the tavern. Earlier that day Schleicher fought with Anna Schüler
over a washboard. Tempers flared and insults flew. When Anna
Schüler called Schleicher a "wobbly minded old woman," a mild
insult given the names women usually called each other, Schleicher
shot back at Schüler "that she lied like a witch and whore." To her
credit, Schleicher suggested that they reconcile their differences
over a drink at the tavern. Schüler agreed and Schleicher paid for
the rounds, but then Schüler refused to forgive. At that point Treher intervened, urging the two women to make up. Seemingly
grateful for this friendly gesture, Schleicher then gave him a cup of
wine, intended for Schüler. Accounts differed as to who poured the
drink, or what exactly was said—and these details would matter
later—but after Treher drank the draft, he immediately felt sick.
Dropping his pants, the distressed man ran outside into the garden
and relieved himself. He became so ill, in fact, that he was offered
a healing potion of theriac, an antidote for poison, and he was bundled off to a bed in the tavern. The Atzenroders were so alarmed
Treher might die that Court Preacher Dietzel was sent for. While
Treher recovered from the attack, rumors of the disturbing events
quickly spread. On May 4 the court heard accusations against

Schleicher that she had attempted to poison the butcher from Gerabronn.[48]

While no one who denounced Schleicher mentioned the word "witchcraft," their careful choice of words make it plain that they suspected Schleicher of the crime. The court adviser was at first unprepared to rearrest Schleicher. In a brief to the count on May 15—while he was drawing up a delicate legal maneuver involving the two Schmieg women—von Gülchen explained that he was reluctant to move against Schleicher because there was no specific evidence that she had attempted to poison Treher. Peter Balduff had not seen her put poison into the cup. Indeed, it was not even clear who had poured the man's drink. The women could not agree among themselves that Schleicher had uttered the threatening words "He'll get it, alright!" before she handed him the drink. Still, he ordered an investigation, asking Court Barber Unfug to examine the herbs and roots that Schleicher allegedly kept in her cottage, and calling for more depositions on the matter.[49]

The reports returning to Langenburg seemed to confirm fears that a much wider conspiracy of witches and poisoners might be at work than first imagined. There were several reasons why von Gülchen now widened the investigation. First, Unfug, fresh from seeking the source of poisoning in the Hürden affair, discovered a cache of suspicious herbs, roots, and other questionable charms wrapped up in a bundle and hidden in Schleicher's little hut. Unfug had found a little crock made of elderwood, a pot shard holding some mysterious salve, fat, butter, or grease; a small sack of unidentified roots pierced through and attached to a flower with a feather; dried flowers that looked like elderwood blossoms; a bundle of herbs that included melissa (the herb of the black Christ), hellebore, and others; juniper; a small box with nothing in it; a small golden-colored bundle; tormentil, hayflowers, and other roots and herbs.[50] Second, new evidence came from Georg Bauer that Schleicher had secretly killed his livestock several years ago.[51] Third, the poisoning of Carl Lang several years prior—which now looked like an attempt at murder—required more investigation.

Taken together with the reports about the attempted poisoning of Treher, the evidence warranted von Gülchen to bring in Schlei-

cher and all of the witnesses for questioning. The court adviser suspected that the old woman had become active again, that the cell
of witches to which she belonged had new orders to sow mischief,
devilry, and terror. As von Gülchen put it, citing an old proverb,
"when the fruit is ripe, it falls from the tree." Better to stop Schleicher now before she went further.

The full interrogation on June 15 confirmed von Gülchen's suspicions about the woman's odd behavior. Before the assembled
court of the court adviser, Court Preacher Dietzel, the chancellery
secretary, the Langenburg steward, and two additional judges
drawn from among the town's citizenry, witnesses were called and
deposed before Schleicher was brought in and confronted with the
evidence. Paul Treher came from Gerabronn. He not only recalled
how he was poisoned at the tavern; he remembered an uncanny
encounter with Schleicher several years prior. He told the court
that while he was at Lindenbronn a dog suddenly ran up to him.
He was surprised to watch the dog leap over a high fence, go into
a pen, leave, and then repeat the feat several more times. He looked
for help, and when a peasant lad came with a gun to shoot the wild
dog, the animal disappeared. Suddenly, standing in its place was a
female figure. Treher recognized Schleicher. She said to him, "Look
here now, butcher, I will tell my lord about all of this." Then she
vanished. He had not seen her before or since. Other witnesses,
including Peter Balduff, Georg Bauer, and Michael Schum, came
in to relate their stories of Treher's poisoning at the tavern. Carl
Lang recounted, now in greater and more ominous detail than
before, how Schleicher had once tried to poison his sauerkraut,
how dreadfully ill he became, and how it had taken him a year to
recover his strength.[52]

With presumptions of guilt running against her, Schleicher was
brought in for interrogation. Von Gülchen admonished her to tell
the whole truth and she would be treated with mercy. The first
words out of her mouth—"I am not a witch, and if I were such a
woman, I would not want to continue to be one"—showed her
desperation. She denied having tried to poison Treher, or that she
had drawn the drink in the first place. His patience at an end, von
Gülchen reminded her that she had indeed poured the man a

drink and that if she did not confess she would be turned over to Master Fuchs for torture.[53]

In the afternoon the questioning turned to the herbs, roots, and amulets the court barber had found in her house. Within a different context these objects could be viewed as a typical peasant woman's herbal pharmacy, remedies for treating illnesses or warding off harm from cattle. When asked about the various preparations, Schleicher said that she did not know the names of all of them, but that she had treated herself with them when she was ill. The melissa, she said, "she had rubbed on her chest." Elderwood blossoms were commonly used in a variety of medical cures, as was the juniper wood, widely known as a blood purifier. Some of the herbs and roots, she said, had been used by her husband for curing sick cattle. Scattered around the barn, the black flowers of the hellebore and tormentil were commonly used to cure sick cows or to ward off harmful spirits.[54] Master Fuchs, she said, had himself given the tormentil to her husband to help heal sick cows.[55]

Unmoved and troubled, von Gülchen again threatened to turn her over for questioning under torture and returned her to prison.[56]

---

*H*E NOW believed he had disturbing evidence that a whole nest of witches, their terror orchestrated by the evil one, was at work all around Langenburg. Between June 20 and 22, he laid out his thinking to Heinrich Friedrich in two long, rambling documents. In the first document he insisted, as a jurist, on the need for Schleicher to confess her crimes, and the imperative that she be made to renounce her master, Satan, and return to godly obedience. While discussing her case, he thought he also saw connections between Schleicher and Anna Schmieg.[57]

In the second document, a long-winded legal brief, von Gülchen organized his thoughts more carefully, informing the count both of the progress to date and how he wanted to proceed. He saw the same pattern in the way that Schleicher and Anna Schmieg used poison and witchcraft, both of them focusing their attacks on unsuspecting victims close to their homes.

A NEST OF WITCHES. *Witch theory imagined that no witch ever worked alone. At night herdes of witch fiends flew off to remote woods, barren heaths, hills, and caverns to plot new terror. Here a nest of witches cooks up a diabolical brew (left) while others, sitting in a ceremonial circle, perform malevolent magic and still others come and go to their dark haunts with their demonic familiars (center) or gather for a witches' dance (right).*

Already in 1668–69 rumors had named Schleicher, *die Spätzin*, as an accomplice of Turk Anna and her daughter. Linking all of their attacks together, von Gülchen found it significant that Georg Bauer, a credible witness, reported the ominous news that people were now saying "that the Turks have come to Regenbach." Implicit was the fear that the devil, whose fiendish armies under the Ottomans were advancing on Austria and the Holy Roman Empire, was unleashing a new horde of demon fiends and witches against the little Christian community of Langenburg. Von Gülchen aimed to have Schleicher reveal her ties to Turk Anna and her daughter, to have her admit that she had worked as a secret agent of Satan since she was a little girl. "If she does not want to admit to all of this," von Gülchen wrote, "then she is to be met with raw, hard words, and she will receive no mercy."[58] Fuchs would press it out of her under torture.

Count Heinrich Friedrich penned his approval for the next stage of interrogation, including the use of torture if necessary, and gave his backing to his court adviser's plan to expose the conspiracy that threatened his domain. He even suggested a legal maneuver in which Anna Schmieg could be brought into the torture chamber with Schleicher. As Anna looked on, Master Fuchs would demonstrate on Schleicher the fate that awaited anyone who remained an unbending enemy of Christ and the state.

CHAPTER IX

Satan in the Heart?

Office of the Langenburg Court Preacher,
February–March, 1672

hile Anna Schmieg experienced the shock of hearing her life reviewed through the lenses of the law and witch theory, she found herself facing another equally disorienting ordeal. It started two days after Anna Fessler had died, when Pastor Wibel had sent report up the hill to his superior, Court Preacher Ludwig Casimir Dietzel. In his short letter he related his shock about Anna Fessler's death: "Eight days ago my wife and I were over there [in Hürden] with her, she certainly looked somewhat bloated, but she did not know the cause." He informed Dietzel that "she may have worried that she had taken a lying-in soup from the old witch and that she had been given the rest [of the poison] in the Shrove cake."[1] Pastor Wibel asked whether he should prepare her earthly remains for burial in the parish cemetery or whether he should wait while the authorities took charge.

One might mistake Pastor Wibel's request as a matter that had little direct bearing on Anna Schmieg's fate. Wibel's insinuations about "the old witch" may never have entered the formal record as evidence against Anna Schmieg, but his note indicated that while the legal inquiry was running its course, difficult religious and pastoral problems had also to be faced in this affair. Once his duty was fulfilled, Wibel then recorded a somber death notice in the Bächlingen parish register. Briefly noting the troubling circumstances of her death, he wrote that ". . . she had eaten a little bun . . . and it is suspected she has died by poisoning."[2]

Pastor Wibel's note drew Dietzel officially into the Schmieg affair. One of Dietzel's duties was to provide spiritual guidance and instruction to prisoners. Given that Barbara Reinhart had used her private sessions with him to recant her confessions, Dietzel likely assumed that he would hear all kinds of lies, evasions, and half-truths from Anna Schmieg. "The first thing one is to do is to ask them, why are you lying in prison [?], and one will soon note through the answer how it stands with their heart."[3] Both from the ordinance that guided Lutheran pastors in this particular ministry and his own experience with prisoners, Dietzel also knew that the difficulties could even challenge his own faith. His task was to engage the most recalcitrant of sinners under the most extreme circumstances:

> Regardless of how he answers, all of your conduct should determine that if he does not understand Christian teaching, then he is to be instructed in it insofar as it is possible. If he is insolent, defiant, or impatient one has to make it clear to him through the sharpness of the law just how big the sin is and instill a terror, contrition and pain in him.
>
> If on the other hand he is timid and frightened so one should console him with the goodness and compassion of the Gospel, and console him and when the humiliating corporal punishment attacks him to remind him to handle himself like any servant of the church would.[4]

Even with these guidelines the task was a troubling one.

Providing spiritual counsel to those imprisoned was a duty that the court preacher shared with parish pastors, sometimes working together in teams. While Dietzel hovered on the margins of the inquiry at first, he still familiarized himself intimately with Anna

Schmieg and the circumstances of her case. When von Gülchen drew up the first interrogation questions, he explicitly requested Dietzel's presence for the "theological" questions that opened the session. He may in fact have consulted with Dietzel, as he had in earlier witch trials, in drawing up the questions about Anna's spiritual state. Dietzel's involvement confronted Anna with a new aspect of the ordeal: confessing her sins in detail to a pastor. That the confessor was the count's personal pastor may have made this prospect even more intimidating. It would be a sometimes subtle, sometimes emotionally violent, interrogation. It made spiritual partners out of two very unlikely Christians: the powerful court preacher and a common miller's wife, a university-educated Lutheran, steeped in theology, and an illiterate peasant woman. That the power lay with the court preacher goes without saying, but one should also recognize that Dietzel felt that his own spiritual welfare hung in the balance. Manuals advising pastors on confessing convicts warned of the terrible burden of getting to know the heart of a convict and holding her secrets in confidence.[5]

All the things that bound Dietzel and Anna Schmieg together also guaranteed mutual disbelief, incomprehension, pain, and, in the end, dismay and betrayal.

———

*L*UDWIG CASIMIR Dietzel brought to the lofty office of Langenburg court preacher a lifetime of loyal service to both the church and to his patron and lord, epitomizing the Lutheran pastorate that had emerged by the end of the sixteenth century. Born in 1617 in Enslingen, Dietzel stemmed from a long line of Lutheran pastors. Both his father and grandfather had been pastors at the time of the Protestant Reformation. From his father he seems to have learned the tenacity of the minister whose life mission it was to bring the Lutheran faith to reluctant villagers at the height of the confessional era.[6] From his mother he had breeding. Elisabeth Dietzel was the daughter of Ludwig Casimir Hartmann, court adviser and chancellery director at Hohenlohe-Waldenburg. As descendants of Johann Hartmann, one of the architects of Hohenlohe's Reformation, the Hartmanns were Lutheran bluebloods, first families of faith and service to the counts of Hohenlohe. That young Ludwig rose above his father's modest station may therefore have been due less to his own merit than to the influence of his mother and her family. After beginning his career modestly enough in 1642 as pastor of Ruppertshofen, Dietzel became, in 1645, the Langenburg town preacher. Five years later, Count Heinrich Friedrich tapped Dietzel as his court preacher.[7] Anna Schmieg would therefore face a confessor not only bred for his office, but known for his staunch loyalty to Heinrich Friedrich, his family, and the government.[8]

Dietzel's education and spiritual devotion also prompted the intensity with which he engaged Anna Schmieg. He received a classical education at the Latin schools at Weikersheim and Öhringen, then went to gymnasium in Speyer in 1632, where he learned Latin, Greek, Hebrew, logic, oratory, and ethics. By the time he enrolled at the University of Strasbourg in 1636, he therefore had the solid and traditional humanist foundation for training as a pastor.[9]

Like Count Heinrich Friedrich and Court Adviser von Gülchen, Dietzel came under the influence of Strasbourg's Lutheran reform movement at the peak of its power. The leaders of the movement in the 1630s and 1640s were dynamic and popular preachers, and professors of theology as well. They equipped their large and devoted following of students not only with an orthodox theological education but instilled in them an ardor for the pastoral office.[10] To them the disasters of the Thirty Years' War—the advance of Catholic powers, the occupation and destruction of Lutheran lands, the hated imperial Edict of Restitution, the suffering of Protestant refugees—had revealed God's wrath and the urgent need for spiritual, religious, and moral renewal. Lutheran pastors needed to meet these challenges directly and personally through pastoral counseling with the laity.

Strasbourg reformers like Johann Schmidt taught that pastors should meet the crisis of the day through direct pastoral work, even meeting parishioners individually in their homes. Professor Johann Georg Dorsch, who taught Dietzel courses in Biblical exegesis, would become famous for his Peace Sermon, calling for moral and spiritual reform through personal penance and contrition of one's sins.[11] Well-known reformer Johann Konrad Dannhauer, another of Dietzel's mentors, urged on his followers the piety of Johann Arndt, the wildly popular Lutheran devotional writer who espoused a revolution in personal spiritual devotion.[12] Later, Dietzel would lionize his professors and praise the influence they had on him. He was not the only one, of course. In the heyday of Strasbourg's reform movement its preachers and professors educated a generation of pastors, theologians, and reformers who helped renew German Lutheranism after the war.[13] During the most difficult periods of the war young Strasbourg-educated pastors went out to churches and parishes throughout southern Germany and rebuilt them. Dietzel also had personal reasons for his gratitude and devotion to his professors and their teachings. Already hard-pressed when he arrived in Strasbourg—hard economic times and inflation impoverished his family in the 1630s—Dietzel suddenly lost his father. Overwhelmed by grief and left penniless, he completed his studies only through the personal intervention of his professors, who arranged a scholarship for him. With their aid Dietzel passed his exams as a preacher in 1641, holding a public disputation on the topic of Holy Communion one year later.[14]

Dietzel's own training and career, in fact, exemplified a broad shift in the Lutheran pastoral mission toward the end of the Thirty Years' War. Whereas the leaders of the Lutheran Confessional Age, known as the "masters of discipline," stressed indoctrination and order, the new generation became "shepherds of the soul," focused on pastoral outreach, education, and spiritual work among the laity. The pastoral message shifted away from fiery "calls to salvation" to actively leading laymen to adopt the Christian life.[15]

During the war Dietzel's own life as a pastor exemplified these teachings. In 1643 soldiers attacked him at his parsonage in Ruppertshofen, and Dietzel had to flee for his life, earning him the reputation of a martyr who willingly faced danger and endured suffering in the service of the Protestant faith.[16] When he was then appointed town preacher in 1645, he became one of the frontline defenders of Lutheranism against the alarming advance of Catholicism in the region.[17] Given Langenburg's vulnerability after the town's sacking and occupation in 1634 and its weakness before the advances of the wily and aggressive Catholic Bishop of Würzburg, Langenburg felt itself under religious siege. In Dietzel the counts and the town saw a vigorous defender of orthodox Lutheranism, one who embodied the steely determination to carry on the tough moral and spiritual struggle.[18] When at the end of the war in 1650 Dietzel became Langenburg's court preacher, he became Heinrich Friedrich's trusted agent in rebuilding the church.

As leader of the Lutheran Church in the territory, and under Heinrich Friedrich's orders, Dietzel had intensified the religious struggle. "Our old stately churches, the true Christian Augsburg Religion and the Faith that alone saves have been hard persecuted and attacked by the Devil," one court preacher wrote.[19] The peace celebrations in Langenburg in 1650 would therefore commemorate the suffering endured during the war, including both public ceremonies and intensified private devotions at home.[20] Only through continued penance, prayer, and individuals converting their hearts to Christ would the peace and the restoration of the true Christian faith be secured. But while the threat from Catholicism abated, the dangers of immorality, impiety, and even apostasy remained.

The shift in the struggle to the moral and interior life of Langenburg's subjects played to one of Dietzel's strengths: his skill in the confessional, to which he brought particular pride and experience. At the time when Johann Ludwig Hartmann, an expert on spiritual consolation, called the confessional "a birthing stool of anxiety and pain," it was said about Dietzel that he left the confessional chamber only with reluctance and regret.[21] In these intimate meetings Dietzel "took particular care for the souls entrusted to him to admonish them to penance and contrition and suffering for the sins that they had committed and then absolved them, so that they could return home justified with joy and consolation through faith in Jesus Christ."[22]

━━

ANNA SCHMIEG brought an entirely different set of expectations and values to her spiritual state. Like other villagers, she experienced religion through a matrix of rituals and social identities as a Lutheran and a Christian, not as doctrine or as an interior experience or state of the conscience, a vital difference with Dietzel. In her trial she affirmed that she had been baptized, that the ceremony had been properly recorded in a hymnal, and that the pastor in Bächlingen had attested to her inclusion in the community of the faithful. She understood baptism's meaning as a covenant with God, saying that "she has not broken her baptismal covenant and attached herself to evil." Whether she had received full instruction in the catechism, and therefore remembered the doctrinal instruction in the Ten Commandments, the Creed, the Lord's Prayer, and the basic schooling in the two sacraments, is open to question. In her trial she did not answer theological questions about the promise of baptism, and when pressed about matters beyond her, she simply said that "she was not educated."[23]

Neither her answers nor her evasions to some of these questions were unusual for a peasant woman, however. She may have wished to deflect her interrogators from pressing closer or, like many other villagers, she may have memorized only parts of the catechism. It is also possible that under these extraordinary pressures she simply could not recall. Even though her stepfather had been a schoolteacher in Crispach, children from farming and rural artisan families attended school spottily in the best of times. In the war years, when she would have gone to school and been catechized, the schools were often disrupted. Attendance at adult catechism in Bächlingen was erratic at best, the pastor reported: "Most stay away, especially the men."[24] Anna seems to have attended sermons, sent her children to catechism classes, attended Holy Communion, and even have gone to confession, like most others. She conformed to communal and institutional expectations.

Still, Anna's moral and religious behavior did raise some concerns within the parish in the years before her trial. Beginning in 1654, and repeating almost every two years thereafter, Dietzel and his team of church inspectors toured the parishes, inquiring into the quality of pastoral oversight, making sure that church services were held regularly and that teachings still conformed to the Augsburg Confession, and checking to see that the laity remained practicing Lutherans.[25] Questions about sorcery and witchcraft routinely came up during these visitations, but Dietzel posed his questions about these dark matters within a general framework of renewing the moral Christian life. Witchcraft, for example, he classed among a large group of sins that included sectarianism, cursing, blasphemy, and desecrations of the sacraments. When he asked the members of Anna Schmieg's parish whether anyone practiced "sorcery" or "witchcraft" in the village, his terms tended to invoke not the frightening associations of a diabolical pact with the devil, but the loose catch-all term of "superstition." To Dietzel "witchcraft" was not a crime but a pastoral concern, a sin, an immoral and impious act barring the way to true Christianity.[26]

Through his parish inspections and the reports he received from Bächlingen's pastors over the years, Dietzel must have been familiar with the challenges to Christian discipline that the Schmiegs posed to the church. Anna and Hans were known for quarrelling with neighbors, breaking the parish peace, drinking and cursing, and skipping church services. The Bächlingen pastor singled Anna out during the 1654 visitation, reporting to Dietzel that the miller's wife and another woman "were so furious with each other that they could no longer speak." A slaughtered goose had provoked this spat. Only the pastor's intervention had restored the village peace.[27] Notoriously, Hans quarreled with the village teamster and skipped church services to work in his fields, while Anna slipped off to drink at one of the taverns.[28]

———

ONE OF the other important clues about Dietzel's views toward witchcraft and people like the Schmiegs lay in the books available to him in the Langenburg libraries. In establishing a professional pastorate Lutheran churches expected their pastors to read and study daily. Every pastor was expected to draw on these readings for instruction, sermons, and devotion. The Bächlingen pastor, for example, had on hand the essential works of a busy pastor: the Bible, the Lutheran catechism, a copy of the Augsburg Confession, the Formula of Concord, the church ordinance, perhaps a work or two of Luther's and other devotional works. Every morning he read sections from the Old and New Testament, as well as from Melanchthon's *Loci Communis*.[29] Throughout the trial Dietzel followed the same routine. His religious studies done, Court Preacher Dietzel then took part in interrogating or confessing Anna in the afternoon.

For his daily study Dietzel turned to the Langenburg court preacher's library, the largest Lutheran library in the region. Only the count's personal library was larger. Books had been added to the collection since the Reformation, and by Dietzel's time the library comprised several hundred volumes.[30] This was no witch hunter's library, however, no treasure trove of early modern treatises on demonology. Still, if Dietzel wanted to read up on sorcery and witchcraft during the witch trials, he would find a few key references on the subject.

One of his predecessors in office had bound the works together in a single volume and carefully noted the places in the Bible that referred to diabolism and magic. The core works were sermons from authors well known in Protestant circles of southwestern Germany: Johann Brenz's *On Sorcery and Its Punishment* (1612), David Meder's *Eight Sermons on Witchcraft, Including on the Devil's Murderous Children, the Witches, Demon Fiends, Sorcerers, Dragon People, Milk Thieves, etc.* (1605), and Daniel Schaller's *Trafficking in Sorcery: Eight Sermons on the Twenty-Eighth Chapter of the First Book of Samuel* (1611).[31] The volume included sermons by less well-known authors, too.[32] The collection was rounded off with works on hail and storms, a cautionary work on sorcerers and soothsayers, a sermon on the appearance of a new comet in the heavens, and a story of a poor girl from Silesia possessed by a demon.[33]

Running through these works was a common concern: warnings to treat witches, storms, and strange occurrences as signs of God's intentions for Christians. These sermons drove home, sometimes crudely so, the message that witchcraft was real and that witches were living everywhere among Christians. All these treatises had been written when the fear of witches permeated sermons following outbreaks of damaging weather, and in which any doubts about the reality of witchcraft were actively combated.

The eight sermons of David Meder, once a Hohenlohe pastor himself, were something of a primer on witchcraft, beginning with the question of "whether there really were witches and demon-lovers" before enumerating the various names for these fiends, the sins they committed, their powers, and how people were seduced into pacts with the devil.[34] That the volume did not contain any of the newer, more skeptical, or more cautious-sounding works about witchcraft did not mean, of course, that Dietzel was unaware of the attitudes of the more cautious writers. Even a Protestant "skeptic" like Johann Matthäus Meyfart did not doubt the reality of witchcraft.[35] He merely cautioned readers that the law could not ferret out these enemies so easily, and that judges and pastors endangered their own salvation when they prosecuted the innocent unjustly.[36]

These works stressed the strength and consolation that faith conferred in the face of misfortunes, advising readers to channel the fear of demons and witches into motivation for spiritual self-improvement. All of these works tended to link witchcraft to wider doctrinal issues, to the recognition of moral truth and the experience of preaching the Gospel to Christians. Together they reinforced the Protestant message of God's absolute sovereignty over nature and human affairs, that all things ultimately come from God, that the devil and witches only work with God's permission so that he might further his plan for mankind. This school of thinking about witchcraft formed a tradition of theological reflection reaching back to the late Middle Ages.[37] Turning away from fear and the power of witches to do harm, these sermons would have focused Dietzel's attention squarely on the site where God's cosmic struggle against evil took place: the human heart.

Meder, in his fourth sermon, "On the Sins and Vices of Witches," argued that witches hid behind a mask of conformity, behind which their hearts had rejected Christ and turned toward Satan. As apostates, they secretly raged against God's discipline embodied in the Ten Commandments. Meder even went so far as to question whether witches might have even lost their humanity, warning pastors that "the demon-fiends act so terribly that they lose all human affections and goodwill toward their neighbors and even become inhuman so that no pious person can get anything good out of them because they are sworn enemies of all human beings." Meder concluded that even witches could be won back to God. Converting a witch's heart might be difficult, but Scripture provided hopeful examples of how hardened apostates had been saved. Once the Word had opened the heart, and Christ had been let in, the alert confessor could then urge the witch to confess her terrible sins and, by showing true remorse, even earn absolution for them.[38]

Court Preacher Dietzel tended to approach confessional sessions with suspects like Anna Schmieg in a similar way. Ever since his first appointment as a Hohenlohe pastor, he had seen in penance and confession the hope of genuine Christian renewal. Meder's views on confession, penance, and conversion echoed those of Johann Arndt, whose *Four Books of True Christianity* were so inspirational to Strasbourg's Lutherans and Dietzel's mentors at the university. In fact, Arndt provided his followers not only with a detailed understanding of the interior landscape of the heart—the seat of "true Christianity"—but also with pertinent advice about how to convert lost souls back to Christ. Conversion began with repentance, then overcoming self-love and love of sin and worldly things. One's will had to be broken. One had to deny all worldly pleasures and allurements. Then the self could be conformed to God's will. There were all kinds of false turns, deceptions, and lies on the long, hard road to complete conversion. Satan permanently cast out from the heart, the Christian could be saved.[39] Multiply such conversions within the community and the whole of society could be healed. Such an approach had guided Dietzel and Heinrich Friedrich in their campaign to restore true Christianity to Langenburg after the war.[40] In confronting a recalcitrant witch the stakes were especially high. Force her into repentance, turn her heart from Satan, and the worst of Christ's secret enemies could be driven out into the open and won over. Convert her and a lasting Christian peace might then be possible.[41]

Dein Jesus Zeigt Sein Leiden an:
Doch geht die Welt, aufs teufels bahn.

FALSE CHRISTIANS. *Lutheran devotional works warned readers that the world teemed with "false Christians" who wore masks of piety while dancing to the tune of Satan.*

$\mathcal{D}$IETZEL'S PRESENCE at Anna Schmieg's interrogation on March 7–8, and most of the sessions thereafter, made it plain that the government intended to ferret out the spiritual and religious roots of her sins along with exposing and prosecuting any crimes that might come to light. Critics of witch trials railed against this dangerous confusion of religion and the law. By drawing confessors into the legal interrogations, or compromising the confidentiality of the confessional, such clergymen not only ran the risk of making a mockery out of a sacred rite, but also ran the risk of corrupting the pursuit of justice with their religious bigotry and zeal.[42] While Dietzel may have seen his pastoral responsibilities as independent of the legal process, he showed no reluctance to coordinate his sessions of spiritual consolation very closely with Anna's interrogations. In fact, he brought to the trial a certain hardness that even von Gülchen at times lacked. His sessions with Turk Anna and her daughter, and especially with Barbara Reinhart and Barbara Schleicher, had been emotional and even violent. He listened carefully to what he heard Reinhart say in the confessional and then compared it to what she had said earlier in the interrogation sessions. When she seemed ready to break, he picked up the tempo of questioning and drove in on her weaknesses, confronting her with the lies, delusions, and false desires that clouded her heart. Reinhart, in defense, accused him of forcing her to say things she did not want to say.

During these difficult confrontations Dietzel was supposed to balance the church's admonition to wait patiently for a true and voluntary confession against the very real spiritual dangers waiting to overwhelm him during the process. But as Johann Arndt and others pointed out, breaking Satan's grip often required a shock, a violent confrontation with the truth. Besides, one had to assume that standing at the witch's side, whispering in her ear and numbing her to the pain of torture, was Satan himself. While witchcraft manuals reassured confessors and magistrates that faith in Christ shielded them against the bewildering attacks of Satan, it was still confusing and frightening to confront evil face-to-face. Getting the truth out of a witch was an ordeal unlike any other.

During the interrogations, and more so during the private sessions with Dietzel, Anna was asked for the first time in her life to account in detail for all of her sins. Part of the reticence she showed arose from the fact that she knew confession not as a private affair, but as a church ceremony that actively *discouraged* Lutherans from detailing their sins. While Martin Luther himself praised the spiritual benefits of confession and penance, advising Protestants to use the rite to prepare for Holy Communion, he also thought it deceptive that enumerating one's individual sins was helpful to salvation. To do so, one Lutheran writer cautioned, led to spiritual peril.[43] Following Luther's reservations, the liturgy tended to reduce confession to ceremonial formulae, asking parishioners to admit their general sinfulness and shifting the focus to instruction in God's Law and the Gospel.[44] The church ordinance renewed in 1654 embodied this same approach toward confession.[45] Anna had never used confession to explore the depths of her conscience or the dark recesses of her heart.[46]

Moreover, Anna and her neighbors had their own ways of blunting the potential of the confession for deep self-examination. Most villagers refused to make confession a regular practice. Ignoring appeals from their pastor to come to confession and communion every two weeks, the villagers of Bächlingen and Hürden tended to come only twice a year. The people "go to [confession and communion] in large numbers at Easter and in the fall, but four, five, or six Sundays go by and no one comes," the Bächlingen pastor complained. "Between Christmas and Easter and during Trinity up to the 13th Sunday no one comes." When Anna and her neighbors did go to confession, they showed up at church in groups. "By custom ten or twelve pairs of them come at one time, even though it would be more helpful with the troubling business if they were to return over and over again."[47]

Finally, the ritual aspect of confession reinforced the attitude that the rite had a magical power to purify the individual.[48] Dietzel recognized the challenge that these customs and beliefs posed to his campaign to use penance as a way to bring about Christian renewal. After the Thirty Years' War he had repeatedly exhorted villagers not to attend confession in such large groups. Perhaps townspeople responded to Dietzel's admonitions, but his lectures seem to have changed little in the countryside.[49]

When villagers like Anna went to Bächlingen for confession, they tended to do so on Saturdays, dressed in their Sunday best. Anna's little group would have gone up to the confessional stool in the choir or the sacristy, recited the liturgy with the pastor, and then received, on bended knees, the absolution.[50] Outwardly reconciled to God, they were then ready to receive communion the next day.

Nothing in Anna's experience or personal makeup therefore prepared her for the probing questions about her sins that she now faced. Very likely she had no idea that her answers to von Gülchen's questions would be taken down in detail and read back to her later on, that a determined court preacher would also hold her accountable during auricular confession for every single word that she uttered. There would be no room for anonymity, evasiveness, or vague professions of belief. Contradictory statements would have to be faced. Her motives would be open to relentless questioning. While confessional manuals warned the faithful about the difficulties of discerning the secret impulses of the human heart—"the heart is deceitful above all things, and desperately wicked: who can know it?" (Jeremiah 17:9)—Court Preacher Dietzel intended to do precisely that.

CHAPTER X

A Daughter's Betrayal

Langenburg Palace Chancellery,
April 30–May 22, 1672

y the end of April, Langenburg's social drama had entered a confusing and dangerous phase. The threat to Anna, her daughter, and Hans is easy enough to understand, but for those in control of the investigations—especially Court Adviser von Gülchen and Court Preacher Dietzel—other perils now became clear. One main reason was that treating the matter in accordance with the normal procedures of the law made an uncertain course of events virtually inevitable. Given modern preconceptions about witch trials—one too readily assumes that the outcome was predetermined—that the law might contribute to an unsettled state of affairs may seem a paradox, but the procedures common by the middle of the seventeenth century made convictions difficult to achieve. Even if von Gülchen believed that Anna Schmieg was a witch, convicting her of witchcraft was an entirely different matter.

Roman law had a name for the procedure that now guided the investigation: the "ordinary procedure," or *processus ordinarii*. This legal course differed sharply from treating witchcraft as a *crimen exceptum,* or "extraordinary crime." Even though witchcraft was still considered one of the most heinous secret crimes imaginable, it was rare by the 1670s for German magistrates to treat it with the haste and urgency of an "extraordinary crime." Among the reforms that had quietly entered judicial practice since the second quarter of the century were thorough preliminary investigations; careful, systematic interrogations; some protections for the accused; strict application of the rules of evidence in Roman law; consultations with jurisconsults at courts and the universities; and more cautious extractions of confessions under torture.

What made Anna Schmieg's trial so uncertain? For one thing, the key witnesses and suspects were all family members. More to the point: it involved a mother and daughter and the complex web of relationships and emotions that bound them together. Sifting through their cover-ups, lies, and deceits meant pitting two family members against each other, and legal experts rightly worried about the justice of confrontations of this kind. The law required magistrates to look for enmity as the motive for witchcraft. But how was one to separate out enmity when it was mixed up with affection, loyalty, and interest? The requirement to consult outside experts—usually university professors—about ambiguous points of law created additional uncertainty. Vexed as he was about some procedures and findings, von Gülchen would have to turn to learned jurists and academic physicians for advice. He had no influence over their views, yet to comply with imperial law he was obligated to follow their advice, whatever that might be. Finally, there were the confessions. For all the court adviser's power over Anna Schmieg, he was utterly dependent on her word in the end. The law demanded it.

The "ordinary procedure" was nonetheless firmly believed to be capable of unearthing the truth about the murkiest and most disturbing events. This search for truth was something that seventeenth-century law shared with science and medicine. Respect for Roman law and its practical applications in society had reached such an advanced state in Italy and the Holy Roman Empire that natural philosophers and physicians often considered its methods as models of rigorous, dispassionate investigation into human and natural events. Even supernatural forces were open to rational investigation.[1] Von Gülchen knew that only patient adherence to these procedures and the evidence they yielded could reveal the hidden truths that he and the government sought. He knew that some witnesses were lying, others covering up; that mundane activities, such as how women baked Shrove cakes, mattered; he also recognized that deception could blind his own judgment. Because the process aimed at a confession, and the confession would reveal the darkest, the most hidden secrets of the heart, he knew that the procedures would unearth the truth.

This is why in his interrogations he circled back over and over to the same questions. In 1668 when the Reinhart confession looked feeble and unclear, when she accused him of coercing her, he was thrown into confusion and doubt. He knew the concerns about persecuting the innocent. And he knew that unfair judges would have to account for their actions on Judgment Day. Von Gülchen was often ill now. It took great effort to work, and at times he may have worked from his bed.

*T*HE SUREST path to the truth regarding the poisoning of Anna Fessler, von Gülchen reckoned, was to focus attention on Schmieg's daughter. This was a brutal tactic. It meant that he not only had to break apart what contemporaries considered the strongest, most "natural" of all affections—that of a daughter for her mother—but that he then had to redirect Eva's loyalty to the authorities and God. Luther and the Lutheran Church had elevated the status of mothers within the household. The Fourth Commandment, to honor fathers and mothers, was such a moral and legal absolute to Lutherans that state laws were built upon it. Mothers had customary powers over education, upbringing, and also the arranging and approving of marriage partners. Reinforcing those bonds had been a high priority at the end of the Thirty Years' War when Langenburg's territorial marriage courts were reconstituted. In disputes over marriage the courts tended to side

with parents against their children.[2] When von Gülchen and Dietzel sat in on these marriage courts, they held the Fourth Commandment and the ideal of filial loyalty to parents in the highest
esteem.

There were legal contradictions and inconsistencies regarding
the sanctity of familial bonds, however. In criminal law some jurists
objected to forcing a child to testify against a parent. Imperial
criminal law allowed a judge to have a suspect be confronted personally with witnesses whose testimonies directly contradicted
theirs.[3] Could one legally make a daughter denounce her own
mother? On this question jurists divided sharply, but von Gülchen
voiced no concern at the time that he was about to enter a hotly
debated legal matter. Administrative, and not criminal, law was,
after all, his expertise. Besides, he was focused on the fact that Eva
should have had direct, firsthand knowledge of her mother's baking and domestic habits. He may also have been drawing on the
belief that witchcraft descended in the maternal line. Perverting
the natural, maternal bonds, witches perpetuated the black arts in
secret by instructing their daughters. They turned natural God-
given loyalties to blasphemous and diabolical purposes. The problem with witchcraft was that it was a secret crime. Break Eva's
bonds to her mother, redirect her loyalty toward God and the state,
make her confess, von Gülchen thought, and he could get at the
secret locked in her heart.[4]

In planning his interrogation von Gülchen laid out his precisely
worded examinations in a carefully thought-through sequence,
paying attention to the emotional rhythm of the questioning, following mundane and factual probing about the baking of the cakes
with sudden and provocative queries about her and her mother's
guilt. At key points he grilled Eva on matters such as how she dis-
tributed the cakes, a tactic that involved confronting her with other
witnesses, especially when he suspected she might be lying. In
Latin and capital letters he highlighted the urgent issues.

In his interrogation that day von Gülchen planned to close the
session with a shock and drive a wedge between Eva and her
mother. At the end of the session, when Eva would be weary, he
planned to jolt her into telling the truth by quoting the words of

her mother against her. Perhaps because she had fallen into despair, Anna had been heard by the jailer to say on April 11 that she blamed her husband and daughter for the tragedy of her whole family.

"Don't let me sit in prison any longer. No one brought me into this business except my husband. I'll fix him so he'll only shake his head in the end. My daughter is worthless, she's not even worth the bread that she eats, since she was the one who took the little cake out of the sack and gave it to little Anna. That's not a good sign. And if I'm a witch then my daughter is one, too, and learned it all from me. I know I'm doomed to walk down the Path of Straw [the road to execution], if only that would happen soon. There's no one else to blame in this but my husband."

After this he would ask the daughter: . . ."You are accused by your own mother, and if it's true that you took the little cake out of the sack and gave it to Anna and put it on the table, then that's one suspicious thing on top of another. Like your mother says, this isn't a good sign; then it was you, the daughter, who must have put something bad or poisonous into it. You should crawl on your knees before the Cross and do penance."

NB: Here the Court Preacher should confront her with what she has learned in the catechism and read to her what penance and contrition really is!

"You should beg to God and the Gracious Government for forgiveness. If you do so, fine, but if you don't, then know that your mother, who is locked up, will be let out of prison and given over to the district officer, but you will stay in the tower, where your mother has been sitting and you'll be chained up even more tightly than her, and in the end all grace will be denied and you'll be turned over to feel the stern force of the law!"

NB: Turn to her in all earnestness, say everything good and earnest to her so that above all else she can be won over.[5]

By confronting Eva with the fact that her mother had suggested that Eva herself might be a witch, von Gülchen hoped to frighten the young woman into an honest confession, one that might betray her mother and her mother's secrets.

ON THE morning of April 30, Eva was brought into the chancellery and faced the court, which included von Gülchen, Court Preacher Dietzel, probably the other two judges, and the court scribe. When faced with sharp questioning, she not only maintained her own innocence but tried to shield her mother. Given the evidence against them, this was a hard front to maintain. Von Gülchen repeatedly confronted her with contradicting statements from her husband and other Hürdeners about the cakes and her role in offering them to Anna Fessler, the neighbors, and the Fessler boy. In response, she tended to offer vague or incomplete answers, sometimes saying she could not remember. Elsewhere she was caught in half-truths and lies. She could not sustain her earlier story, for example, that Anna Fessler had wanted the cakes. Her neighbor had not in fact asked for them, she admitted. She was also caught in false statements about the size and shape of the cakes. She was forced to admit that "the cakes that she gave little Anna were prettier and had risen more than the others." In perhaps an attempt to save herself while imperiling her mother, she insisted—in contradiction to her mother's story—that her mother had called her in from the barn, put cakes into her apron, and ordered her to take them to Anna Fessler's house. "At that," she said, she "went over to Anna's house and gave her to eat a yellow one that her mother told her to, and set the others on the table."[6]

As the morning session wore on and she struggled to assert her own innocence, more and more of her answers put the blame on her mother. When von Gülchen pressed her on whether she helped to make the Shrove cakes and what exactly she knew about how they were made, her answer proved damning for her mother:

> She didn't help her mother make the dough. She put one little egg into the bowl, a little curdled milk and then left, but she didn't do anything else with it.
>
> Her brother Michel carried the dough from the sitting room into the kitchen and stayed there while she [her mother] baked the

cakes. Her brother doesn't know how her mother made the cakes. Michel wasn't at home, but returned when her mother was finished with the dough, since he helped her cut it, and helped her as above.[7]

Other damaging statements tumbled out. When asked whether her mother considered Anna Fessler an enemy, she responded that "when Anna Fessler accused her mother of spreading poison on the pasture, then her mother became her enemy." Quickly recognizing the importance of this story, von Gülchen scrawled "*NB*" in the margin. She was even forced to confirm a tale that the *Kutscherin* had told her, that her mother, when drunk, had muttered under her breath to the devil.[8]

If she was trying to protect her mother—and the vague answers she sometimes gave suggest that she was—the strategy tended to break down in the afternoon session. When pressed hard whether she believed her mother guilty in the death of Anna Fessler, she wavered. She "could not say whether her mother is guilty or not—the little cakes were given to her by her mother, and more than this she doesn't know." When von Gülchen followed up, asking her "whether she herself is also guilty in the crime and she helped her mother," she retreated. "No," she insisted, "she didn't help her mother. It's unjust to say that she did. Her mother has to bear the responsibility."[9]

After one more question, the session came to its climax. Court Adviser von Gülchen's instructions made it clear that by reading her mother's two denunciations of her to Eva, he wanted her to turn against her mother and admit Anna was a witch. Right after these statements, the court preacher then bore down on Eva, reminding her of the lessons from the catechism about penance and confession, admonishing her that any mercy she might expect from God and the authorities now depended on her telling the full, complete truth.[10] Standing before the court, Eva then listened as the scribe read out her mother's bitter remarks about her daughter's worthlessness, her account suggesting that Eva had acted suspiciously on Shrove Tuesday, and that if Anna was a witch then so, too, was her daughter.

Despite the emotional blow of these words, Eva responded immediately. "She is no witch," Eva defended herself: "Her mother might be one, but she has to answer for that herself." She admitted that Anna Fessler's rapid demise after eating the cake had raised suspicions that she had been poisoned. She quickly blamed her mother for this: "And the suspicion is on her mother, because she [Eva] did nothing with the baking of the cakes and didn't help, as she has said."[11] The court adviser's brief *NB* in the margins of the protocol said it all. He now had the legal testimony against Anna Schmieg he sought. Eva's vague statements were giving way to clear denunciations against her mother.

⸻

$\mathcal{H}$AVING DRIVEN the first wedge between Eva and her mother, von Gülchen stood back from the interrogations to take stock. For two weeks he tended to other government business, reviewed the trial protocols, and considered what to do. While he had gained a foothold against Anna from Eva's answers, he still needed more evidence to make sure that Anna would confess. On May 16 and 17 he laid out his thinking in a long, carefully drafted plan of interrogation that he submitted to Count Heinrich Friedrich for review and approval.[12]

While Eva may have convinced him that she did not help her mother make the cakes, her absence from the kitchen left him with no direct evidence about how the Shrove cakes might have been poisoned. "In my view," he wrote Heinrich Friedrich, "the miller's wife is still thoroughly suspicious as the one who poisoned the cake but not by *ratione facti progyny* [by reason of the evidence of the child]." Leaping ahead of the evidence, however, and, relying instead on "reasonable knowledge" and "administrative reasoning" (*ratione scientia et ministery*), he came to the conclusion that Eva must know that her mother was guilty. To prove his view he still needed *certain evidence* that Anna had made the dough and what exactly she had mixed into it.[13]

His plan would unfold in two parts. On May 21 he would interrogate Eva and focus on all the details about the Shrove cakes: What did she know about how the cakes were baked? Did she help? Why did she take the cakes to Anna Fessler? Why did she urge the "largest and the prettiest" on Anna? What did her mother tell her to say? Weren't her mother and the Fesslers enemies? Were there two batches of dough? Similar questions were to follow about the cakes that were baked and brought to the other neighbors. After pressing Eva about whether she thought her mother guilty of witchcraft and poisoning, he would then bring in Anna and have them face each other. In this second part—to take place May 22—he would also interrogate the son, Michel, and then submit Anna Schmieg to further interrogation. "And if after all of this no confession is brought out then she is to be spoken to sharply, to confess to the truth, and to threaten her for the first and last time with the executioner and questioning under torture."[14]

What was striking in this exhaustively laid-out plan was the intense focus on every aspect of how one woman and her daughter baked batches of cakes and gave them away. The blending of the material and the factual with the magical and the demonic still figured in his questions. She would be pressed on her knowledge of whether witches could be saved, for example, and whether she knew that witches have marks of the devil on them. Von Gülchen wanted to know whether Anna had foretold her own fate when she had remarked that she expected to be led out to Gallows Hill. Witches could see into the future, after all. She would be questioned whether she had been procuring extraordinary amounts of milk, the implication being that she was stealing milk from the neighbors' cows through sympathetic magic. And she would have to explain about "the repulsive toad that lived in her barn: Was it not really her demon lover?"[15]

Von Gülchen's blending of the mundane with the magical and the demonic was not unusual. Though this trial ran much more along the lines of the natural and the empirical, it still fit perfectly with witch theory. The devil and witches were experts in using natural laws and forces for their nefarious ends. Paradoxically—to us—the fear of the demonic and the need to prove it at work in the mundane drove judges like von Gülchen to focus ever more sharply on the purely human.

THE SESSION that unfolded on May 21 would turn out to be a decisive turning point. Under von Gülchen's intense questioning, and later in a brutal face-to-face encounter with her mother, Eva broke her equivocations and silences. Von Gülchen asked her twenty-four questions, revolving around the three alleged poisonings (Anna Fessler, her son, and the teamster's wife). In the background lay the government's suspicion that the plots might be part of a wider conspiracy not yet fully uncovered.

In her responses that morning Eva held herself up as a dutiful daughter carrying out her mother's commands. She now said that her mother had told her exactly what to say to her neighbors, making Eva merely the obedient instrument of her mother's will, and she now admitted that she had qualms about what her mother had really been up to that day. "Her mother ordered her to do it," Eva said, and to say to Anna Fessler, "Eat the little cake, it's baked with good butter, it won't hurt you."[16] More damning, her mother, she said, had not simply mixed up all of the cakes together in her apron, as someone with innocent intentions toward Fessler would have done. Instead her mother had "given her a special one" separate from the others and with instructions to urge this particular one on Anna Fessler. Eva repeated her innocence in the matter of the cakes, vehemently insisting that the cake she gave Fessler also came from her apron and that she had not secretly pulled it from a sack. Her mother was also the one who the next morning ordered her to take another special cake to the Fessler's boy.

Eva then took her story yet further:

The part she broke off from this little cake [meant for the Fessler's boy] she didn't eat, but brought it back home instead. What she did with it, she simply doesn't know anymore. She didn't want to eat any of it, because, God knows, she knew that her mother wished she would eat just a little bit of it, and that it was pure poison and it would kill her heart.

On the night that little Anna [Fessler] died her mother set little cakes on the table, and because they had quarreled with each other before, Eva said that, had she eaten one, the poison in it would kill her heart. For this reason she [Eva] ate none of them, and she also refused to eat from those that she took to Anna Fessler's little boy the next day at her mother's bidding.[17]

Eva was now saying that she herself feared that her mother had poisoned the cakes that day and she worried she, too, would have been murdered.

Even more damaging testimony followed. She could not provide any useful testimony about how the cakes had been baked. Beyond breaking an egg or two Eva professed that she had nothing to do with the baking of the cakes. Had her mother made more than one batch of cake dough that day? Had Eva been able to confirm this, it would have been a very suspicious sign indeed, but Eva did not know. She did affirm that her mother's hatred for Anna Fessler might have driven her to vengeance: "Her mother was little Anna's enemy because her cows damaged her mother's [pasture]. Then Eva warned Anna Fessler about her mother, saying 'that she started to act as if she meant to poison the pasture.' " Clarifying her thoughts, Eva then said, "Yes, she believes that because little Anna died so quickly, her mother must be guilty of having done it, especially because she expressly ordered her later [to lie] and say that she had taken the little cake out of her apron and not out of the sack."[18]

On the question of the third alleged poisoning, she again portrayed herself as a dutiful daughter executing her mother's wishes. She delivered the teamster's wife Shrove cakes just as her mother ordered. She added a new detail: "The little cake that she brought the *Kutscherin* came from a basket that her mother had put out of the way and which had never held anything before. Four little cakes were lying in the basket. Her mother had in fact said to her, 'eat as much as you like from these little cakes.' "[19]

Eva indicated that her mother had indeed made two different batches of cakes, one of which was poisoned, and that she was using her daughter to carry out her wicked plots. Something new and more disturbing emerged in Eva's testimony before the court that day. In her answers she developed the outlines of a previously hidden reason why the cakes had gone to the neighbors on Shrove Tuesday. She suggested that her mother really meant the cakes for her, Eva, and her husband, Philip. When, earlier, von Gülchen pressed her that she had brought suspicion on herself by urging one special cake on little Anna, Eva admitted that this had been the case, but that originally "her mother had said that she [the deponent] should eat it, or if she didn't like it, to take it to Anna Fessler. "Her mother began to treat her horribly as soon as she wanted to leave [the mill] and move to Nesselbach to be with her husband [Philip]. The Benzin [Anna Fessler] became her mother's enemy when she advised Eva, not to stay in Hürden but to move to Nesselbach instead."

Eva's revelation caught von Gülchen's attention. Next to Eva's account the court scribe marked "*NB*" in bold letters and added: "Her mother therefore wished her all kinds of bad luck, [and] if it had worked, it would have gone badly for her."[20] Leaving nothing to doubt about her wariness in dealing with her mother, Eva went on to say that "she was grateful that she had seen through her mother because her mother had said that she would bake little cakes one more time and that Eva would never again in her life eat a little cake from her mother. Who knows what would have happened to her husband if he had come to Hürden for Shrove Tuesday because her mother really wanted to get him, too." Eva said plainly that the reason she refused to eat her mother's cakes was that "her mother had hung a great curse on them."[21]

The breach was in the open now. Eva was not just distancing herself from her mother—family members often backed away from helping one of their own during a witchcraft accusation—she was also suggesting that the plot was wider and more sinister than anyone suspected: *Anna Schmieg was trying to poison her own daughter and son-in-law.*

IN THE meantime, von Gülchen had Anna led into the chamber. The "confrontation" that then followed between daughter and mother was short and carefully staged. One cannot discern what either woman was thinking about the enormity of the betrayal that was about to unfold. Yet the emotional fury Eva's treachery triggered in Anna is unmistakable. Von Gülchen set twelve questions to Eva. The fact that Eva seemed not to waver as she affirmed all the incriminating points against her demonstrated the openness of her breach with her mother. What gave Eva's denunciations so much force was that they were done face-to-face. The session resembled skirmishers firing volleys at each other, Eva affirming a fact and her mother spitting back a furious rejoinder, here and there lacing her responses with the insults and biting sarcasm for which she was notorious.

The strongest confrontations came early in the session. When Eva contended once again, in response to von Gülchen's prodding, that her mother had become Anna Fessler's enemy, her mother would hear none of it. "God punish her body and soul if she had been little Anna's enemy." The scribe noted accusingly that "she threw her tongue around in her mouth just like the Cattle Woman [Barbara Reinhart] had done before." Eva's testimony about her muttering in a strange way under her breath led Anna to admit that "she talked to her pigs just like other people do when feeding their cows." When Eva said that she had heard rumors that her mother was talking to the devil, Anna bristled. Recognizing that this slander came from the teamster's wife, Anna retorted that she "lies like a loose whore." The most important standoff took place over whether Anna had ordered her daughter to take cakes to Anna Fessler or not:

> Eva: Yes, and says further to her mother's face: you called me in from the barn and said: "Go over to Benzen Michel [Michel Fessler] and tell him he should fetch Philip [Eva's husband] over for Shrove Tuesday, we don't get together anymore for Shrove Tuesday, give a cake to little Anna [Fessler] just like you would give something spe-

cial to Hans [Eva's father]." And you said that I was to eat one, too, and that if I didn't want it that I should give it to little Anna.

The miller's wife swore vehemently it wasn't true. She didn't send Anna [Fessler] a little cake—she would have been out of her mind to do such a thing—but instead sent Eva to Anna's husband, Michel, to tell him to fetch her daughter's husband [Philip] from Nesselbach.[22]

But for one crucial detail, Eva and Anna were now telling the same story. Wanting to bring her family together for a traditional Shrove Tuesday celebration, Anna had sent her daughter over to look for Michel Fessler—Anna later even conceded that she had given Eva three Shrove cakes as a gift for Michel—to ask Michel to fetch Eva's husband, Philip, for the holiday. The point they hotly disputed was whether Anna Schmieg had also given Eva a cake meant particularly for her daughter or Anna Fessler to eat. On this point Schmieg was adamant: she did no such thing.

The logic of such a confrontation was to put the accused on the defensive. Observing an accuser and a suspect carefully, one could discern who was telling the truth. Experienced magistrates therefore knew how to interpret their facial expressions, gestures, tone of voice, and emotions.[23] Only when the miller's wife vindicated herself by telling how she had sent her daughter on an errand to Michel Fessler—not his wife—was she seen as forthright. After that, however, her responses seemed equivocal. At other times she responded with silence. But magistrates also knew that silence could be a sign of guilt: her muteness drew the court's attention. When Eva testified that her mother did not like Hans Barthel Walther's wife, her mother did not deny it. "Neighbors are often enemies with each other," Anna said. To Eva's statement that her mother must bear the guilt for Anna Fessler's death, Anna "swore repeatedly: if *she* sent little Anna a cake and she is guilty in her death, then God should send her a sign." At the end of the session she had almost nothing to say when Eva affirmed that "if Anna [Fessler] died then her mother must bear the sin for it." When the story came out about sending her daughter off for wine, Anna did not deny it, screaming at Eva "that the Devil should come and take her so she can leave this world[!] . . . "If I did it, then I did it, I can't deny it, but neither can I affirm it."[24]

———

WHEN THE court convened once again around one o'clock on the next afternoon, May 22, Court Adviser von Gülchen turned to the next step in his plan: a short interrogation of Michel Schmieg. Michel not only maintained his innocence in the affair—he said he had simply helped his mother carry the cake dough into the kitchen—but he also tried to support his mother's account. When asked directly about his mother's baking, he said "he can't say that his mother did anything wrong with the little cakes that she baked." This statement was too vague to be helpful to his mother in the end, however. He did confirm his sister's innocence regarding the baking of the cakes: "She simply did not work around the dough much," he said. In fact, Eva was away in Bächlingen at the time, fetching wine and taking care of the cows. Even his father, Hans, had been away from home when his mother finished preparing the dough.[25]

The high point of the session came once he left the room. Anna was led back into the chamber and was subjected to the most searching interrogation she had yet endured. Not only was von Gülchen much better informed about the affair, he now knew precisely where she had been evasive or inconsistent and was prepared to confront Anna with her own words.

From the start of this session Anna's answers were confusing and evasive. When asked whether she had in fact said that it was not a good sign if her daughter had taken the Shrove cake out of a sack and given it to Anna Fessler, she responded that "maybe she had said it, maybe not." She continued: "If I did, you can cut my head off." Von Gülchen asked her pointedly: "Did you say that 'if you are a witch then your daughter must be one, too, that she would have learned it from you?' "Writing "*NB*" in bold letters in the margin, the scribe then noted what happened next: Anna fell silent, and remained silent for a full half hour.[26]

WHEN SHE finally spoke, she refused to answer the question directly and instead "talked about strange things." "If it turns out that you are in fact a witch," von Gülchen pressed on, "then do you stand by the view that you must have taught witchcraft to your daughter as well?" Anna denied she was a witch and said that therefore she could not have taught her daughter the dark arts.[27]

One of the telling signs of her contradictions was her response to questions about her attempted suicide. Had she wanted to hang herself after Anna Fessler's death because she had been cried out "for twenty miles around" that she was a witch? If so, then what did her actions say about her conscience? Her reply:

> The outcry and the appearances are as they are. Her neighbors know better about it, and without a doubt the outcry came from them. She herself does not believe that anyone with a good conscience could hang herself. She admits that she said to Hubfritz's wife that she wants to hang herself.
>
> [Appolonia] was brought out and confronted the miller's wife eye-to-eye and she stood by her earlier statement.[28]

Here Anna not only acknowledged her reputation as a witch, but she also showed no sign of resisting her public image or even questioning whether her neighbors were right or not. Her admission that she wished to take her own life, knowing that suicide pointed to a guilty conscience, was even more damaging. Yet she still refused to say that she was a witch. "She took consolation in the mercy of the authorities, but she was no witch. God would not want any part of her soul if she were a witch."[29]

When asked whether her body bore the mark of a witch, Anna insisted that she had never seen one on herself. Yet she went on to say that "she wants to have herself looked over, and if one finds a sign on her she wants to confess it and have herself burned."[30] Did she say this defiantly? Or was she simply meeting her tormentor's accusations with her old sarcasm, taunting him to prove it? It is

even possible that a calculation lay behind her challenge. If the executioner examined her—and she could somehow appeal to his
loyalty as her husband's kinsman—then the charges against her
could be shown to be baseless. It is also possible that she had begun
to harbor doubts about herself—How could one be sure of one's
identity in the face of such relentless questioning?—and the horror of this recognition was beginning to sink in. It is possible that
after four months in chains the terrible strains of the interrogations
were bringing her to exhaustion.

When pressed further about witches and witchcraft, Anna
showed her revulsion at what witches do and what fate awaited
them. She repeated: "If she were a witch God would want no part
of her soul." As if to hold out some consolation, she was asked
"whether she believed that a witch can be saved and enter heaven?
Whether she will convert, and show remorse for having turned to
the Devil, and turn back to God? Whether she believed that Turk
Anna had been saved?"

Anna knew the orthodox Lutheran teaching on sinfulness:
"They say that, yes, there is no sin so great that if one wants to
show contrition and sorrow for it, he can be saved." But she
doubted whether this would in fact happen. "She believed it difficult, however, that witches should be saved because they denied
God." She then insisted, once again, that she knew nothing of
witchcraft. Even if she knew, as she said she had heard in a sermon,
that "the devil can teach witches to work with poisonous herbs,
roots and powders and can harm men and animals," she denied
knowing anything about such vile things. When pressed about
whether she was familiar with "poisonous spiders and toads and
the like" or whether she had heard that Turk Anna had put such
poisonous things into the bread that she gave to women and children in Regenbach, "she said she can't say anything about such
things, she doesn't want to say . . . leave her in peace, one can't make
her say things."[31]

When questioned specifically about how the cakes were made,
Anna gave less ambiguous answers. She vehemently swore "on her
soul before God" that she had not made two separate batches of
dough and cakes. Similarly she swore that she would go to Holy

Communion on her testimony that she had not baked a special cake that was prettier and larger than the others. When she could not remember certain details, she might truly have forgotten them and was not being evasive.[32]

The court then followed up, inquiring about her gloomy prophecies on her fate. Again she wavered. When she was arrested and had to part from Hans, she admitted that she "had taken leave from her husband with the hand and said that they would never again see one another." When pressed whether she had also said "that she would be led out the High Way [to her execution]," she did not answer directly, saying at first that "if she had wished this then it would be an awful wish." But when the court brought in the government lackey who swore that she had said it, she admitted to it. But she remained recalcitrant about other charges: that she had harmed Eva Büchlerin from Forst with a shot in the arm, that Büchlerin was her enemy and she had sought revenge against her, or that her cows gave abnormally large amounts of fat and milk. She swore, too, that she knew nothing about a "horrible toad" living in her barn, which Anna Heinckelin swore she had seen the day the Heinckelin child drowned in the river near the mill.[33]

Yet Anna continued to leave open the possibility that she may not know everything that was in her own conscience. For Anna as for Luther, the conscience was not a faculty of the mind kept alive by an internal dialogue with oneself, but one prodded into awareness periodically from without, through penance and Holy Communion. Neither was the conscience preoccupied with the details of individual sins. The conscience made one aware of one's total sinfulness.[34] Perhaps it was here that doubts crept into her words before the court. When pressed hard once again to tell the truth, to admit her or Eva's guilt in the death of Anna Fessler, Anna was, in part, clear about the answer: "God punish her life and soul if she knew [who was guilty], but she cannot say—she doesn't have remorse since she didn't do it."[35]

When Anna resumed her testimony, the court scribe noted the tentative tone of her final words: "If she does not have a good conscience, then she does not want to get out [of this affair] alive. She wants to have herself killed; here she is, you may do with her what you will."[36] To the scribe—and later that evening to von Gülchen when he read over the protocol—her statement came close to an admission of doubt. Anna might yet reveal the truth about who she really was and what she had done. For Anna, however, her words might well have been the kind of testy defiance and sarcasm for which she had long been known.

Now other testimony that she had given—whether spoken honestly or thoughtlessly or perhaps even defiantly—came back to haunt her. In her first interrogation she had suggested that Master Fuchs look into her conscience; he could tell if she was a witch. To make a new point—that the next time the court examined her it might well be under torture—von Gülchen brought Master Fuchs into the chamber. Seeing him, Anna became agitated. Von Gülchen asked her to confirm her earlier statement about the executioner's powers. She emphatically denied ever having said such a thing, but when one of the jailers was brought in and testified to the contrary, she recanted. She had meant to say, she insisted, that Fuchs could tell a witch by finding the marks of a witch on someone's body. Never had she meant that he had supernatural powers of discernment. Only God knows a witch.[37]

While Anna was answering these questions, von Gülchen was quietly sizing up his executioner. Could he trust Fuchs? Only a few weeks earlier von Gülchen had heard that Fuchs and Hans Schmieg were related, raising the ticklish question of the executioner's loyalty were he ordered to torture a kinsman's wife. Was it true, he suddenly asked Fuchs, that he and Anna's husband were bound to each other as godparents? "No," Fuchs replied. Whether this was true or not—the nature of Fuchs's close ties to Schmieg would remain a mystery—is unclear.[38] Apparently satisfied, however, von Gülchen dismissed him.

After warning Anna one last time that she must tell the truth, he had her returned to her cell. He then commanded the jailer to cut her rations, allowing her meat and wine only on Fridays and Sundays. Her daily fare was to be only soup, bread, salt, and a bit of fat.[39]

Despite Eva's unsettling revelations and Anna's fierce denials on May 21 and 22, von Gülchen still did not have the answers he sought. Retiring that afternoon to his chamber, he reflected on their testimonies and how to get at the truth that still eluded him. Resolved on a new course of action, von Gülchen took up his pen and wrote to Heinrich Friedrich.

CHAPTER XI

A Mother's Revenge?

Langenburg Palace Chancellery,
May 22–June 3, 1672

he end of May was a time of confusion. Despite driving a breach between mother and daughter, von Gülchen had been unable to sort through all the contradictions and evasions in their stories. He found Eva's testimony inconsistent and vague on key points. Loyalty to her mother still overrode duty to conscience, God, and the authorities. The court adviser still believed the secret to breaking the affair open was for Eva to "tell the complete truth." If she did so, she might gain the grace and forgiveness of God, and mercy for herself.[1]

As he reflected on the case on May 22 and 23, he pinpointed the places where her stories were not credible. Eva knew that the cakes were poisoned. He also thought she knew where her mother had stored the cakes, since he suspected Anna of having made two batches. It was also odd that Eva knew her mother hated the Fesslers and yet never suspected anything wrong with her cakes. Von Gülchen thought he knew why Eva broke into pieces the cake meant for the little Fessler boy: her conscience prevented her from giving him a poisoned cake intact.[2] In return for her honesty, von Gülchen could offer Eva a favorable judgment. Break her silence and her loyalty to her mother, and the truth would spill out.

He considered Anna in an entirely different light. He had no doubt that she had poisoned her neighbor or that she was a witch. However, scrupulous jurist that he was, he knew he had to secure a direct confession to prove her crimes. One might think von Gülchen's reading of the situation prejudicial, that a presumption of her guilt sprang from his belief in witches and guided his thinking. Such a view would be a misreading not only of von Gülchen, but of other similarly trained jurists confronting cases of witchcraft and poisoning. Well-trained jurists thought deeply and methodically about difficult-to-interpret evidence as they struggled to gain a clear understanding of events.

Von Gülchen did so by thinking carefully about the "cause" in the case, the real reason behind this whole murky affair.[3] One should not confuse von Gülchen's "cause" with a modern understanding of "motive." He did not think of "cause" as we might today, as a connected sequence of events culminating in an act of revenge. To a seventeenth-century jurist "cause," or *causa,* was a legal concept defining the *particular objective conditions between two parties* that explained murder or harm.[4] In cases of murder, poisoning, or serious injury, the law required a magistrate to look for one and only one "cause": enmity or bitter and unresolved hatred between enemies. When enmity was left unresolved, so the law presumed, it became a force propelling individuals to violence. This was why the state preached penance and Holy Communion so insistently: Only religious absolution could dissolve enmity and allow individuals and the community to heal. Given that Anna had never resolved her enmity with the Fesslers, it seemed only logical that some violent assault, if not murder, would follow. Moreover, by searching for the legal "cause" of the crime, von Gülchen was laying the foundation for questioning Anna under torture.

⸻

*B*UT IF enmity was implicated in these events—and what we know about Anna's temper and ferocity make it worth exploring further—then how? Was there a crisis at the mill so desperate that it could actually provoke Anna to murder?

Answers to these questions take us back at least a year before the events on Shrove Tuesday, when the Schmieg family entered one of the most difficult transitions a peasant family had to undergo. After decades of working the mill, raising a family, and fighting off enemies, Hans and Anna were getting old. Hans no longer had the strength to do all the required labor at the mill. The Schmiegs were therefore planning their retirement. At the same time, their children—Michel and Eva—had reached the age when they needed to be settled, preferably by marriage, which also meant providing an inheritance for each of them through dowries or marriage portions, enabling them to marry, acquire property, and establish their own households. In a peasant society, these two transitions—an old couple's retirement and their children's marriages—were often interwoven and managed as a single transaction. Relinquishing control over the patrimony, parents settled into retirement as dependents on the young couple who then assumed ownership of the family's property.

Guiding this transition were a variety of laws, customs, and practices governing inheritance, retirement, and marriage. In Hohenlohe, custom and the law were complex: Some properties were impartible, passing intact to a single heir, while others might be divided up among the children. Still other parts of the settlement might involve payments stretching out over a number of years. While these customs gave parents and children a great deal of flexibility, they also brought uncertainty and conflict. For good reason Hohenlohers were known for their manipulations, cunning, and even deceit in managing this delicate life transition.[5]

Around the time that Hans and Anna had begun to consolidate their gains at the mill and consider how to pass on their hard-won legacy, scandal struck the family. In the summer of 1670, Eva struck up a romance with Philip Küstner. At the time, Eva was only eighteen; Philip, twenty-one. Daughters were expected to delay serious courtship and marriage, especially ones who, like Eva, came from families with property to manage and wealth to defend. Because parents held the purse strings, and church laws forbade children to marry until parents gave their consent, daughters waited until they were at least twenty-five or twenty-six before becoming engaged and married. Besides, Hans and Anna intended Michel to marry first and assume the Schmieg legacy. Once Michel was settled into the mill, Hans and Anna could retire. Later, when Eva could be married into the Preuninger family, the wealthy millers from the Moses Mill in Bächlingen, the Schmieg legacy would be secure. Anna Schmieg might have been an outsider, but her children and her children's children would be entrenched village insiders.[6] A furtive romance was one thing, but the timing for a serious courtship was all wrong.[7]

Even if Eva had been free to carry on a courtship, it is doubtful that her parents would have intended her for a man who was, by many reports, a lazy rogue with dismal prospects. But Eva found him irresistible. They met when a number of young people went to a nearby village to help cut flax in the fields. Afterward, the two found themselves in a group going to Zottishofen, where young people could drink wine and have a bit of fun away from their elders, neighbors, and the pastor. Eva and Philip walked home together. When later that summer Philip and his friends went down to the Jagst River to swim, Eva came to watch. On two occasions she went up to him and offered him a bunch of flowers. By then "it was well known that he loved her."[8] How many times Eva and Philip met, and where and when they began to make love, is not entirely clear. Philip claimed that he and his buddies visited her on a couple of occasions in her parents' mill. By the spring of 1671 their relationship had become more intimate. On one occasion Eva went up to Nesselbach to help Philip's father, Conrad Küstner, and his family make hay at their little farm, bringing the Küstners a gift of her mother's prized cherries. Soon thereafter they met again at a village dance just a couple of miles from Hürden. Eva recalled behaving "properly" at the dance and that she had not stayed for the drinking, and when the boys became rowdy, she insisted that she and the *Kutscherin*'s maid returned home together.[9] But Philip boasted that they had in fact drunk wine together, that she flirted with him at the dance, and that she had given him little gifts. "Several times she asked him to come to her."[10]

On Saturday night, March 17—a week before Easter—Phillip stole down from Nesselbach and came to the mill at Hürden. He rapped on a shutter and woke Eva. The two of them slipped past her parents room and, "because it was cold," went back to her bedroom. At first they sat together, but then Eva, still dressed in her shirt, went to the bed and lay down. He was an awkward lover, it seems. "It was a long time until day came," she remembered, "and he left her, and the deed was done only one time. She went downstairs with him, and closed up the house." About six weeks later they made love again, although they had differing accounts about whether they actually had sexual intercourse.[11]

In this region of Germany the custom of *Fenstern*, or "letting your lover in through the window," was something young women and men often did. Parents might wink at a midnight rendezvous, so long as the couple were engaged and a marriage date had been set. In this case, however, Anna and Hans did not know about their daughter's nighttime rendezvous. Eva never mentioned that he had promised marriage or that indeed, she wanted to marry him at all.[12]

In the middle of August, Eva knew that she was pregnant, but she kept the secret from her parents for another month. Anna seems not to have suspected anything. On September 23, Eva finally admitted her condition. The Schmiegs were "wretched." Hans proposed marrying Eva to the Preuninger's son, but Eva refused because she was pregnant. Enraged, old Hans threatened to beat his daughter. Meanwhile, the Walthers and their girls—one of whom had returned from the dance in Dünsbach with Eva—put out the rumor that Eva had been raped. Distressed, Eva "escaped and went to the Heinckelins' house and had no desire to come out or go away."[13] Someone had alerted the marriage court in Langenburg, and one of the district officers came down to Hürden to seize Eva and bring her in for a hearing. Anna Heinckelin related: "When the daughter of the miller's wife was about to be taken away on account of her whoring, she ran to the Jagst [river] and wanted to drown herself. Her [Heinckelin's] husband, however, jumped in after her and brought her back to shallow water and that same night she slept in their bed at their house."[14]

WHEN THE Marriage Court convened at Langenburg on September 25, the two young people stood before the magistrates accused of fornication. Presiding was Court Preacher Dietzel, assisted by Assum and a scribe. The court examined Eva first and then Philip. Dietzel naturally wanted to find out whether they had violated the stern proscriptions against dancing and drinking, even though the most important issues were clearly the matter of fornication, Eva's pregnancy, and the lack of an intent to marry. Dietzel found that neither the Schmiegs nor the Küstners were aware of the liaison. When the families were asked for a resolution of the matter, both said that "they should get married and should be brought to honor. They wish to become subjects of Langenburg, and plead for their release from prison."[15]

The blow to the Schmiegs was devastating. Such transgressions were not just violations of God's laws, but a flagrant breach of the public peace. As Hans and Conrad Küstner said, the arrest and imprisonment of the two young people—acts that tarnished their parents' honor as well—"threw us parents into such despair that we cannot find words to express the shame and grief." The parents begged Heinrich Friedrich for mercy. "Now they have confessed their sins and misdeeds, and shown that they are sorry from their hearts, and plead with us to the High God, . . . to take them back into the count's good grace."[16] They knew that a public penance and fine loomed, but banishment of Eva and Philip from the territory was a possibility as well.

For Hans and Anna Schmieg one more disturbing consequence of this disaster was the collapse of their hopes for a secure future. With Eva's scandal the Schmiegs lost the possibility of an alliance with the Preuningers from the Moses Mill. The debacle further jeopardized the plans to pass the Hürden mill to their son, Michel. The Küstners were small peasants with a farm in Nesselbach, and they could not even bestow a reasonable marriage portion on Philip.[17] Rumor also had it that he acted a bit crazy, that he was a village idiot.[18]

To seal this unwanted marriage Hans Schmieg made a fateful promise: to give Philip half of the mill as a marriage portion and bring him into the family. Even in the best of circumstances it would have been an unwise decision: The mill and its attached properties could support a single family, but hardly more. To divide the property—still encumbered by debts—with a man of dubious abilities and no resources was folly. The disaster also collapsed the marriage plans for Michel. With the mill suddenly committed else-where, Michel's fiancée and her family broke off the engagement. Whether old Hans intended to carry through with his promise to Philip, however, we will never know. Yet how else could the dishon-ored couple marry and their families regain the favor of the count?

With this capitulation the Schmiegs and the Küstners had not reckoned that the government would make a public example out of the couple as well. Punishments of young people engaging in premarital sex were fairly common. It may have been the couple's blatant admission of having sex without intending to marry that drew attention to the case.

After two weeks in prison, Eva and Philip were released. Hein-rich Friedrich then magnanimously announced that the couple would not be expelled from the territory. A wedding procession would be arranged in which the young couple walked to church in Bächlingen, but escorted by a government officer. Traditionally parents and family members followed the couple joined by other villagers. After wending their way to the church the couple would declare penance for their sins before the entire congregation. To demonstrate "punishment and public revulsion" against their wan-tonness, the count further decreed that Eva and Philip wear wreaths of straw on their heads. While the authorities of other Franconian territories sometimes shamed a pregnant woman by making her wear a wreath of straw—and not flowers—on her wedding day, no Langenburger had ever been forced to endure such a humiliation before.[19]

The prospect of such a public spectacle dealt as much of a blow to the honor of the parents as it did to Eva and Philip. The Schmiegs and Küstners begged the count not to make them endure the humiliating ordeal:

The government's decree [that the couple] not only wear straw wreaths to church but also be accompanied by the district officer not only strikes at the delinquents but especially at us heartsick parents. . . . It cuts deep into our hearts, yes, right into the bone marrow, because no one ever remembers such a disgrace taking place before in the parish of Bächlingen.[20]

The plan to shame Eva and Philip created concerns among the citizens of Langenburg, who were worried by this innovation in punishing violations of the marriage laws. The count's ministers advised Heinrich Friedrich to drop the order that the couple wear the wreaths and reduce their fines to 35 gulden. But the government kept the plan to make a public example out of the couple and their parents so as to deter others from sin. When the wedding took place, the couple was escorted by a district officer. After Eva and Philip declared penance for their sins, Pastor Wibel mounted the pulpit and preached a stinging sermon on God's commandment against adultery, which further embarrassed the couple and their parents.[21]

Throughout the winter of 1671–72 tensions mounted in the Schmieg household. Philip moved in with the Schmiegs, and their baby, Margaretha, was born on December 4.[22] Hans then refused to turn over half of the mill to his new son-in-law. Both Eva and Anna—Anna in particular—were angry with Hans on this point. Insulted, Philip refused to live any longer with the Schmiegs and moved back to Nesselbach. His departure put pressure on Eva to join him, but she felt conflicted. In turning to Anna Fessler as a friend, Eva confided in a woman who had also experienced humiliation and hardship in starting her own marriage. Only a little older than Eva, Anna had also become pregnant out of wedlock and been disciplined for her sins by the marriage court. Like the Küstners, the parents of Anna Fessler's new husband had also been unable to settle on her and Michel a suitable marriage portion. Like Eva, Anna Fessler had begun her marriage penniless, dependent, and shackled to a man with no property and little income. Still, Anna Fessler counseled Eva to leave her parents' household and join her husband.[23] When Eva's mother learned of this, it only angered her more.

Meanwhile, Hans Schmieg was unable to pay Eva's fine to the government in a timely way. One month before Anna Fessler died, on January 20, Hans turned to Count Heinrich Friedrich and petitioned for relief. The prince acceded to his request, but he also sent Hans a warning to pay the fine in full the next quarter.[24]

―――

IN LIGHT of the family disgrace and the reneged promise on the mill, von Gülchen had a plausible theory: Using the Shrove Tuesday festivities as a cover, Anna, perhaps goaded by Hans, had plotted to murder their son-in-law and maybe others. Responding to his mother-in-law's invitation to come to the mill to celebrate Shrove Tuesday, Philip would have eaten his own death. In fact, the murder of a man who had disgraced his family or failed miserably to support his household adequately might meet with sympathy in the village. On occasion, even the courts sympathized with women who meted out rough justice in such a way.[25] Traditionally women were closely associated with secretive murders by poison.[26] Anna would likely have had the poison on hand, too. Millers were among the few people who could buy arsenic and other poisons to control vermin.[27] A rogue gold digger threatening the household's very survival might be justly dealt with in this way. Neighbors would understand.

If this was true, it is also unlikely that Anna originally intended to poison the Fesslers. Michel Fessler threatened to accuse Anna of killing his cow, and Anna may have known that his wife had helped alienate her daughter. But Michel had not in fact lodged a formal accusation against Anna Schmieg—the court had suspended its sessions in 1671. Besides, given that Anna knew what her neighbors thought of her and also knew the lore about witches poisoning new mothers, her loud protest that she would have been out of her mind to attack Anna Fessler had a ring of truth. That she may have meant to poison her own daughter is also possible. After all, Eva brought the debacle on the family in the first place.

If these were Anna's intentions, the plot's connections with witchcraft appear in an intriguing new light. Consciously or not, Anna had long been playing upon her neighbors' fears of witches. Her reputation as a "hellish woman" went back to at least 1654. Everyone knew that Turk Anna and her minions had slaughtered cattle and children with poison. When Anna discovered the Fesslers grazing their cattle on her field, her curses recalled the terrible work of these known witches. Some women lived with the reputation of being a witch for a long time, knowing how to turn it to their advantage to intimidate neighbors.[28]

Anna may have acted impulsively, adding poison she had on hand to the cakes, in a fit of anger, not considering the consequences. She may have thought that the murder would be blamed on natural causes or that blame would fall on someone else. Anna had not counted on the fact that when Eva took some of the cakes and went looking for Michel Fessler—to have him round up Philip—that Michel would not be at home. At the door instead stood her friend, Anna.

*E*ARLY IN the morning of June 3, von Gülchen renewed his interrogations of Eva. The court assured her that her recent testimony had been welcome and that if she continued in this vein she could gain the mercy of God and the government. From the start Eva indicated that "she wanted to tell everything that she knew and that was true and not be silent about anything on account of her love for her mother." She then renounced the pact she said she had made with her mother to remain silent. That she had "not immediately talked in the beginning," Eva explained, "was her mother's fault because she had expressly forbidden her, that she should say nothing, that she should protect her and consider that she is her mother." Now when asked about her mother and Anna Fessler, Eva replied that "her mother had been little Anna's enemy ever since she had announced that the pasture was poisoned and then when she counseled Eva that she should leave her mother and move with her husband to Nesselbach."[29]

This was no surprise, of course. What Eva then said, however, damned her mother. Asked about taking the cakes to the Fesslers and the events immediately after, she gave the court this account:

> Her mother gave her several cakes to put into her apron and told her to take them to the oxherd Michel's house, and she put a special one in Eva's hand and said, eat it. But she [Eva] excused herself and [said she] did not want to eat it. At that her mother ordered her to put it into the sack and give it to Anna Fessler, which she did.
>
> On Saturday evening, however, she [Eva] came from Nesselbach to her mother and said: "What did you do to the little cake, people are saying everywhere that Fessler died from it. If you did something to it, say so." Her mother then responded, "God in heaven show mercy on me, what have I done? I didn't do anything. All you have to say is that you didn't put the little cake into a sack, but that you instead put it in your apron."
>
> Eva then reminded her mother, "You know exactly how you gave me the little cake, [saying] I should eat it, but I didn't want to. You then shoved the little cake into my sack and ordered me to take it to the *Benzin*. If I'm called to Langenburg and asked about it, I'll say how it all happened." To which the mother said: "God in heaven show mercy. If you say that, and I have to go to Langenburg, I will never come home again." Eva then said: "Do as you like" and she left the house. Then her mother said, "Now I will never see you again."[30]

Eva not only affirmed her own innocence, she also directly accused her mother of poisoning the cake and binding her to silence about it. Answering the court's next questions, Eva rounded out her story. "Her mother had told her that Anna should eat the cake, that the cake was made with milk and fat, that it won't hurt her."[31]

Von Gülchen went over the questions again with Eva. She now embellished the story, highlighting her mother's enmity and calculated malice. Eva stood by her testimony that she did not want to eat the cakes because her mother had cursed them and that they "repelled her heart." Yet she still refused to admit that she consciously knew that the cake was poisoned. In fact, she suggested that she had not even told her husband, because of the horrible truth it might point to. "The reason," she said, "was that she was worried that she had that kind of a mother."[32]

The high point in the session was the confrontation. The court adviser choreographed it so that mother and daughter were forced to face off against each other over and over again. When the first question about Fessler was put to them, Anna denied being Fessler's enemy. But Eva turned on her—the first of many times that day—and said: "All year long you didn't mean well by little Anna, you were always threatening with her." At this rebuke Anna Schmieg "fell on her knees, lifted her hands up pleadingly, and implored several times that she had never been little Anna's enemy."[33]

---

*A*FTER THE shock of this first denunciation and the resulting clash of testimonies, the session settled into a back-and-forth on the details of the Shrove cakes. Eva challenged her mother's testimony at almost every turn, the exchanges becoming verbally violent as the bond between them broke. Sometimes Anna's denials were forceful and direct, a few times she acquiesced with what her daughter said, but at others times Anna provoked the court to punish her if she had done wrong. With these denials she often said that others (God, the court, her daughter, her neighbors) seemed to know more about her and her deeds than she knew herself. Anna's grip on her own identity seemed to be weakening.

When Eva accused her mother of baking a special cake that she separated from the others—a sign that it was poisoned—Anna fiercely denied it. She added that if she did so, then "she wished that God would punish her body and soul on the spot, and that they could cut off her head right here in the chancellery." When Eva testified that Anna first offered her the cake, and only when she had refused did her mother order her to take it to Anna Fessler, Anna Schmieg denied it. But she qualified her answer, saying that she could not take an oath on whether or not she had uttered such words. If she had, "then she wanted her head to be cut off." She then denied having said prophetically to her daughter that if she were arrested and taken to Langenburg she would never come home again. But then she admitted that "she really wanted to leave, but if she did so, she would become everyman's witch, and the world would be witness against her."[34]

When the session resumed in the afternoon, Anna repeated her conditional answers, most of which caught the ear of the magistrates and were carefully noted in the margins of the protocol. When Eva accused her again of having instructed her to lie about the cakes, she "denied it forcefully, she would give up her life if it were true." She broke down, admitting that she and her daughter had fallen out over the matter of Eva's moving to Nesselbach. She admitted that her neighbors saw her as a witch and that she was rumored to have a witch's mark. When her daughter was led away briefly and Anna stood alone before the magistrates, she even suggested that the poisoned cake was intended for Philip. "If her son-in-law had been offered the cake then he would have eaten it, moreover: he would have had enough"—a comment the court took to mean that the cake would have been his last. She vacillated on whether she had made two batches of cakes. In invoking God, the court, her neighbors, and later in the day, the executioner once again, as better witnesses than she, Anna signaled uncertainty about who she actually was. Those vacillations alternated with adamant denials that she had poisoned the cakes.[35]

Late in the afternoon, frustrated with these answers, Court Adviser von Gülchen applied more pressure. He bluntly asked Anna and Eva which of them was guilty in Fessler's death. At first Anna denied any guilt; when pressed further, she wavered and said "she thought that both of them shared the guilt in it." Following up, the magistrates pressed the pair harder, first together, then separately. Though Anna had given the court an opening, in this moment both mother and daughter refused to confirm or clarify it.

———

*A*T THE end of the day Anna Schmieg faced the court alone. The questioning turned to the heart of the matter: Was she a witch? They asked her to see herself through the eyes of others—her daughter, her neighbors, Satan, the executioner. It was as if she were being asked to peer into the mirrors others held up to her, and then view herself through the images they reflected. Von Gülchen pressed Anna twice, about her own statement—sometimes denied, sometimes affirmed—that "if her daughter were a witch then she must have learned it from someone." Maddeningly, however, Anna allowed that she had indeed said those words, but that "she hoped that she [her daughter] was no witch." Von Gülchen pressed her harder. "Right now you say you are not a witch, but if it were to come out that you are one, would you then reconcile yourself to the contents of the rest of the interrogation?" Anna only replied that "her daughter will certainly know, she only has to say so. If Eva can say that she isn't a witch, then she has not learned it from anyone." As for herself, she has a clear conscience.

When it came to the neighbors, Anna admitted that they either saw her as a witch or treated her antagonistically. She thought that the teamster's wife and Michel, the peasant from Forst, considered her a witch. Some people—again the teamster's wife and this time Anna Fessler—had been her enemies ever since they had incited her daughter to move away from the mill. If she had wished to be led out to her execution sooner rather than later, as one of the government lackeys alleged, Anna said, it was because "everywhere, the Hürdeners especially, have hammered in on her . . . they were so hard with her she would rather die than suffer this [treatment] longer."[36]

What seems to have upset her more than anything else was the accusation of her neighbor from Forst, a woman Anna thought she had treated kindly. "What the woman from Forst knows only Jesus Christ can see." In her entire life she never harmed her; and if she [woman from Forst] stated that she has harmed her, then: "O holy angels, that my soul should know such a person living here among us. On my soul what can I say? On my soul, like anyone else—I can say but little." Imploring God, she seemed astonished, the scribe noted, not just by the accusation, but by what the accusation against her meant about who she was. "Oh, you Holy Trinity, O, Lord Jesus Christ! O Lord, may you show us [all] what I am."[37]

Questions about Anna's knowledge of witchcraft—the witch's mark, her familiarity with poisons and poisonous creatures—elicited denials, inconsistent answers, and even bewilderment. When asked about the rumor that she had a witch's mark, first she admitted that she had heard it, "but then wavered and became inconsistent and completely incomprehensible in her speech." About the witch's mark itself she admitted that God himself would have marked her with a sign if she were one. Yet she never testified whether she had seen such a mark on her body, saying at one point: "What do I know? She would like to have herself looked over, you can do with her what you want." In the last questioning of the day, when asked whether she believed Master Endris to have the power to "see" whether someone was a witch or not, she admitted that "she had heard it from other people, but not from Endris himself."[38]

By the end of the day Anna Schmieg had not confessed to poisoning and witchcraft. Her daughter had not simply provided the court with damaging evidence against her mother. In betraying Anna, Eva left her mother completely isolated. While Hans remained loyal, he had been unable to help in any material way. Worn by the relentless questioning and cut off from her family, Anna at times no longer seemed sure of her answers. What if she were a witch after all?

CHAPTER XII

Corpus Delicti

*Langenburg Chancellery and
Altdorf University, Faculty of Law,
May 31– June 19, 1672*

nna Schmieg was not the only one under strain. Even as Court Adviser von Gülchen completed his interrogations of Eva and Anna, the witch scare threatened to explode into a full-blown crisis. By the middle of May the contagion had spread beyond Hürden to new corners of the territory. With the arrest of Barbara Schleicher alarms were raised in Atzenrod and then spread to the suburbs of Langenburg, Lindenbronn, and even beyond the borders in the direction of Gerabronn. Once again the palace at Langenburg became the source of many of these rumors as court servants returned home and passed on the stories they had heard about the investigations. At the end of May a strange new dimension of the scare unfolded when von Gülchen heard reports of a frightened young woman from Unterregenbach—where memories of Turk Anna's reign of terror remained fresh—so overwhelmed by doubt and fear that she denounced herself as a witch.

On May 31, Ursula Baumann, maid to the Langenburg court

rope-maker, turned herself in to the church authorities. Already in the Langenburg trials, girls and young women had stirred up fears of witchcraft, telling tales about older women cavorting with the devil, or worshiping strange idols in barns, or cursing the meadows and keeping animal familiars. Ursula was fourteen or fifteen, the age at which the devil liked to approach young women, seduce them, and bring them into his service.[1]

She told Court Preacher Dietzel and her pastor how a mysterious, dark stranger had slipped into her bedroom at night and beguiled her into witchcraft. Dressed in black, the man looked to her like a peasant, not the lowly and poor sort but a wealthy farmer, the kind of suitor a poor village maid might dream about. But he appeared "completely wild and disorderly." She quickly agreed to slip away with him to a dance, and "climbing on a pitchfork used for shoveling manure, the peasant sitting up front and she behind him, they flew out the door and into the woods." When they arrived at the secret dance, the revelers were forced to swear not to run away. Then, holding Ursula's hand—much as a stern schoolteacher might do—the dark peasant made Ursula write out something in blood. At the end of the evening she bowed to him and kissed his buttocks. The reverie had so frightened her, she had never gone back to him.[2]

When von Gülchen heard about this startling confession—a black parody of village courtship—he decided to treat it not as a crime but as a spiritual and moral problem.[3] Returning Ursula to the care of Dietzel and her pastor on June 14, von Gülchen ordered the girl to swear off Satan, to return to the care of her guardian, and to pray three times every week with her pastor.[4] Still, village nerves were rattled. In July anxious men brought fresh concerns about Ursula to Langenburg. Von Gülchen warned her once again to stay at home, attend church, go to school, and work diligently.[5]

———

*W*HILE FEARS of witchcraft mounted, von Gülchen still faced an even more vexing problem: proving that Anna Schmieg was a witch. One might have thought that by breaking up the conspiracy between mother and daughter he had turned the corner. Having driven the truth into the open, von Gülchen, one might expect, was now in a position to force Anna to confess under torture and thereby bring the ordeal to a conclusion. But when he retired to the chancellery, read over the protocols, and thought about the case, problems began to multiply.

The root of these problems was a classic legal dilemma involving the proof of witchcraft. In relying on the "ordinary procedure," von Gülchen had acted properly, but he now ran headlong into the problem of testing the evidence of an occult crime against the normal standards of proof, something that would be difficult, if not impossible, to do. But if his evidence failed to meet the standard for questioning under torture, he could go no further. Where earlier judges cut through this dilemma by suspending the ordinary rules of proof, now the insistence on following these rules created obstacles to a successful prosecution. Judicial skeptics doubted that witchcraft could be proved at all.[6]

Von Gülchen faced this dilemma squarely and pored over the evidence in the case. He found an ingenious solution. He would set aside the exasperatingly ambiguous evidence concerning witchcraft and press forward against the ordinary crime of poisoning alone. Laying out all the trial protocols before him, he drew up on June 3 a twenty-one-page legal opinion called *Extract of the Protocols of the Most Complete Inquisition into the Cause of Poisoning Involving the Old Miller's Wife of Hürden*.[7] It was dry, densely written in Latin and German, factual, and abstract. For the first time, von Gülchen tested his case against Anna.

As legal reforms took hold after the Thirty Years' War, jurists adopted a specialized form of legal reasoning expressly designed to weed out partisanship and prejudice. Having reached the end of a general inquisition, a judge reviewed the testimony and other evidence and, using a technique called "subsumption," selected certain findings as "legally relevant." Properly executed, this mental exercise forced the judge to classify the evidence "objectively" and to weigh the relative certainty of all of the facts, thereby making it clear what could and could not be proved. Subsumption was meant to make the judge into a blind instrument of the law.[8]

Von Gülchen followed the two guiding principles of this technique. He suppressed his own personal opinions or interpretations. First, he lined up the evidence. No evidence was cited that was not strictly recorded in the protocols of the sessions over which he had presided. He dismissed from consideration the rumors he had heard, such as the jailer's reports about Anna's mutterings in prison. These accounts had not been formally recorded and therefore had no legal bearing on the case as he now described it. Following the second principle, he then painstakingly maneuvered each separate bit of evidence into the legal categories that could justify questioning Anna under torture. In thinking through the evidence this way, von Gülchen was engaged in the legal fiction of imagining himself an eyewitness to events as they unfolded before his eyes. This peculiar way of reasoning about the signs of a crime Carpzov likened to "seeing" events "in the bright light of the day."[9] In his mind's eye von Gülchen was treating the evidence like little windows onto the events in question.

To establish a case against Anna at all, von Gülchen had first to line up his evidence regarding her reputation and the signs of her animosity toward neighbors and family members. He had to prove that Anna did not simply have a "bad reputation," but that she lived in "legal infamy" concerning the specific crimes in question. The complaints of Anna's disgruntled neighbors against her antisocial or immoral behavior were largely beside the point.[10] Instead he showed that her infamy (*mala fama*) related directly to the crimes that had taken place on Shrove Tuesday. The evidence of Anna's *inimicitia odium*, or vicious enmity, toward others came next, including Eva's testimony that her mother "hated" the Fesslers. Von Gülchen referred to Anna's own words—"neighbors were often enemies with each other"—to prove her hatred for the Walthers. He wheeled out Eva's admissions that she had been on bad terms with her mother ever since she wished to leave the mill and join her husband in Nesselbach. Underscoring this especially odious form of enmity—hatred of one's own blood—von Gülchen quoted Eva saying that she had been born an enemy of her mother and that her mother had always wished her ill.[11] The sheer mass of facts was overwhelming and built a strong opening to his case.

Then von Gülchen turned to less traditional evidence: the signs pointing to Anna's guilty feelings and troubled conscience. He went beyond the requirements of the *Carolina* that might reveal the normally hidden condition of a suspect's heart and conscience. If he piled up a sufficient amount of this kind of evidence, he might compensate for its weak legal quality.[12] First, von Gülchen listed the signs pointing to a guilty conscience: rumors that Anna and Eva were "anxious;" Anna's troubling farewell to her husband; her despair; the suicide attempt; her hesitation when asked about baptism; and her admission that "she had become everyone's witch" and that "the world had become too narrow for her." Her shocking "preoccupations" pointed to guilt as well, including her saying that "it doesn't matter to her if she has to be burned or cut up, that others will follow, too." The rumors that "there are two witches in Hürden"—which she admitted could only refer to her and her daughter—seemed tantamount to a confession. Even her despairing admission to the guards that she preferred to die rather than to suffer any longer, that she knew she was an object of scorn and derision, was taken as evidence of a guilty conscience.[13]

He then looked for signs of a confession, the "queen of evidence."[14] But his evidence was ambiguous at best and relied on the assumption that hardened witches lied and dissembled. Anna's words could not be taken at face value. Instead he treated them as pointers to a troubled conscience struggling to free itself from the grip of Satan and reveal truths that only the conscience might know. Here he cited every scrap of testimony that might indicate that Anna had killed Fessler. Straying from the rules—his prejudice intruded into the document at this point—von Gülchen even listed the secondhand reports that Anna had "muttered under her breath" and cursed her daughter.[15] But these statements amounted at best to what jurists considered to be "remote and apparent evidence," far short of the standard necessary to justify questioning under torture.

Von Gülchen then came to the heart of the matter: the evidence of murder (*corpus delicti*) and poisoning (*indicia intoxicarum*). He had no finding of fact that Fessler had indeed been murdered. Dr. Thym's inspection of the body had proved inconclusive. So he copied down the testimony of those who had witnessed Fessler's illness and death, noting their belief that she had been poisoned by eating Anna's cake. He bolstered this with statements from Anna herself that seemed to point to murder, such as her admission that she did not know whether Fessler had died from eating the cake and her refusal to take an oath about whether the cake in fact harmed her. But these statements could not stand in for a *corpus delicti*. To strengthen his evidence, von Gülchen launched into a detailed excursus about his suspect and how Anna's obstinate refusals to admit to the more credible accounts of her daughter pointed indirectly to murder. To make a suspicious death into a murder von Gülchen had to show that Anna's cake had poisoned Fessler and that Anna had actually poisoned her cakes (*indicia intoxicarum*). But his evidence was once again weak and indirect. The best he could do was point to the refusal of the Walthers' dog to eat even a scrap of Anna's cake, an odd incorporation of popular belief into his deduction of poisoning. In a similar fashion he reasoned that Anna's secretive way of baking the cakes—out of view of her daughter and without any help from her son or husband—suggested that she had laced them with poison.[16] Pointing to Eva's testimony, he then went through ten additional suspicious facts that strongly suggested poisoning. But no one had seen Anna poison her cakes. Besides, no poison had been found at the mill.

After this meticulous review, looking still more deeply into some of Eva's statements, von Gülchen concluded that Anna had plotted to murder her own daughter and son-in-law, and others as well. He speculated about what might have happened had Eva eaten one of the cakes and Philip returned to Hürden that night to celebrate Shrove Tuesday with the Schmiegs. Then he linked this speculation to troubling reports from neighbors about the incredible quantities of fat that seemed to materialize in Anna's kitchen and the mysterious ability of her old decrepit cow to produce four or five times more milk and butter than the younger and healthier cows of her neighbors.[17]

His case for witchcraft was weak, however. Even though he called the affair "a case of poisoning," von Gülchen had actually treated the evidence as if he were investigating the composite crime of poisoning and witchcraft. But he had come across very little of the evidence the law required to prove witchcraft. To proceed with a charge of witchcraft or sorcery, he would have to produce one of four specific types of testimony: that Anna had taught witchcraft; proof that she threatened someone with sorcery or witchcraft; signs that she associated with known witches or sorcerers; or findings that she possessed the paraphernalia of sorcery, such as manuals of charms or collections of poisonous toads and powders.[18] He had no such evidence. Relating to the fourth type of evidence, von Gülchen did list the reports of Anna invoking the devil's name, cursing and muttering charms over her cakes. But each of these "facts" was ambiguous. What peasant did not curse or occasionally invoke the devil's name? As if to acknowledge the weakness of this evidence, von Gülchen did not even attempt to subsume the data under a separate category of "sorcery and witchcraft." Instead he shuffled it together with the other testimonies.[19]

The evidence of poisoning also seemed to fall far short of what he needed to press the case against Anna. In fact, he had no proof of a crime at all! A general inquisition had first and foremost to establish the fact that a crime or crimes had taken place, but von Gülchen had been unable even to establish the *corpus delicti*, or the physical confirmation of a crime. His thin paragraph of testimony attesting to the fact that Fessler had died after eating Anna's cake rested on no material proof. The autopsy was inconclusive. Even if the report had clearly ruled the death a poisoning, the evidence suggested at least two different types of poisonings.

But the quandary abut the *corpus delicti* made von Gülchen's case against Anna even more uncertain than this. A magistrate did not have the authority to establish the *corpus delicti* on his own. When medical experts came to uncertain conclusions or disagreed with each other about a cause of death, a magistrate was obliged to seek the advice of additional experts.[20] Only when a new review board agreed and ruled conclusively on the cause of death would von Gülchen have his *corpus delicti*.

Recognizing that he needed both legal and medical advice, von Gülchen first considered consulting the University of Strasbourg, which had so deeply shaped his legal and religious thinking. Then he changed his mind.[21] Strasbourg had no faculty of medicine. So he bundled up the protocols of the interrogations, Dr. Thym's autopsy report, and his own extract of the protocols, and handed them over to a courier with orders to ride to Nuremberg and its university at Altdorf.

ALTDORF'S FORTUNES had improved considerably since von Gülchen's student days at the university in the 1630s. Despite the decline of its political influence, Nuremberg had assumed new cultural influence at the end of the Thirty Years' War in part through the flowering of the intellectual life of its university at Altdorf. Despite its seeming isolation—Altdorf lay twenty kilometers from Nuremberg—this little Protestant university had become a hub of intellectual activity in the region, stimulating new interest in the natural sciences, medicine, technology, literature, and the practical arts.[22] Burghers from Nuremberg frequented the disputations in law and theology and attended lectures at the university's new public anatomical theater—one of the first in the Holy Roman Empire. Governments turned to Altdorf's jurists, physicians, and theologians for their advice concerning the practical problems of rebuilding states and societies shaken by the war.[23] The single, large building of the university—built around a courtyard—created an intimate setting for this academic work. Professors and students alike lived in the village. This close-knit academic community was an ideal setting for the detached, scholarly reflection that Anna Schmieg's case now required.

The Schmieg case first came to the attention of Altdorf's three professors of law: Ernst Cregel, Johann Christoph Wagenseil, and Johann Wolfgang Textor, who brought to the law both pragmatism and experience that grew out of their considerable service as consultants to princes, territorial governments, and cities across Europe.[24] Having risen to the highest offices of the law faculty and university by this time, Ernst Cregel (1628–74) brought a lifetime of expertise in public, municipal, feudal, and church law to the cases that came to his attention.[25] His younger colleague, Johann

A . Das Schloß .
B . Der Hortus Medicorum .
C . Das Collegium .
D . Das Rathaus .

E . Die Kirche .
F . Das Pfarrhaus .
G . Die Stattschul .
H . Der Herrn Diaconorum wohnungen .

ALTDORF. *Altdorf University (top center) dominated the little town of Altdorf. Professors and students lived only a few minutes' walk from the Collegium, the central university building, and formed a tight-knit academic community.*

Wagenseil (1633–1705), had a European-wide reputation. Having traveled across Germany, Spain, Holland, Italy, and France, he had earned a French doctorate of laws in 1665 in Orléans and had taken up his post at Altdorf in 1668. Drawing on this wide experience, Wagenseil contributed to the new politico-historical approaches to the laws and institutions of the Holy Roman Empire popular since the end of the Thirty Years' War.[26] He had firsthand experience of the political and legal challenges of restoring order to a little state like Langenburg. To him legal problems were to be understood as firmly rooted in the current circumstances of Germany's laws and political institutions. An insistence on order and discipline revealed itself in a stern "Spanish bearing" and the habit of having his wife follow him by half a step.[27]

Altdorf's third professor of law, Johann Wolfgang Textor (1638–1701), was fast earning a reputation as one of the most powerful and original legal minds of the day. He also brought to the perplexing case from Langenburg a native's knowledge of the Hohenlohe and its princes, laws, governments, and people. Born in Neuenstein—the old castle town and seat of Hohenlohe family power—Textor had grown up in a family of jurists known for their service to the counts and their governments. For thirty years his father had served as chancellery director in Neuenstein. Schooled in the nearby town of Öhringen, Textor went on to study law at Jena and Strasbourg before earning his doctorate in law at Strasbourg in 1663.[28] Between 1661 and 1666 he served as chancellery director for the joint family government of the Neuenstein line of the family. From this position he had been involved in the long and bitter lawsuit against Langenburg and Count Heinrich Friedrich's claims against the family lands at Weikersheim. Quite likely he was personally acquainted with Heinrich Friedrich and von Gülchen. Swearing never to reveal the princely family's secrets, he left Neuenstein for Altdorf in 1666, but he remained an adviser to the princes of Hohenlohe-Neuenstein.[29]

At Altdorf he had distinguished himself quickly for his advocacy of public law and his razor-sharp legal mind. In 1667 he had acquired a reputation as an advocate of the concept of "reason of state" through his widely read treatise on public law in the German states.[30] To his experience and interest in public law, he also brought a formidable knowledge of Roman law. Since 1670 he had been Professor of the Pandects, the professor responsible for teaching the classical writings of Roman jurists. "So good was his memory," his biographer wrote, "that Textor knew the entire *Corpus Juris Civilis* [the books of Roman civil law] by heart." Textor saw civil society in entirely different terms than von Gülchen. An iconoclast, he rankled orthodox Lutherans around him by arguing against religious zealotry in any form, going so far as to insist that

D. JO.   WOLFGANGVS TEXTOR. JCT
Neuensteinio – Hohenloicus

JOHANN WOLFGANG TEXTOR. *Dr. Johann Wolfgang Textor
the Elder (1638–1701), legal adviser to the counts of
Hohenlohe-Neuenstein, professor of institutes and Roman
law at Altdorf University.*

public order could not rest on dogmatic religion but on reason of
state alone. So sharply did he attack opponents and cut to the heart
of complex legal issues that his colleagues nicknamed him the
Ictum ingeniosum, the "Clever Sting."[31]

WHEN THE problem of evidence in the Schmieg affair came to
his attention, the young Textor was so intrigued that he quickly

organized a formal disputation based on it. The only university disputation at Altdorf that this distinguished jurist of public law
would hold on criminal law, it was published later that summer as
A Legal Disputation on the Corpus Delicti in Murder.[32] A variety of
reasons likely drew Textor to the case: his old ties to his native land
and the legal and political issues of the Hohenlohe princes he still
served; his interest in rethinking the law and public order along
secular lines; his flair for seizing upon controversial issues; and his
passion for debate.

Most of all, Textor saw the affair as an opportunity to think
through the problems involving evidence with implications far
beyond Anna Schmieg and the witch trials at Langenburg.[33] On
June 19 the disputation took place in the Welser Auditorium, also
called the Theological Hall. Textor presided at the center podium.
Below him stood the respondent, his student, Mauritius Hieronymus de Venne. Surrounding them were the deacon and the rector
of the Law Faculty, Cregel, Wagenseil, and perhaps other jurists

AN ALTDORF DISPUTATION. *Altdorf disputations were lively and well-attended affairs.*
Here a student makes his argument before the professors, assembled on the dais before him,
while fellow students and members of the public look on.

from the Nuremberg area. Rounding out the audience were the students, required by university statute to attend, and members of the public.[34] The disputation was in Latin.[35]

The debate opened by laying out the question at hand: How was a magistrate to establish the evidence of a crime in cases of murder? At the back of his mind Textor had the puzzle of the missing *corpus delicti* in the Schmieg case to consider, but in the debate he broadened the subject to consider the wider issue of evidence in murder cases in general, especially murders that took place in secret and left scant traces behind. First, the key concept had to be defined. The *corpus delicti* had to be understood in two ways, he argued. Naturally the term referred to the physical evidence itself—in this case, a victim's body or cadaver. The evidence of murder also had to be grasped as the product of a magistrate's formal reasoning about the circumstances surrounding the crime. Textor made it clear that two types of crime presented few problems in establishing a *corpus delicti*: conventional murders or arson that left solid material evidence; and crimes like adultery, sodomy, or incest, which left residual traces behind. But a third class of crimes—secret or occult crimes like poisoning and witchcraft—left no material traces at all, posing grave challenges to a judge investigating an alleged wrongdoing because he had to consider evidence of an indirect, uneven, and confusing quality.[36] To resolve this dilemma—which was also von Gülchen's dilemma—Textor argued that a judge had to think beyond the evidence and make *legal presumptions* about what had happened and who was likely to be guilty.[37]

Textor and his student then broke the problem down into four parts. In the first part he asked the conventional question—what constitutes the *corpus delicti* in murder?—but he then attacked it in a startlingly original way. Naturally, Textor argued, the first requirement for establishing the *corpus delicti* is a body. Normally one could tell from the cuts and wounds on a corpse that someone had been murdered. The second requirement was the malicious intent of a killer to murder someone. Here, Textor saw a huge problem: poisonings rarely left physical signs on a victim's body. Where was the *corpus delicti* when findings of violence were impossible to see?[38]

The significance of Textor's line of reasoning can be grasped when one considers the problems of secret or occult crimes like the ones ascribed to Anna Schmieg. The traditional way of establishing evidence worked well when people witnessed a stabbing in a tavern or saw an assailant deliver fatal blows in a brawl. In these cases a murder weapon could be established by witnesses who saw the assault. Poisonings and witchcraft left no such weapons behind, and no witnesses who saw the poison poured or the sorcery performed. The cadaver itself rarely showed outward signs of violence. Lacking confirmation, the courts either dropped the prosecution or suspended ordinary legal procedures and, despite not having physical proof, moved right to convicting, sentencing, and punishing the accused murderer.[39]

Given his strong conviction that the ordinary procedures of the law served as a bastion of order, Textor found both of these solutions distasteful. However, he thought, if a judge could determine that the wounds and the other circumstances of the crime could be *presumed* to point to a killer's malice or his intention to kill someone, then he could treat these crimes using ordinary rules of evidence and judicial procedure. He need not argue that judges suspend the rules of evidence and procedure and treat sorcery, witchcraft, and poisoning as exceptional crimes. By looking at the body and its wounds and all the other outward circumstances of the crime, a judge could presume a murderer's intent to kill. "We say that the *corpus delicti* in murder is nothing more than the malicious intent to kill someone extracted from the wounds left behind on the body or other legitimate signs that appear *by presumption*."[40] Textor thus provided judges with a new legal concept that justified treating occult crimes through normal judicial procedures.

In other words, Textor created a novel tool that established a *corpus delicti* in difficult-to-prove crimes: "presumptive malice." He collapsed the invisible and immaterial aspects of the crime—the killer's intention and the occult workings of poison or a curse—into the material evidence of the body. A judge could read the evidence of an occult crime in an entirely material way.

Textor then turned to the second aspect of the problem: establishing the lethality of the wounds by consulting medical experts in cases of suspicious deaths. Only then, Textor insisted, could a judge be confident that a murder had actually taken place.[41]

Investigators typically found a number of wounds on a victim's body, some of them inconsequential, and others lethal. In cases of poisoning, however, an inspection often turned up no obvious injuries or wounds. The solution, Textor argued, was for medical experts to establish the lethality of wounds, though he admitted that relying on the opinions of physicians and surgeons opened the legal process to potential difficulties.[42] The experts might fail to arrive at a conclusion. (Textor likely had the autopsy report from the Schmieg case in mind.) Witnesses might question the experts' credentials. Physicians might disagree with one another over the cause of death and then refuse to take an oath on their findings. None of these issues, Textor argued, need pose insuperable problems to a careful judge.[43]

Then he laid out the four basic steps for physicians or surgeons to give a judgment on the lethality of particular wounds. First, the experts should carry out an autopsy. Next, they were to inspect the wounds—both inside and outside the body—diligently, systematically, and accurately. Then the experts were to determine the lethality of the wounds. Finally, for their findings to be recognized, the experts then had to make a formal declaration of their conclusions before a court.[44] In this way Textor insisted on integrating the arguments of medicine and its allied sciences with the law when establishing the fact of a crime.[45]

Textor finished by taking up two other issues. In the third part of the disputation he discussed how a defendant might contest the evidence of murder. A defendant might argue that she had acted out of self-defense, for example, or she might present an eyewitness who contradicted the arguments for murder. Moreover, a closer inspection of the wounds on the victim's body might show that they were not lethal after all or that they proved self-defense. Of course, a suspect with a notorious reputation might have a difficult time proving that she did not harbor any intention to murder someone. Throughout this discussion Textor insisted repeatedly that a magistrate follow the rules of evidence alone. If a judge found the evidence insufficient at any stage of the trial, he was obligated to purge the defendant of the charges and set her free.[46]

Finally, Textor reviewed the evidence necessary for a judge to proceed to questioning a suspect under torture. General suspicions provided no legal grounds for taking this step. Instead, he argued, the law required "urgent and grave signs" that a crime had actually taken place, such as wounds on a body or witnesses who saw the fight or who heard the exchange of fighting words. In cases of poisoning, the finding of poison and the evidence of enmity between the suspect and the victim could justify torture.[47] For this step Textor came down on the side of caution and the Romano-canonical legal tradition and its standards of evidence. One had to have two eyewitnesses—not just one—before proceeding to torture.[48] If the evidence proved inadequate, then a court must purge the charges.

———

*T*EXTOR RARELY mentioned witchcraft. Poisoning interested him much more. And while contemporaries often linked poisoning and witchcraft, Textor tended not to run the two together as a composite crime. When he did mention witchcraft, he simply considered it as one of a class of crimes known to produce evidence that was difficult to prove. In this regard Textor's disputation is noteworthy for not treating poisoning and witchcraft as exceptional crimes. He treated the evidence for these crimes like the evidence for any other. Textor's arguments about *corpus delicti* quietly turned attention away from the exceptional quality of *any* evidence, and insisted on subjecting it to more material and ordinary concepts of the law. Of greater significance in the long run, however, was his insistence on applying the legal concept of "the lethality of wounds," opening up the evidence in occult crimes to systematic examination through academic medicine. One did not have to contest witchcraft to undermine it. By developing more useful, convincing, and utilitarian concepts, one could simply ignore it.

In the short term his ingenious but novel concept of "presumptive malice" seems to have found no adherents. His argument may have appeared odd because it implied collapsing two procedural steps normally kept apart from each other at the time: the ruling on the fact of a crime at the end of a General Inquisition and the discovery of a specific murderer's intention to kill during the Special Inquisition that followed it.[49]

But the immediate issue was not an abstract issue of jurisprudence. Did von Gülchen have sufficient evidence against Anna Schmieg? Textor was arguing that he did. Using "presumptive malice," von Gülchen might rule that he had a *corpus delicti*. But there was a condition: Making that ruling required medical experts finding that poison had actually killed Anna Fessler.

CHAPTER XIII

A Question of Poison

Altdorf University, the Medical School, June 4–July 2, 1672

he pivotal questions in the Schmieg affair were now laid at the door of Altdorf's faculty of medicine. The reluctance of Dr. Andreas Thym and Barber-Surgeon Unfug to rule on Anna Fessler's death meant that Langenburg now depended on a more learned appellate body of physicians to resolve the controversy and establish what had killed Anna Fessler. Yet seeking another medical ruling brought new risks: physicians not only held differing views about poisoning and bewitchment, but tended to favor naturalistic explanations of illness and disease.

Like jurists, physicians were truth-seekers. Yet they often had to search through incomplete and indirect evidence to discover the truth. While they prized visual evidence, they also were forced to rely on the oral testimonies of others. They strained to establish absolute certainty but often had to weigh evidence that led only to gradations of certainty. Baldus long ago pointed to the common nature of their epistemological activities: "The judge is like the physician: the physician knows the disease. . . . first in an oblique and inappropriate way through the urine. . . . This is what the judge does when he sees by speculating and ponders to know the truth through plausible and similar things. Second, the physician sees by touching the pulse, and the judge when he touches the truth through open testimonies."[1] This affinity between the two types of professionals involved more than similarity in general philosophical outlook. Through the development of forensic medicine physicians were required to reason through evidence in the same way that jurists made expert medical testimony acceptable to a court of law.

Yet legal and medical professionals sometimes found themselves at odds. They might vie with one another in offering different explanations of a suspicious death. They might balk at taking oaths about medical testimony considered merely to be their best knowledge. Textor argued that if judges received contentious, divided, or equivocal medical testimony, they could rein in the physicians by forcing their testimony to conform to the standards of the law. Jurists were careful to retain the ultimate power. When he sent for the advice of Altdorf's physicians, von Gülchen therefore ran the risk of injecting controversy or an unfavorable ruling into his proceedings on the Schmieg affair.

Ever since jurists had pressed for a stricter concept of the "lethality of wounds," the courts had become dependent on the opinions of medical specialists. And when legal reformers went further and urged courts to seek out the opinions of university-educated physicians, and not just local surgeons, they made the law a dynamic instrument that relied on new medical and scientific developments in surgery, anatomy, physiology, and toxicology. Meeting these legal demands had helped propel German universities and their faculties of medicine to the forefront in the developing field of forensic medicine in Europe.

━━

THE MEDICAL school at Altdorf may not have been as highly regarded as those at Jena, Leiden, or Leipzig, but its faculty was widely considered an innovative center of the empirical sciences and medicine. Home to the German Academy of Naturalists, the city was a center of activity for research on plants, animals, and insects. Closely connected to the city's learned societies, skilled artisans were known for making finely crafted instruments and measuring devices to aid scientific research.[2] The region's naturalists, scientists, and physicians in turn inspired a flowering culture of writers, poets, and painters, many of whom were known for their vivid depictions of plants and insects.[3] The large and active community of physicians in Nuremberg maintained intimate ties to Altdorf and the university's teaching and research programs in medicine. Moritz Hofmann, the leading physician at Altdorf at this time and a key figure in the Schmieg affair, had started out as a municipal physician in the city and drew on his close ties to Nuremberg's physicians in organizing them into their own learned society.[4]

Reflecting a scientific culture that prized firsthand observation, the medical faculty distinguished itself as a pioneer in developing new observational and empirical approaches to medicine and sci-

ANATOMICAL THEATER AT ALTDORF. *At Altdorf's Anatomical Theater professors of medicine demonstrated their skill while instructing students and Nuremberg burghers in the wonders of human anatomy.*

ence. When the university established its first medical garden in 1626, professors and students began to study plants and their medicinal properties firsthand; botany made its way into the medical curriculum. In 1650 the university built a public anatomical theater, fostering research in the growing field of anatomy and surgery. As interest in anatomy grew, Altdorf's physicians held open lectures and dissections at the theater, teaching Nuremberg's burghers about the wonders of the human body.[5] In 1657 the university opened its own observatory, testimony to the growing interest in astronomy. Later, in 1682, ten short years after the Schmieg affair, the university built one of the first university chemical laboratories in the empire.[6]

At the center of these innovations was Moritz Hofmann, who had set the intellectual tone in the medical faculty since the end of the Thirty Years' War. Driven from his home in northern Germany during the war, Hofmann (b. 1622) had arrived in Nuremberg in 1638 and studied under his uncle, Georg Nösler, a professor of medicine at Altdorf. Two other professors, Kaspar Hofmann and Ludwig Jungermann, tutored him as well. But Moritz Hofmann refused to follow in his mentors' footsteps. Eschewing the philosophical approaches to medicine popular at the time, he left for Italy in 1641, enrolling at the University of Padua to study anatomy and botany.[7] At the time, one of Padua's best-known graduates, William Harvey, was still stirring controversy with his theory about the circulation of the blood.[8]

According to Hofmann's training, knowledge of the human body gained through visual observation was superior to the untested knowledge of books. His enthusiasm for observation spilled over into all of his work. He assembled, described, and classified a collection of more than 2,000 specimens of plants. He claimed to have discovered through his own dissections the tiny ducts of the pancreas, first in a chicken and then in a human body.[9]

When Hofmann returned to Nuremberg in 1644, earning his doctorate in 1645, he became a municipal physician. As the old guard passed away, he moved over to Altdorf, assuming the key professorships in medicine, first becoming professor of anatomy and surgery, and then assuming Kaspar Hofmann's old chair in medi-

MAURICIUS HOFFMANN Fürstenwaldens. Marchicus
Med. Doct. in universitate Altdorffinâ Anatom. Chirurg.
ac Botan. Prof. Publ. Hortiq; Medici Præfectus.
et Reipubl. Norimbergensis Practicus.
Ætat. XLIII.

MORITZ HOFMANN. *Dr. Moritz Hofmann, doctor of
medicine at Altdorf University, professor of anatomy,
surgery, and botany, and municipal physician of the City
of Nuremberg.*

cine in 1649. When Jungermann died, he took over the position in
botany as well and became director of the university medical garden.[10] The building of Altdorf's anatomical theater was Hofmann's
project, and he presided over the public dissections. Like his contemporary at the University of Jena, Werner Rolfinck, Hofmann took
on the task of reforming the curriculum to include surgery and
anatomy. Widely sought out by princes, Hofmann served an illustrious clientele that included the Elector of Brandenburg, the mar-
graves of Culmbach and Ansbach, and the Duke of Württemberg.[11]

Despite his embrace of firsthand observation, Hofmann's ideas about the human body still rested on views of physiology that could readily accommodate invisible, spiritual, or supernatural influences on the body. Like Harvey, Hofmann may have appeared to belong to a progressive camp of physicians when he championed the idea of the circulation of the blood—he proved the theory for himself through dissection—but he still held to the old Aristotelian concept that blood contained the vital energy or "animal spirits" that carried life throughout the body.[12] These invisible "animal spirits" had their origins in the heart, which was considered the almost mystical seat of life in the body.

Hofmann's younger colleague, Jacob Pancratius Bruno (1629–1709), tended to approach medicine from the older vantage point of Galenic medical philosophy. Like Hofmann, Bruno had learned medicine in Altdorf at the feet of a family patriarch. His father, Jacob, had been professor of philosophy at Altdorf. Although the young Bruno left to study medicine at Jena, he had returned to Altdorf to participate in disputations in 1649 and 1652 under Hofmann's supervision.[13] He had then assumed a chair in medicine at Altdorf in 1662.

While Bruno did not reject the empiricism of his teacher and senior colleague, his first instincts were to analyze medical problems through Galenic and Aristotelian categories. Bruno vigorously defended Galen, whom he called "the Prince of Doctors." Galenists saw the body's health depending on humoral pathology, a delicate balance of "complexions"—qualities like hot and cold, wet and dry—and "humors," or fluids, like blood, phlegm, bile, and black bile. Understanding the complexions and humors of the organs and the different parts of the body helped a Galenic physician to diagnose illness and disease and prescribe a course of healing.[14] Not surprisingly, bodily fluids fascinated Bruno. As the humor that transported the vital animal spirits throughout the body, blood was the likely source of any problem when the life energy or spirit ebbed away.[15] He was not adverse to proceeding by observation, however.[16]

Between them, Bruno and Hofmann drew on the medical epistemologies of the empirical branches of medicine—surgery, anatomy, botany—as well as the still widely respected concepts of Galenic medical philosophy. Eclecticism and syncretism were, after all, the hallmarks of medical thought and practice in the middle of the seventeenth century.[17] The Altdorf library register from the 1650s and 1660s shows Hofmann and Bruno reading extensively in almost every field of medicine.[18]

In any event, Hofmann and Bruno found common ground in the Schmieg case precisely at the point where anatomical empiricism always came up short: connecting firsthand observation with understanding the causes of illness and disease.[19] On the art of medical diagnosis, Hofmann and Bruno saw eye-to-eye. When diagnosing the course of a fatal illness, both of them turned for guidance to Galen, his Renaissance commentators, and their own extensive experience.

DRAWING ON their expertise and relying on the reports and legal opinions from Langenburg, Bruno and Hofmann came to an unambiguous conclusion about the Schmieg incident:

> From our basic and reasonable experience we cannot conclude or adjudicate otherwise than that the Anna Fessler in question must have consumed poison, and very probably Arsenic, by means of the little cake which she ate (because no other suspicious food is mentioned in the records). In this way she lost her life in the most wretched way.[20]

While one might not be surprised at the finding of poisoning, their confident assertion that they knew the specific poison seems perplexing. In his autopsy report Thym mentioned finding part of the cake in Fessler's stomach, but he made no allusions to arsenic or any yellow substance that might have resembled it. Von Gülchen had not mentioned finding evidence of poison or the paraphernalia of poisoning and witchcraft at the mill. How then did these professors conclude that Fessler had died of acute arsenic poisoning?

Hofmann and Bruno supported their finding by laying out the empirical evidence, beginning with the initial reports of Barber-Surgeon Unfug and the postmortem observations of Dr. Thym. They first noted the sudden and unexpected onset of Fessler's illness, describing how she had experienced "unexpected anxiety welling up from around the diaphragm in the belly." Then they related how other telling symptoms of poisoning rapidly set in, including Fessler's "restlessness, continuous vomiting, struggling, and painful torments." These signs testified to a "clamoring" of "the most vehement and lethal kind." Then they went to the postmortem observations that Thym and the barber-surgeon made about the appearance of the corpse, paying particular attention to the "foam around her mouth" and "the swelling from the crown of her heart to the legs." Finally they noted the symptoms of poisoning inside the cavity of her chest: "the ruptures in the bowels" and the suspicious-looking "dark colored and spotted muscle striations on her left side." As to the condition of the heart, the "left sphere of the ventricle" had been "completely corrupted." The only counterindication was a "spleen excessively swollen from jaundice."[21]

Interpreting the signs of poison was an exceptionally difficult task. Even the best anatomists, like Hofmann, knew not to confuse the most vivid descriptions of the symptoms of an illness with a proper diagnosis. This was why Hofmann and Bruno then turned to the evidence that clinched the case for poisoning: the condition of Anna Fessler's blood. They noted that her physical symptoms displayed "a peculiar corrupting and congealing of the blood and a powerful dispersal of the life spirits." In his autopsy report Dr. Thym had confined his observations about the condition of the blood and heart to a very small section. But Hofmann and Bruno took Thym's few marginal observations and made them the focus of their report. The pooling up and congealing of the blood around the heart, they argued, pointed clearly to poisoning.[22]

In identifying the condition of Fessler's blood as the key evidence, these two physicians were guided by Galenic physiology and humoral pathology. The old argument among physicians about which of the organs ruled the body—the heart, as Aristotelians argued, or the heart in combination with the liver and brain, as the strict Galenists argued—was resolved here in favor of the heart. Poison had attacked Fessler's life spirits right at their source.

But Hofmann and Bruno could not make their ruling without also confronting and refuting the theory that might undermine their finding. Dr. Thym had discussed at length the possibility that Fessler's body had generated the poison on its own and that over time a noxious accumulation of toxins had finally overwhelmed her heart. "In no way," Hofmann and Bruno argued, "could such a fatal course of events come about from an 'internally generated poison.'" To back up their argument they turned to the reports from Fessler's husband, mother, and sister concerning the young mother's recent state of health. Finding their accounts convincing, Hofmann and Bruno determined that "the deceased had been fresh and healthy at the time that she was single and then later when she was married and she must therefore have been lively and brisk from having sufficiently pure blood." The only evidence that gave them pause was the accounts that Fessler had not completed her lying-in and had experienced "some *cachexia* or wasting away in which she had suffered for several days from jaundice and swollen legs." But these symptoms had already subsided before she ate the cake, they argued, "because she did not complain about it any longer, but instead ate and drank enough and without a doubt could have started to keep house once again."[23]

But the counter theory could still not be dismissed so easily. Thym had found evidence of jaundice in the spleen after all. Even if her swellings and the jaundice had subsided, they wondered, might she not have suffered from a natural predisposition to *cachexia*, wasting away? Many pregnant women and new mothers were afflicted with this debilitating syndrome. But they finally set this theory aside on the grounds that Fessler was too young and energetic at the time of her death:

Even assuming that she had a predisposition towards wasting away, what leads away from this diagnosis is that the predisposition to consumption creates long and slow changes and such a quick death and the changes that set in afterwards could not have taken place without some violent and life-threatening external cause. For a young woman of 27 years like the deceased it can in no way be presumed that such corruption of the blood could go on internally in a hidden way.[24]

While they could not rule out the possibility that some naturally occurring toxins had been present in Fessler's body, they thought her too young and healthy for this silent and slow illness to have killed her.

—

*B*UT WHY *arsenic?* Nowhere did Hofmann and Bruno offer evidence for the presence of arsenic in Fessler. Dr. Thym had briefly mentioned finding a portion of undigested cake in Fessler's stomach, but Hofmann and Bruno did not cite this fact as evidence for their claim. Von Gülchen had no evidence of arsenic or any other poisons in Anna Schmieg's kitchen. On this point Hofmann and Bruno were not following the evidence at all but actually asserting their own erudition. In forensic medicine erudition trumped evidence—even, paradoxically, empirical evidence.[25]

What enabled Hofmann and Bruno to make sense of the Schmieg affair was a well known procedure for identifying poisoning and arsenic in one of the standard manuals of forensic medicine. In following this procedure—described in the best-known manual of forensic medicine at the time, Paolo Zacchia's *Quaestiones Medico-Legales* (1630)—the Altdorfers selected only certain facts from the reports and then, maneuvering them into the appropriate categories, they diagnosed Fessler's illness as poisoning.[26] They first established a chronology of poor Fessler's demise: her original state of good health, the sudden onset of illness after eating the cake, the turning point, and then the appearance of her body after her death. They then matched Fessler's symptoms with the textbook descriptions and their meanings from the manual. Hofmann and Bruno were following the standard practice of the day.

Their reasoning about poison and arsenic also followed a template laid down by authorities on the subject. Knowing how important it was to work through the erudite and esoteric debate about poisons and their origins, they began with the source of the toxin. When they called attention to certain symptoms, they could have copied them almost verbatim from Zacchia's list of the symptoms of acute poisoning: anxiety, restlessness, swelling, vomiting, violent tremors, and extreme pain.[27] In highlighting certain parts of Fessler's body, Hofmann and Bruno showed that they knew the likely places where erudite forensic experts knew to look for signs of poisoning. Like Zacchia, Hofmann and Bruno took the view that poison tended to attack only particular parts of the body: the blood and the heart.[28] Naturally they gravitated to the postmortem descriptions of the corrupted blood around Fessler's heart.[29] In reasoning through the evidence like Zacchia, Hofmann and Bruno lent authority and weight to their opinion. In doing so, they also translated the confusing facts about Fessler's death into a textbook case of poisoning.

The same reasoning was at work when the Altdorfers sided with Langenburg in arguing that Fessler had ingested a cake with arsenic. Widely known in ancient and medieval medicine, arsenic was the most feared poison of the sixteenth and seventeenth centuries.[30] Zacchia mentioned arsenic in his work more than any other type of poison. When Hofmann and Bruno identified arsenic as the toxic agent, they were simply following the conventional wisdom and deduced its presence from the medical literature. But like other authorities, they did not understand how arsenic worked on the human body. Instead, Hofmann and Bruno implied that the arsenic worked in the same naturalistic way described by Zacchia.[31] Given that arsenic could explain the mysterious onset of Fessler's illness, they did not even have to face directly the evidence of sorcery or witchcraft.[32] Moreover, they may have thought that arsenic or *Mauspulver* (mouse powder) would have been readily available to a miller's wife, since millers were legally authorized to use arsenic to keep the rats under control.

ON JULY 2 the Altdorf medical faculty drew up its report. Concise and to the point, it bore no comparison to a university disputation like Textor's. Here the professors joined ranks and, addressing

OPINION OF THE MEDICAL FACULTY AT ALTDORF. *Bearing the seal of the University of Altdorf, and the signature of the dean, senior physician, and doctors of the Medical Faculty, the Altdorf Faculty of Medicine announces its ruling of poisoning in the Schmieg affair.*

themselves as a collegial body to the Langenburg court, had the university affix the seal of the medical faculty at the bottom. Theirs was a legally binding judgment.

The Langenburg court now had its *corpus delicti*. Fessler had died by arsenic poisoning. Anna Schmieg was a textbook poisoner.

CHAPTER XIV

Impasse

Langenburg, June 3–September 4, 1672

hile the Altdorf Medical Faculty met and deliberated, the court at Langenburg intensified its hunt for witches. Court Adviser von Gülchen began to realize he was uncovering a plot of terror, coordinated through a diabolical conspiracy aimed at the foundations of Langenburg's Christian political order. Count Heinrich Friedrich and Court Preacher Dietzel backed him in this view. Only a few weeks earlier Louis XIV's armies had marched on the Netherlands, storming across weak and vulnerable territories of the western empire and sending shockwaves through the ranks of the German princes.[1] When tales about Barbara Schleicher, the suspected witch from Atzenrod, were followed by disturbing new reports about Hans Schmieg, the Langenburg authorities suddenly faced the prospect that the foreign and domestic threats might feed on each other—much as they had during the Thirty Years' War—sowing disorder quickly and unpredictably. As suspects came and went before the court, and the same personnel heard testimonies from all of the cases at the same time, gossip spread throughout the district. Directing these trials, trying to take in the new information, and hearing about still more undocumented rumors, von Gülchen thought he saw connections between all of the events.

Or so it seemed. The best evidence for a wider conspiracy came through the renewed prosecution of Barbara Schleicher, the *Spätzin*, in June. She had been under a cloud of suspicion since her release in 1669.[2] Now in the spring of 1672, Paul Treher, from Gerabronn, accused Schleicher of slipping poison into his wine at a nearby tavern, and how he had become deathly ill, and she had repeated over and over again, "He won't die, he won't die." He went on to relate an encounter with a spirit, a powerful dog, that frightened him and later materialized as Schleicher. Other witnesses from the tavern confirmed these details, the most damaging testimony coming from Carl Friedrich Lang, the tavernkeeper, that Schleicher had once tried to poison him with sauerkraut, and that he was therefore not surprised when Treher turned deathly ill from the wine.[3]

The most damaging evidence was that on May 11 the Langenburg chamber secretary had discovered a pharmacy in a cabinet in Schleicher's house. Barber-Surgeon Unfug's inventory of all the herbs and roots seems to have been precisely the kind any peasant woman would have put together to treat illness and wounds, but just having one now put Schleicher under suspicion.[4] She said that she used them mostly on herself, tying them into a bundle and wearing them around her neck. Dried elder blossoms were widely used against all kinds of ailments. It was said that the great Dutch physician Hermann Boerhaave himself never passed by an elder tree without tipping his hat out of respect for its healing properties.[5] Melissa balm was used against colds and influenza.[6] Verbena could have been used for a variety of ailments and for warding off demons.[7] And there were additional herbs commonly used in treating sickness in animals.[8]

Schleicher did not defend herself very well, however. She failed to explain the normal household uses of her herbs and could not even identify some of them. While she likely did not know their names, such answers, taken as refusals, hinted at secret knowledge that roused the suspicions of the court.

Von Gülchen saw proof of a wider conspiracy, one that now included Schleicher, and he had no doubts about her guilt. Like Anna Schmieg, she worked witchcraft through poison. That she preferred putting poison into wine or soup and not into Shrove cakes was just a variation on a theme. Like Anna Schmieg, she kept her activities hidden by working within the village. Von Gülchen also recalled a connection made between Schleicher and the terrible Turk Anna.[9] This evil had to be stopped before they and their partners did more harm.

The court adviser knew that the testimony against Schleicher was strong—stronger, in fact, than that against Anna Schmieg. He had at least two credible eyewitness accounts about her poisonings, and he had confirmed that she kept a secret trove of poisons in her larder. He knew what litany she had to confess to: that she had worked with Turk Anna and her daughter to poison cattle in the territory, that she had allied herself with Barbara Reinhart to poison horses and cows in Count Heinrich Friedrich's barns, that she had poisoned both of her husbands, that she had attempted to poison both Treher and Lang, and that she had done all of this after having met and been seduced by "black Hans," the devil.[10]

Von Gülchen sent his views to the count, who suggested making Anna Schmieg watch when Schleicher was tortured, thus frightening her into a confession and forcing the conspiracy into the open. To the court and people he commanded, the message was clear: witches had joined together and were at work around Langenburg.

Meanwhile, people from villages in the Jagst Valley sent in new accusations against Hans Schmieg. While he was passing through a village, a former neighbor claimed she had heard him utter a threat against the Heinckelins, the couple who had testified against his wife before the inquisition. She passed on the rumors from Heinckelin's wife that Anna Schmieg was now turning herself into a mouse, a rat, or a toad, and escaping into the night to seek revenge on her enemies, saying that

a toad wandered around her house, and that she could not say anything else but that it was the Miller's wife, and that she had murdered her child. And since the Miller thinks they will never give him back his wife and they want to destroy his mill, he wants to get even with Heinckelin, to burn down the Heinckelins' house and barn, and that he knows how to bring Heinckelin to the gallows so that he slaps his hands to his head.[11]

Another story made the rounds, even more damaging, for it linked Hans explicitly to the diabolical conspiracy. In midsummer a district officer reported that the butcher's son in Bächlingen had bought a mandrake—a magical herb—from a doctor who was passing through the village. The lad had sold it to the very interested Hürden miller. Shortly thereafter while on an errand to Weikersheim, the poor boy had mysteriously died.[12]

Mandrake was a root known since Roman times. Roman naturalists, like Pliny and Dioscorides, and Renaissance herbalists depicted the poisonous root as bearing an uncanny resemblance to an old man with a black beard. It was said to scream and groan when it was dug up, often from the soil under the gallows, and the hapless person who failed to shield his ears might die from the shrieks.[13] Seventeenth-century healers carved the root into the likenesses of men and women, most of them about a foot or so in size, and even gave them clothes. Some were described to look like toads, dragons, or some other wondrous animals. They sold them on a lively black market, sometimes for tidy sums of money. In folklore this strange root had legendary powers. Hidden in a box or buried near a house or barn, the mandrake drew wealth and prosperity to its owner. It could help a pregnant woman in childbirth. But it could also be used to hurt others, by dealing death or illness to cattle. Its associations with sudden death and damnation were widely known. The owner, not surprisingly, was suspected of being in league with Satan.[14]

Between the mandrake and the spurious stories, Hans Schmieg came under renewed suspicion of sorcery and witchcraft. On August 14 the court brought him in for questioning once again about the black cats' heads at the mill, the mandrake, and the new reports of threats against his neighbors. Hans blamed the matter of the cats' heads on his hired hand. One of the several mill hands he had recently hired must have cursed the works, and he swore that the cat's head had been recommended to him as the way to lift the curse.[15] He denied threatening to burn down the Heinckelins' house or that his wife assumed the shape of a toad and slipped out at night to attack them. Questioned as a source of these rumors, Michel Fessler wavered and admitted that he had heard these stories only secondhand. When the court brought in Georg Heinckelin to confront Hans, the old miller accused his neighbor of spreading lies about him in the taverns. Hans hotly denied the rumor that he had stolen hay from government barns.[16]

In a session on August 19, Hans admitted that he had kept the mandrake, "about a hand's span in length," in a box in his barn. He had indeed gotten it from the butcher's son in Bächlingen and kept it for three months. But he denied the reports that any wealth had come to him through it or that it gave the ominous appearance of a dried-out old frog with a black beard.[17] When asked what he used it for, he denied using it for anything.[18] When Eva was brought in and queried about the strangely carved root, she said that she had stumbled upon it by accident in the barn and that it had frightened her, but that she had not known what it was. When Anna told her it was a mandrake, she said she threw it into the river.[19]

At another time, and absent suspicions against his wife, it is unlikely that the court adviser would have pressed the matter very far. He might have simply admonished Hans, fined him, or singled him out for church discipline as he had done with others. The mandrake had long been thrown away, and its uses were ambiguous at best. No one had even accused him of using the mandrake to work sorcery against the butcher's son or anyone else. The reports about the threats to his neighbors were also weak. Schmieg's tough words, as he himself admitted, could simply be explained by his need to defend himself.

In a gathering atmosphere of fear, von Gülchen could not take Hans's reasoning at face value. Witch panics tended to take hold of the governments of small German territories where court personnel had close relationships to the people and events. Tainted by the suspicions surrounding Anna and Eva, and given Hans's earlier admissions that he engaged in sorcery to fix mechanical problems at the mill, von Gülchen may have found it hard not to see him involved in the witches' conspiracy. Moreover, Hans's enemies saw the opportunity to settle old scores.

⸻

$\mathcal{T}$HE TWO rulings from Altdorf cleared the way for von Gülchen to renew his prosecution of Anna, this time as the object of a special inquisition into specific charges of poisoning and witchcraft. If she still refused to confess, he could now lawfully question her under torture.[20] With the other investigations gathering momentum, he could finally put his case against her to the test.

The questions about whether, how, and why a crime had been committed were set aside. Using the Altdorf rulings, the Langenburg court now *knew* that Anna had poisoned Fessler. The court needed to produce the confession. The court adviser's aim for Anna was *büssen*—meaning "to confess one's sins and do penance." His words came right out of the Lutheran liturgy, and they blended the legal and the religious purposes of a criminal trial. She should confess

> out of concern for the salvation of her soul, that her hard and obdurate heart be softened, her tongue not speaking as up to now to the Devil, but addressing God the Holy Spirit and lead and urge her into the dear truth, so she would then be consoled once again, and could be assured of the grace of God and human forgiveness. But if not, then she would become a curse, turned over to God's wrath and denied grace from the authorities, [turned over] for temporal and eternal punishment where it is said: "Woe oh woe, from woe in all eternity God protect us, Amen!"[21]

Assuming that the shock of interrogation could finally break the devil's grip on her heart and conscience, von Gülchen then laid out the seven articles against her, beginning with the poisoning of Anna Fessler. Schmieg was to confess to keeping poisonous substances for the task, and also to admit to the fact that her cake, and nothing else, had killed her neighbor. Freed from the devil, she could then reveal to the court her true identity: that she was a fiend, a minion of the devil, a witch. The legal procedure, in short, was meant to unmask Anna Schmieg.[22]

───────

*T*HE COURT summoned Anna to the chambers of the chancellery on the morning of July 26 and demanded she confess to having sent poisoned cakes to Anna Fessler. She denied the charge, replying that the court "can turn her over [to the executioner], she will gladly give her life. . . . She fell to her knees, and prayed the little prayer: Help Savior, help me in my worry and need."[23] She remembered this prayer from a popular Lutheran hymn of the time. According to procedure, the court then let her know she could have legal counsel with her in the session. She refused. Choosing to stand alone, she said she would confront her daughter and her neighbors herself.

The court now read the list of articles that von Gülchen had drawn up, point by point, giving Anna a chance to confess. Over and over again, she denied them all. Weeping, she insisted she had not poisoned Fessler and that she had not baked any special cakes that day. In the middle of her denials Anna suggested that her daughter and the *Kutscherin* had probably baked cakes and sent a poisoned one to Fessler. The emotional strain of the session mounted as the morning wore on. She admitted trying to hang herself, but said it had nothing to do with a bad conscience. The executioner would not get anything else out her. When Eva's written testimony was read to her, she exclaimed that "she should have drowned her daughter at birth," that Eva was a useless wench, a "wanton slut and likely a witch as well."[24]

The climax of the morning session came in the confrontation between Anna and Eva. Anna countered her daughter's accusations with such shocking oaths and vile language that the scribe invoked God's protection when he heard her. "The Miller's wife denied it all," the scribe recorded, "and swore an oath—God save us all!—that the Devil may take her, and God may punish her in body and soul—she can swear by two fingers raised to God, that her daughter tells lies." When Eva repeated her damning account of how her mother had given her special cakes to take to the Fessler household, Anna responded, saying that she had only wanted to follow her husband's wishes and send for their son-in-law to come to the mill for Shrove Tuesday.

Her responses to the remaining articles were the same: she categorically refused to confess. When confronted by the accusation that she must have been seduced by the devil since she had been considered a witch for so long, she denied it and taunted, "Prove it!" Von Gülchen returned to her muttering and cursing and her infuriatingly ambiguous statements, such as "If I am witch then my daughter is one, too" or "If they burn me, they burn me, but they should burn the *Kutscherin* as well." While showing the strain of the morning's violent confrontation with her daughter, her angry answers were laced with defiance and sarcasm. Von Gülchen had them noted before returning her to prison at noon.[25]

That afternoon the court applied additional pressure. Schmieg forcefully denied witchcraft. She admitted that her cows gave inordinate amounts of milk, but said it was purely natural. When asked why her neighbor, the woman from Forst, accused her of giving her a "witch's shot" in the arm, she replied she did not know, and followed up by saying: "My neighbors want to make a witch out of me; then they can have me killed. I know for certain that an injustice is being done to me."

The height of the session, indeed of the entire day, came when the court called in all of Schmieg's neighbors from Hürden along with Eva. For the first time, Anna confronted all of her accusers and enemies. First the neighbors, then Georg Hermann's wife of Eberbach (in the form of a deposition), and finally her daughter: All were asked whether they would swear an oath in Anna's presence that their denunciations were true. Over the bitter vehemence and repeated denials of Anna Schmieg, they all said that they would. While she was briefly led away, they solemnly swore an oath, sealing their testimonies before the court.[26] Thus they put their own salvation in peril should it be discovered that they were lying.

When Anna returned and refused to confess one last time, with equal vehemence, Master Fuchs was brought in. Still she refused to confess. Because the executioner's touch dishonored his victim and his instruments disfigured her body, he ran the risk of unleashing curses and revenge if he acted unjustly. Following custom, he asked her forgiveness for what he was required to do. Anna became furious. "She wanted to hit him in the face with all her strength [and said that] she would rather be cut to pieces than that she confess."[27]

———

$\mathcal{T}$HAT EVENING Master Fuchs, along with the chancellery secretary and a court scribe, came to the tower, showed her his instruments of torture, and gave her one last opportunity to confess. She not only refused to do so, she uttered the curse that every executioner and judge feared most, threatening "to charge those people who brought her into this game before God on the Judgment Day." If someone uttered this rare curse on the day of their public execution, it could halt the entire judgment process and even invite additional torture.[28] But Anna was out of public view. Then, remembering, she said "that her husband had told her never to let the Master touch her; in her whole life he [Fuchs] had never called her a witch or a whore."[29]

In the painful session that followed, everyone present, including the court officers and even the law itself, was at risk along with Anna Schmieg. To proceed to torture and not elicit a confession was tantamount to an admission that the law had failed, that the evidence was deficient, that the truth remained elusive or unknown, or worse, that the judge and the court were committing an injustice.

Master Fuchs began the session by hoisting her up on the strappado. Her hands tied behind her back and then lifted off the floor, she refused to confess: "the Devil can take her, she's never seen any poison in her whole life." When Fuchs went to the next degree of torture, placing her thumbs in the thumbscrews and tightening them "until the blood ran out," Anna remained defiant. The chamber secretary approached her, asking her finally to speak the truth: "At this she said that it helps her soul not one bit, she can confess nothing, she asks for God's sake that they believe her, so that she can earn her place in heaven."[30] Torture had failed.

———

*V*ON GÜLCHEN struggled over the best way to respond to this new and troubling dilemma. Without a licit confession, one could not convict someone of a crime. Had his evidence been deficient after all? Had he proceeded improperly? Given the heightened concerns about torture in the late seventeenth century, without new evidence he could not subject her legally to torture again. Should she be purged of the charges and set free?

Von Gülchen turned back to the weakest link in all of the evidence: Eva's testimony against her mother. He brought Eva in alone for questioning on August 14, focusing more sharply on her role in the familiar events. Did she not have a reputation as a witch herself? Why had she attempted suicide? Why had she been so reluctant at first to talk about Anna Fessler's death? Had she not also baked cakes with the teamster's wife and delivered them to Fessler on her own earlier that day and without her mother's knowledge?

Eva admitted that she had baked cakes with Hans Barthel Walther's wife, the *Kutscherin*, on the morning of Shrove Tuesday and taken them to the Fesslers around midday. Otherwise, she repeated her familiar denials and affirmed once again her suspicions that her mother had cursed the cakes.[31] What was particularly clear in all of this questioning, however, was that Eva was the lone and key witness to the accusations against her mother. Moreover, her reputation, inconsistent behavior, and lies made her less than entirely credible.

———

*T*HE TRIAL was at an impasse. On August 19 von Gülchen sent copies and extracts from the interrogation protocols of all three cases—Barbara Schleicher, Hans and Anna Schmieg—by courier to Altdorf with a request for an opinion. Just how deeply his legal doubts ran at this point we do not know.

After considering the evidence for sorcery and possibly witch-craft against Hans, Textor and his colleagues curtly dismissed almost all of it. None of the evidence pointed to serious breaches of the law, and none of the evidence justified holding the old miller longer, let alone questioning him under torture as the Langenburg court would have liked. They did agree that he had "offended the community" with his cat heads, the mandrake, and his harsh talk about his neighbors, but none of these raised any suspicions at all regarding sorcery, let alone witchcraft. They recommended a 20-reichstaler fine and a short stint in prison. Schleicher was a differ-ent matter. Because she had confessed to witchcraft under torture but later refused to confirm the confession, it was licit to subject her to questioning under torture again. However, if she did not confess fully this time and no new evidence was brought forward, she, too, should be let go. The court could have her flogged and banished from the land.[32]

The opinion regarding Anna Schmieg, however, represented a stinging rebuff to the government of Langenburg. The law made it clear that only if a court found new evidence against a suspect could it subject her to a second round of torture. Finding neither a confession nor new evidence, the Altdorf professors refused to jus-tify torture of Anna a second time. Because Anna's case was more complex and vexing than the other two, their opinion went on for fourteen pages. The jurists came right to the point: "In the docu-mented circumstances [Anna] Elisabeth Schmieg is not to be ques-tioned under torture, but instead because no strong evidence has come forward against her, she is to be released from prison." No evidence proved that Schmieg's cake delivered the poison to Anna Fessler; the poison, in fact, could just as likely have come from Heinckelin's cakes that Fessler ate earlier in the day or some other source. Next, the court had not proved Anna's bad reputation. The testimony about her reputation was simply too vague, not clear in its origins, and not at all specific to the crime. Moreover, what the Langenburg court considered as Anna Schmieg's "confession" regarding her reputation was not a legal confession at all. Langenburg, the jurists then argued, had not even proved that Anna had enmity with Anna Fessler. Even Michel Fessler gave contradictory statements on this matter. When the court also argued that Schmieg had "tacitly" confessed to the crime herself when she said that her son-in-law "would have enough" if he ate from her presumed poisoned cake, the Altdorf jurists argued that this was at best an ambiguous statement open to different readings.[33]

Then Altdorf homed in on the gravest shortcomings in the case. The jurists pointed out that not a single witness testified to having seen Anna Schmieg poison the cakes. She was not known to buy poison or keep poisonous substances on hand. It was ridiculous to conclude from the fact that she had baked cakes "in secret" that she had therefore baked different batches of them, let alone poisoned any of them. Furthermore, the daughter's testimony was dubious on many counts. Not only did the law not allow children to testify against their parents, but Eva was the lone witness to the key accusations. Roman law required two to constitute full proof. Besides, they went on, her character was questionable and her answers therefore not credible.[34]

Most of all, the jurists argued, the legal reasoning was seriously flawed and much of the evidence ambiguous and inconclusive. The entire chain of events von Gülchen claimed to have reconstructed for the Shrove Tuesday murder was built on "conjectures and presumptions" that Altdorf found "dubious" and "deficient." Even the evidence that supported his theory they deemed "altogether imperfect," "insufficient," or even "irrelevant." The evidence taken to point to diabolism—Anna's muttering, the "witch's shot," her drinking, threats, and curses—were much too ambiguous and open to conflicting interpretations.[35]

When the jurists turned their attention to Eva and her testimony, they were just as skeptical. They allowed that she could be questioned "under the first degree of torture," that is, shown the executioner's instruments, because it was she who had brought the cakes to Fessler and urged her to eat them. But this did not prove that Eva murdered her since the intention to kill her could not be proved. In fact, the major problem was that no one could prove where the poison came from.[36] It was not witchcraft that they doubted, but the overall evidence, and von Gülchen's reasoning about it that failed the test.[37]

The Altdorf jurists eviscerated Langenburg's argument that Anna Schmieg was a witch and a poisoner. But the Altdorfers offered the Langenburg government a solution to the dilemma it was in. The court, they concluded in their brief, could simply banish the mother and daughter from the territory. Their moral conduct, attempted suicides, and proven thieving alone would justify such treatment. They were offering Langenburg a fig leaf to cover up the embarrassing impasse.

CHAPTER XV

Politics

*Langenburg Chancellery and
the University of Strasbourg,
September 7–October 8, 1672*

or two days, September 7 and 8, Court Adviser von Gülchen pored over the Altdorf opinion, reread the trial documents, and planned his counterattack. "Against all hope," he lamented, "the Altdorf jurists went right to [the evidence] with the poisoned cake, and they will not allow that the miller's wife be brought in again for torture."[1] Still committed to the rule of law, he decided to shore up the evidence on the critical points and then send off for a new, and—he hoped—more sympathetic opinion from the University of Strasbourg. It was a weakness in imperial law that no decree prohibited courts from seeking a second ruling when they disagreed with the first.

Von Gülchen's plan was not just a cynical political maneuver. The devastating rebuff from Altdorf exposed points in Langenburg's thinking that were taken for granted in the little principality and that shaped the very way that "facts" were seen, felt, and experienced. Von Gülchen and the Altdorf jurists saw different realities.

For his new report he aimed at making the weak points so strong that they would amount to that elusive "full evidence" necessary to justify the extraordinary step of a second round of questioning under torture. All new testimonies would be sealed with formal oaths. He would prove that the poison could only have come from Anna Schmieg's cakes and that she was a witch. All day Sunday, September 8, he worked on the plan, sending it in the evening to Heinrich Friedrich. He reassured the count, who had to approve (and pay for) his new course of action: "Have no doubts, an opinion quite different from the Altdorfers will come back!"[2]

Heinrich Friedrich supported his adviser's new tack. What choice did he have? Order von Gülchen to purge Schmieg of the charges and release her? Ignore the Altdorf opinion and continue on against Schmieg in defiance of their ruling? Neither of these courses of action would show his people that he and his government had found the evil in the land and were protecting them from it. In the most serious challenge to public order since the end of the war, his government would not fail. Approving the plan, Heinrich Friedrich made a suggestion here and there, and in the meantime backed the idea of pressing ahead with the punishment of Barbara Schleicher.[3]

Von Gülchen lost no time in summoning witnesses from across the territory to the chancellery for new depositions. These men and women had given their views several times before, but now he asked them to address specific weaknesses in the evidence and seal their testimonies with oaths. On September 12 they all trudged up to Langenburg and paraded before the court. First, he tried to tie Anna's reputation specifically to the poisoning of Fessler through new testimony from Barbara Truckenmüller, Fessler's younger sister, and Anna Heinckelin. Truckenmüller told how Anna Heinckelin had brought cakes over to her sister and her sister's delight in them. This neighbor woman's cakes clearly had not harmed her. Von Gülchen's hopes that Heinckelin might provide specific testimony against Schmieg were disappointed, however. Even though she had once mentioned Schmieg's name in association with the strange drowning of her child, she now recalled only vague impressions about Schmieg's reputation, none of them particularly damning. "She had heard since then from people [about Anna Schmieg's reputation as a witch] but she does not want to accuse anyone in particular." The closest she came to making the denunciation von Gülchen longed to hear was when she recalled that "several years ago when they were hauling in witches someone said that the miller's wife had also been named" and further recalled that the big black toad creeping around her barn must be Schmieg's familiar spirit. The village elders—Lienhard Finck, Hans Albrecht, and Michel Franck—were no better. "In general," old Finck said, "she is known as a witch."[4]

Only Michel Fessler and Philip Küstner, Anna's son-in-law, delivered new bits of information. Asked about the origins of Anna's enmity for him and his wife, Michel again said that he first witnessed it over a year ago when she flared into a rage over his cows grazing in her meadow. He continued that his wife, as Eva's friend, had counseled the distressed young woman to leave her mother and move with her husband to Nesselbach. Philip added new details to this story, commenting on the uneasy atmosphere in the mill in the weeks leading up to Shrove Tuesday. When asked whether his mother-in-law hated him and whether he had been promised half of the mill, he replied:

Yes. At the time that they lived together in Hürden she already treated him like her enemy. In the beginning she spoke reassuring words to him. Afterwards, when he only asked for a piece of bread she cursed it in the name of the Devil and gave it to him. . . .

Had the miller offered him half of the mill? Yes. But his father-in-law no longer wanted to abide by it because he wanted to give it to his son, and he [Philip] couldn't bear this treatment from him for long.[5]

He noted that the entire time he lived with the Schmiegs (since late fall 1671) that Eva and her mother had fought constantly.[6] This little account of what went wrong between Philip and the Schmiegs went right to the "cause" von Gülchen needed.

But Michel Fessler's and Philip's testimonies were not enough.

Eva was the pivotal witness, and her testimony vital. On September 12 officers of the court first visited Eva in her cell. When the executioner showed her his instruments, Eva swore that her story was true, "all of this while tears and heavy sobbing poured from her."[7] Then on September 14 von Gülchen had Eva confront her mother once more, affirm her testimony to her face, and then swear a solemn oath. Von Gülchen carefully crafted the oath to address all the legal and ethical problems that made Eva's testimony so problematic: her dubious feelings for her mother, her lies and deception. True, he could not change the fact that she was still a child testifying against her mother, and that this objection could still pose a problem for jurists not wanting to relax the strict rules governing testimony. But it might make Eva seem more credible.

Imposing an oath was a solemn step, for it forced someone to put her own soul and salvation in peril. First, von Gülchen asked twelve villagers to step forward, one at a time, and take an oath that his testimony was true. Then he turned to Eva and asked whether she understood the punishment that awaited her if she was lying. She replied: "Yes, she can do it with a clear conscience. The oath and perjury have been fully explained to her and she stands completely by it." He then led her through fifteen points in her testimony, one by one, and Eva affirmed each with a simple yes. Anna listened, apparently without a word, until she was asked what she thought. "If her daughter were speaking a single word of truth," she spoke with biting sarcasm, "then she would gladly offer her head and have them cut it off."[8]

Then Eva took the oath: "Every point [in the testimony] that has been read aloud to me is true, and I testify to this not out of enmity, envy or untruthfulness against my mother but out of obedience to the command of our merciful Lordship to prove my own innocence, so help me God and his holy Gospel."[9]

After her daughter had taken the oath, Anna looked Eva squarely in the face and said, "If you could swear an oath to all this, then you are lost, lost forever."[10] Anna Schmieg had the last word.

WHEN ON September 19 von Gülchen had executed every part
of his plan, he briskly drew together his thoughts for the Strasbourg jurists, requesting their permission to question Anna one
more time under torture and their advice about what to do with
Eva. He first went over the various parts of the Shrove Tuesday
scheme as he understood it. Then he sketched out, for the first time
in writing, the diabolical plot he thought he had uncovered. By
"her speech, gestures, expressions and things like this the government and the whole community consider the miller's wife to be a
witch," a witch just like Schleicher, and just like Barbara Reinhart
and Turk Anna, the two witches who had been burned a few years
ago. "Why had all of this happened?" he asked at the end of his letter. "Witches' bread. Turk Anna passed on her poisoned bread in
secret. The documents say so!" Imagining the conspirators to have
crisscrossed the land in a web of secret dealings, he pointed to Hans
Schmieg's trips to Binselberg, Michel Schmieg's trips to Dünsbach,
and Eva's errands on behalf of her mother. All these places were the
haunts where Turk Anna had been known to poison cattle and
children. That Anna Schmieg had poisoned cattle and people in
exactly the same way as had Turk Anna—by her baking—was no
accident! The miller's wife had learned this devilish craft directly
from Turk Anna, the witch matriarch.[11] The skeptical Altdorfers
would never have allowed such wild imaginings. To the Langenburg court, however, the conspiracy was obvious. Would Strasbourg's jurists see it this way, too?

IN HINDSIGHT, it seems almost inevitable that Langenburg would
turn to Strasbourg to help resolve its crisis. All the key players at the
court—Count Heinrich Friedrich, Court Adviser von Gülchen,
and Court Preacher Dietzel—had been educated and formed at
Strasbourg as young men. Still an intellectual and cultural power-
house of Protestant Europe, a source of advice for many south
German Protestant princes, territories, and cities, it was not the
same beacon of fervent Lutheran orthodoxy and piety that it had

been in the 1630s and 1640s.[12] By the early 1670s the threat of war with France and the development of new political and legal interests had given Strasbourg and its university a more secular outlook.

In the wake of the Peace of Westphalia, jurists began to face the hard reality that the empire had no unitary system of laws, that Roman law overlay a messy patchwork of local, territorial, and church laws. At Strasbourg this realization, made more acute by war, was, in part, what made the law faculty particularly receptive to public law, and the *usus modernus* school of thought.[13] Strasbourg's university and its law faculty were noted for lively debates, sharp differences of opinion, and controversy over politics, religion, and law.[14]

One of the debates that played a part in shaping the university jurists' views toward witchcraft involved the controversy over politics and the nature of the state. Since the late sixteenth century a number of Strasbourg professors, taking up the ideas of Jean Bodin, had advanced the arguments for divine-right monarchy and absolutism for the Holy Roman Empire and its territories. Shaken by the French Wars of Religion, Bodin had argued for a theocratic view of government and the importance of maintaining religious confessional orthodoxy in the face of public strife and discord. According to this view, worldly government was an expression of the divine order. Kings, princes, and magistrates, as God's representatives on earth, had to keep the divinely sanctioned order.[15] In one of the most widely regarded works on demons and witches of the late sixteenth and seventeenth centuries, *On the Demonomania of the Witches* (1580), Bodin had continued this line of political thinking.[16] He warned princes and magistrates that witches, as servants of the devil, represented the most dangerous threat to God's sovereignty and public order on earth. When confronted with witches, a magistrate had the sacred duty to enter the cosmic struggle on the side of God and, using the full powers of the state, eradicate these enemies or allow the state to descend into chaos.[17] So heinous did Bodin consider the witch's pact with Satan that he thought magistrates justified in suspending the normal rules of justice and prosecuting witchcraft as an exceptional crime.[18]

These theocratic values had been implicit in Heinrich Friedrich's and von Gülchen's policies when they had set about restoring Langenburg to order after the Thirty Years' War. Langenburg was now a beleaguered earthly manifestation of a divine order that could be maintained only by conforming to the absolute unitary will of God. In appealing to Strasbourg to authorize him to renew the torture of Anna Schmieg, von Gülchen hoped to expose the witch conspirators in his own land and save it from their evil.

At Strasbourg these theocratic views about the state, religion, and the law still had a formidable champion in the deacon of the Faculty of Law: Johann Rebhan (1604–89). Son of a Lutheran preacher and adviser to many Protestant princes, Rebhan brought to his understanding of politics and the law the precepts, piety, and understandings of Lutheran orthodoxy.[19] Surely jurists like Rebhan would understand the urgency of protecting the godly by rooting out the "evil people." But Rebhan was engaged in a fierce controversy with his colleagues over the nature of the state and civil society.[20] By the end of the Thirty Years' War, a number of jurists and other professors had become supporters of Hugo Grotius and his powerful arguments that one understand the state as grounded in natural law. Followers of this school of thought tended to view government and society in more secular terms and played down witchcraft as a dire threat to public order.[21]

As a former student of his old mentor Rebhan, whose thinking mirrored his own, von Gülchen expected a sympathetic hearing. Had von Gülchen known of the changed intellectual climate at Strasbourg, he might have had more sober expectations. In recent years Strasbourg had tended to rule on witch trials with caution. True, the law faculty had supported the prosecution of witchcraft when trials surged in southwestern Germany from the 1650s to the mid-1660s. But they showed distaste for such fantasies as tales of witches flying through the night, orgies with Satan at the witches' Sabbath, and stories of witches copulating with demons. And while they held firmly to the idea that the weak and sinful made pacts with the devil, by the mid-1660s they also tended to rule against the excesses of the law in prosecuting witches.[22] When they held university debates, they also expressed caution about the standard of evidence necessary to prove material harm, the strength of eye-witness accounts, the rights of the innocent, and the problem of unjust prosecutions.[23]

Moreover, grave questions about torture had been raised in the university community. In 1658, Jacob Schaller, professor of philosophy and ethics, had published a treatise marshaling all the compelling arguments against torture: that it stupefies the senses and makes it impossible to get at the truth; that it produces false confessions; that the Bible does not justify it; that torture produces tyranny and injustice; that nature itself abhors torture; and that especially in cases of occult crimes torture produces injustice.[24] Schaller echoed the scathing arguments of Friedrich von Spee, the most famous skeptic about torture and the witch trials in the seventeenth century.[25]

ON SEPTEMBER 26 the law faculty met for the first time to review and discuss the Schmieg affair. It does not take long to suspect that in composing their forty-three-page opinion, the Strasbourgeois had to tame serious differences of opinion. The document was replete with doubts, qualifications, hair-splitting legal distinctions, and surprisingly, even dubious leaps over the evidence. Not even the elegance of their Latin and German—Strasbourg had long prided itself on its achievements in humanist letters—could hide the fact that the professors had struggled to arrive at a unified position.

In fact, the jurists started out arguing that despite the fact that they harbored very grave doubts about the evidence, their decision was not an obvious one: Anna Schmieg's "denials up to this point do not allow for a purging of the charges, but rather that she be further questioned under torture."[26] There they came to it: *Langenburg would be allowed to subject Anna Schmieg one more time to questioning under torture.*

Their conclusion, they made clear, had not come easily. Moreover, they recognized that their ruling was an extraordinary one, not just *unsupported* by findings in the law, but indeed *unsupportable* by the law:

> True, to outward appearances it might seem that the evidence brought against the imprisoned miller's wife is not in this way proven, nor can it be proved, as found in the common written law and especially in the imperial law of the Holy Roman Empire's Ordinance on Criminal Law. We cannot deny that this matter is somewhat difficult to see this way so that we should not be able to adjudicate and speak the law this way without a great deal more research and reflection. If the suspect were not such a well known godless and dishonorable old woman, who even wants to kill herself and then at the same time mocks the executioner's torturing her, we would not speak the law or adjudicate in the same way. These last two indications point either to a weak-minded person who is not in full command of her senses or to someone with a thoroughly evil and desperate disposition. Without these other concurring circumstances which we presume in this present case we would have ordered in this criminal matter, as in other places, a milder course of action.[27]

The Strasbourg jurists were admitting that, strictly following imperial criminal law and the common standards of evidence, they could not legally prove Anna Schmieg a poisoner and a witch. In developing their opinion this way, they hinted at the concern that an occult crime like witchcraft could not be proved within the law and its rules of evidence. They did not go so far as to urge Langenburg to treat this case as an exceptional crime, nor did they recommend suspending ordinary law and its rules of evidence. But they came very close to doing so.

Were it not for the fact that other intervening "circumstances stood in the middle of this case," they went on, they would have recommended clearing Anna of the charges. So weak did they consider the evidence against Anna that their opinion seemed at first to build an argument forbidding von Gülchen from subjecting Anna to torture a second time. But the "concurrent evidence"

THREE HAGS. *In seventeenth-century German culture, old and masterless women were feared as potential threats to the moral order of the patriarchal family, the church, and the state. Here Jacques de Geyn suggests these fears in this study of three slightly sinister old women.*

pointed to something very disturbing, indeed the gravest crime of all: that Anna Schmieg was "a godless, barbaric and crazy old woman."[28] Strictly speaking, their words were a legal and political judgment. Schmieg's behavior betrayed her not simply as an impious or immoral woman, but as a traitor against God and the state.[29]

Where did they see evidence of Schmieg's spiritual treason? For one, they found her curses so out of the ordinary, and invoking the devil so powerfully, that she had likely renounced God altogether. When she swore that "God punish her, the Devil should take her, she wants no part of the Kingdom of God," she renounced any hope of ever gaining salvation.

Equally significant, they thought, was what they considered her other godless behavior, especially her brutal treatment of her children. They expressed their horror at how she had wished that she had drowned her daughter as a baby, that she had also openly called her son-in-law a "no-good rogue." Her heavy drinking and her dishonoring confession and holy absolution showed she had given herself over to the evil one. Anna Schmieg's life was an affront to the Ten Commandments.

The jurists read Anna's notoriously brutal sarcasm without any sense of humor or irony. When she responded to questions about her attempt at suicide by saying that "she had tried to hang herself over the donkey's stall" because "she wanted to do it on the same spot where smoochers like to go" they took it as a sign of a guilty conscience. (That her answer showed her contempt for her son-in-law and his love affair with Eva by desecrating the place where the peasant lovers probably had their rendezvous did not occur to them. In dialect the word for "smoocher" or *Küsser* sounds very much like Philip's family name: Küstner.) They were just as appalled by what they understood as her mockeries about torture.[30]

For the Strasbourg jurists, Anna's renunciation of God and family made her a likely poisoner.[31] Still, they refused to ignore or explain away the serious legal doubts about the evidence against Anna. At the end of their opinion they returned to the points that troubled them and went through each of them again, this time suggesting specific remedies that might lift the clouds of uncertainty. The easiest issue to treat was dispelling the doubt that someone else close to Anna Fessler—Barbara Heinckelin or her own sister, Barbara Truckenmüller—might have slipped poison into Fessler's food. Here the Strasbourgeois suggested arguments that foregrounded the suspicious timing between Schmieg's alleged attack—in the evening around Ave Maria—and the onset of the illness soon thereafter. They also suggested that the legal rule concerning enmity between suspect and victim—none was documented between Fessler and the other women—might suffice to close off further speculation about other suspects.

What about the lack of a confession from Anna? The more she hardened in her contradictions and denials, they cautioned, "the more suspicious and less innocent" she appeared to be. Yet they could not escape the fact that there was no firm evidence of guilt. While Schmieg should be forced to tell the truth, they recognized that "for this reason [alone] one would not cut off her head."[32]

Some of von Gülchen's "new evidence" could also be turned to good use against Anna. The neighbors' vague statements about Schmieg's reputation, for example, might not be specific enough to help in prosecuting the particular crime at hand, but they amounted to adequate "general indications" concerning her godless life. The village men's testimonies concerning Schmieg's reputation as a village witch might be considered sufficient enough to link her to specific local attacks on cattle. The jurists also thought that Langenburg could use Schmieg's secretive behavior concerning the cakes in combination with her general reputation to make "strong enough evidence to justify further questioning under torture."[33]

What about Eva, her suspicious behavior, her half-truths and inconsistent stories? The clever Strasbourg jurists thought they could answer these objections through one of those subtle qualifications in the law. "We are assured by the rule in criminal law that in cases *where the truth is not otherwise to be found* as well as in the provision in the ordinary law concerning testimony of a bad quality that otherwise would have to be refused" that such testimony could be used.[34] Despite reservations about Eva's testimony, one could use it against her mother.

Still, they found her part in the affair suspicious and disturbing, her answers unconvincing. Like von Gülchen, they did not consider her the prime suspect. Again concurring with his view, they thought she should be questioned one more time under the threat of torture. If she finally told consistent stories, the charges should be dropped. But they advised that if this were to happen, she should be made to live in another village. It would be an offense to Michel Fessler, the widower, to have to see someone everyday who had had such a suspicious role in his wife's murder.[35]

━━━

WHY DID Strasbourg recommend one more round of torture for Anna Schmieg where Altdorf stood foursquare against it?

When the Strasbourg jurists nudged aside their doubts, implicit in their reasoning was a vision of the state, society, and the individual unlike the Altdorfers'. In Anna Schmieg's words and behavior the Strasbourgeois thought they saw evidence of a grand cosmic political and spiritual struggle. Like strands of a finely woven tapestry, the cosmic and the political were woven seamlessly together. God's kingdom legitimized and supported the rule of divinely ordained kings and rulers on this earth and their magistrates, who upheld the laws. The earthly kingdom, like a finely polished mirror, reflected back and took part in the great cosmic struggle of good against evil, light against darkness, God against Satan.

The Strasbourg professors invoked the idea of divine-right sovereignty from Bodin. Populating a mystical political landscape along with God, princes, magistrates, and ministers, witches posed the gravest danger to the commonwealth. Magistrates had the sacred duty to eradicate them. Underpinning this view was Scripture, too. "But if thou do that which is evil, be afraid; for he beareth not the sword in vain: for he is the minister of God, a revenger to execute wrath upon him that doeth evil" (Romans 13:4).

Tellingly, the Strasbourgeois cited Bodin several times.[36] At the critical juncture in their reasoning about the dubious quality of some of the evidence, for example, they cited Bodin's warning that of all crimes witchcraft was the most difficult to prove with the law. When they went on to argue for setting aside the logic of the normative law and brought to the fore their concerns about *lèse-majesté*, their reasoning was completely consistent with Bodin. But their long and detailed discussions about the poor quality of von Gülchen's evidence could have been lifted from the pages of any judicial skeptic. Awkwardly they tried to reconcile their skepticism

with their alarm. While not directly advising von Gülchen to suspend the ordinary rules of the law and treat witchcraft as an
"exceptional crime," they were in effect doing so. It was a strained
argument, and they knew it.

In contrast, Textor at Altdorf held that the commonwealth had
its origins not in God's will but in natural reason and natural law.
These were the compacts that men entered into to make worldly
kingdoms and republics and that limited the powers of the state
and its ruler.[37] Textor did not disregard religion as essential to the
commonwealth, but he recognized the importance of separating
religion from politics.[38] He saw the atheist or the Epicurean as the
worst enemy of religion, not the apostate or traitor against God's
sovereignty.[39]

Running throughout the Altdorf opinion one also finds the
assumption that the state, its ruler, and its civil servants were duty-
bound to follow the law and its operations. The Altdorf jurists
clearly supported kings and princes, but the state comes off as more
circumscribed in its powers, less absolute, and more restricted by
treaties, constitutions, and patchworks of laws. His reference point
in politics was not God's heavenly kingdom but the political realities of the Holy Roman Empire after the Peace of Westphalia.[40] In
Textor's mature work no king or ruler could subvert or circumvent
the fundamental laws of the state.[41] Invading foreign armies, not
demons or witches, were the only imminent dangers to the commonwealth that might force a ruler to do so. Shorn of their quasi-
sacral roles, magistrates were simply virtuous and efficient civil
servants.[42] It is hardly surprising that Textor and the Altdorfers had
passed over all of von Gülchen's evidence of a pact with the devil
without the slightest mention.

It was not the first time nor the last that these political values
clashed. In the thrall of the new political thinking about the Holy
Roman Empire and the state, Textor, when a law student at Strasbourg, had argued for reconciling religious differences as a way to
put the empire and its principalities on stable footing. He was
obviously thinking about the religious zeal that had made the
Thirty Years' War so long and destructive. Textor's views had not
been well received by some in the Lutheran orthodox community.

Rebhan himself denounced the "sectarianism" of some jurists at the time.[43] The Schmieg case, the Textor controversy: both were stalking horses for the big battles over the nature of the state and the role of religion in guiding state policy.

───

*T*HE STRASBOURG jurists discussed the Schmieg case for two weeks before writing up their opinion on October 8. In one last significant gesture they wrote a separate letter to Count Heinrich Friedrich and the court that accompanied the opinion. "We wish from our hearts that God the Almighty would exterminate all evil and that the incarcerated prisoner may calm her heart and conscience to the extent that she give to God and the High Authorities her confession and contrition for her sins, and at the same time find her way to Eternal Salvation."[44] The sentiment, one imagines, fell on sympathetic ears at Langenburg.

CHAPTER XVI

A Vengeful Heart

Tower of Langenburg Castle,
September 4–November 4, 1672

uring the long months she had been confined to prison, Anna's world had collapsed. She was not entirely deprived of company. She talked with the jailer; and the jailer's wife, taking pity on her, took her out of her cell now and then, offering her meals in her own small room. Messages from Hürden occasionally reached her, and her husband, Hans, somehow got food, drink, and fresh straw to her. These contacts were all under surveillance; the jailer even reported Anna's mutterings to the court adviser.

The routine social exchanges that had defined her sense of who she was—her roles as miller's wife, mother, and neighbor—had withered. Anna felt cut off from support, abandoned, and betrayed. It is no accident that at this time she was overheard to say in her cell that if she ever got free from prison she would leave Hürden and never return. For a peasant to abandon house, property, and kin was virtually a death wish. Besides, she may well have been weaker after months of imprisonment. We know that she nursed injuries to her legs. Anna Schmieg's sense of self was firmly set in social relationships, and all of these were in tatters.

The pastors who would begin confessing Anna understood a person's identity in quite different terms. Following Johann Arndt, whose religious thought ruled at the Langenburg court, they had a more layered and dynamic view of the individual. Like Luther, Arndt found the core of the person in the inner self—the heart—where a cosmic struggle was waged. This inner self could reflect the image of God or have the image of Satan imprinted on it. The former was pure love, faith, and conformity to Christ. The latter was pure evil, enmity, and loyalty to Satan.

Arndt's work was a manual on how to read the signs of a Christian life and thus also the signs of a godless one.[1] For Arndt the sins planted in the heart and nourished by Satan were so numerous they could never be counted, but included among them were selfishness, pride, lying, blasphemy, cursing, hate, envy, and others.[2] As Arndt had written, "through remorse and pain the heart is broken, torn apart, beaten down and then through faith and forgiveness of sins is healed, consoled, purified, changed and improved."[3] Outwardly such repentance would show itself in tears, wailing, and cries of remorse. Bringing about this crisis of the soul in hardened malefactors might require striking terror in them.[4] One experienced Lutheran confessor cautioned, "It is not enough that she confess in general to being a poor sinner but she must use the time of her imprisonment to go through her entire life and look deliberately at all of her special sins so that she can stand judged before the Divine Majesty."[5]

Following Arndt's ideas, Court Adviser von Gülchen and Court Preacher Dietzel planned to confront Anna with her own words to reveal a heart secretly in the grip of Satan. Anna's religious education and regular practices had not prepared her for private auricular confession, let alone one as intensive and probing as this one. The Lutheran Church had preserved confession, even after Luther vehemently denounced the way it was practiced.[6] Anna had no experience in confronting a pastor, let alone a team of them, who would relentlessly examine her every word, act, and gesture, query her about them, and then press her to admit that they had a different meaning.

Drawing on his religious knowledge as much as his knowledge

of the law, von Gülchen planned and scripted the entire process very carefully. Here was the final act of the play, the scene when terrible revelations would be unveiled. It also mobilized, at one time or another, almost every member of the government hierarchy beyond von Gülchen: the count, who reviewed and commented on every order that was drawn up; Court Preacher Dietzel; the Langenburg chamber secretary; Pastor Wibel of Bächlingen; the pastor of Unterregenbach; the Langenburg court magistrates; Master Fuchs; the court scribe; and the jailer.

———

*T*HE FIRST session opened on Monday, October 21. The court preacher began with a "long lecture," urging Anna "to empty her heart" and confess. To this first appeal Anna denied she was a witch. But soon after came a surprising admission. After Dietzel and Anna had prayed the Lord's Prayer together, he asked if she could pray further with a "good conscience." She denounced her daughter:

> No, in the name of God, I see very well how it is going. Here I am, do with me what you want. If I have to suffer then my daughter should suffer with me as well since she brought me into this misery.
>
> My daughter was a whore, and still is a whore and if she were not protected then she would act like a whore again. She [Eva] had hardly recovered from her pregnancy when a man from Michelbach went after her, and she said she wanted him more than she wanted her husband.
>
> I confess that I long for revenge against my daughter.[7]

In German, Anna said she had a *rachgieriges Herz*, a heart with an uncontrollable hunger for revenge.

Though Anna admitted despising her daughter, she would not admit it came from Satan. In response to the twenty-eight questions that Dietzel then put to her, most of them theological, she maintained her faith. When asked if the devil, like God, can create things, she begged ignorance, saying that she did not know and had nothing to do with the scoundrel. On other points of theology she followed Dietzel's cues, saying that "she thinks often on Christ's suffering, death and resurrection . . . [that] she must now suffer herself to be sure she is innocent." She pronounced that "she is as innocent as Lazarus," "has the Holy Spirit in her heart," and is a true member of the Christian Church.[8]

Toward the end, Anna could not restrain herself, however. Again the thought of her daughter triggered her outburst. She said that if there were one child she would not have baptized, it was her daughter. She wished she "had drowned her in her first bath." Over and over, the scribe recorded, she wept. "They do an injustice accusing her of poisoning." She was not like the others, she pleaded. "She has always hoped, especially today, that she will be home again tomorrow, but now they should just lead her away [for execution]."[9]

Von Gülchen had planned for a day of interrogation to be followed on the next by torture. Anna affirmed her innocence even in the face of Master Fuchs and his instruments. Yet when Fuchs applied the thumbscrews, something remarkable, and very disturbing, happened. Anna felt no pain.[10] So the protocol records, and so the executioner, an expert in these matters, reported after the session. All who witnessed it knew that witches still in the grip of Satan felt no pain.

Anna might have felt different about this claim. It was recorded that she again anxiously cried out to Jesus lines from the Lutheran hymn "Help, Savior, Help Me" and at one point shouted, "My God, my God, leave me not!"[11] Her apparent lack of pain might have been imputed to her ability to sustain her innocence under torture. To Anna these were signs of her lack of guilt and God's favor. Master Fuchs worried that the devil had his grip so strongly on her that she might not break under torture at all.[12]

When Dietzel pressed her the next day about how she could withstand such pain, she replied: "She cannot say or answer where the insensitivity comes from, she is not a learned person, she hopes she has it from God. . . . That no blood came from her right hand she has her dear God to thank." When pressed again, she said that God was her consolation. "She lifted up her hands several times and said: 'Oh, you Son, protect me, your daughter

will be plagued with evil.' " Most of these responses, not surprisingly, drew on prayers and hymns commonly taught in Lutheran
instructions on the catechism. When asked where she learned her
answer to a question about the Resurrection, she simply said, "In
church."[13]

By alternating the sessions with the pastors with interrogations
under the executioner—in our modern view a sadistic attempt to
break her will—the court was lining up the evidence of her words
with the signs of her body. Every confessor, Lutheran and Catholic
alike, was familiar with Jeremiah's warnings about a deceitful heart.
The sessions revealed a deep facet of Baroque Lutheran culture:
words, bodily gestures, and actions pointed to the more important
but hidden realities within.

When Anna's answers still failed to satisfy and she returned to
the executioner one more time, on October 24, a new, disturbing
sign was discovered: a mark on her body. When asked about it, she
said that it was painful, coming from a boil or wound. But the executioner, pricking it with a needle, saw it differently: "He considers it a witch's mark. In fact it does not bleed!" Taunting her to her
face, Master Endris pricked the mark and looked for blood. But she
did not flinch. Her final answer was that she had borne this mark
for forty years or more. Perhaps it was a mark of shame, but it was
not a mark of the devil.[14]

---

*T*HE TURNING point came the next day, October 25, when Anna
"opened her heart." Using a script written by von Gülchen, Court
Preacher Dietzel joined the battle for her heart and soul. "If you
want a great victory[,] so you have to overcome yourself, your
anger, arrogance, ambition and evil desires. In such a way you overcome the Kingdom of Satan."[15] Confronting Anna with twenty-
nine carefully chosen phrases from her own words, he challenged
her to believe that their real meaning was the *inverse* of what she
thought.

In the counseling style of Arndt, Dietzel asked Anna to consider
her soul and salvation, especially now that she had been told she

would soon die. He threw her wish "to appear before God with the people who unjustly accuse her of poisoning and witchcraft!" back at her: "Since she committed the crime in secret, how could there be any witnesses?" She must realize "that her conscience is the best witness and that hers is painfully wounded and, at bottom, wicked."[16] She herself needed to *divulge* that she had poisoned Anna Fessler.

Dietzel's challenge to her conscience seems to have jolted Anna. She wavered, first replying with the equivocal language she had often used in the past. "If she were guilty in giving the cake then God would have the plague throttle her." Then she admitted that she gave her daughter little cakes to give away, but that "it is a great sorrow in her heart that she cannot affirm anything else. She knows she is expected to admit it, but she cannot. She believes on her soul that with all the witches you have never had such a situation as you have with me." Knowing what they expected her to say, she wavered one final time before telling Dietzel, "She will take onto her conscience that she gave this little cake and let herself be judged for it." After further questioning Anna almost seemed to want to please the preacher. She slowly gave in to her guilt, at first couching it in religious terms, conceding that "the devil may have given her the poison."[17]

But when Anna finally admitted to poisoning the cakes, she did so in more mundane terms:

> A vagabond gave her a bit of poison for the little cake. He had asked for a drink at the teamster's house but he had been turned away, thinking that he was full of vengeance and wanting to burn up his pigs. She put a bit of this poison into the little cake, but it was meant for her daughter and not for Fessler. At this point she began to cry and pleaded: "for God's sake, guide me and talk to me." She poisoned a few cakes (but not many). They were sitting in a bowl. Her daughter may have taken one and taken it to the teamster's wife.[18]

The poisoning, Schmieg confessed, came from her "vengeful heart." When pressed whether the poison was meant for Eva, Anna freely admitted it.

Her revelations were selective, however. No lurid confessions about meeting the devil or flying off to the witches' Sabbath tumbled out of her. She refused to implicate her daughter, son, or husband in her crime. She concentrated her responses on the state of her heart, the enmity within it, and on the past, as the pastors urged her to do. Dietzel confronted her with her former words on her innocence, pressing her to search her memory. "She should say that she is innocent and be purged, or she is lying to conceal great wrongs."[19] In order to free the authorities from the possible charge that they were committing an injustice, they needed Anna to admit all of her crimes. With her heart now opened, she remembered one more terrible sin.

Long ago, when she was a maid in Unterregenbach, a friend of her kinsman's, "a real whorish scoundrel," "came to her, and they fornicated together in the barn, but they did it only one time."[20] Whether a rape or consensual sex, clearly Anna considered it a shame—in her lifetime there was no end to sermons preaching against the sin of youthful lust and sex. As such, the story had meaning as part of confessing her sins, very much as the state and church authorities had hoped.

The court preacher never reached the end of his script for this session. Nor did he need to. Still, he searched the meaning of her words, over and over, once again telling her that they meant the opposite of what she intended. He instructed her that when she said she was a member of the community of saints, what she really meant was that she was a servant of the devil. When she invoked God, she was really appealing for aid from Satan. This was the topsy-turvy logic of witchcraft. Her admission of these reversals seemed the clearest evidence that Anna had been a witch all along.[21]

But Anna could not help herself. She admitted, too, that a spirit had come to her in prison, "taken her by the throat and wanted to go to bed with her. Crying, lamenting, and begging forgiveness, she confessed to being seduced one other time in Regenbach, by a lad from Sonnhofen who had misled her with promises of marriage."[22]

Even though the official record tried to capture the drama of the confession, at times Anna seemed to have a completely different understanding of this process. She seemed to cling to the notion that this confession was a ritual process like any other, that it would cleanse and purify her. Sin, repentance, and forgiveness were all still actions, not affects. She expected her confession to heal her shattered self and mend relationships with others. Before Dietzel told her that even sins as heinous as witchcraft and poisoning could be forgiven, her shame kept her from confessing them. Now, Anna wanted to make amends to her daughter. "She would like to have her daughter brought before her, wants to fall down at her feet, and beg her forgiveness."[23]

Anna's belief that this confessional rite could heal her broken life—going back to her childhood—explains why painful memories came tumbling out of her at times. Remembering her mother's death and going to her uncle's house for help, Anna said "she did not stay long with him because he had so many children and she misbehaved so badly." Without prodding, she then recounted the other sad details of her childhood, and her own guilt, so common among children, that she bore moral responsibility for it all.[24] Showing her contrition, she recited prayers "on her knees with her hands outstretched." The session was over.

———

*T*HAT NIGHT Anna slept better than on any other since coming to the prison. Perhaps it was from sheer exhaustion, or relief that her ordeal was reaching its end. Yet that observation, freely offered by her and confirmed by the jailer, was no innocent or casual comment. It reinforced the Lutheran belief that true peace could come only from an unburdening of the heart.[25]

This initial confession did not end the ordeal for Anna, however. Unaware of this, she actually had only begun the process of what the court considered a full confession. Another long and emotional cycle of sessions, seven of them to be exact, lay before her. As von Gülchen wrote on October 26, "the miller's wife has made a good start towards a confession and conversion." Why was this only a "good start"? The law required that Anna's testimony provide the kind of detailed descriptions of crimes that only an eyewitness could give. This was why the court adviser drew up a list of twenty specific questions and charges, calling for all of the details, as yet unrevealed, about how she poisoned the cakes, where, when, and how her seduction by the devil had occurred; and a listing of the lifetime of crimes she had alluded to in one of her sessions.[26] Only then could the secular government know the full scope of harm that had been done and bring justice to the people under its protection.

These sessions also turned the pastors and court officers, indeed the entire court, into firsthand witnesses of a cosmic drama. Given his devout faith and his fears of wider conspiracies besetting his land, Count Heinrich Friedrich followed these sessions closely. Playing out before him and his fascinated court was the struggle between God and Satan. A curtain had been raised, revealing a stage that normally lay just beyond sight. "There is so much to learn about the evil spirit through these cases," von Gülchen wrote.[27] They were watching Christ and the Gospel reclaim a sinful heart, showing that God was actively at work among them. They had an obligation to bring the process of penance and conversion to its full conclusion. In her "good start," von Gülchen for the first time struck an optimistic note regarding Anna. He hoped that she could be made once again "a child of God."[28] Anna herself expressed doubts on this matter, still, she was to be fully confessed so that no doubts remained.

———

$\mathcal{F}$ROM OCTOBER 25 on, the court records show a changed Anna Schmieg. Her old identity—the tough miller's wife who defended herself, husband, family, and honor from neighbors and enemies—gave way. Whereas before she tended to present herself in relationship to family, kin, and neighbors, now she more often presented herself in terms of her false beliefs (apostasy), her relationship with God and the devil (diabolical conversion), and its effects on her heart (revenge, hate, envy). A self that had been hidden now came into view.

We know that Anna's confession and conversion were made

under immense spiritual, psychological, and emotional pressure. When her admissions did not fully satisfy the court and she was pressed to elaborate on the details of her secret life as a witch, she balked. Asked whether she wanted to go to her execution settled and peaceful, she replied "that she cannot say anything more than that she is a witch, but cannot say that she did anything."[29] On October 29 she was tortured again, this time repeatedly with the strappado. Wailing and pleading, she still hesitated. When the torture was renewed, she confessed, in a confused and disordered way, to a long list of crimes.

Three matters about her secret identity and deeds interested the court officers in particular. She first had to explain how she was seduced by the devil. Confused by what they wanted, she resisted turning what she had presented as the moral lapse of a young woman at her kinsman's house—sleeping with a young man—into a demonic encounter. However, when "talked to more closely, she said that she had fallen from God and he [the youth] had baptized her in the name of the Devil." When pressed for more details, she blurted out that she called him "Heinrich Zacharias, the thief!"[30] On the second matter—the details of the poisoned cake—she affirmed her earlier account but claimed that her daughter and son were innocent in the affair. Regarding her husband, she admitted that he had had strange dealings involving the mandrake and the cat's head, leaving it open as to whether this pointed to his involvement in witchcraft and sorcery or not. Her other crimes remained a sticking point. She insisted that she had done no other harm to people and cattle, but when pressed further, admitted to having poisoned the cows by feeding them bread she had tainted with spiders. When compelled to reveal the names of her accomplices, she offered that there were legions of them: whole groups of vagabonds—men, women, even serving girls—and then a long list of people from Hürden and nearby villages (Nesselbach, Bächlingen, and Forst) who joined her at the witches' dance.[31]

When not facing physical force, Anna underwent psychological torture. Her life and its events were searched through, the meanings of old memories inverted, disturbing crimes and mysterious misfortunes ascribed to her. The course of her life was not

WITCHES' SABBATH. *The witches' sabbath was imagined as a topsy-turvy riot of the senses, a perversion of Christian virtues. A demon leads a long line of revelers around a mountaintop—the legendary Blockesberg in Thuringia—while other demons and witches couple, dance, conjure, and worship the devil.*

simply interpreted, it was turned upside down. She did not make her admissions freely. At one point, hoping that a general confession would be enough, Anna quoted Luther back to her tormentors. "It would take more than a lifetime to repent all of her sins."[32]

In the context of Lutheran confession this would have been a standard admission, but even this was read as a perversity. Only a vividly detailed recounting of a lifetime of sin and crime would do:

> If she does not tell the truth then tell her that the Evil Spirit is Master of her heart, tongue and conscience. The good spirit and angels will come to her and comfort her. She should consider that already as a maiden of 14 or 16 she was seduced into witchcraft. Now she is 60 or 61 years old; it is no shame for her to confess what she must have done here and there over 45 years. [Otherwise] she would be more harshly punished, and what she denies will not be forgiven.[33]

Law blended with theology to compel her to trace her identity as a witch back to an entire life of sin and crime. Anna's life story had to be rewritten, empirically verified, and then affirmed "voluntarily" in her own words.

The exact words—the clinching evidence that she had committed the alleged crimes—would be read aloud before the court so that the state could show it had exercised its duty to expose and punish the crimes that had racked its people for a number of years. Anna's confession would also demonstrate that the truth of religious faith was open to empirical observation and confirmation.

But Anna would not give them that satisfaction. As late as November 1, his frustration showing, von Gülchen wrote Heinrich Friedrich that "the miller's wife has not yet shown a full and complete repentance." He despaired of finding the right tactics to get her to say the words required.[34] In the end, he simply drew up a detailed list of fifteen charges and presented them to her on Monday, November 4. All she was required to do was affirm each one. And she did. This document became her legal confession.

———

𝓑EFORE ACCEPTING her confession, the court had to reconcile her statements with those of other witnesses, members of her family in particular, in order to ascertain exact guilt and clear unwarranted accusations. Only then could justice be done.

The meeting with her daughter took place on Saturday,

November 2. The court needed the women's testimonies to match perfectly in order to apportion guilt and innocence. Eva still denied categorically being a witch. Despite her previous remorse, Anna was harsh one last time, insisting that if she were a witch then Eva must be one, too. Eva responded, "If her mother is a witch, then she does not want to be her daughter any longer." Anna relented, saying "she has lied and her daughter is not one" and exonerated Eva of all responsibility in the poisoning.[35]

The matter did not quite rest there, however. Eva had discovered a mark on her back and claimed Anna was responsible. Her mother, she said, had "carved little pieces out of her back and taken out some black hairs and bristles from a sow and that for a long time she has not been able to wear a bodice to church and that this had gone on for more than a year."[36]

Whether birthmarks, scars, or blemishes, the court saw them as a witch's marks, and both mother and daughter were despondent over them. For Eva the marks brought up feelings of rejection: "Her mother said to her more than 100 times, that had she known she would not be able to do anything with her, that she would have drowned her in her first bath!" Anna, in turn, broke down, lamenting, "Oh my God, she had never her entire life thought of leaving a mark on her daughter."[37]

Mother and daughter left each other that day feeling perhaps strangely united now that their stories were exactly the same. Anna filled in the last details about the poisoned cakes, and Eva confessed that after delivering her baby last winter she had, in fact, committed adultery with a man from Sonnhofen. Other small details in the poisoning of Anna Fessler were reconciled: the number of cakes and their color, even Anna's feelings about her son-in-law. If there was no clear evidence of reconciliation, at least Eva showed pity over her mother's fate. "When the daughter was let out into the district servant's house, she said good night to her mother, saying that she forgave her everything." But she also left her mother with a preachy last word: "She should in the future stay by the truth and tell no more lies about her."[38]

Anna had no opportunity to reconcile with her husband and son, however. In her meeting with her son, Michel, before the court on November 2, Anna stayed firm in denouncing him. She said he was with her when she poisoned the cakes and knew all about the crime. Michel vehemently denied it and condemned her for dragging them all down with her. "Mother, you think that just because you are no good that we all are worthless, too; moreover, you have done a great deal of evil, and it's too much wanting to bring all of that home to us."[39]

On November 4 her meeting with her husband, Hans, had testy moments but went better. With him standing there, she withdrew her statement that he had gone to the witch's dance with her on the Katzenstein. But she then went on to charge him with sexual affairs and dealings with the mandrake. For his part, Hans recalled urging her during her long imprisonment to make her peace with her hopeless situation, remembering the times he had sent her food and telling her to pray and ask for a merciful judgment. When he was discharged from the court and she was pressed about her retractions, she said that "he had been angry with her because she is such an angry wretch" but that otherwise he had participated in no wrongdoing.[40]

———

WITH HER formal confession, written and approved on November 4, Anna's earlier identity as the miller's wife and a mother vanished altogether. What took its place was a new and terrible one: that of a witch. In fifteen detailed charges, her official confession revealed her secret life: her seduction by the devil when she was fifteen or sixteen, her drowning one of her own children in the millrace, her attempt to murder Eva and her son-in-law with Shrovetide cakes, but killing her neighbor instead, her harm to neighbors and their animals, as well as a life of cursing, drinking, and godless behavior, and a suicide attempt.[41]

After visiting Anna on the day she affirmed this confession, Dietzel reported a final time about the state of her heart and soul. The court preacher was visiting her and Barbara Schleicher every day now, looking for signs of conversion and offering them consolation. To the court it was essential that she be shown to repent and

ANNA SCHMIEG'S CONFESSION, NOVEMBER 4, 1672. *Reviewing all of the evidence and testimony, Court Adviser von Gülchen drew up a final list of fifteen crimes for Anna Schmieg's final confession. As they were read aloud, Anna affirmed each charge with "Ja," or "yes," her words duly recorded in the margin by the scribe.*

that this repentance be witnessed and described, if at all possible. He believed she stood on the threshold of conversion. After talking with her on November 4 about "purifying her heart," she seemed "sorrowful" about her past and "inclined to admit her wrongs and hereby to show repentance as if she were left standing on this, her Mt. Sinai."[42]

CHAPTER XVII

Poor Sinner

Langenburg and Gallows Hill,
November 8, 1672

hile Anna Schmieg and Barbara Schleicher awaited their fate in prison, up in the chancellery's chambers Court Adviser von Gülchen prepared the final act. On the evening of November 7 he had written to Count Heinrich Friedrich with a report about the prisoners and his plans for the ceremonial sentencing and execution.[1] By Friday morning, November 8, the town and its citizens had been informed of their duty to attend.[2]

When the prince scribbled his approval of these measures, he added one provision of his own. Taking no chances, he authorized the court adviser to take any additional means necessary to maintain public order. Authorities feared that an execution might not go properly. If the accused did not confirm her confession in public, or the executioner botched the execution, or, perhaps worse, the accused publicly cursed the authorities, these could be taken as signs of divine disfavor or injustice.[3] Crowds had been known to react violently to such unexpected disruptions during an execution. Given the fears that had swept this region since 1668, and the popular support for the accusations of Langenburg's witches, such a public tumult was unlikely.

The material and institutional preparations were by far the easiest. The majestic palace and town square were readied to become the main stage in the drama, with teams of artisans working for days. In the Castle Tower the walls had been repaired, doors reinforced, and new chains and iron balls laid aside for the prisoners. In the courtroom carpenters set up a new table and chairs for the judges. For the court officer who would preside over the session, the ancient ceremonial armor was repaired and polished, and a new staff, symbolic of the court's authority, made. On Gallows Hill the stocks were rebuilt, special ropes laid aside for the executioner's use, stakes erected, and cords of wood piled up.[4] A band of five guards was organized, drummers assembled, and boys from the Langenburg school readied to sing hymns.[5]

The script for the ceremony was brought from the archives, and the various officials rehearsed their roles and the lines they were to speak. Every word, every gesture to be made before the court, was written out, reviewed, and approved in advance.[6]

Anna and Barbara Schleicher were readied as well. Court Preacher Dietzel visited the two witches and talked to them about their sins. At first he was angry that Schleicher had refused to affirm her confession, but then she relented, and she and Anna were moved to a full and contrite confession one last time. He offered them absolution and Holy Communion.[7] He also had to counter the popular misconception that criminals were somehow different from the rest of the laity. In Lutheran teaching everyone was a liar and a sinner. What made the prisoners different was that their sins were more visible to the community and so their deaths were opportunities to see how penitent Christians might meet their end. In fact, the prisoners, having confessed fully and then willingly meeting their deaths, would immediately go to heaven to stand before God. The execution was therefore two dramas at once. The state showed its power to apply the law, restore justice, and punish the guilty. And citizens were invited to watch the drama of salvation. A public execution was a sermon in action.

There was more to it than this, however. In visiting the prisoners and hearing their confessions the week before, Dietzel was also carrying out his duty as a state official. Here the church itself was implicated in a kind of spiritual violence. Every good pastor relied upon a variety of spiritual, psychological, and physical tactics—backed up with the implicit threat of renewed torture to make sure that the confession held. With Barbara Schleicher there had not been much trouble. On November 5 in one last brief session before the chancellery and members of the clergy, she had given a full confession. Under Dietzel's stern lecturing, she had broken down completely. As the chancellery scribe read out the list of thirteen crimes, she responded with a simple "yes" to them all.[8]

Anna had been an entirely different story. It may have been her tenacity and the difficulty in getting her to confess that made the authorities worry that she might not accept the new part assigned her in this drama, that of the remorseful sinner. Dietzel ministered to both women through the day of the execution. Only the state of their hearts mattered now. He likely counseled them to be grateful that through this punishment God made their sins visible to them so that they could feel contrition and accept forgiveness. They were to accept willingly their punishment and hold no malice against the authorities for carrying out their Christian duty. Christ himself had been crucified with criminals. Paul, who had persecuted Christians, had been converted and accepted into heaven. And Dietzel might have consoled them, as advice manuals recommended, that the physical suffering lasted a short quarter of an hour and "they should not let themselves be confused by the assembly of the masses but instead consider that it was God's will that they be held up as an example to fear God and frighten people away from sin and vice."[9] He may have held out the old words of consolation: "Today you will be in heaven."[10] The three days before the date of sentencing and execution would remind Langenburg's Christians of the three days of Christ's suffering on the cross.[11] The day of the execution was set for a Friday, an unmistakable reference to Good Friday.

As villagers, Anna and Barbara had never received this intense individualized counseling and instruction. Now they embodied the Christian ideal of the poor sinner. They ate better than ever before, in part to strengthen them for the ordeal. But the food was also meant as a gesture of reconciliation from the authorities who were about to torture them publicly and then put them to death. Even after all this individual counsel and care, Anna was still reported to be unsteady, even melancholy and troubled. On the day before the executions von Gülchen seemed nervous when he heard that she appeared "not completely penitent but feisty" and then later in the evening relieved to learn that she and Schleicher appeared "peaceful" and mentally and physically well. He was most concerned that the women be alert and sober for the sentencing and execution.[12]

AFTER A ritual last meal and a final moment with a pastor, the two women were bound and escorted from their cells to the courtroom. First to arrive, wearing his ceremonial armor, Chief Justice and Town Steward Georg Friedrich Assum descended from his coach and went into the courtroom. Behind him came the Twelve, the court judges, or assessors, including the mayor of Langenburg, five notables from the town, and six others from the leading families around Langenburg. Many of these judges had taken part in the interrogations of Schmieg and Schleicher and knew the women well. When they were all inside, they remained standing as the court steward, holding the ritual staff, called the court to order in the name of Count Heinrich Friedrich. The clerk summoned the judges to raise three fingers and swear the oath binding them to shed blood only in the name of the imperial criminal law.

After the court's jurisdiction was affirmed and the chief justice pronounced that the court was prepared to carry out its duties, he called out, "Was anyone present wishing to make use of this criminal court?" When the judges responded that there was, the preliminaries came to an end.

Anna and Barbara were then led into the court, escorted by Master Fuchs. An officer representing Heinrich Friedrich presented the formal accusations against them and requested that the court scribe read them aloud. Led forward to the center of the court, surrounded by the justices, Anna Elisabeth Schmieg and Barbara Schleicher had to confess one more time, openly and publicly.

This was the moment of danger. Were Anna now to curse the judges as she had cursed the executioner before she was tortured, "asking them to join her for God's Judgment in the Valley of Jehosaphat," the proceedings might break up. She could be tortured again, but the curse would have had a shocking effect and raised the question about whether an injustice was about to be committed.[13]

Because of these dangers, instead of asking the women to speak for themselves, the count's officer spoke for them, saying that the two poor sinners had freely confessed their crimes and were ready to be given over to justice. The scribe read of Anna's use of witchcraft and murder, as well as her seduction by Satan. He pronounced that she had done so many evil things that she could not even remember them all.[14] He then read out a list of Schleicher's crimes, which included witchcraft, murdering two husbands, turning herself into a wolf, and attempting to commit suicide. Whoever these two poor sinners had been before that day, they were now publicly branded as witches, poisoners, and murderers.[15]

Then came the sentencing. The members of the court stood up and filed out to the district office house across from the palace so that they could officially deliberate and approve the sentence. This was a formality, as the sentence had already been worked out in advance. Still, the court scribe noted the buzz of excitement as the judge and the assessors left. When they returned, he brought the court back to order. Clearly and loudly the scribe repeated the women's crimes and that they were deserving of punishment for the ill ways in which they had lived their lives. The sentence: Anna and Barbara were to have their flesh torn by red-hot tongs and then be "burned into dust" at the stake.

However, in recognition that they had seemed contrite about their crimes, converted to God, confessed, and repented, their pain and suffering would be lessened. After Master Endris tore their flesh with tongs, they would be granted the mercy of not being burned alive. Instead he was to strangle each of them with a rope and then burn their bodies at the stake.[16] It was a traditional display of mercy and power on the part of Count Heinrich Friedrich and his court.

One last symbolic act remained. Chief Justice Assum turned to the court assessors and asked them whether the sentence had been decided as the court scribe had read it. Together they replied yes. Assum then rose, broke the ceremonial staff in two, and threw the pieces to the floor. With this old legal gesture, the blood court was symbolically breaking its staff over the lives of the prisoners.[17] Then he said, "God help their poor souls." Heinrich Friedrich's representative then asked that the executioner carry out the sentence. According to prescription, the command to the executioner was repeated three times. At the close the chief justice forbade everyone present, on penalty of bodily punishment, from seeking revenge for this act of justice. No one was to take up violence against the law or question what was being done. The court scribe repeated his admonition.

The executioner then led the women out of the court, across the drawbridge, and over into the market square, where they joined the procession that had assembled. Drummers beat out a cadence, schoolboys sang hymns, and the sober procession marched down Langenburg's long main street and out the gate at the east end of the town.

Once past the town gate, Anna's and Barbara's expulsion from the community was complete. From many perspectives, as we have seen, Anna's emotional world was not like our own. It would be wrong to assume that Anna and Barbara felt the same anxiety and fear that we would today as they climbed the "Path of Straw" to Gallows Hill. The belief that someone who received absolution before an execution, and who did not sin again by resisting, would go right to heaven may help explain why prisoners rarely resisted at this point. Most tried to meet their fate as best as they could. Considering the suffering of the last ten months, Anna may have welcomed her end. She and Schleicher may also have been fortified for the ordeal with wine. Prayer may have brought them solace. However she felt about her fate, no record mentions her resisting or cursing the executioner or members of the court.

The scene at the gallows must have been crowded. The execution was seen as an example, and it was considered essential that the Langenburg schoolchildren be let out of school to join the procession. There, with the rest of their neighbors, they would have watched Anna and Barbara torn with hot irons and then strangled with a rope. After the bodies were burned to ashes, the last ritual gesture was made. "Lord Chief Justice," Master Endris asked, "Have I carried out the law?" To which Assum would have replied, "If you have executed what the law and the sentence require, then the law has been fulfilled."

This verbal exchange was critical for the execution to have fulfilled its purpose. At this moment the law, formally in suspense ever since Anna's arrest, had been restored. The breach in public order that had opened on Shrove Tuesday was now mended. Count Heinrich Friedrich had seen to it. The chief justice and the assessors filed back into town and into the courtroom. Once they took their seats, it was announced that justice had been done. A lavish feast awaited them.[18]

$$=$$

*B*y burning Anna and Barbara and burying their ashes at the gallows, the officials meant to erase every physical trace of the two women's lives. Yet in the seventeenth century every life was a moral lesson in one way or another, to anyone who paused to think about it. These lessons in life were meant to be told and retold. Lutheran funeral sermons aimed precisely at this transformation of a person's life into an exemplar of the Christian life.

Later that day of the executions, Pastor Wibel returned home to Bächlingen. He had visited Anna daily over the last week to ten days, working together with Court Preacher Dietzel in ministering to her, prodding her to confess, and moving her to repent and ask for divine mercy. It was his duty to record every baptism, marriage, and death in his parish. The entries usually mentioned just the bare facts of their lives. His entry for Anna Schmieg would be different. He wanted to make sure that anyone who read the death register in the future would know how to understand her life and death. Pastor Wibel opened the death register and pen in hand, wrote:

> The 8th of Nov. Elisabeth, Hans Schmieg the Miller of Hürden's wife, for sorcery and witchcraft, who 40 years ago gave herself to the devil at Regenbach, who did a great deal of various evil things over many years to people and cattle, bound at Langenburg to the stake and then strangled and burned.[19]

In this remarkable entry Wibel confidently summed up Anna Elisabeth Schmieg's life and death. She was no enigma to him. The events surrounding her—events that make up the last prosecuted incidents of witchcraft in the region—were to be understood as sorcery and witchcraft. He was among the last people to have talked to her, after all. He knew firsthand the tragic course of her last year. Through it, her identity—a terrible identity that had been kept secret, he believed, for forty years or more—had finally been revealed. Someone—it is not clear who—called attention to this entry by placing the large letters NB in the margins of the book.

While Pastor Wibel meant to end Anna Schmieg's life story with this short entry, it is doubtful that he had any idea that her story would not end there, that it would have unexpected echoes and consequences.

CHAPTER XVIII

Ruin

Langenburg, Hürden, and the Hohenlohe,
November 10, 1672–November 9, 1693

he executions of Anna Schmieg and Barbara Schleicher did not bring an end to the scare over sorcery, witchcraft, and poisoning in and around Langenburg. More plots were uncovered. The more serious problem in the aftermath of the executions involved ending trials for witchcraft throughout the territory and mending the breaches in the social and political fabric that had been torn open. The trials came to an end as village communities worked through the last, bitter social dynamics that had propelled the trials from the start. This occurred during the winter of 1672–73, after Anna's execution, with the Schmieg family unraveling in a final spasm of venomous recriminations and accusations.

The events that would wind down the scare revolved around Eva. Despite the mountain of records in which she figures so prominently, she may be the most difficult of all the people caught up in the witch panic to understand. The trial records and other records that mention her consistently cast her in a negative light: as a suspected witch, a loose and immoral young woman, a liar, at times a lost soul, perhaps even a mentally unbalanced individual. In contemporary terms she might be seen as traumatized and even self-destructive. While these judgments come easily to us today, accepting them uncritically would be wrong.

Throughout the tumultuous events of the last year and a half, Eva was actually doing what every young peasant woman tried to do: balance her desires for independence, affection, and support with the exacting demands of Lutheran moral discipline, parents, marriage, and property. The records of marriage courts from the seventeenth century are full of cases of young village women who, through a misjudgment, lack of support, or bad luck, failed to carry off the delicate balancing act necessary to navigate this important transition into adulthood. Within the norms thought to govern this stage of life, the surviving records make Eva appear to embody two moral extremes. On the one hand, she was defiant, self-indulgent, excessively independent, even reckless. When her father wished to arrange a favorable match for her with the son of the miller from the next village, she refused. That match could have secured the Schmiegs an alliance with the Preuningers from Bächlingen, thereby helping to consolidate their position in the region. Eva instead sought out her own partners, even facing scandal and shame for her actions.

On the other hand, Eva was close and loyal to her parents, especially to her mother. Even after she married, she and her new husband had lived at the mill with her parents in Hürden and then, when Philip had left the mill and pressured his wife to join him, she remained with her family, and as daughters are supposed to do, she helped with the many daily chores around the mill. The authorities had expressed the view that by placing devotion to her parents over her husband she had dishonored the estate of marriage. During her own trial for witchcraft and poisoning, moreover, she had defied the court's power and threats for a long time in order to protect her mother, before finally giving in and testifying against her. Perhaps these two traits—obedience to family and defiance of social norms—were closely related.

Whatever the case, along with these complicated feelings came one more: fear. She had been the object of her mother's venom. Eva herself had said she sensed this hostility, so much so that she refused to eat her mother's food. How the young woman ever came to terms with such a terrifying rejection is nowhere made clear. On the night of her release from prison she would relive this fear for her life in a way that would play itself out as the final undoing of her family.

═══

ON FRIDAY, November 15, one week after her mother's execution, Eva was set free from prison. As she later told the story to the authorities, she made her way that evening down the dark path from the town to Bächlingen and then on to Hürden and her parents' mill. When she entered the kitchen, she found her brother, Michel, with his new fiancée, Barbara Fleisch. From Eva's account there was immediate dislike and suspicion between her and Michel's fiancée. "You are an enemy to me," Eva recorded Barbara saying, "I don't like seeing you!" "Go away," Eva replied, and left the kitchen to take care of the cow in the barn. When she returned, she noticed that her brother and his fiancée had moved across the room to the bench and that a tankard of wine was waiting for her on the big kneading trough, probably the same one that her mother was said to have used to prepare the poisoned Shrove cakes. "Eva, there is a glass of wine, you said you were so thirsty," Barbara said to her. "Drink it up." When she drank from the glass, however, it tasted "like bitter gall" and she went outside to throw up. When she returned, Barbara taunted her. For several days, Eva reported, she felt fine, but then on the following Wednesday she had terrible pains in her stomach.

Her suspicions began to mount when she saw her brother that week acting anxious, as if he had a guilty conscience. She recalled that "since her imprisonment her brother Michel had said to her several times that her mother laid in wait for her many times, that she told him everything, and that once he wanted to try it out on her!" Perhaps thinking about the allegations that Michel helped her mother to prepare the poisoned Shrove cakes, she believed her brother and his fiancée were attempting to poison her now. She also reported that the couple had been sleeping together at the mill, taking over her father's room, and acting as if they were married and masters of the mill. On November 22 she went to Pastor Wibel with her accusations.[1] Her illness persisting off and on through the winter, she was given medications designed to purge the poison.

Court Adviser von Gülchen sent a team of court officers to Hürden to hear Eva's complaint in person. Losing no time, he had Michel and Barbara arrested and brought to Langenburg for interrogation.[2] For almost three months the pair would be held there, accused of violating the marriage laws and attempting to poison Eva.[3] In the background, unmentioned, was the suspicion that deadly witchcraft once again was in play.

The trigger for part of this new crisis involving the Schmiegs was once again a disputed courtship and marriage. Tied up in this, of course, was the unresolved matter of the inheritance of the mill at Hürden. Eva's illicit love affair and forced marriage to Philip Küstner had dragged her parents into approving a match they both actually resented, with Hans ultimately renouncing his promise to devolve half of the mill to Philip and Eva as their marriage portion. Michel's courtship of Barbara Fleisch began sometime during the investigation and trial of his parents. One could easily interpret this alliance—done without his family's approval—as an effort to take over the mill during the confusion occasioned by the trials. During the trial that followed, Eva protested—as one might expect—that she did not begrudge her brother the mill.[4] One should not take her protestations at face value, of course, since she had to prove to the court that no enmity lay behind her accusation. But there can be little doubt that her brother's alliance with Barbara Fleisch was a direct threat. Not only had Michel grown up at the mill and knew its operations, but he might be able to draw on Barbara's family connections in the neighboring county to raise money and support for the mill. Eva and her husband, Philip, stood to lose their share and perhaps any other inheritance.

Among the charges that Eva made against her brother and Barbara Fleisch was a violation of the marriage ordinance. One need not indulge in elaborate psychological explanations to see in this accusation Eva's fears that Michel and Barbara would not only take over the mill but assume the leading positions. The threat, Eva thought, was Barbara: it was she who urged her to drink the poisoned wine. There was little doubt that enmity lay between the two young women. Even Michel himself admitted early in the new interrogations that Barbara told him his sister was his enemy.[5] The poisoned drink—whether it was real or not—was once again an expression of the venomous relations within the Schmieg family.

As the trial wore on into February 1673, the parties stuck to their stories. Eva denounced their behavior as shocking and scandalous.[6] Michel and Barbara denied that they had tried to poison Eva and asserted that they had become engaged with the full knowledge and approval of Barbara's father. While Michel admitted that his mother strongly disapproved of the match when she had heard about it in prison, he related that his father not only knew of it but had relented and approved it. The couple's claims that they had not slept together were not quite as credible. The common custom in this part of Franconia was that engaged couples could sleep together so long as a marriage was planned. Still, punishments for illicit sexual relations were quite common.

In the villages around Langenburg the trial spawned new rumors and suspicions about the Schmiegs and witchcraft—suspicions that settled not on Michel and Barbara but on Eva. When the men from the surrounding villages were asked about Michel, they had little to say. He may have been obstinate and defiant. Some claimed he had a bad reputation like his father, but this kind of general report was too vague to be actionable.

Hans Barthel Walther related that Eva had returned from prison bragging that she was now a witch finder. She proved this new reputation, if not for spying out witches then for spitefulness, by denouncing two other women in the village for witchcraft. Leonhard Widman recounted how she had accused him to his face of slipping away at night to the witches' dance on the Katzenstein with her mother. In other reports Eva even accused Georg Heinckelin's wife (who had lost a child to a drowning accident near the mill), of killing her own children several years before. Regarding Michel, she spread stories that he was interested in cats, hinting that he was engaged in sorcery.[7] Perhaps she had returned from prison frightened and wary. Maybe she was getting revenge on her mother's tormentors. Only two people stuck by her. The district officer's wife, who ministered to her when she was ill, offered a sympathetic picture of her and her condition. Pastor Wibel showed understanding for her, confirming that she had been ill and saying that when her mother was spoken of she could not be moved, and even laughed, "as if she were sparing herself some sadness about her difficult situation."[8]

In Hürden itself Eva was increasingly seen as an irritant and a source of public disorder. One senses fear that she could use her credibility with the government to make new accusations and extend the trials even further. One hears in these accounts a pro-phylactic effort to protect themselves against her slander, to taint her reputation further as a means of self-protection.

Then came the surprise: After many interrogations Michel Schmieg confessed. On January 12, 1673, he admitted putting poison into his sister's wine that Friday night when she had come home from Langenburg. Moreover, he said he used the same pow-dered poison his mother had given him for the Shrovetide cakes. He exculpated his fiancée, saying she knew nothing of the plot.[9] Michel's confession may have been true or he may simply have lost hope of getting out of prison. He may even have figured that if he confessed, he could clear Barbara's name.

---

*I*N THE meantime, the insinuations against Michel's father, Hans, intensified. The accusations surrounding him had always been closely related to those against his wife. Like the suspicions against his wife, that witchcraft and sorcery ran deep within the Schmieg family, fears had been driven by villagers who suspected him of harming them. They had been reawakened in late July and August when Hans was overheard to be plotting revenge against the Heinckelins for testifying against his wife, and the court had pun-ished him in September for "use of magical objects" and released him.[10]

Suspicions lingered, however, especially among his old enemies in Bächlingen. On November 12—four days after his wife's execution and the same day his daughter was released and returned to Hürden—Hans was arrested on new suspicions of sorcery and possible witchcraft. Since that time he had languished in prison in Langenburg.

The suspicions against Hans reveal how much villagers distinguished different types of sorcery and witchcraft based, in part, on the kinds of work that men and women performed. The accusations against Anna had involved food, health, and reproduction.[11] In contrast, these involved his work as a miller. He was suspected of using sorcery to repair and protect the millwheels in their daily operation. Whereas local women exhibited most of the animus against Anna, those who accused Hans tended to come from farther afield, a fact that mirrored the wider circuit of his work and contacts as a miller compared to the contacts his wife nurtured in Hürden. The suspicions against Hans never had quite the same intensity, or density of social interactions, as did those focused on Anna. Instead they tended to focus on objects of exchange within the barter and market economy: cats, the mandrake, illicit trade in grain and cattle.

The case against Hans illustrates not only a persistent ambivalence surrounding particular cultural practices among villagers, but that this ambivalence could be mobilized for opportunistic purposes. Before the Thirty Years' War the clergy pressed villagers about "magical and superstitious practices." By the time of Hans's case the tendency to view certain magical practices as potentially diabolical had spread more widely. While it may be a change within the culture, it also suggests a certain opportunism among villagers who knew how to manipulate these attitudes to denounce their enemies. The accusation that landed Hans Schmieg in prison this second time, for example, involved an old magical practice. His new accuser, Martin Stütz of Bächlingen, accused Hans of locking the door of his cottage with a charm when Hans passed three times through a twisted tree, invoking the name of the devil each time.[12] Had this account come to light during a routine church visitation, it would likely have earned a reprimand to leave off the magic and superstition. Within the current charged context, however, the accusation was enough to start anew the investigation against Hans.

Using sorcery and possibly witchcraft, Hans, so the Langenburg court suspected, may have planned to spring his convicted wife from prison, strip the mill of its possessions, then move away and carry out a sustained campaign of revenge against the Schmiegs' enemies. Popular suspicion fell on the Schmieg children, Michel and perhaps even Eva, as co-conspirators. The court turned up evidence that Hans may have enlisted the help of Kling Appel from Dörnmütz to provide a charm that would unlock doors to help Anna flee from prison in October. Appel's reputation as a cunning woman—she said she only helped "people with a good heart"—had drawn villagers to Dörnmütz for years.[13] As payment, Hans allegedly smuggled Anna's church coat out of prison and gave it to her. In the meantime, he and Michel were spiriting their belongings out of the mill and sending them to family members in the distant villages of Pfedelbach and Berndshofen. Depending on who told the story, the plot may also have involved Eva. Once Anna escaped prison, the Schmiegs would flee the territory.

Suspicion eventually also fell on Master Endris. He was not only related to Hans, but was one of the few Langenburgers to keep his company on occasion. Fuchs's access to the prison and reputation for knowing magical charms suggested that he could be of help. Hans himself implicated Fuchs, raising the possibility that he was seeking revenge for the harm Fuchs had done to his entire family. At the initial hearing on November 12, Hans accused Fuchs of teaching him the charm.[14] As the witch finder who had helped start the panic, Fuchs was now in danger of becoming one of its victims.

Once the court gained a rough idea about the allegations against Hans, he was left in prison until the court was ready to press the investigation seriously. Once Michel confessed and awaited a special inquisition into his crimes as "a witch master," the court renewed its questioning of Hans. On February 13 the court pressed him on several matters: his activities with magical objects like the mandrake and cat heads, the charms he had learned, and the possibility of a wider conspiracy involving the mill and revenge against his neighbors.[15] The old miller refused to break. In a conversation overheard by a guard, Hans told Michel that all was lost. The court would never relent. He despaired of ever being free again.[16]

———

THE TRIALS of the Schmiegs came to an abrupt and surprising end. On the night of February 16 father and son slipped out of their prison cells, climbed over the town walls, and fled into the night.[17] Their daring escape stirred the court and raised additional fears. To von Gülchen the Schmiegs' escape pointed to their "guilty consciences" and he sent out alerts to all of the territory's districts and neighboring lordships to be on the watch for the pair. Had they escaped through their cunning? Negligence on the part of the watchman? Or had someone with access to the prison and the keys helped them? One cannot help but suspect that Hans and Michel escaped with help from inside the palace. Perhaps they bribed the jailer or played on his sympathy. After all, the jailer had let Hans get food and wine to Anna when she had been locked up. It is even possible that Endris Fuchs let them out. The escape conveniently removed Hans as the only witness to testify against Fuchs and his magical arts.[18] For his negligence the guard came under investigation and was eventually fined.[19] While von Gülchen continued to hunt for them, the Schmiegs vanished.

Well into the summer of 1673 and even into the following winter, the fears about the old miller-sorcerer and his "witch master" son lingered. The authorities were afraid that such diabolical criminals might return to make good on their threats of revenge. Rumors had the two in disguise moving secretly between villages in the next territory near Ingelfingen, about eight to ten miles from Hürden.[20] Hans was described as "cleanly shaven around the mouth" and wearing a green cloak and black hat.[21] Other rumors told of Hans visiting his brother in nearby Berndshofen or even meeting secretly with Anna's aunt near Amlishagen in Blaubach.[22] Naturally, Eva, the only surviving member of the Schmieg family in the district, was thought to know their whereabouts. And she

proclaimed she did. When questioned by the authorities, she said
that Hans and Michel had moved among relatives and friends in
Orlach and Jungholtzhausen, eventually making their way to Heidelberg, where they were working in a sawmill.[23] Father and son
had disappeared and would never be heard from again.[24]

————

*W*HY DID these rumors generate such a reaction from the
authorities? Certainly they wanted to arrest two dangerous fugitives from justice. A more pressing concern lay behind the alarm,
however: the mill at Hürden. Hans Schmieg had threatened to
burn it down, and the government was concerned that he just
might make good on his threat.

In one way or another, the mill had stirred the strongest, most
enduring, and most contested emotions during the entire Schmieg
trials. The whole affair revolved around its disposition. Of course,
the government had also seized the property of Barbara Schleicher
in Atzenrod, and it made sure that her house and land had been
sold off and occupied again. But hers was not nearly as vital a part
of the seigniorial and village order as the mill at Hürden. The property was not simply the patrimony of the Schmiegs. It anchored
the village of Hürden, along with the surrounding communities,
and the economic and social relationships that tied into it. For
Heinrich Friedrich it was one of the district's largest properties and
a source of rents and dues. Its vital and inherent function was the
milling of grain and its distribution in the region. For all these reasons the Langenburg government intervened soon after Anna
Schmieg's execution in order to arrange the disposition of the
property. If the breech in the rural social order was to be healed, it
would be healed here.

The government worked for almost a year arranging the sale of
the mill. In fact, Court Adviser von Gülchen took extraordinary
interest in the mill and, in particular, in a fair and just settlement for
Eva and her husband.[25] Von Gülchen's work had begun with getting estimates about the cost of the mill and checking the surveys
of the land that belonged to it. He had Hans's debts on the mill tal-

lied. In addition, the costs of the trials had to be figured in. An extra problem was that the mill was run-down and in need of repair. Ironically, one of the bids would come from Moses Preuninger, the Bächlingen miller. Had Hans Schmieg had his way, Preuninger's son would have made the ideal husband for Eva. So Preuninger's interest in the mill at Hürden went back at least a couple of years. In making his bid Preuninger described the mill this way: "Not only the house but the barn too is completely run-down, and indeed falling into ruins almost by the hour. The millwork itself, the millrace, the stones, and the wheels are in such bad shape that they also must be repaired. It will take a considerable sum of money [to fix it all up.]"[26]

As an experienced miller, Preuninger knew what he was talking about. He was also a shrewd bargain hunter. His bid of 550 gulden for the mill was 350 gulden less than Hans had paid for it more than twenty years ago. Even though von Gülchen and Heinrich Friedrich favored settling the mill on Eva and Philip Küstner, the couple could not come up with the necessary money.[27] In July 1673, Preuninger won the bid and, as the mill passed into his possession, rumors of Hans Schmieg's ghostly appearances began to make the rounds. Hans Barthel Walther and Leonhard Widman, Hans's old enemies from Hürden, seem to have been the authors of these sightings.[28] Perhaps their fears were triggered by the change of guard at the mill. Or perhaps they simply wanted to make sure that a vigilant eye kept the sly old miller and his son away.

In all of these events after Anna Schmieg's trial, one can see the extremely meticulous hand of the authorities intervening to restore order. While the Langenburg court ruthlessly pursued Hans and Michel, raising the prospect of spreading additional fears of witchcraft, Heinrich Friedrich's officers refused to allow new suspicions to grow into additional witch trials. Their restraint helped end the accusations. Instead of pursuing the possibility of witchcraft in a number of new directions—Eva Küstner, Endris Fuchs, Kling Appel, or Barbara Fleisch—they simply did not follow up. It was not for lack of evidence or for a lack of belief in witchcraft. Count Heinrich Friedrich and his court advisers simply wanted to restore order after all of the confusion of the last several years.

The officers worked toward that end in countless small ways. When the Hürdeners denounced Eva, von Gülchen intervened. In the course of her trial, it seems the court adviser developed some protective instincts toward the young woman. In return for the testimony that was bought at such a high price, he had promised aid and mercy. He forced the young woman's detractors to apologize, pressed them to forgiveness, and reconciliation with Eva. No more rumors of her being a witch made it to official ears after that.

When the government settled the mill, its debts, and inheritance obligations, it restored a web of relationships that had been strained or destroyed by the witch trials. Once a source of controversy and fears, the mill became ordinary once more. The Langenburg chancellery reached right down to the level of issuing orders about how to distribute the smallest items from the old mill—bedding, utensils, and chickens and geese, among other things—exercising its power to turn conflict into gratitude and indebtedness.

———

*T*HE RUIN that settled on the Schmieg family eventually touched Eva almost as disastrously as it did her father and brother. When the mill passed out of the Schmiegs' hands, she lost land, social position, and a secure income. From the home where she had grown up, Eva took away a bed, bed linens, utensils, a cow, fodder, some chickens and geese. She did secure the remaining share of her inheritance from the mill—200 gulden and a claim to an annuity on the mill's kitchen garden—to be paid out to her and her young daughter, Margaretha, over a number of years as an inheritance. Other than this, however, she had been forced to leave her family home and move in with her husband and his parents in their house in Nesselbach.

Eva found neither support nor stability in her marriage. The evidence suggests that she and Philip never fully reconciled after the marriage settlement came apart in the winter of 1671–72. In fact, she admitted to seeing other men and expressed a desire to leave Philip. In the bits and pieces of testimony from the time after the

execution of her mother, it is clear that she kept her distance from
Philip. In July 1673 her great-aunt explained

> that he treated her harshly on account of her and her father's deal-
> ings, but she was not to blame for that. She therefore came to me
> to complain bitterly and ask that I come once to see her. If her hus-
> band cannot mend his ways, then she cannot stay with him. At
> which she [the great aunt] advised Eva that she cite her husband
> before the government, but the young woman said she had already
> done so, that nothing would help.[29]

The final breach in their marriage came in 1675. By this time
she had given birth to two more children, a second daughter, Barbara, and a son, Hans Jörg.[30] Late in 1674 the war with France had
also widened. When Saxon troops moved into Langenburg territory and set up camp near Nesselbach, Eva had a scandalous affair
with one of the soldiers. On January 16, 1675, Eva's mother-in-law
appeared before Pastor Wibel to charge her daughter-in-law with
sleeping with the regimental musician.[31] The taint of witchcraft
clung to Eva's reputation, and one can see evidence of the heavy
prejudices against her everywhere in the records about this affair.
Once sympathetic to the young woman and otherwise restrained
in his reports, Pastor Wibel referred harshly to her as "the witch
from Hürden" in his account to the chancellery. The case then
went to the marriage court, where the old stories about her reputation as loose and wild, as a whore and adulterer, now returned.

The remarkable thing about the protocols of this investigation is
that all of the parties, Eva included, basically agreed that she had
openly broken her marriage vows. The soldier, a trumpeter in a
Saxon regiment, had been billeted in the Küstner household. Eva
told the story to the marriage court this way:

> On Thursday, that is, two days before the Saxon people were to
> break camp in Nesselbach, she and the trumpeter had a glass of
> wine at her father-in-law's house. In the evening she had to feed
> the cattle as usual. After that he asked her to sleep with him. He
> wanted to give her money. She refused him, and said that she has a

husband. But he came to her in the night and fell into her bed. The room had no door. As he laid down next to her in the bed, he said to her that she should sleep with him. She said no. But he stayed with her for half an hour. He only did it with her one time. And gave her only half a gulden and 3 batzen. The next day the young man came to her and said that she should give back the money that he had given her. She didn't want to. But she finally gave back the 3 batzen.[32]

One cannot easily sort out Eva's part in this affair. She had never internalized the sexual restraint and discipline that the marriage ordinance demanded. She never reconciled with Philip. She seems to have considered married life under the authority of the Küstners in Nesselbach burdensome and oppressive. Her in-laws, not surprisingly, never ceased to make clear their displeasure with her and repeatedly condemned her for loose morals. To escape she admitted she often went out at night, seeking the company of other men. Philip said she could have protected herself by sleeping in the room in the house that had a key.[33] We might see the affair as a rape, although Eva gives no evidence of such coercion or violence. In fact, the money that changed hands suggests that she might even have been engaging in prostitution. The Küstners closed ranks against her with Philip testifying that he did not want her as his wife any longer and admitting that they had not slept together as man and wife ever since she had told him of the affair.[34] As far as he was concerned, the marriage was at an end.

Count Heinrich Friedrich, in turn, decreed on March 20 that Eva "has broken the Sixth Commandment, her marital duty and loyalty, all Christian discipline and violated and mishandled her honor." Because her husband refused to reconcile with her, the prince formally declared them divorced. Then the hard judgment fell. Eva was to be banished permanently from Hohenlohe. She was granted the right to assign her 10-gulden annuity from the mill at Hürden to Philip and the children, and she was allowed to take 3 or 4 gulden with her when she left. The remainder of her belongings were forfeit.[35]

Eva expressed only one wish: a chance to say goodbye to her

children. So, on March 22, in the presence of the district officer and the Küstners—her in-laws did not trust her—she bid farewell to them. She gathered up most of her clothes but left them her coat and a few other things.[36]

———

*E*VA'S FATE after she left Nesselbach in March 1675 remains largely a mystery. Yet there is a hint that she eventually found a measure of stability after all.

In November 1693—eighteen years after she left the territory—a letter arrived at the Langenburg chancellery. It had been written on Eva's behalf by a notary in Heilbronn, the imperial city about thirty miles to the west. Eva did not explain her life in any detail, only that she had been living there for a long time and worked as a servant for Heilbronn's mayor. Honorable witnesses, the mayor included, she said, could testify to her improved character, even though "it is written that my parents have a terrible name and reputation." She was writing on behalf of her son, Hans Jörg. When the mill at Hürden was sold, it was agreed that her own inheritance from it—about 200 gulden at the time—would go to her children. Her daughter Margaretha, the daughter born shortly after she married Philip, had been secure in this inheritance. But she wanted to advance the claim of her son so that he would get his fair share.[37]

One of the many tragedies associated with the Schmieg family then repeated itself. Eva had a broken relationship with her mother, Anna, and that conflict had spilled over into the terrible events of 1672. Now Eva entered into a conflict with her own daughter, Margaretha.[38] The alienation apparently dated from the time that Eva had been forced to abandon the girl in 1675. Her father-in-law, Conrad Küstner, had raised Margaretha and looked after her interests. That was due to the dissolute life that Eva's former husband, Philip, had fallen into after his marriage to Eva was dissolved. In 1676 he was cited for once again getting a servant girl pregnant out of wedlock, fled the country and returned, under humiliating circumstances.[39] In any event, Margaretha disputed her mother's claim that she had a brother at all. She claimed that her mother must have had the boy with another man long after she had left Nesselbach.[40]

The dispute dragged on for several years, Eva never clearly establishing the right of her son to acquire a share of the mill. The whole affair, in fact, slipped into the wearisome kind of dispute over money and inheritance so common to the region. One of the ways that families were defined, after all, was in their claims to a common property and the right to gain access to it. Property disputes made and unmade families in Hohenlohe.

Margaretha eventually married. We will never know what she was told about her grandmother and mother or the witch scare of 1668–72. What we do know is that despite the fact that she never remembered her grandmother, she remained deeply attached to Anna's herb garden at the mill and the income it generated. The small plot drew an income of only 10 gulden a year. She fought fiercely for it, seeking justice in her claim. Margaretha's was the last recorded claim a descendant of the Schmiegs had on the old mill and what little remained of Anna Schmieg's property.

CHAPTER XIX

Stories

or a few more years, accounts that might revive memories of Anna and her witchcraft circulated in the region. Like the stories about Turk Anna, the reports of Anna Schmieg had the potential to frame perceptions of otherwise inexplicable misfortunes or to stir fears about other witches. In the tales about the disappearance of Hans and Michel Schmieg, such memories of Anna had played a part. When the authorities accused Eva of adultery, Pastor Wibel and others recalled Anna, associating Anna's reputation for witchcraft with Eva, which contributed to the decision to banish her from the land. Rumors about other witches might also stir memories of Anna Schmieg. Around the time of Eva's banishment in 1675 villagers near Ingelfingen—a small town associated with rumors sighting Hans and Michel Schmieg—told church officials about a Gypsy woman thought to be practicing sorcery and witchcraft. From Crispenhofen came a more detailed account about "people who bought from a woman a mandrake and roots to use on their cows, and these roots caused the milk to sour."[1] In 1677–78 a formal accusation of witchcraft was leveled against Barbara Kutterolf of Langenburg. The court unmasked the accuser as a liar, full of malice, and motivated by personal gain.[2] In the end, these opportunities to use Anna's memory to stir new accusations of witch-craft went nowhere.

Two contemporary stories about Anna Schmieg's life and death survived, however. Both of them were *official* stories and therefore served *public* ends. Out of Anna's trial records came the Langenburg state account. Composed as Anna's official confession to witch-craft, it was posted around the town of Langenburg and perhaps elsewhere for the public to read and then affixed to the official trial dossier in the chancellery. This official record was one more way the government healed the breach in the body politic. Details of Anna's life were adapted to the familiar German Baroque story of the witch: a terrifying moral tale about a mother and neighbor turned evil through diabolical seduction, apostasy, bondage to the devil, and a lifetime of secret and heinous crimes. The account not only justified her conviction and execution, but proved once again the threat of witchcraft to the state and Christian society and legit-imized the government's authority to protect itself and its people from this menace. Court Adviser von Gülchen had written it, but without the cacophony of voices—rumors, depositions, reports, testimonies, interrogations, and uncertain medical opinions and dissenting legal voices—that might undermine its stability or authority.[3] His authorship remained hidden from public view, thereby lending it authenticity and unquestionable authority.

By the 1680s other events had overtaken Langenburg, and the official account of Anna Schmieg faded into the territory's past. These changes were the by-product of developments unrelated to the witch trials. Once France invaded Holland, the standoff between France and the Holy Roman Empire and the Habsburg monarchy that had contributed to the atmosphere of tension in Langenburg gave way to open war in 1674. Langenburg turned its attention to all of the pressing matters that came with it: the quartering of troops, the levying of taxes, and so on. In 1675, Court Adviser von Gülchen, so pivotal in carrying out the witch trials, died. Heinrich Friedrich's trusted minister had been not only experienced with witch trials, but also a leader who tended to see the administration of the law through the lens of Lutheran penitential theology. His successor had another worldview. That

same year Count Joachim Albrecht died, and the Kirchberg lands
fell to Heinrich Friedrich and Langenburg. While retaining a
powerful sense of his world as imperiled, the count devoted the
rest of his reign to consolidating the pieces into a new state. He
died in 1699.

Even when it underwent sweeping changes, a small territory
like Langenburg guarded its records and official accounts fiercely.
In the old regime, archives were instruments of rule. They were
legal expressions of dynastic power, privileges, and freedoms. Not
all accounts of criminal trials came to be identified as so vital in
serving these state purposes that they were marked for preserva-
tion. Anna Schmieg's was one, however. Beginning around 1680,
the Langenburg chancellery officials undertook a reordering of all
of the state's records. When this process was completed in 1701,
they had created the Common Archive of Langenburg, which
remains largely intact to the present day.[4] Top among the eight categories of records were those pertaining to the "Privileges and
Freedoms of the Counts of Hohenlohe." Next came the chancellery records themselves, organized by historical periods. Within
the next, and probably largest, subset of records, "General Administration of the County of Langenburg," were the court records.
Here Anna Schmieg's dossier found its place. No longer classed
narrowly as a "witch," her account was listed as one of a few hundred "criminal cases."[5]

The archivist placed a cover sheet describing her case this way:
"Concerning: Elisabeth Schmieg, the miller's wife from Hürden,
shown occupied with witchcraft, and who, through magical
means, executed people and cattle, on which account she was convicted and burned."[6]

This unknown chancellery official was the first to present the
trial in rough chronological fashion. Court Adviser von Gülchen
grasped the trial as a sequence of legal acts, roughly divided into
the steps of a General Inquisition and then a special one. The
archivist thought in these legal terms, too, but he arranged the documents by their dates, beginning with the first official report of
Anna Fessler's death. Each of the 139 pieces of the dossier were
placed in virtually perfect chronological sequence. Each document

represented one distinctive administrative act. This cataloguing did not set a new interpretation on Anna's life and trial, yet perhaps for the first time chancellery officials who glanced through the dossier could see her trial as an unfolding of separate legal acts. The mass of details was now subsumed into a legal-administrative testament to Langenburg and imperial justice.

Other contemporary accounts of Anna Schmieg's life also survived: short notices about her death preserved in Lutheran church records became the basis for new stories in the eighteenth century. Pastor Wibel's entry in the parish death register may have been short, but over the years as additional entries were made, it also stood out as the biography of Bächlingen's only witch. His account of Anna's life therefore served as a reminder of the cosmic struggle with Satan that had reached right into the lives of the members of Bächlingen's parish. Ironically, Bächlingen's most notorious parishioner had become one of its best remembered.

Later, around 1750, one of Pastor Wibel's descendants served as court preacher at Langenburg. Johann Christoph Wibel, a formidable Lutheran churchman not only entered the bitter fight with Hohenlohe's Catholics in the Great Easter Conflict (1744–50), but also shored up the Lutheran Church, systematizing Langenburg's church administration and writing the first Protestant church history of the land in three volumes.[7]

New stories about Langenburg's witches—Anna Schmieg among them—served Wibel's purposes perfectly. He cited them as an example when he wrote up advice for pastors about the difficult task of counseling criminals, cautioning his successors: in this pastoral mission you will encounter apostates, servants of the devil, the most heinous sinners of all.[8] They, too, merited the pastor's compassion and instruction.

In his history of the church in Hohenlohe he held up the witches as examples of the evil that Satan had visited on the land. While in general he noted that Hohenlohers had been sober churchgoers, he wrote that occasionally "fanaticism" arose. Concerned about the new threat of Pietism and "religious enthusiasm" in general, Wibel placed the witches of Langenburg in a long line of "sectarians" and "false prophets," noting that "various women,

five altogether, were burned in Langenburg for their admitted sorcery and poisonings."[9]

While brief, the references to Anna Schmieg and the other
witches became factual evidence in a story of the triumph of
Protestantism and the Reformation. But Wibel described Langenburg's witches only as nameless "various old women" who were
only one of God's scourges, listing beside them other natural
calamities like wars, pestilence, storms, earthquakes, and cattle diseases.[10] Wibel called pious readers to take particular note: These
stories "should serve as an encouragement to us, to turn from all
ungratefulness toward God and his sacred Word, the pure Evangel-
ical teaching, to which we confess and adorn us with a holy conversion so that faith and conscience are preserved to the end."[11]
Scripture still attested to the dangers of sorcery and witchcraft.[12]

———

By the early 1800s, witches were no longer incontrovertible
facts, however. For a century or more the stories about Anna
Schmieg and Langenburg's witches were no longer cited. Between
1906 and 1913, however, that changed in a sensational way. The
Langenburg witches and Anna Schmieg were given three new stories for a modern society. Through them Anna Schmieg became a
mythical figure, a local heroine, a martyr, a saint.

The creator of these new stories was Agnes Günther. Born in
1863 in Stuttgart, and married to a Lutheran theologian and deacon, Günther came to Langenburg in 1891.[13] She was a pious
Lutheran, but her piety drew not from the orthodox tradition but
from the more emotional, subjective, even mystical strains of
Lutheran Pietism.[14]

Enriching this piety was experience of the spirit world. Günther's spirit guide, Gisela, was a life-long companion, and the inspiration for her literary works and the central figure haunting them.
This spirit guide had a previous life in Langenburg in the seventeenth century, where she was persecuted as a witch and burned.
Agnes Günther then created a literary figure, also called Gisela, part
spirit, part historical figure. Already in 1903 Günther's husband,

Rudolf, was incorporating into his written work and public lectures references to the records of Anna Schmieg and Barbara Schleicher and the terrible "witch madness" that had seized people.[15] "The fear of witches must have run through the people like an infectious epidemic," he wrote.[16] Günther alluded to the impact that the records of this time had on her in her 1913 play *On the Witch Who Was a Saint* (*Von der Hexe die eine Heilige war*):

> It was a terrible and bitter time in the German land. Smouldering fires where witches were burned marred the landscape and an unspeakable lament rose to heaven—dripping blood from her hands, and eyes seeing far into the distance—that was the witch. And a knight hid and protected her . . . ; in a small princely residence town [Langenburg] two hours away. Looking into the many old strewn about papers, makes the heart beat with rage today.[17]

The "old papers" were the records of Anna Schmieg's and Barbara Schleicher's trials for witchcraft in 1672.

‎———

*G*ÜNTHER CONCEIVED her first literary work, a play called *The Witch* (*Die Hexe*), while imagining herself in the terrible circumstances of Anna Schmieg and Barbara Schleicher.[18] That these two women were victims of ignorance, persecution, and superstition went without saying. For Günther the primary inspiration for her work was her spirit guide, Gisela, not the trial records. On February 16 and 19, 1906, Günther staged her play, in the Langenburg Palace. Newspaper accounts reported that the great hall was overflowing, that the effect of the play on the audience was stunning. It recounted the story of Gisela, young Countess of Thorstein, an orphan at the time of the Thirty Years' War. Her affinity with nature and deep piety attracts suspicions of witchcraft. Even her protector, the Count of Brauneck, is worried and keeps her apart from him in a separate room of the castle. When a hailstorm destroys the crops, the peasants blame Gisela for their misfortune and clamor for her to be tried as a witch. Giving in to the mob, the count has his son, Heinz, and the court preacher interrogate Gisela. Later, left alone in a chamber of the castle, she is tortured by an evil woman who tries to pry from her the secrets of witchcraft. Heinz, now obviously in love with Gisela, rescues her and takes her to a nearby castle, where she is nursed back to health. At the end of the story, however, the witch-hating peasants storm the castle, the young count and his father coming too late to save her. In her dying gasp Gisela pleads that the count treat the poor ignorant peasants with mercy. Her last act is that of a saint.[19]

Günther incorporated Gisela—the Langenburg witch—into two additional literary works that appeared in 1913. *The Witch Who Was a Saint* opens with Gisela in a castle. It then moves to Heaven, where Gisela has a conversation with an angel called "Suffering" in which she describes the senseless cruelty and persecution she had experienced. She is told that she is "no poor butterfly crushed in the dust. You are an actor in a theater for the gods and human-kind."[20] Gisela then relates her retreat to the Castle of Silence, where bread appears magically in her hands as she distributes it to children. Her lover, Count Heinz—her "fool"—had rescued her and consoled her. Later, when she had been burned at the stake, Heinz bends over her and weeps. Taking solace in God's eternal bread, Gisela, dying, asks God's blessing on the fields and the poor who draw sustenance from it:

> And now come, all of you, and take the bread! You who are tired, old, the widow with the careworn face, the poor servant girl marked by suffering, come through summer and winter, through good years and bad years. I see you coming, a long procession, span-ning the centuries. . . . My body has long fallen into ashes, no one recalls the witch any longer. Come and take this, the bread that gives you love.[21]

No longer a destroyer of human life, she is Ceres, the goddess of grain, a transfigured saint who sustains it. Hers was a model Chris-tian soul who knows the suffering of the world and sacrifices her-self for others. She becomes the bread of life.

Even more popular was Günther's novel, *The Saint and her Fool.*

Its sensational effect on its readers, primarily women, helped make it into one of the most widely read sentimental novels of the first half of the twentieth century. Günther had begun to conceive this story while staging her earlier play in 1906. Set in the present, it tells the story of Rosemarie, a princess of Brauneck (Langenburg) who grows up so sensitive and inward-looking that her father and stepmother consider her abnormal. Harro, count of nearby Thorstein, befriends and encourages her visions. Their budding romance is ripped apart by father and step-mother, Charlotte. Rosemarie is eventually reunited with Harro, and they marry. It becomes clear that Rosemarie, who increasingly has visions of Gisela, not only embodies the spirit of Gisela, but her husband has mystical connections with Gisela's lover. In a hunting accident Princess Charlotte kills Rosemarie. Before she dies, the union of Gisela/Rosemarie with Heinrich Friedrich/Harro is brought to a spiritual climax.[22]

Highbrow literary critics deplored the novel's sentimentality, dismissing it as kitsch. That did not stop its success: *The Saint and her Fool* went through over 140 editions, selling more than a million copies.[23] Film versions were made in 1928, 1935, and 1957. Drawing thousands of visitors, Langenburg became a popular destination for travelers inspired by the story's loving depiction of the town and its environs as the quintessential German *Heimat*, or homeland. So complete is the literary magic that some visitors to Langenburg are shocked to learn that no countess of Langenburg has ever been a witch.[24]

Günther struck a nerve in the German reading public. In an era of industrialization, urbanization, the emergence of a working class, and challenges to women's roles, some writers embraced the "new woman" of the twentieth century. Others, like Günther, looked to the past for conservative models of feminine virtue.[25] Her heroines embodied idealized virtues from an age that was ending: gentleness, deference, self-sacrifice, stillness, piety, but with a powerful inner vision.[26] Given not only rapid change but also the ordeals of World War I, the Weimar Republic, and the Nazi era, this positive treatment of suffering and sacrifice appealed to many women. Clearly, too, the evocation of a landscape arousing deep attachments to home resonated with the *Heimat* movement of the time.[27]

The novel was also buoyed by the discovery of the "witch craze" in the late nineteenth and early twentieth centuries. Witches became heroines of the homeland movement, local figures who could counterbalance a masculine German nationalism that played down regional identities and traditions.[28] Taking the lead in creating these new images of witches were local historians, civil servants, schoolteachers, and church pastors who rummaged through archives and published accounts in newspapers and the reports of local historical societies.[29]

---

*T*ODAY, AGNES Günther's Gisela is but one of several images of Anna Schmieg and the Langenburg witches. Some are historical fragments, others draw on folklore; still others circulate quietly among neighbors. The forms are just as varied: a play, historical entries in travel books, a display in a museum exhibition, academic articles and books. Like Günther's tale, they blur the line between history and fiction.

The most coherent and clearly formulated of these new stories was written and staged in the late 1950s: *The Witch from Hürden: A Play for the Homeland*.[30] Like Günther, the play's author, Frau Ingaruth Schlauch, was a Lutheran clergyman's wife. Also, like Günther, the stimulus for her work came from reading church records: Pastor Wibel's old death notice about Anna Schmieg.[31] She, too, took the historical facts to draw moral lessons about her time.

In the late 1940s and 1950s, a wave of refugees, many of them displaced from eastern Germany at the end of World War II, settled in Hohenlohe's close-knit villages and small towns. Many pastors helped ease the tensions created by this immigration and integrate the newcomers into community life. Such was the purpose of Schlauch's new play, performed in the parish of Bächlingen in the late 1950s.[32]

The drama was set in Germany after the Thirty Years' War, with its hardship and the settling of foreigners in the region. It opens with villagers in Bächlingen blaming their misfortune in a recent storm and flood on the witchcraft of the miller's wife, Ursula Schmieg from nearby Hürden. Schmieg, we soon learn, is a stranger who had made a fortunate match with the miller. She is proud, educated, and has a disturbing way of teasing the locals about their superstitious beliefs. Her directness is misunderstood. She is a healer and a wise woman. Secretly neighbors come to her for help. When she jokingly advises a young maid how to win over a wealthy peasant, the rumor circulates that she uses love magic. The neighbors—some of them the very same neighbors who had privately welcomed her help—gather at the tavern and denounce her for witchcraft.

In this play Ursula Schmieg is a beacon of enlightenment. At her trial she chastises the court judge for his ignorance and cowardice: "I expected better than this from the likes of you. You are possessed by superstition. Indeed to you, so well educated, I speak, I plead, you can't be serious. You must know that there are no witches!" As her accusers come before the court, she offers calm and reasonable explanations. Instead of using his reason, the judge, reading the notorious passages about women and witchcraft from the *Malleus Maleficarum*, condemns her for witchcraft. But in contrast to Günther's tale of Gisela, this play ends on a happy note. Dressed in white like a queen and saint, invoking memories of Gisela going to the pyre, Ursula Schmieg goes to the marketplace to meet her fate without fear. Then the count arrives and sets her free, condemning the judge for stirring up the mob: "Are you listening to these people's gossip? . . . You're pandering to [prejudiced and ignorant] people." In another gesture reminiscent of Gisela, Ursula invokes the count's mercy to forgive the people.

Around the same time, more clearly historical references to Anna Schmieg became a small but firm part of local history. The same longing for regional identity that Agnes Günther had drawn on was now being used to forge local identities firmly set within the new Federal Republic of Germany. In introducing Franconian Hohenlohe to readers, for example, Rudolf Schlauch, Ingaruth's husband, drew on the memory of Anna Schmieg to illustrate part of the region's past. His work emphasized the close identification of the ruling House of Hohenlohe with the land, towns, villages, and people.[33] Pride of place went to Langenburg, its castle, and the other castles of the region. But he also pointed out the beauty of the Jagst Valley, in particular, the scenic mills along the river's course. He wrote of Hürden's mill and the history of the Schmieg family.[34]

In the 1980s and 1990s a series of widely visited museum exhibitions on witchcraft and the witch hunt circulated in Germany. These exhibitions typically displayed trial records, commentaries by academic historians, material artifacts, paintings, woodcut images, newspaper accounts, literary images, fictional accounts, images from fairy tales and children's books, and even films. While historians and archivists guided visitors to view these materials in light of academic historical research, the complex juxtaposition of artifacts, documents, and images created multiple, sometimes even contradictory, impressions of witchcraft.

In one exhibit in Schwäbisch Hall Anna Schmieg became a complicated emblem of Hohenlohe's witchcraft persecution. The 1988 exhibit represented the first public effort aimed at integrating local witch stories into the regional history of the Swabian-Franconian borderlands. In the exhibition catalog, historians and archivists emphasized a historical understanding of witchcraft.[35] One section of the exhibit included Anna Schmieg's trial records: the decree announcing her and Barbara Schleicher's judgment, the description of Schleicher's sack of herbs, and the thick bundle of archival records of Schmieg's trial.[36] At some points witches were presented as innocent victims of a blind and cruel legal system. Other times, witches appeared as scary figures from Grimm's fairy tales. In yet others the image of the witch as a wise woman and healer, repressed by male physicians, was emphasized. And in the folklore section one could view a picture of Bächlingen and Hürden, where locals still knew about Anna Schmieg as a witch and "where one today still hears reports of superstition and customary practices aimed at protection against witches."[37]

What accounts for the resurrection of these stories about Anna Schmieg and the Langenburg witches? The desire for regional identity remains strong, and regional history bolsters those identities, which balance the complex and changing national identity of modern Germans. In a Germany still coming to terms with its Nazi past and the persecutions of Jews, foreigners, and other minorities, the trials of witches can hold up a sobering lesson about what happens when prejudice and zeal take over the legal machinery of the state. But the witch can stand as a symbol of resistance against Christianity or misogyny, holding out the hope of women's freedom, nonconformity, and alternative religions and lifestyles. In our technologically driven age, she can even evoke a nostalgic longing for wisdom.[38] Still, we first encounter her as children, of course, learning that some women are full of malice or, in more modern children's tales, are funny, rebellious, or witty— the confident nonconformists who snub conventions and go their own way.

In the early 1990s, when Gottlob Haag, a local poet and writer, set out to write about witches in Hohenlohe, few of his neighbors knew any stories, let alone admitted to believing in witchcraft. So the stories he relates were devices for invoking the remote and lonely Hohenlohe landscapes and wizened, cunning women, falsely persecuted:

> If you want to know more about them [the Hohenlohe witches], you should first search yourself, throw a glance into your own past and become completely self-aware. For only if you know where you ultimately come from will you know where you are going. Sure of yourself, then you can comfortably go out on the eve of a new moon, cross the way and go over to the witches' field, to the witches' tree. . . . You should come to it without asking "how" or thinking "but," come to it without guile and falseness, like a child, wrapping your arms around the trunk of the linden tree in order to feel the power that flows out from it and into yourself . . . These are no wicked faces that you are allowed to look upon. They are the faces of wise women, old as the stones, furrowed with the runes of the ages, from whom radiates a deep knowing. Many of them have gone through the fire, yet their countenances have not been thereby destroyed, for their knowledge made them immune to it.

Uninjured [were] their souls and spirits which were thrust into the embers in order to destroy them, for they were also not made of the transitory stuff of the earth.[39]

Less poetic yet no less ardent are the few whispered stories still told about Anna Schmieg in Hürden, Bächlingen, and Langenburg. Not long ago one Hürdener, spying two visitors, a researcher from America and his wife, peering at the mill, called out across the way. "You know, a witch used to live there!" Under the shade of a tree she then told them a short tale. In her story Anna Schmieg did not even have a name. She was "the witch of Hürden," a vague memory of the woman who once lived at the mill.[40]

Notes

Works frequently cited have been identified by the following abbreviations:

ALAL   Hohenlohe-Zentralarchiv Neuenstein, La 75: Archiv Lang-
                enburg, Amt Langenburg

ALGAL   Hohenlohe-Zentralarchiv Neuenstein, La 5: Archiv Langen-
                burg, Gemeinschaftliches Archiv

ALKI   Hohenlohe-Zentralarchiv Neuenstein, La 15: Archiv Lang-
                enburg, Kanzlei I

ALKaI   Hohenlohe-Zentralarchiv Neuenstein, La 40: Archiv Lang-
                enburg, Kammer I

ALRI   Hohenlohe-Zentralarchiv Neuenstein, La 35: Archiv Lang-
                enburg, Regierung I

ALSBR   Hohenlohe-Zentralarchiv Neuenstein, La 160: Archiv Lang-
                enburg Sonstige Bestände, Rechnungen

HDA   Hans Bächtold-Stäubli, ed., *Handwörterbuch des deutschen
                Aberglaubens* (Berlin: Walther de Gruyter, 1927–42), 10 vols.
                Reprint with preface by Christoph Daxelmüller, Berlin:
                Walther de Gruyter, 1987. Citations are to the reprinted
                edition.

HZAN   Hohenlohe-Zentralarchiv Neuenstein

KB1276   Landeskirchliches Archiv Stuttgart, Kirchenbuch B1276,
                          Bächlingen, vol. 1.

PGO   Gustav Radbruch, ed., *Die Peinliche Gerichtsordnung Kaiser
                          Karls V. von 1532 (Carolina)* (Stuttgart: Philipp Reclam, 1962)

CHAPTER 1 *Death on Shrove Tuesday*

1. This narrative of the events on Shrove Tuesday rests on testimonies given before
authorities between February 21 and 29, 1672. ALGAL 529/1, February 21, 1672; ALGAL
529/2, February 22, 1672; ALGAL 529/3, February 22, 1672; ALGAL 529/5, February 22,
1672; ALGAL 529/6, February 22, 1672; ALGAL 529/4, February 23, 1672; ALGAL
529/29 & 31, February 27–28, 1672; ALGAL 529/31, February 29, 1672.

2. ALGAL 529/29 & 30, February 27, 1672.

3. "Hund," in *HDA*, vol. 4, cols. 470–90.

4. ALGAL 529/29 & 30, February 27, 1672.

5. ALGAL 529/29 & 30, February 27, 1672.

6. Across Europe towns and large villages greeted twilight and the encroaching dangers
of the night with a variety of protective measures. See A. Roger Ekirch, *At Day's Close:
Night in Times Past* (New York: W. W. Norton, 2005), 15–23.

7. ALGAL 529/29 & 30, February 27, 1672.

8. ALGAL 529/29 & 30, February 27, 1672.

9. "Katze," in *HDA*, vol. 4, cols 1107–24.

10. ALGAL 529/29 & 30, February 27, 1672.

11. ALGAL 529/29 & 30, February 27, 1672.

12. ALGAL 529/29 & 30, February 27, 1672. In popular culture Shrove cakes were
thought to have spiritual or magical uses similar to the consecrated bread of the
Eucharist. "Fastnacht," in *HDA*, vol. 2, cols. 1259–60.

13. While recent studies have added to our understanding of witch trials, few can explain
how or why villagers experienced some mundane events as witchcraft. See especially
Robin Briggs, *Witches and Neighbors: The Social and Cultural Context of European Witchcraft*
(New York: Viking, 1996); Brian Levack, *The Witch-Hunt in Early Modern Europe*, 3rd ed.
(Harlow: Longman, 2006); Wolfgang Behringer, *Witchcraft Persecutions in Bavaria: Popular
Magic, Religious Zealotry, and Reason of State in Early Modern Europe*, trans. J. C. Grayson and
David Lederer (Cambridge: Cambridge University Press, 1997). On the connection of
witchcraft with motherhood and pregnancy, see especially Lyndal Roper, *Witch Craze:
Terror and Fantasy in Baroque Germany* (New Haven: Yale University Press, 2004). In the
Hürden affair I am arguing that generalized fears surrounding motherhood and child-
birth could trigger a credible accusation of witchcraft only under very specific and
unusual circumstances.

14. KB1276.

15. ALGAL 529/29 & 30, February 27, 1672. Anna Fessler's husband noted Eva Küstner's
customary gifts to his wife.

16. On women, pregnancy, and the lying-in, see especially Ulinka Rublack, "Pregnancy, Childbirth, and the Female Body in Early Modern Germany," *Past and Present*, no. 150 (1996), 84–110; and Eva Labouvie, *Andere Umstände: Eine Kulturgeschichte der Geburt* (Cologne: Böhlau, 1998).

17. A wide variety of legal and customary protections were available to pregnant women. Labouvie, *Andere Umstände*, 77–102.

18. Roper, *Witch Craze*, 127–59.

19. ALGAL 529/29–30, February 27, 1672.

20. ALGAL 529/29–30, February 27, 1672.

21. ALGAL 529/1, February 21, 1672.

22. ALGAL 529/29–30, February 27, 1672.

23. Protestant church visitation records give varying and poor reports about the availability of midwives in the parish of Bächlingen. In 1658 the account reported midwives doing their work well, but two years later the pastor of Bächlingen complained that his parish had no midwives at all. ALGAL 554/17, 1658; ALGAL 554/20, 1660.

24. Shrove Tuesday celebrations remain part of village culture in southwestern Germany to the present day. See Tübingener Arbeitskreis für Fastnachtsforschung, *Dörfliche Fastnacht zwischen Neckar und Bodensee*, Volksleben, vol. 12 (Tübingen: Vereinigung für Volkskunde, 1966); and Adolf Spamer, *Deutsche Fastnachtsbräuche* (Jena: Eugen Diederich, 1936). On feast days in general, see Ingeborg Weber-Kellermann, *Saure Wochen, Frohe Feste: Fest und Alltag in der Sprache der Bräuche* (Munich: C. J. Bucher, 1985).

25. Robert Scribner, "Cosmic Order and Daily Life: Sacred and Secular in Pre-Industrial German Society," in Kaspar von Greyerz, ed., *Religion and Society in Early Modern Europe, 1500–1800* (London: George Allen & Unwin, 1984), 18–19.

26. "Fastnacht," *HDA*, vol. 2, cols. 1256–57.

27. About the traditions associated with the baking of cakes in German folklore, see "Kuchen," in *HDA*, vol. 5, cols. 645–89. Bede made the reference to the Germans' baking customs in his *De Temporum Ratione*, cited in "Kuchen," col. 657.

28. Karl-Sigismund Kramer, *Volksleben im Fürstentum Ansbach und seinen Nachbargebieten (1500–1800): Eine Volkskunde auf Grund archivalischer Quellen*, Beiträge zur Volkstumsforschung herausgegeben von der bayerischen Landesstelle für Volkskunde, vol. 13 (Wurzburg: Ferdinand Schöningh, 1961), 103–4.

29. Because so many villagers shared the same Christian names, locals often distinguished individuals by their nicknames. The records often call Michel Fessler "Benzen Michel" because the old Swabian name, "*Benz*," a name for oxen or cattle, referred to Michel's trade as a local cattle driver or cowherd. To distinguish his wife from all of the other "Annas," his wife was naturally called *Benzin Anna*. See Hermann Fischer, *Schwäbisches Wörterbuch* (Tübingen: H. Laupp'sche Buchhandlung, 1904), vol. 1, col. 853.

30. ALGAL 687/119, November 15, 1669.

31. The Lutheran church ordinance of 1687 laying down the seating order for villagers in the Bächlingen church likely reflected the customary seating practices in the parish. Women were assigned seats by social rank, marital status, and age. ALAL 992, 1687.

32. In the tax assessment of 1670 the government assessed the Hürden mill at more than

twice the value of the other properties in the hamlet. ALSBR 888, April 23–October 28, 1670. On the hierarchy of wealth in this region, see Thomas Robisheaux, *Rural Society and the Search for Order in Early Modern Germany* (Cambridge: Cambridge University Press, 1989).

33. ALGAL 529/29–30, February 27, 1672.

34. ALGAL 529/29–30, February 27, 1672. Michel Fessler may not have known that his wife had talked several times to Eva.

35. ALGAL 529/29 & 31, February 27–28, 1672.

36. ALGAL 529/29–30, February 27, 1672.

37. ALGAL 529/1, February 21, 1672.

38. ALGAL 529/29–30, February 27, 1672.

39. ALGAL 529/30, February 27, 1672.

40. ALGAL 529/30, February 27, 1672.

CHAPTER II *The Autopsy*

1. The harsh words describing Langenburg's people were from the territory's ruler, Count Heinrich Friedrich, Lord of Langenburg and Count of Hohenlohe-Langenburg. ALKI 20. *Ruggericht Ordnung*, 1654.

2. ALGAL 529/1, February 21, 1672.

3. See Sabine Sander, *Handwerkschirurgen: Sozialgeschichte einer verdrängten Berufsgruppe*, Kritische Studien zur Geschichtswissenschaft, vol. 83 (Göttingen: Vandenhoeck & Ruprecht, 1989).

4. These duties were described in the Langenburg Court Barber Ordinance of 1627. ALGAL 282.

5. Wolfgang Adam, "Lesen und Vorlesen am Langenburger Hof: Zur Lesefähigkeit und zum Buchbesitz der Diener und Beamten," in Wolfgang Brückner, Peter Blickle, and Dieter Breuer, eds., *Literatur und Volk im 17. Jahrhundert: Probleme populärer Kultur in Deutschland*, Wolfenbütteler Arbeiten zur Barockforschung, vol. 13 (Wiesbaden: Otto Harrassowitz, 1985), pt. 2, 477.

6. About bath masters, their medical knowledge, and their place in early modern towns, see Werner Danckert, *Unehrliche Leute: Die verfemten Berufe* (Bern: Francke, 1963), 64–87.

7. For a contemporary description of the craft of the surgeon, see the widely read manual by the French royal surgeon, Ambroise Paré, translated into German as *Wund Artzney oder Artzney Spiegell* (Frankfurt a. M.: Caspar Tötell, 1635).

8. *PGO*, Article 147, 94. For an introduction to the *Carolina* and imperial law, Rudolf Stintzing remains a standard starting point: *Geschichte der deutschen Rechtswissenschaft*, 2 vols. (Munich: R. Oldenbourg, 1880–84). On the law's development, see Winfried Trusen, "Strafprozess und Rezeption: Zu den Entwicklungen im Spätmittelalter und den Grundlagen der *Carolina*," in Peter Landau and Friedrich-Christian Schroeder, eds., *Strafrecht, Strafprozess und Rezeption: Grundlagen, Entwicklung und Wirkung der Constitutio Criminalis Carolina*, Juristische Abhandlungen, vol. 19 (Frankfurt a.M.: Vittorio Klostermann, 1984), 29–118. For wider and comparative perspectives on the law, see John H. Langbein, *Prose-*

cuting Crime in the Renaissance: England, Germany, France (Cambridge, Mass.: Harvard University Press, 1974); and Gerald Strauss, *Law, Resistance, and the State: The Opposition to Roman Law in Reformation Germany* (Princeton, N.J.: Princeton University Press, 1986).

9. *PGO*, Article 147, p. 94.

10. *PGO*, Article 149, p. 95.

11. *PGO*, Articles 37 and 50, pp. 47, 53.

12. Robert Jütte, *Ärzte, Heiler und Patienten: Medizinischer Alltag in der frühen Neuzeit* (Munich: Artemis & Winkler, 1991), 116–18.

13. ALGAL 529/2, February 22, 1672.

14. ALGAL 529/2, February 22, 1672.

15. In the seventeenth century, jurists came to interpret the *Carolina's* requirement to consult "medical professionals" as requiring consultations with physicians and not just barber-surgeons.

16. Esther Fischer-Homberger, *Medizin vor Gericht: Gerichtsmedizin von der Renaissance bis zur Aufklärung* (Bern: Hans Huber, 1983), 43–52.

17. See Gottfried Welsch, *Rationale Vulnerum Lethalium Judicium* . . . 2nd ed. (Leipzig: Ritzschianis, 1662), 129–30.

18. ALGAL 529/3, February 22, 1672.

19. Stadtarchiv Hall, 2/74, 8–10. My thanks to Terence McIntosh for this reference and a copy of the document.

20. For an introduction to the Galenic tradition in the universities, see Andrew Wear, "Medicine in Early Modern Europe, 1500–1700," in Lawrence I. Conrad, et al, eds., *The Western Medical Tradition, 800 B.C. to 1800 A.D.* (Cambridge: Cambridge University Press, 1995), 215–361, especially 251–64.

21. On the importance of William Harvey and his reception, see Wear, "Medicine in Early Modern Europe," 325–40.

22. Allen Debus, "Chemistry and the Universities in the Seventeenth Century," *Estudos Avançados* 4, 10 (1990), 184–85. Rolfinck came to be known for his massive synthesis of anatomy, *Dissertationes Anatomicae Methodo Synthetica Exaratae* . . . (Nuremberg: Endter, 1656).

23. Johannes Theodor Schenck, *Disputatio Medica Inauguralis de Vulneribus, Andreas Thymius Waltershusa Thuringus [Resp]* (Jena: Disputation, 1662).

24. Stadtarchiv Hall, 2/74, 8–10.

25. Stadtarchiv Hall, 2/74, 8–10.

26. Physicians relied upon their patients for valuable understanding about their body and health; see Barbara Duden, *The Woman Beneath the Skin: A Doctor's Patients in Eighteenth-Century Germany*, trans. Thomas Dunlap (Cambridge, Mass.: Harvard University Press, 1991).

27. Only in the late seventeenth century did forensic experts make the case that physicians conducting autopsies rely exclusively on their own observations for their diagnosis of the cause of death. One of the first proponents of this new approach was Johannes

Bohn at Leipzig. See his *De Renunciatione Vulnerum, seu Vulnerum Lethalium Examen* . . . (Leipzig: Thomas Fritsch, 1711). First edition published in 1689.

28. ALGAL 529/3, February 22, 1672.

29. ALGAL 529/3, February 22, 1672.

30. ALGAL 529/3, February 22, 1672.

31. "Daniel Sennert," *Allgemeine Deutsche Biographie* (Leipzig, 1889), vol. 29, 74. Debus, "Chemistry and the Universities," 184–85. I am grateful to Seymour Mauskopf and Michael McVaugh for this insight into the connections between Thym, Rolfinck, and Sennert.

32. Daniel Sennert, *Operum Omnia* (Lyon: Ioanni Antonii Huguetan & Marci Antonii Ravavd, 1650), 3 vols.

33. Sennert, *Opera Omnia*, vol. 3, Pars. 1: *De morbis occultarum qualitatum in Genere*, 521–41.

34. Sennert, *Opera Omnia*, vol. 3, Pars. 1, 522–24.

35. Sennert, *Opera Omnia*, vol. 3, Pars II: *De Morbis Malignis, Occultis, & Venenatis, ab Interno Humorum Vitio*, pp. 542–58; and Pars V: *De Venenis Externis in Genere*, 604–20.

36. Sennert, *Opera Omnia*, vol. 3, Pars II, 542–46.

37. Sennert, *Opera Omnia*, vol. 3, Pars II, 545–46.

38. Sennert, *Opera Omnia*, vol. 3, Pars II, 548.

39. ALGAL 529/3, February 22, 1672.

40. ALGAL 529/3, February 22, 1672.

41. ALGAL 529/3, February 22, 1672. Reading the signs of illness or death was a challenging and frequently difficult matter. For a comparable case, see Guido Ruggiero, "The Strange Death of Margarita Marcellini: *Male*, Signs, and the Everyday World of Pre-Modern Medicine," *American Historical Review* 106, 4(2001), 1141–58.

CHAPTER III *A Confusing and Suspicious Affair*

1. The description of the court adviser's illness comes from the court preacher, who worked almost daily with him. Ludwig Casimir Dietzel, *Leichenpredigt Herrn Tobiae Ulrichi von Gülchen* (Schwäbisch Hall: Hans-Reinhard Läidogen, 1675).

2. ALGAL 529/5, February 22, 1672.

3. ALGAL 529/6, February 22, 1672.

4. Johann David Wibel later rose to the rank of town pastor of Kirchberg and eventually court preacher of Langenburg before he died. Hohenlohe's church historian, Johann Christian Wibel, was his grandson. For a biography, see Otto Haug, *Pfarrerbuch Württembergisch Franken*, pt. 2: *Die Kirchen- und Schuldiener*, Baden-Württembergisches Pfarrerbuch, vol. 2, pt. 2 (Stuttgart: Scheufele, 1981), 501.

5. ALGAL 529/5, February 22, 1672.

6. The italics are the author's, but they reflect the focus of von Gülchen's thinking that night. ALGAL 529/5, February 22, 1672.

7. Dietzel, *Leichenpredigt Herrn Tobiae Ulrichi von Gülchen*.

8. Dietzel, *Leichenpredigt Herrn Tobiae Ulrichi von Gülchen.*

9. Dietzel, *Leichenpredigt Herrn Tobiae Ulrichi von Gülchen.*

10. On the trend toward pragmatic approaches to the law, see Michael Stolleis, *Geschichte des öffentlichen Rechts in Deutschland,* vol. 1: *Reichspublizistik und Policeywissenschaft 1600–1800* (Munich: C. H. Beck, 1988). Some jurists extended the logic of this new thinking about the law to reassess the Holy Roman Empire and its legal foundations, but von Gülchen was not inclined in this direction. See Constantin Fasolt, *The Limits of History* (Chicago: University of Chicago Press, 2004).

11. Dietzel, *Leichenpredit Herrn Tobiae Ulrich von Gülchen.*

12. In his university disputation von Gülchen addressed the classic question about the jurisdictional authority of the institutions of the Holy Roman Empire and argued for the empire as the guarantor of public order and stability. Wilhelm Ludwell and Tobias Ulrich von Gülchen, *De Foro Competente Quam Divina Favente Clementia* (diss., Altdorf University, 1639).

13. On Strasbourg's Lutheran Orthodoxy and Johann Schmidt, see Johannes Wallmann, *Philipp Jakob Spener und die Anfänge des Pietismus,* Beiträge zur historischen Theologie, vol. 42 (Tübingen: J. C. B. Mohr, 1970), 1–34.

14. "*Schlecht und recht das behüte mich / dann ich harze dein.*" Psalms 25:21.

15. Dietzel, *Leichenpredigt Herrn Tobiae Ulrichi von Gülchen.*

16. Civil servants like von Gülchen were a distinctive social caste in high demand following the Thirty Years' War. See Robert von Friedeburg and Wolfgang Mager, "Learned Men and Merchants," in Sheilagh Ogilvie, ed., *Germany: A New Social and Economic History,* vol. 2: *1630–1800* (London: Arnold, 1996), 164–96; and Michael Stolleis, "Grundzüge der Beamtenethik (1550–1650)," in Roman Schnur, ed., *Die Rolle der Juristen bei der Entstehung des modernen Staates* (Berlin: Duncker & Humblot, 1986), 273–302. On the early modern state, see Paul Münch, "The Growth of the Modern State," in Ogilvie, ed., *Germany: A New Social and Economic History,* vol. 2: *1630–1800,* 196–232.

17. See Dietzel, *Leichenpredigt Herrn Tobiae Ulrichi von Gülchen.*

18. ALGAL 234, 1616. The chancellery ordinance was drawn up in 1616 and renewed after the Thirty Years' War.

19. ALGAL 234, 1616.

20. ALGAL 529/29, February 27, 1672.

21. Benedict Carpzov, *Practicae Novae Imperialis Saxonicae Rerum Criminalium, Pars III . . .* (Wittenberg, 1670), §10–15, pp. 177–78.

22. Dietzel, *Leichenpredigt Herrn Tobiae Ulrichi von Gülchen.*

23. Cited in Franz Wieacker, *A History of Private Law in Europe with Particular Reference to Germany,* trans. Tony Weir (Oxford: Oxford University Press, 1995), 139.

24. ALGAL 529/29–30, February 27, 1672.

25. ALGAL 529/29–30, February 27, 1672.

26. ALGAL 529/29–30, February 27, 1672.

27. ALGAL 529/29–30, February 27, 1672.

28. ALGAL 529/29–30, February 27, 1672.

29. ALGAL 529/29–30, February 27, 1672.

30. ALGAL 529/29–30, February 27, 1672.

31. ALGAL 529/29–30, February 27, 1672.

32. ALGAL 529/29–30, February 27, 1672.

33. ALGAL 529/29 & 31, February 28, 1672.

34. ALGAL 529/29 & 31, February 28, 1672.

35. ALGAL 529/29 & 31, February 28, 1672.

36. ALGAL 529/29 & 31, February 28, 1672.

37. ALGAL 529/31 & 32, February 29, 1672.

38. ALGAL 529/31 & 32, February 29, 1672.

39. ALGAL 529/31 & 32, February 29, 1672.

40. ALGAL 529/31 & 32, February 29, 1672.

41. ALGAL 529/31 & 32, February 29, 1672.

42. ALGAL 529/31 & 32, February 29, 1672.

43. ALGAL 529/31 & 32, February 29, 1672.

44. ALGAL 529/31 & 32, February 29, 1672.

45. ALGAL 529/31 & 32, February, 29, 1672.

46. Dietzel, *Leichenpredigt Herrn Tobiae Ulrichi von Gülchen.*

47. Dietzel, *Leichenpredigt Herrn Tobiae Ulrichi von Gülchen.*

48. ALGAL 529/31 & 32, February 29, 1672.

CHAPTER IV *Warding Off Evil*

1. Veit Ludwig von Seckendorf, author of a standard manual on politics, *Teutscher Fürsten-Stat, oder Gründliche und kurtze Beschreibung, welcher Gestalt Fürstenthümer, Graff- und Herrschafften im H. Römischen Reich teutscher Nation* . . . (Frankfurt: Th. M. Goetzen, 1656), imagined the ideal prince ruler immersed in daily governance, much like Count Heinrich Friedrich.

2. Matthaeus Merian and Martin Zeiller, *Topographia Germaniae*, vol. 8: *Topographia Franconiae, Das ist Beschreibung und Eÿgentliche Contrafactur der Vornembsten Stätte und Plätze des Frankenlandes* . . . (Basel: Bärenreiter, 1962) (first published in Frankfurt, 1654), 3.

3. Gerhard Taddey, "Neue Forschungen zur Baugeschichte von Schloss Langenburg," *Württembergisch Franken* (1979), 13–46.

4. Wolfgang Adam, "Lesen und Vorlesen," 475–88.

5. For a description of Heinrich Friedrich's library, see Wolfgang Adam, "*Der Ablenkende*: Ein Mitglied der Fruchtbringenden Gesellschaft und seine Bibliothek in Langenburg," in Paul Raabe, ed., *Bücher und Bibliotheken im 17. Jahrhundert in Deutschland: Vorträge des vierten Jahrestreffens des Wolfenbütteler Arbeitskreises für Geschichte des Buchwesens in der Herzog*

August Bibliothek Wolfenbüttel 22. bis 24. Mai 1979, Wolfenbütteler Schriften zur Geschichte des Buchwesens, vol. 6 (Hamburg: Dr. Ernst Hauswedell & Co., 1980), 186–207. The library's holdings suggest that Heinrich Friedrich kept well informed about current political, legal, and religious issues of the empire.

6. Daniel Casper von Lohenstein and Andreas Gryphius were two of the best-known German writers of the Baroque era.

7. Adam, "*Der Ablenkende.*"

8. On Johann Arndt and the devotional movement he helped inspire, see Karl Holl, "Die Bedeutung der grossen Kriege für das religiöse und kirchliche Leben innerhalb des deutschen Protestantismus," in his *Gesammelte Aufsätze zur Kirchengeschichte*, vol. III: *Der Westen* (Tübingen: J. C. B. Mohr, 1929), 302–84; Winfried Zeller, *Der Protestantismus des 17. Jahrhunderts*, Klassiker des Protestantismus, vol. 5 (Bremen: Carl Schünemann, 1962); Eric Lund, "Johann Arndt and the Development of a Lutheran Spiritual Tradition" (Ph.D. diss.: Yale University, 1979); Johannes Wallmann, "Reflexionen und Bemerkungen zur Frömmigkeitskrise des 17. Jahrhunderts," in Manfred Jakubowski-Tiessen, ed., *Krisen des 17. Jahrhunderts: Interdisziplinäre Perspektiven* (Göttingen: Vandenhoeck & Ruprecht, 1999), 25–42; and Thomas Kaufmann, *Dreissigjähriger Krieg und Westfälischer Friede: Kirchengeschichtliche Studien zur lutherischen Konfessionskultur* (Tübingen: Mohr Siebeck, 1998).

9. Adam, "Lesen und Vorlesen," 480.

10. Adam, "Lesen und Vorlesen," 480.

11. The quote is from his funeral sermon, Johann David Wibel, *Trauer-Sermon und Leichen-Predigten welche der Naechtlichen Beysess- und Beerdigung des verblichenen Leichnambs des Weiland Hochgebohrnen Grafen und Herrn /Herrn Heinrich Friderichen Grafen von Hohenlohe und Gleichen / Herrn zu Langenburg und Cranichfeld . . .* (Öhringen: Johann Fuchs, 1699). The war and the flight from Langenburg left deep marks on Heinrich Friedrich and the members of his family. See Frank Kleinehagenbrock, *Die Grafschaft Hohenlohe im Dreissigjährigen Krieg: Eine erfahrungsgeschichtliche Untersuchung zu Herrschaft und Untertanen*, Veröffentlichungen der Kommission für geschichtliche Landeskunde in Baden-Württemberg, Reihe B, vol. 153 (Stuttgart: W. Kohlhammer, 2003), 232–36.

12. On the Habsburg political and religious ambitions at the height of the Thirty Years' War, see Martin Heckel, *Deutschland im konfessionellen Zeitalter*, Deutsche Geschichte, vol. 5 (Göttingen: Vandenhoeck & Ruprecht, 1983), 145–50; and R. J. W. Evans, *The Making of the Habsburg Monarchy, 1550–1700: An Interpretation* (Oxford: Oxford University Press, 1979).

13. For a discussion of the Thirty Years' War in Hohenlohe, see Kleinehagenbrock, *Die Grafschaft Hohenlohe im Dreissigjährigen Krieg*.

14. On the economic crisis of war years, see Robisheaux, *Rural Society*, 201–26.

15. Cited in Kleinehagenbrock, *Die Grafschaft Hohenlohe im Dreissigjährigen Krieg*, 262.

16. On the flight of the Hohenlohe family in 1634 and its plight during the war, see Kleinehagenbrock, *Die Grafschaft Hohenlohe im Dreissigjährigen Krieg*, 229–66.

17. Kleinehagenbrock, *Die Grafschaft Hohenlohe im Dreissigjährigen Krieg*, 266–69.

18. *Trauer-Sermon Heinrich Friedrich*.

19. Adam, "*Der Ablenkende*," 186–87.

20. Heinrich Friedrich wrote this account late in life for his own funeral sermon. It is preserved in the Hof-Prädikatur Library in Langenburg. The quote is cited in Kleinehagenbrock, *Die Grafschaft Hohenlohe im Dreissigjährigen Krieg*, 232.

21. ALGAL 234/54, January 1651.

22. For a standard assessment of the Peace of Westphalia, see Heinz Duchhardt, *Das Zeitalter des Absolutismus*, Oldenbourg Grundriss der Geschichte, vol. 11, 2nd ed. (Munich: R. Oldenbourg, 1992), 9–13.

23. ALGAL 609/5, August 21, 1650. An annual Feast of Peace was celebrated throughout the 1650s, the last recorded instance occurring in 1659. ALGAL 609/14, October 12, 1659.

24. ALKI 20/10, June 27, 1654.

25. For a full discussion of the courts, see Gustav Adolf Thumm, *Die bäuerlichen und dörflichen Rechtsverhältnisse des Fürstentums Hohenlohe im 17. und 18. Jahrhundert*, Forschungen aus Württembergisch Franken, vol. 6. (Benningen/N.: Neckar Druck & Verlagsgesellschaft, 1971), 214–65.

26. Thomas Robisheaux, "Peasants and Pastors: Rural Youth Control and the Reformation in Hohenlohe, 1540–1680," *Social History* 6 (1981), 281–300.

27. ALKI 20/10, June 27, 1654.

28. The term "rituals of retribution" is from Richard J. Evans, *Rituals of Retribution: Capital Punishment in Germany 1600–1987* (Oxford: Oxford University Press, 1996). See also Richard van Dülmen, *The Theatre of Horror: Crime and Punishment in Early Modern Germany*, trans. Elisabeth Neu (Cambrige, Mass.: Basil Blackwell, 1991).

29. Adam, "*Der Ablenkende*," 188. The poem was written by a Lutheran preacher of the region, Johann Philipp Härpffer.

30. Karl Otmar v. Aretin, *Das alte Reich 1648–1806*, vol. 1: *Föderalistische oder hierarchische Ordnung (1648–1684)* (Stuttgart: Klett-Cotta, 1993), 242–47.

31. See Norbert Schoch, *Die Wiedereinführung und Ausübung des öffentlichen römisch-katholischen Gottesdienstes in der Grafschaft Hohenlohe-Waldenburg im 17. und 18. Jahrhundert verglichen mit den Bestimmungen des Westfälischen Friedens und der hohenlohischen Hausverträge* (diss., Tübingen, 1958); and his "Eine Gegenreformation in Hohenlohe," *Württembergisch Franken* 50, N.F. 40 (1966), 304–33.

32. Volker Press has suggested, probably rightly, that the counts converted to Catholicism in order to seek patronage and opportunities for advancement in imperial Catholic circles in southern Germany and in Vienna. Volker Press, "Das Haus Hohenlohe in der frühen Neuzeit," in his *Adel im Alten Reich: Gesammelte Vorträge und Aufsätze*, ed. Franz Brendle and Anton Schindling (Tübingen: Bibliotheca Academica, 1998), 180–81.

33. Robisheaux, *Rural Society*, 237–42.

34. ALKI, 22/34, March 28, 1670.

35. ALKI 22/44, May 27, 1670; ALKI 22/45, June 21, 1670; ALKI 22/47, August 4, 1670; and ALKI 22/49, August 12, 1670.

36. Robisheaux, *Rural Society*, 247–54.

CHAPTER V *A Secret Crime?*

1. Only in April did Eva testify to returning to the Fessler household the next morning. ALGAL 529/36, April 30, 1672.

2. ALGAL 529/36, April 30, 1672.

3. ALGAL 529/29 & 30, February 28, 1672.

4. ALGAL 529/29 & 30, February 28, 1672.

5. ALGAL 529/31, March 7, 1672.

6. ALGAL 529/31, March 7, 1672.

7. ALGAL 529/31, February 27–28, 1672.

8. Wieacker argues that the "modern use movement" in the law emerged as a rigorous reasoning process about facts and procedures, that is, a particular legal cognitive process. Von Gülchen in large part embodied this process but at key points diverged from it. On the movement, see Wieacker, *History of Private Law*, 159–98.

9. Georg Adam Struve's manual of criminal-law procedure, first published in 1670, was a standard reference in the late seventeenth century. Struve himself exemplified the "modern use movement" in the law. The edition consulted for this study is the seventh edition: Georg Adam Struve, *Jurisprudentia Romano-Germanica Forensis*, 7th ed. (Jena, 1697). Von Gülchen followed Struve closely. I am grateful to Peter Oestmann for his advice about the importance of "*die kleine Struve*," or the "little Struve," as a standard reference.

10. ALGAL 529/33, March 6, 1672.

11. Von Gülchen was typical of most jurists in seeing law and theology as supporting one another. His intention to begin his first interrogation of Schmieg by proceeding "theologically" suggests that sin and crime were indistinguishable for him. For him theology was not abstract doctrine, but a set of living and practical concepts able to reveal moral and spiritual truths.

12. ALGAL 529/33, March 6, 1672.

13. For a discussion of how early modern magistrates blended the secular and the sacred in their work, see Stuart Clark, *Thinking with Demons: the Idea of Witchcraft in Early Modern Europe* (Oxford: Oxford University Press, 1997), 560–71.

14. While the court scribe seems to have recorded many of the direct colloquial expressions of Schmieg, he also distanced himself from her speech by summarizing answers and presenting much of her testimony in the impersonal third person. When she cursed or mentioned the devil, he invoked a blessing in the protocol with large letters: *S. V.*, or *Salve Venie*. On this interplay of peasant and bureaucratic voices, see David Sabean, "Peasant Voices and Bureaucratic Texts: Narrative Structure in Early Modern Protocols," in Peter Becker and William Clark, *Little Tools of Knowledge: Historical Essays on Academic and Bureaucratic Practices* (Ann Arbor: University of Michigan Press, 2001), 67–93.

15. ALGAL 529/31, March 7, 1672.

16. ALGAL 529/31, March 7, 1672.

17. ALGAL 529/31, March 7, 1672.

18. The condemnation of suicide went back to St. Augustine. Lutherans affirmed this Augustinian position and condemned suicide often and vehemently in sermons and ordinances. See Georges Minois, *History of Suicide: Voluntary Death in Western Culture*, trans. Lydia G. Cochrane (Baltimore: Johns Hopkins University Press, 1999), especially 116–47. For a case study of two Lutheran lands, see Vera Lind, *Selbtsmord in der frühen Neuzeit: Diskurs, Lebenswelt und kultereller Wandel am Beispiel der Herzogtümer Schleswig und Holstein*, Veröfftenlichungen des Max-Planck-Instituts für Geschichte, vol. 146 (Göttingen: Vandenhoeck & Ruprecht, 1999).

19. ALGAL 529/31, March 7, 1672.

20. ALGAL 529/31, March 7, 1672.

21. Sönke Lorenz, "Der Hexenprozess," in Sönke Lorenz, ed., *Hexen und Hexenverfolgung im deutschen Südwesten*, Volkskundliche Veröffentlichungen des Badischen Landesmuseums Karlsruhe, vol. 2/2 (Karlsruhe: Badisches Landesmuseum Karlsruhe, 1994), 71.

22. ALGAL 529/31, March 7, 1672.

23. ALGAL 529/31, March 7, 1672.

24. David Sabean, *Power in the Blood: Popular Culture and Village Discourse in Early Modern Germany* (Cambridge: Cambridge University Press, 1984), 30–36.

25. ALGAL 529/31, March 7, 1672.

26. ALGAL 529/31, March 7, 1672.

27. ALGAL 529/31, March 7, 1672. The italicized sentence is underlined in the protocol. Two *NB*'s (for *nota bene*) are added in the margin for added emphasis.

28. ALGAL 529/31, March 7, 1672.

29. ALGAL 529/31, March 7, 1672.

30. ALGAL 529/31, March 7, 1672.

31. ALGAL 529/31, March 7, 1672.

32. ALGAL 529/31, March 7, 1672.

33. ALGAL 529/31, March 7, 1672.

34. ALGAL 529/31, March 7, 1672.

35. ALGAL 529/31, March 7, 1672. The emphasis is the interrogator's with an additional *NB* in the margin.

36. ALGAL 529/31, March 8, 1672.

37. ALGAL 529/31, March 8, 1672.

38. ALGAL 529/31, March 8, 1672.

CHAPTER VI *The Outsider*

1 ALGAL 529/31, March 7, 1672.

2 Max Miller and Gerhard Thaddey, eds., *Handbuch der historischen Stätten Deutschlands*, vol. 6: *Baden-Württemberg*, 2nd ed. (Stuttgart: Alfred Kröner, 1980), 24–25.

3. On the agricultural crisis of the early war years, see Robisheaux, *Rural Society*, 201–26.

For views on the general crisis, see Wilhelm Abel, *Agricultural Fluctuations in Europe: From the Thirteenth to the Twentieth Centuries* (London: Methuen, 1980); and *Massenarmut und Hungerkrisen im vorindustriellen Europa: Versuch einer Synopsis* (Hamburg: Paul Parey, 1974); Henry Kamen, "The Economic and Social Consequences of the Thirty Years' War," *Past and Present*, no. 39 (1968), 44–61; John Thiebault, *German Villages in Crisis: Rural Life in Hesse-Kassel and the Thirty Years' War, 1580–1720* (Atlantic Highlands, N.J.: Humanities Press International, 1995); and William W. Hagen, "Seventeenth-Century Crisis in Brandenburg: The Thirty Years' War, the Destabilization of Serfdom, and the Rise of Absolutism," *American Historical Review* 94 (1989), 302–35.

4. See Robisheaux, *Rural Society*, 130–31.

5. On female domestic servants, see Renate Dürr, *Mägde in der Stadt: Das Beispiel Schwäbisch Hall in der Frühen Neuzeit,* Geschichte und Geschlechter vol. 13 (Frankfurt: Campus, 1995).

6. Dürr, *Mägde in der Stadt,* 159.

7. In 1630 the Haffner household was assessed at 1,505 gulden putting it in the top 5 percent of all households in the district.

8. ALKI I, 33/4, n.d.

9. Ann Tlusty, *Bacchus and the Civic Order; The Culture of Drink in Early Modern Germany* (Charlottesville: University of Virginia Press, 2001), 158ff.

10. Quoted in Robisheaux, *Rural Society,* 221.

11. Robisheaux, *Rural Society,* 215.

12. The ordinance governing inheritance required that wards manage the property of their charges fairly and honestly, and that they bring them up with Christian virtues and honor, standing by them and helping them to establish their own households through marriage. ALKI 33/4, n.d.

13. The parish register of Bächlingen records the baptism of Hans Martin, the Schmiegs' first child, on May 28, 1640, or about three years after Anna's marriage. KB 1276.

14. Robisheaux, *Rural Society,* 210–16.

15. Cited by the author of *Zimmern Chronicle.* K. A. Barack, ed., *Zimmerische Chronik,* Bibliothek des Litterarischen Vereins in Stuttgart, vols. 91–94 (Tübingen: H. Laupp, 1869), vol. 3, 132.

16. For a description of the early modern population regime, see Michael Flinn, *The European Demographic System, 1500–1820* (Baltimore: Johns Hopkins University Press, 1981); and Jan de Vries, "Population," in Thomas A. Brady, Jr., Heiko A. Oberman, and James D. Tracy, eds., *Handbook of European History, 1400–1600: Late Middle Ages, Renaissance, and Reformation,* vol. 1: *Structures and Assertions* (Leiden: E. J. Brill, 1994), 1–50. To understand the effects of high mortality rates on peasant families over several generations, see Arthur Imhof, *Lost Worlds: How Our European Ancestors Coped with Everyday Life and Why Life Is So Hard Today,* trans. Thomas Robisheaux (Charlottesville: University of Virginia Press, 1996).

17. The Bächlingen parish register records only eight, but a ninth, named Michel, was also listed when he died at age six years. KB 1276.

18. KB 1276.

19. KB 1276.

20. ALAL 40, August 25, 1651.

21. ALAL 40, August 25, 1651.

22. Gustav Bossert, *Bächlinger Ortschronik*, HZAN Sammlung von Manuskripten 36 [19c], n.d. [ca. 1870], unpaginated.

23. ALGAL 190/5, December 16, 1647.

24. ALAL 40, August 25, 1651.

25. ALSBR B865, 1649/50, May 23, 1649.

26. ALAL 40, August 25, 1651.

27. ALSBR B865, 1649/50.

28. ALSBR B866, [1650/51?].

29. ALSBR B870, 1654/55, no. 11 of the court protocol & punishments posted November 15, 16, 17, 1654. Wihrt was fined 1 gulden and Schmieg 2 gulden and 30 kreutzer.

30. Eva Labouvie, "Verwünschen und Verfluchen: Formen der verbalen Konfliktregelung in der ländlichen Gesellschaft der Frühen Neuzeit," in Peter Blickle, ed., *Der Fluch und der Eid: Die metaphysische Begründung gesellschaftlichen Zusammenlebens und politischer Ordnung in der ständischen Gesellschaft*, Zeitschrift für historische Forschung, Beiheft no. 15 (Berlin: Duncker & Humblot, 1993), 138–39.

31. ALSBR B870, 1654/55, Gericht protocol & punishments posted November 15, 16, 17, 1654, no. 72.

32. The Bächlingen pastor reported the incident during the church visitation. ALGAL 554/12, 1654.

33. See David Sabean's discussion of how pastors and state officials in the Duchy of Württemberg forced recalcitrant villagers into obedience through confession and communion in Sabean, *Power in the Blood*, 37–60.

34. On confession and social discipline among Lutherans, see Hans-Christoph Rublack, "Lutherische Beichte und Sozialdisziplinierung," *Archiv für Reformationsgeschichte* 84 (1993), 127–55.

35. ALSBR B871, 1655/56, Ruggericht, April 17–18, 1656.

36. ALKI 1 118/2, October 28, 1658. The emphasis was Hohenbuch's.

37. ALKI 1 118/2, October 28, 1658.

38. ALKI 1 118/2, October 28, 1658.

39. Invoking the "common good" was a common way of mobilizing protests against governments in the seventeenth century. See Winfried Schulze, "Vom Gemeinnutz zum Eigennutz: Über den Normenwandal in der ständischen Gesellschaft der frühen Neuzeit," *Historische Zeitschift* 243 (1986), 591–622; and Renate Blickle, "Nahrung und Eigentum als Kategorien in der ständischen Gesellschaft," in Winfried Schulze, ed., *Ständische Gesellschaft und soziale Mobilität*, Schriften des Historischen Kollegs, Kolloquien no. 12 (Munich: R. Oldenbourg, 1988), 73–93.

40. ALKI 1 118/2, October 28, 1658.

41. ALSBR B879, 1661/62, March 27, 1662.

42. ALSBR B879, 1661/62, March 27, 1662.

43. ALSBR B879, 1661/62, March 27, 1662.

44. The expression "evil woman" (*böse Frau*) evoked different meanings depending on the speaker and the context. When educated Lutheran state officials used the term, it carried diabolical connotations. To Hürden's young women the name drew on socioeconomic, religious, personal, and even generational complaints against an older and wealthier neighbor woman. To older men it implied a communal judgment involving a woman's general bad reputation. On older women and witchcraft, see Briggs, *Witches and Neighbors*, 15–61; Levack, *The Witch Hunt*, 149–55; Diane Purkiss, *The Witch in History: Early Modern and Twentieth-Century Representations* (London: Routledge, 1996); Lyndal Roper, *Witch Craze*; and Alison Rowlands, *Witchcraft Narratives in Germany: Rothenburg 1561–1652* (Manchester: Manchester University Press, 2003), 135–79.

CHAPTER VII *Sorcery at the Mill*

1. ALGAL 529/8, March 18, 1672.

2. ALGAL 529/8, March 26, 1672.

3. ALGAL 529/14, April 29, 1672.

4. On the social dynamics of villages in the wake of a witchcraft accusation, see Rainer Walz, *Hexenglaube und magische Kommunkation im Dorf der Frühen Neuzeit: Die Verfolgungen in der Grafschaft Lippe*, Westfälisches Institut für Regionalgeschichte, Landschaftsverband Westfalen-Lippe, Forschungen zur Regionalgeschichte, vol. 9 (Paderborn: Ferdinand Schöningh, 1993).

5. ALGAL 529/29 & 30, February 27, 1672.

6. ALGAL 529/64 & 67, August 14, 1672.

7. ALGAL 529/7, February 28, 1672.

8. Angelika Albrecht, Otmar Reichmayer, and Konrad Bedal, "Glück zu! Zur rechtlichen, wirtschaftlichen und sozialen Stellung des Müllers," in Konrad Bedal, ed., *Mühlen und Müller in Franken*, 2nd ed. (Bad Windsheim: Fränkisches Freilandmuseum, 1992), 126–62.

9. Cited in Albrecht et al., "Glück zu!" 138–39.

10. Müller, Mahler, Roggenstehler,
   sag, womit erhälst dein Schwein?
   Kaufst Getreide nicht um einen Heller,
   muss ja fett wie du doch sein.
   Andre müssen sich ernähren,
   du tust fremdes Gut verzehren.
   Gleich ein Habicht Räuber lebst
   und in lauter Diebstahl schwebst.

Cited in Johannes Mager, Günter Meissner, and Wolfgang Orf, *Die Kulturgeschichte der Mühlen* (Leipzig: Edition Leipzig, 1988), 156.

11. Johann Heinrich Zedler, *Grosses vollständiges Universallexikon aller Wissenschaften und Künste* (Leipzig: Johann Heinrich Zedler, 1739), vol. 22, 190–91.

12. Mager et al., *Die Kulturgeschichte der Mühlen*, 156–61.

13. ALGAL 453/1605–6.

14. ALSBR B861, 1645/46.

15. Richard van Dülmen, "Der infame Mensch: Unehrliche Arbeit und soziale Ausgrenzung in der Frühen Neuzeit," in Richard van Dülmen, ed., *Arbeit, Frömmigkeit und Eigensinn: Studien zur historischen Kulturforschung* (Frankfurt a.M.: Fischer, 1990), 106–40.

16 ALKaI 1072, Inventory, Bartholomei 1637.

17 ALKaI 1072, Abschiedsbrief Bartholomei 1637.

18. ALKaI 1072, June 21, 1637.

19. ALKaI 1072, July 29, 1640.

20. ALKaI 1072, January 29, 1641.

21. ALAL 40, August 25, 1651.

22. On the "common good," see Schulze, "Vom Gemeinnutz zum Eigennutz." Disputes over subsistence lay at the center of most popular peasant unrest of the seventeenth century. See Winfried Schulze, "Herrschaft und Widerstand in der Sicht des 'gemeinen Mannes' im 16./17. Jahrhundert," in Hans Mommsen and Winfried Schulze, eds. *Vom Elend der Handarbeit* (Stuttgart: Klett-Cotta, 1981), 182–98; Renate Blickle, "Nahrung und Eigentum"; and Thomas Robisheaux, "Peasant Unrest and the Moral Economy in the German Southwest, 1560–1620," *Archiv für Reformationsgeschichte* 77 (1987), 174–86.

23. ALAL 924, September 23, 1642.

24. So pervasive and intractable was the problem that Steward Hohenbuch kept a separate protocol of decrees and punishments between 1646 and 1650 involving violations of market ordinances, ALAL 340.

25. ALSBR B855, 1639/40.

26. ALSBR B857, 1641/42.

27. ALSBR B8651649/50, May 23, 1649.

28. ALSBR B865, 1649/50, May 26, 1649.

29. ALKaII 6/6, October 11, 1650.

30. Only two short documents survive concerning the affair: the *Urfehde*, or oath, that Schmieg swore in 1649 to accept his punishment and not seek revenge for the treatment he suffered, and his petition from August 25, 1651, pleading for mercy, relief from the fine, and help from the government in countering the abuse from his neighbors.

31. ALAL 40, August 25, 1651.

32. ALAL 40, August 25, 1651. On the legal practice of the Urfehde, see St. Chr. Saar, "Urfehde," in *Handwörterbuch zur deutschen Rechtsgeschichte*, gen. ed. Adalbert Erler (Berlin: Erich Schmidt, 1998), vol. 5, cols. 562–70.

33. ALAL 40, August 25, 1651.

34. ALAL 40, December 24, 1651.

35. Hans was a forest officer in 1650 and headman of Bächlingen one year later. ALSBR B865, 1649/50, January 7, 1650. ALKI 621, April 24, 1651.

36. ALAL 494, January 6, 1651.

37. ALSBR Schatzungsanlage 1663, p. 442.

38. ALAL 494, October 11, 1655. Schmieg's debts totaled 300 gulden in 1663, among the highest levels of debt in the two villages of Bächlingen and Hürden. ALSBR 1663.

39. ALAL 477, April 26, 1651; ALAL 477, October 25, 1651; and ALAL 432, April 12, 1653. One striking instance of the favor shown Schmieg occurred in 1654 when Schmieg asked that he be paid 51/2 gulden on an old debt. The debt went back to the time of Heinrich Friedrich's father, Count Philip Ernst, and involved financial support to Hans and Anna for taking care of two children of Court Adviser Assum when they were orphaned. The Schmiegs were apparently engaged to care for the children of one of Heinrich Friedrich's closest advisers. ALAL 40, October 25, 1654; ALAL 477, October 25, 1654.

40. ALSBR B870, 1654/55, no. 47.

41. ALSBR B871, 1655/56, April 17–18, 1656.

42. ALSBR B870, 1654/55, no. 73.

43. ALSBR B871, 1655/56, April 17–18, 1656.

44. ALAL 477, April 26, 1651.

45. One example of these tensions involved Georg Arnold making false accusations against Schmieg and Hans Häfner in 1666–67. B882 Amtsrechnuingen des Amts Langenburg 1666/67.

46. Fischer-Homberger, *Medizin vor Gericht*, 74–80.

47. "Polizei- und Rügordnung vom 15. September 1588," in Gunther Franz, ed., *Die evangelischen Kirchenordnungen des XVI. Jahrhunderts*: vol. 15, *Württemberg*, pt. 1, *Grafschaft Hohenlohe*, gen. ed. Emil Sehling (Tübingen: J. C. B. Mohr, 1977), 579.

48. ALGAL 554/12, 1654.

49. ALGAL 554/12, November 24, 1654.

50. ALGAL 554/16, 1656.

51. Hohenlohe Bibliothek 1U/1, 1619.

52. "Polizei- und Rügordnung," 579.

53. ALGAL 529/61, April 11, 1672.

54. On the medical folklore associated with cats, see "Katze" in *HDA*, vol. 4, cols. 1107–24.

55. ALGAL 529/7, February 28, 1672. "Katze," cols. 1115–17.

56. ALGAL 529/7, February 28, 1672.

57. Nicolaus Remigius, *Daemonolatria, Das ist von Unholden und Zauber Geistern . . .* (Frankfurt a.M., 1598), 156–57.

58. ALGAL 529/61, April 11, 1672.

59. ALGAL 529/61, April 11, 1672.

60. ALGAL 529/61, 1672. "*Er gestehe wan Ihm kunffig einer uf sein Mist komme so er Ihn rechschaft heraus sehen.*"

61. ALGAL 529/61, April 11, 1672.

CHAPTER VIII Wider Conspiracies

1. On the dishonorable status of executioners, see Richard van Dülmen, "Der infame Mensch: Unehrliche Arbeit und soziale Ausgrenzung in der Frühen Neuzeit," in Richard van Dülman, ed., *Arbeit, Frömmigkeit und Eigensinn: Studien zur historischen Kulturforschung* (Frankfurt a.M.: Fischer, 1990), 106–40; Kathy Stuart, *Defiled Trades and Social Outcasts: Honor and Ritual Pollution in Early Modern Germany* (Cambridge: Cambridge University Press, 1999), 149ff.; and especially Jutta Nowosadtko, *Scharfrichter und Abdecker: Der Alltag zweier "unehrlicher Berufe" in der Frühen Neuzeit* (Paderborn: Ferdinand Schöningh, 1994).

2. On the healing craft of executioners, see Stuart, *Defiled Trades and Social Outcasts,* 149–85.

3. On the Württemberg trials, see Edward Watts Bever, "Witchcraft in Early Modern Wuerttemberg" (Ph.D. diss., Princeton University, 1983).

4. Gunther Franz, *Der Dreissigjährige Krieg und das deutsche Volk: Untersuchung zur Bevölkerungs- und Agrargeschichte,* 4th ed. (Stuttgart: Fischer, 1979).

5. On the Esslingen witch trials, see Erik Midelfort, *Witch Hunting in Southwestern Germany, 1562–1684: The Social and Intellectual Foundations* (Stanford, Calif.: Stanford University Press, 1972), 154–56; Günter Jerouschek, *Die Hexen und ihr Prozess: Die Hexenverfolgung in der Reichstadt Esslingen,* Esslinger Studien, Schriftenreihe, vol. 11 (Sigmaringen: Jan Thorbecke, 1992); and Gisela Vöhringer-Rubröder, "Reichstadt Esslingen," in Lorenz, ed., *Hexen und Hexenverfolgung im deutschen Südwesten,* vol. 2, 353–56.

6. *Ein erschröckliche, jedoch war /hafftige und erbärmliche /Newe-Zeitung /von Häxenmeisteren . . . 1665* (Augsburg, 1665). Cited in Midelfort, *Witch Hunting in Southwestern Germany,* 157.

7. Thomas Fritz, "Hexenverfolgungen in der Reichstadt Reutlingen," in Johannes Dillinger, Thomas Fritz, and Wolfgang Mährle, eds., *Zum Feuer Verdammt: Die Hexenverfolgungen in der Grafschaft Hohenberg, der Reichstadt Reutlingen und der Fürstpropstei Ellwangen,* Hexenforschung, vol. 2 (Stuttgart: Franz Steiner, 1998), 163–308.

8. ALKI 377/2, May 14, 1652.

9. In the trials in Neuenstadt, Weinsberg, and Möckmühl between 1656 and 1658, up to thirty-two suspects were cited for witchcraft. In the early 1660s, towns and villages of northern Swabia—including Böblingen, Leonberg, Marbach, Waiblingen, and villages around Stuttgart—reported suspicions and trials. Cannstatt, Heilbronn, and Weinsberg— all near or along the main thoroughfare to Hohenlohe—tried witches in the mid and late 1660s. Reports about other trials filtered into Hohenlohe from the north and east, including Rothenburg o.d.T. See Midelfort, *Witch Hunting in Southwestern Germany,* 221–22; Alison Rowlands, *Witchcraft Narratives in Germany*; and Traudl Kleefeld, Hans Gräser, and Gernot Stepper, *Hexenverfolgung im Markgraftum Brandenburg-Ansbach und in der Herrschaft Sugenheim,* Mittelfränkische Studien, vol. 15 (Ansbach: Historischer Verein für Mittelfranken, 2001). On the trials in Southwest Germany the best standard reference is Lorenz, ed., *Hexen und Hexenverfolgung im deutschen Südwesten.*

10. About the role of rumors and gossip in shaping disputes and misfortunes as "witchcraft," see especially Rainer Walz, *Hexenglaube und magische Kommunkation.* On the role of

stories and communicative power to shape perceptions during intense local conflicts, see also Pamela Stewart and Andrew Strathern, eds., *Witchcraft, Sorcery, Rumors, and Gossip* (Cambridge: Cambridge University Press, 2004); and Charles L. Briggs, ed., *Disorderly Discourse: Narrative, Conflict, and Inequality* (New York: Oxford University Press, 1996).

11. Rowlands, *Witchcraft Narratives in Germany: Rothenburg*, 221–22.

12. ALGAL 525/3, October 24, 1668.

13. ALGAL 525/3, October 24, 1668.

14. ALGAL 525/3, October 24, 1668.

15. ALGAL 525/81, March 8, 1669.

16. ALGAL 525/271/2, November 24, 1668.

17. ALGAL 525/30, November 25, 1668.

18. ALGAL 525/4, October 28, 1668.

19. Suspicions and trials for witchcraft multiplied in Ansbach between 1665 and 1670. Traudl Kleefeld, "Hexenverfolgung im Markgraftum Ansbach im 16. Jahrhundert, unter besondere während der Regierungszeit des Markgraften Georg Friedrich (1556–1603)," in Kleefeld, Gräser, and Stepper, *Hexenverfolgung im Markgraftum Brandenburg-Ansbach*, 1–88. For a wider regional perspective, see also Wolfgang Behringer, *Witchcraft Persecutions in Bavaria*, 331–33.

20. ALGAL 525/11, November 7, 1668.

21. ALGAL 525/14, November 9, 1668.

22. ALGAL 525/21, November 16, 1668.

23. ALGAL 525/24, November 17, 1668.

24. See especially Roper, *Witch Craze*, 204–21.

25. ALGAL 525/26, November 23, 1668.

26. ALGAL 525/34, December 2, 1668.

27. ALGAL 525/63, February 3, 1669.

28. ALGAL 525/63, February 3, 1669.

29. ALGAL 525/77, February 28, 1669.

30. ALGAL 525/80, March 6, 1669.

31. ALGAL 525/80, March 6, 1669.

32. ALGAL 525/81 March 8, 1669.

33. ALGAL 525/3, October 24, 1669.

34. ALGAL 525/81, March 8, 1669.

35. ALGAL 525/84, March 10, 1669.

36. ALGAL 525/89, March 16, 1669.

37. ALGAL 525/94, May 24, 1669.

38. ALGAL 525/95, May 28, 1669.

39. Several widely read treatises drove home the criticism that magistrates bore a partic-

ularly heavy burden of responsibility for persecuting the innocent during witch trials, among them Friedrich von Spee's famous *Cautio Criminalis, seu, De Processibus Contra Segas Liber* . . . 2nd ed. (Frankfurt a.M.: Ioannis Gronaei Austrij, 1632), and Johann Mattäus Meyfart in *Christliche Erinnerung an gewaltige Regenten und gewissenhaffte Praedicanten wie das abscheulihe Laster der Hexerey mit Ernst ausszurotten* . . . (Schleusingen: Peter Schmid, 1636). For a general discussion of the ordeal of magistrates during witch trials, see Clark, *Thinking with Demons*, 560–71.

40. ALGAL 525/96, May 29, 1669.

41. See Thomas Robisheaux, " 'The Queen of Evidence': The Witchcraft Confession in the Age of Confessionalism," in John Headley and Hans Hillerbrand, eds., *Confessionalization in Europe, 1550–1700: Essays in Honor and Memory of Bodo Nischan* (Aldershot: Ashgate, 2004), 175–206.

42. ALGAL 525/119, July 29, 1669.

43. ALGAL 525/110, July 1, 1669.

44. ALGAL 525/122, August 4, 1669.

45. ALGAL 378/2, June 9, 1670.

46. ALKI 378/8, [June 1670?].

47. The dossier is missing documents that explain how the case was resolved.

48. ALGAL 527/3, May 4, 1672. This account is my own and draws together the four stories presented to the district officers on that day. The discrepancies in the accounts are minor. What remained unclear from these accounts became the pivotal issues in the trial of Barbara Schleicher: who poured the drink, what was in the glass, and what was said between Schleicher and Treher.

49. ALGAL 527/8, May 15, 1672.

50. ALGAL 527/2, May 15, 1672.

51. ALGAL 527/11, May 17, 1672.

52. ALGAL 527/16, June 15, 1672.

53. ALGAL 527/16, June 15, 1672.

54. On the healing and magical properties of black hellebore, see "Nieswurz," in *HDA*, vol. 6, cols. 1083–85; and M. Grieve, *A Modern Herbal* (New York: Dover, 1931), vol. 1, 388–89.

55. ALGAL 527/16, June 15, 1672.

56. ALGAL 527/16, June 15, 1672.

57. ALGAL 527/17, June 20–22, 1672.

58. ALGAL 527/17, June 20–22, 1672.

CHAPTER IX *Satan in the Heart?*

1. ALGAL 529/6, February 22, 1672.

2. KB 1276.

3. The quote comes from the Hohenlohe Church ordinance of 1578. Franz, ed., *Grafschaft Hohenlohe*, 290.

4. Franz, ed., *Grafschaft Hohenlohe*, 290.

5. Dietzel's approach to the confessional seems close to the advice offered by one of Franconia's best-known Lutheran confessors of the day, Johann Ludwig Hartmann from Rothenburg o.d.T. Hartmann's two confessional manuals found a wide readership in the late seventeenth century. Dietzel makes no mention of Hartmann, but Hartmann's manuals and other works were available in the Court Preacher's Library. See Johann Ludwig Hartmann, *Absolution-Buch nechst Nothwendigem Bericht /wie ein Seelsorger bey so vielerley Fällen nach den Zeiten und Leuten im Beicht-Stuhl sich zu verhalten* (Rothenburg: Noah von Millenan, 1679); and his masterwork on Lutheran confessional practices, *Hand-Buch für Seelsorger . . .* (Nuremberg: Wolfgang-Moritz Endter, 1699).

6. On the uneven progress of the Reformation in rural Hohenlohe, see Robisheaux, "Peasants and Pastors."

7. The best study of the Lutheran pastorate is Luise Schorn-Schütte, *Evangelische Geistlichkeit in der Frühneuzeit: Deren Anteil an der Entfaltung frühmoderner Staatlichkeit und Gesellschaft dargestellt am Beispiel des Fürstentums Braunschweig-Wolfenbüttel, der Landschaft Hessen-Kassel und der Stadt Braunschweig*, Quellen und Forschungen zur Reformationsgeschichte, vol. 62 (Gütersloh: Gütersloher Hausverlag, 1996). On the pastorate in Hohenlohe during the Thirty Years' War, see Kleinehagenbrock, *Die Grafschaft Hohenlohe im Dreissigjährigen Krieg*, 140–228.

8. The source for Dietzel's biography is his funeral sermon: *Der Weiland Hoch-Ehrwürdig-Hoch-Achtbar und Hochgelehrte Herr Ludwig Casimir Dietzel /Hoch-Gräfl: Hohenloh: Langenburg: 43 jähriger wohl—verdienter Statt-Pfarrer /Hof-Prediger und Superintenddent derselbsten* (Rothenburg: Noah von Millenau, 1696). Hereafter cited as *Leichenpredigt Ludwig Casimir Dietzel*.

9. *Leichenpredigt Ludwig Casimir Dietzel*.

10. Several universities played prominent roles in the Lutheran orthodox reform movement, including Wittenberg, Jena, and Rostock. For the South German lands Strasbourg assumed leadership, drawing students from the entire region. On Strasbourg's Lutheran orthodox movement and its leaders, see Johann Adam, *Evangelische Kirchengeschichte der Stadt Strassburg biz zur französischen Revolution* (Strassburg: J. H. Ed. Heitz, 1922), 384–90; Zeller, *Der Protestantismus des 17. Jahrhunderts*, li–liii; Wallmann, *Philipp Jakob Spener*, 1–34; and Lund, "Johann Arndt," 244–53. For recent approaches to Lutheran orthodoxy, see Kaufmann, *Dreissigjähriger Krieg und Westfälischer Friede*.

11. Johann Georg Dorsch, "Friedenspredigt" in Zeller, *Der Protestantismus des 17. Jahrhunderts*, 249–60.

12. Lund, *Johann Arndt*, 251–52.

13. Some prominent Lutheran reformers influenced by Strasbourg were, among others, Joachim Lütkemann and Philipp Jakob Spener.

14. *Leichenpredigt Ludwig Casimir Dietzel*.

15. On the new Lutheran pastoral style, see Kaufmann, *Dreissigjähriger Krieg und Westfälischer Friede*, 102–12; also Holl, "Die Bedeutung der grossen Kriege für das religiöse und kirchliche Leben." On Hohenlohe, see Frank Kleinehagenbrock, " 'Nun müsst ihr doch

wieder alle Katholisch werden': Der Dreissigjährige Krieg als Bedrohung der Konfession in der Grafschaft Hohenlohe," in Matthias Asche and Anton Schindling, eds., *Das Strafgericht Gottes: Kriegserfahrungen und Religion im Heiligen Römischen Reich Deutscher Nation im Zeitalter des Dreissigjährigen Krieges*, 2nd ed. (Münster: Aschendorff, 2002), 59–122.

16. *Leichenpredigt Ludwig Casimir Dietzel.*

17. Kleinehagenbrock, "Der Dreissigjährige Krieg als Bedrohung der Konfession."

18. Kleinehagenbrok, *Die Grafschaft Hohenloh im Dressigjährigen Kreig*, 153–60.

19. Kleinehagenbrock, "Der Dreissigjährige Krieg als Bedrohung der Konfession," 59.

20 Kleinehagenbrock, *Die Grafschaft Hohenlohe im Dressigjährigen Kreig*, 298–99.

21 Rublack, "Lutherische Beichte," 133.

22 *Leichenpredigt Ludwig Casimir Dietzel.*

23. ALGAL 529/31, March 7–8, 1672.

24. HZAN Kirchenvisitationen 12/1654.

25 Under the direction of Count Heinrich Friedrich, Dietzel revived the Reformation practice of visiting local parishes to restore the territory's Lutheran church. In the 1650s and 1660s the team of visitors included Dietzel, Court Adviser von Gülchen, the Langenburg town steward, and a scribe. If the frequency of the parish inspections is a measure of the intensity of reforming popular religious beliefs and practices, then Langenburg's postwar effort was more systematic and sustained than those carried out in the wake of the Reformation. Church visitations took place in 1654, 1656, 1658, 1660, 1672, and 1675. HZAN 554/1–19, 1654–75.

26. HZAN 554/12, 1654. HZAN 554/17, 1658. These Hohenlohe visitations illustrate the point that the clergy often understood "witchcraft" as a variety of "superstition." See Clark, *Thinking with Demons*, 472–88.

27. HZAN 554/12, 1654.

28. HZAN 554/16, 1656.

29. HZAN 554/12, 1654.

30. I am grateful to Pastor Wilhelm Arnold Ruopp of Langenburg for opening the old Court Preacher's Library (Hof-Prädikatur Bibliothek) to me and providing me with catalogues and access to its volumes.

31. Johann Brenz, *Von Zauberey und ihrer Strafe: Ein Predig, gehalten über d. Evangelium Matth I d. 2.* (Frankfurt, 1612); David Meder, *Acht Hexenpredigten, darinnen Von des Teuffels Mordkindern, der Hexen, Unholden, Zauberischen, Drachenleuten, Milchdieben, etc.* . . . (Leipzig: Jacob Apelo, 1605); and Daniel Schaller, *Zauber Handel: Acht Predigten uber das Acht und Zwangste Capittel des Ersten Buchs Samuelis* . . . (Magdeburg: Johan Francken, 1611).

32. Other titles included Joachim Zehner, *Fünff Predigten von den Hexen, ihren Anfang, Mittel und End in sich haltend und erklärend* . . . (Leipzig: Thomas Schürer, 1613); Johann Hipolyt Brenz, *Von Zauberey und ihrer Straffe: Ein Predig Gehalten uber das Evangelium Matth. 8. Wie ein Ungestimme sich im Mer Erhebt* . . . (Frankfurt a.M.: Johann Saur, 1612); and Abraham Lang, *Zwo Wetterpredigten aus dem 18. Psalm des Königlichen Propheten Davids* . . . (Jena: Heinrich Rauchmaul, 1613).

33. One additional theme running throughout this sermon collection was how God used storms and other troubling upheavals in nature to signal his wrath and displeasure with sinners and how pious Christians should look to faith to meet misfortune. See Abraham Scultetum, *Warnung für der Warsagerey der Zäuberer und Sterngücker* . . . (Amberg: Michael Forster, 1609); Johann Georg Sigwart, *Ein Predig von Hagel und Ungewitter* . . . (Tübingen: Johann Allexandro Cello, 1613); Jacob Herrbrand, *Ein Predig von dem erschrockenlichen Wunderzeichen am Himmel dem newen Cometen oder Pfawenschwantz* . . . (Tübingen: Georg Gruppenbach, 1577); and Tobias Seiler, *Daemonomania: Oberaus schreckliche Historia von einem besessenen zwelffjährigen Jungfräwlein zu Lewenbert in Schlesien* . . . (Wittenberg: Georg Müllern, 1605).

34. Meder, *Acht Hexenpredigten darinnen Von des Teuffels Mordkindern*.

35. See Stuart Clark, "Glaube und Skepsis in der deutschen Hexenliteratur von Johann Weyer bis Friedrich von Spee," in Hartmut Lehmann and Otto Ulbricht, eds., *Vom Unfug des Hexen-Prozesses: Gegner der Hexenverfolgungen von Johann Weyer bis Friedrich von Spee*, Wolfenbütteler Forschungen, vol. 55 (Wiesbaden: Otto Harrassowitz, 1992), 15–34.

36. Meyfart, *Christliche Erinnerung*.

37. Erik Midelfort argues that Lutheran writers like Benz and Meder were part of a long tradition in southwest Germany, reaching back to the late Middle Ages, of viewing witchcraft in providential terms. While Brenz argued this point more consistently than Meder, they saw moral problems in ascribing misfortune directly to witches. Meder also warned his readers of the difficulties in prosecuting witchcraft. For a full discussion of this intellectual tradition, see Midelfort, *Witch Hunting in Southwestern Germany*, 36–56.

38. David Meder, "Von den Sünden und Lastern der Hexen," in his *Acht Hexenpredigten*, 47–61.

39. Arndt laid out his original thinking in 1606 in four books, which he later expanded to six. In Book I he argued that Christianity had fallen into a crisis, that many people masqueraded as Christians, hiding their true identities behind a mask of conformity. To win them over, one had to break open the heart and let God's Word win it away from Satan. In Arndt's view the societal crisis of Christianity could only be overcome by working systematically on the hidden and interior battlefield of the heart. One might think that by assuming the process of conversion to be a long and drawn-out affair that Protestant pastors like Dietzel might despair of converting suspected witches. But Dietzel never voiced doubts about converting witches. In fact, the hope of conversion heightened the drama during Anna Schmieg's interrogations. For a discussion of Arndt's view of conversion, see Lund, *Johann Arndt*, especially 140–213.

40. Kleinehagenbrock, *Die Grafschaft Hohenlohe im Dreissigjährigen Krieg*, 276–79.

41. Kleinehagenbrock, *Die Grafschaft Hohenlohe im Dreissigjährigen Krieg*, 282.

42. Friedrich von Spee's *Cautio Criminalis* warned confessors against being drawn into witch trials and forcing the innocent into false confessions. Even Protestant moderates like Johann Meyfart cautioned that religious zeal might compromise legal procedures and lead to moral and social chaos. See his *Christliche Erinnerung*. For a sharply critical perspective on zealous Protestant pastors and their role in the witch trials, see Johann Leib, *Consilia, Responsa ac Deductiones Juris Variae, Cumprimis Vero Processum Contra Sagas Concernentia* . . . (Frankfurt a.M.: Hermann Sande, 1666). For a recent discussion, see Clark, "Glaube und Skepsis."

43. Johannes Dilherr, *Weg der Seligheit* (Nuremberg: Wolfgang Endter, 1646), 223–24.

44. Rublack, "Lutherische Beichte," 131.

45. The church ordinance renewed after the Thirty Years' War was the Hohenlohe Church Ordinance of 1578. For the provisions governing confession and Holy Communion, see Franz, ed., *Grafschaft Hohenlohe*, 284–89.

46. Rublack, "Lutherische Beichte," 147–48.

47. HZAN 554/12, 1554.

48. Rublack, "Lutherische Beichte," 134–35.

49. HZAN 554/17, 1558.

50. Rublack, "Lutherische Beichte," 134.

CHAPTER X *A Daughter's Betrayal*

1. At this same time, natural philosophers, just like jurists, were also applying progressively higher evidentiary standards to preternatural events and encountered similar difficulties in proving their reality. See Lorraine Daston, "Marvelous Facts and Miraculous Evidence in Early Modern Europe," *Critical Inquiry* 18 (1991), 93–124.

2. Robisheaux, *Rural Society*, 105–20.

3. Because such confrontations often damaged the honor of respectable people, Benedict Carpzov warned magistrates to use the tactic only rarely. "*Ad quam tamen confrontationen, utpote quae non minimus actus praejudicialis est, odiosus, & species suggestionis, nec parum famam viri honesti laedit. . . . absqve indiciis sufficientibus neutiqvam est deveniendum.*" Benedict Carpzov, *Practicae Novae Imperialis Saxonicae Rerum Criminalium, Pars III . . .* (1670), Qu. 114, §77, 134.

4. ALGAL 529/38, May 16–17, 1672.

5. ALGAL 529/37, April 30, 1672.

6. ALGAL 529/36, April 30, 1672.

7. ALGAL 529/36, April 30, 1672.

8. ALGAL 529/36, April 30, 1672.

9. ALGAL 529/36, April 30, 1672.

10. ALGAL 529/37, April 30, 1672.

11. ALGAL 529/36, April 30, 1672.

12. ALGAL 529/38, May 16–17, 1672.

13. ALGAL 529/38, May 16–17, 1672.

14. ALGAL 529/38, May 16–17, 1672.

15. ALGAL 529/38, May 16–17, 1672.

16. ALGAL 529/36, May 21, 1672.

17. ALGAL 529/36, May 21, 1672.

18. ALGAL 529/36, May 21, 1672.

19. ALGAL 529/36, May 21, 1672.

20. ALGAL 529/36, May 21, 1672.

21. ALGAL 529/36, May 21, 1672.

22. ALGAL 529/36, May 21, 1672.

23. Carpzov, *Practicae Novae Imperialis, Pars III*, Qu. 114, §75–79, 134.

24. ALGAL 529/36, May 21, 1672.

25. ALGAL 529/41, May 22, 1672.

26. ALGAL 529/41, May 22, 1672.

27. ALGAL 529/41, May 22, 1672.

28. ALGAL 529/41, May 22, 1672.

29. ALGAL 529/41, May 22, 1672.

30. ALGAL 529/41, May 22, 1672.

31. ALGAL 529/41, May 22, 1672.

32. ALGAL 529/41, May 22, 1672.

33. ALGAL 529/41, May 22, 1672.

34. David Sabean, "The Production of Self During the Age of Confessionalism," *Central European History* 29 (1998), 4–5, 15–16.

35. ALGAL 529/41, May 22, 1672.

36. ALGAL 529/41, May 22, 1672.

37. ALGAL 529/41, May 22, 1672.

38. Some documents suggest that Hans and Endris Fuchs's brother were related to each other as godparents. Regardless of the nature of their ties, Hans and Fuchs knew each other well and helped each other from time to time.

39. ALGAL 529/41, May 22, 1672.

CHAPTER XI *A Mother's Revenge?*

1. ALGAL 529/18, May 22, 1672.

2. LGAL 529/18, May 22, 1672.

3. ALGAL 529/42, May 23, 1672.

4. Von Gülchen's reasoning about the "cause" at the root of this affair resembles Benedict Carpzov's thinking when he relied on Article 24 of the *Carolina* to show how to deduce an unknown truth from established facts. Ultimately, von Gülchen's reasoning rested on the *Carolina*, too. See Carpzov, *Practicae Novae Imperialis*, Pars III, Qu. 123, §27–35, 204–5.

5. Regarding inheritance customs and property conflicts in this region, see Robisheaux, *Rural Society*, 121–46.

6. My argument about the Schmiegs' marriage and inheritance strategy is consistent with peasant marriage strategies throughout the region, especially among families with sizable properties and wealth.

7. The story of Eva and Philip's romance rests on the accounts presented to the Lutheran

Marriage Court in September and October 1671. Eva's and Philip's accounts match each other in all significant details. ALGAL 701/1–7, September 25–November 8.

8. ALGAL 701/1, September 25, 1671.

9. ALGAL 701/2, October 6, 1671.

10. ALGAL 701/1, September 25, 1671.

11. ALGAL 701/2, October 6, 1671.

12. ALGAL 701/2, October 6, 1671.

13. ALGAL 701/1, September 25, 1671.

14. ALGAL 529/30, February 27, 1672. The story was related by Barbara Trückenmuller.

15. ALGAL 701/2, October 6, 1671.

16. ALGAL 701/2, October 7, 1671.

17. Tax registers list Conrad Küstner in 1670 as one of six "full peasants" from Nesselbach. ALSBR B888, April 23–October 28, 1670.

18. At the beginning of the Marriage Court's first session, Philip was asked directly whether he was crazy and if he had ever been confined to the Langenburg madhouse. Philip denied the story, but he did allow "that God had once let him fall down." ALGAL 701/2, October 6, 1672.

19. Karl-Sigismund Kramer, *Volksleben im Hochstift Bamberg und im Fürstentum Coburg (1500–1800)*, Veröffentlichungen der Gesellschaft für Fränkische Geschichte, Reihe IX, vol. 24 (Würzburg: Ferdinand Schöningh, 1967), 127–28.

20. ALGAL 701/5, October, 30, 1671.

21. ALGAL 701/6, November 3, 1671.

22. KB 1276.

23. This account of the events in the winter of 1671–72 has been pieced together through the testimonies of Eva, Barbara Truckenmüller, and Anna Heinckelin.

24. ALRI B4 Supplikenprotokolle über das Amt Langenburg 1660–1717, no. 211, January 20, 1672.

25. I am grateful to Claudia Ulbrich for this suggestion. The dire circumstances of the Schmiegs by February 1672 make a murder plot against a son-in-law entirely plausible, especially when one takes into account Anna's aggressiveness and explosive temper in the face of threats to her household. On village women, marriage, and the household economy, see Claudia Ulbrich, *Shulamit und Margarete: Macht, Geschlecht und Religion in einer ländlichen Gesellschaft des 18ten Jahrhunderts* (Vienna: Böhlau, 1999). For a discussion of women and murder, see Ulinka Rublack, *The Crimes of Women in Early Modern Germany* (Oxford: Clarendon Press, 1999), 224–29.

26. The long early-modern tradition of associating women with poisoning has never been adequately explored. All of the Italian Renaissance physicians who wrote on the subject and were influential in German forensic medicine also assumed the association, including Ferdinand Ponzetti, Girolamo Cardano, and especially Giovanni Baptista Codronchi, who also stressed poison's connections with demons. I have used the 1618 edition of his famous 1595 work, *De Morbis Veneficis, ac Veneficiis, Libri Qvattvor* (Milan,

1618). Typically, too, witchcraft, poisoning, and women were closely associated in the demonological literature, such as the widely read work of Johann Georg Gödelmann, *Von Zäuberern, Hexen und Unholden: warhafftiger vnd wolgegründter Bericht Herrn Georgji Gödelmann, beyder Rechten Doctor und Professorn in der Hohen Schbul zu Rostock, wie dieselbigen zuerkennen und zu straffen*, trans. Georg Nigrinus (Frankfurt a.M.: Nicolaus Basse, 1592). For some introductory comments on the issue, see Fischer-Homberger, *Medizin vor Gericht*, 364–76.

27. The most commonly available poison to control rodents was arsenic. Cities like Nuremberg and Strasbourg controlled its sale; by law, apothecaries had to register sales of arsenic and other poisons with the authorities. L. Lewin, *Die Gifte in der Weltgeschichte: toxikologische, allgemein-verständliche Untersuchungen der historischen Quellen* (Berlin: Julius Sprenger, 1920), 164–66.

28. Christina Larner makes this point about Scottish women and witchcraft; see her *Enemies of God: The Witch-Hunt in Scotland* (Baltimore: Johns Hopkins University Press, 1981), 89–102, especially 97: "The witch had the Scottish female quality of *smeddum*: spirit, a refusal to be put down, quarrelsomeness." This point accords with Ingrid Ahrendt-Schulte's point that German women also used a reputation for witchcraft and sorcery to fight off their enemies. See her *Zauberinnen in der Stadt Horn (1554–1603): Magische Kultur und Hexenverfolgung in der Frühen Neuzeit*, Geschichte und Geschlechter, vol. 21 (Frankfurt a.M.: Campus, 1997).

29. ALGAL 529/41, May 22 and June 3, 1672.

30. ALGAL 529/41, May 22 and June 3, 1672.

31. ALGAL 529/41, May 22 and June 3, 1672.

32. ALGAL 529/41, May 22 and June 3, 1672.

33. ALGAL 529/40, June 3, 1672.

34. ALGAL 529/40, June 3, 1672.

35. ALGAL 529/40, June 3, 1672.

36. ALGAL 529/40, June 3, 1672.

37. ALGAL 529/40, June 3, 1672.

38. ALGAL 529/40, June 3, 1672.

CHAPTER XII *Corpus Delicti*

1. For a discussion of the prominence of children and adolescent girls in the late-seventeenth-century witch trials, see Roper, *Witch Craze*, 181–221. It is possible that anxieties about premarital sex and courtship ran higher after the Thirty Years' War as Protestant churches renewed their campaign to enforce the marriage laws. Women also ran higher risks of punishment for unlawful sex than men. On the punishment of women for violating marriage laws, see Rublack, *Crimes of Women in Early Modern Germany*.

2. ALKI 379/1, May 31, 1672.

3. ALKI 379/2, June 8, 1672.

4. ALKI 379/3, June 14, 1672.

5. ALKI 379/4, July 9, 1672; ALKI 379/6, July 20, 1672.

6. A number of scholars stress judicial skepticism in the decline of witch trials. While I agree with this assessment, it seems more likely that the skepticism regarding witchcraft was largely a consequence of a much broader movement in jurisprudence insisting on procedural correctness and rigorous standards of evidence in Romano-canonical law, among many things. On judicial skepticism regarding seventeenth-century trials, see especially Clark, "Glaube und Skepsis;" and Brian P. Levack, "The Decline and End of Witchcraft Prosecutions," in Bengt Ankarloo and Stuart Clark, eds., *Witchcraft and Magic in Europe: The Eighteenth and Nineteenth Centuries* (Philadelphia: University of Pennsylvania Press, 1999), 1–94.

7. *Extractus Protocollorum Inquisitionum Absolutissmus in Causa Veneficii die alt Müllerin zu Hürden*. The document was one of several that von Gülchen drew together to send off to the University of Altdorf to seek advice. The others, including his letter to the Altdorf professors, have been lost. ALGAL 529/43, June 3, 1672.

8. Wieacker, *History of Private Law*, 141–42.

9. Carpzov, *Practicae Novae Imperialis*, Pars III, Qu. 120, *De incertis seu verisimilibus indiciis omnibus delictis communibus, quorum neutrum per se solum sufficiens est ad torturam*. In this Quaestio, Carpzov discusses evidence (*indicia*) and the standards of proof. Metaphors about sight and light recur throughout this discussion. One example is §13, 178: ". . . *nec obstat, quod ijusmodi indicia certa & indubitata ad condemnandum sufficiant, ac proinde torturam excludant; ubi enim probationes luce meridiana clariorers extant. . . .*"

10. The assumption that witch trials targeted women who engaged in "antisocial" behavior is therefore frequently misleading. The concept "antisocial behavior" is an anachronism that mischaracterizes the nature of conflict in agonistically structured village cultures where *conflict was presumed to be normal.* Villagers routinely engaged in conflict to defend their person, honor, family, rights, and resources. An attack demanded a response, and those who failed to do so invited reprisals, an escalation of the dispute, or the arousal of suspicion about even more serious crimes. When von Gülchen reviewed the evidence against Anna, he unsurprisingly left aside a great deal of the evidence about her "antisocial behavior." See Walz, *Hexenglaube und magische Kommunkation im Dorf.*

11. ALGAL 529/43, June 3, 1672.

12. The *Carolina* laid out the different types of evidence, and, while the court adviser followed those guidelines closely, he was no doubt aware that all of the evidence fell into the weakest category, the category that Carpzov termed "remote and apparent" (*remota et verisimilia indicia*). The doctrine of evidence, according to Carpzov, distinguished *indicia* into three types: the *indicia communia remota* or *non suffientia*, that is, evidence of a general nature, like reputation, but which was alone insufficient for proceeding to torture; the *indicia communia proxima* or *sufficientia*, evidence so strong that it clearly justified torture; and the *indicia propria*, the evidence peculiar to particular crimes (like poisoning or sorcery and witchcraft). These signs or "arguments indicating a crime" were the same as circumstantial evidence in the Anglo-American tradition. Circumstantial evidence could convict someone of a crime. *Indicia* could not. *Indicia* could only provide "sufficient indication" of guilt so that further questioning under torture could be justified. See Carpzov, *Practicae Novae Imperialis*, Pars III, Qu. 123, §1–21, 201–8.

13. ALGAL 529/43, June 3, 1672.

14. See Robisheaux, " 'The Queen of Evidence.' "

15. ALGAL 529/43, June 3, 1672.

16. ALGAL 529/43, June 3, 1672.

17. ALGAL 529/43, June 3, 1672.

18. Carpzov, *Practicae Novae Imperialis,* Pars III, Qu. 122, §60–69, 199–200.

19. Sometime after he composed his review, someone went over von Gülchen's *Extractus Protocollarum,* separating the evidence for witchcraft (*Hexerey*) from that of poisoning (*Vergifftung*). In doing so, this anonymous reviewer affirmed the late-seventeenth-century tendency to treat witchcraft and poisoning as entirely different crimes.

20. Article 147 of the *Carolina* laid down this requirement in imperial criminal law. By the middle of the seventeenth century, however, Carpzov argued for a higher standard of review, calling for physicians, preferably those trained in anatomy, to carry out forensic medical examinations. For technical discussions about the rules of proof, and Carpzov's role in helping set the terms of the discussion, see Karl Alfred Hall, *Die Lehre vom Corpus Delicti: Eine dogmatische Quellenexegese zur Theorie des gemeinen deutschen Inquisitionsprozesses* (Stuttgart: W. Kohlhammer, 1933); and Bernhard Heitsch, *Beweis und Verurteilung im Inquisitionsprozess Benedict Carpzov's: Zur Geschichte des Inquisitionsprozesses von der Constitutio Criminalis Carolina bis zu Benedict Carpzov's Practica nova imperialis Saxonica rerum criminalium* (diss., Göttingen University, 1964).

21. ALGAL 529/43, June 3, 1672.

22. Rudolf Endres, "Nürnbergs Stellung im Reich im 17. Jahrhundert," in John Roger Paas, ed., *Der Franken Rom: Nürnbergs Blütezeit in der zweiten Hälfte des 17. Jahrhunderts* (Wiesbaden: Harrassowitz, 1995), 36–39.

23. See Wolfgang Mährle, *Academia Norica: Wissenschaft und Bildung an der Nürnberger Hohen Schule in Altdorf (1575–1623),* Contubernium: Tübinger Beiträge zur Universitäts- und Wissenschaftsgeschichte, vol. 54 (Stuttgart: Franz Steiner, 2000).

24. Michael Stolleis, *Geschichte des öffentlichen Rechts,* 237–38.

25. Cregel published no treatises and directed only a handful of disputations. See the short biography in Georg Will, "Ernst Cregel," in his *Nürnbergisches Gelehrten-Lexicon oder Beschreibung aller Nürnbergischen Gelehrten beyderley Geschlechtes nach Ihrem Leben, Verdiensten und Schrifften . . .* (Nuremberg: Lorenz Schüpfel, 1755), pt. 1, 220–22.

26. Wagenseil was part of a movement insisting on the importance of history and politics to grasp the law and the institutions of the Holy Roman Empire. The complex legal, political, and religious realities of the empire simply could not be adequately understood through the old legal fiction of a continuous history reaching back to Rome. Wagenseil did not draw radical conclusions from history like some of his better-known contemporaries. See Notker Hammerstein, *Jus und Historie: Ein Beitrag zur Geschichte des historischen Denkens an deutschen Universitäten im späten 17. und im 18. Jahrhundert* (Göttingen: Vandenhoeck & Ruprecht, 1972); and especially Constantin Fasolt, *The Limits of History* (Chicago: University of Chicago Press, 2004). On Wagenseil, see Georg Will, "Wagenseil, Johann Christoph" in his *Nürnbergisches Gelehrten-Lexicon* (Nuremberg: Lorenz Schüpfel, 1758), pt. 4, 144–55.

27. See Will, "Wagenseil."

28 For a sketch of Textor's life, see Georg Will, "Textor, Johann Wolfgang," in his *Nürn-bergisches Gelehrten-Lexicon*, pt. 4, 17–21.

29 Only the general outline of Textor's service to the House of Hohenlohe are known. See Partikulararchiv Öhringen (Oe 10), 118/2/16, 1666–72.

30. Along with Samuel Pufendorf and Jacob Brunnemann, Textor should be considered among the pivotal figures advocating "reason of state" in the reestablishment of public order after the Thirty Years' War. His own critique of the political institutions and laws of the Holy Roman Empire—*Tractatus Juris Publici de Vera et Varia Ratione Status Germaniae Modernae* (Altdorf: Schönnerstädt, 1667)—appeared the same year as Pufendorf's more famous *Severini de Maonzambano Veronensis: De Statu Imperii Germanici ad Laelium Fratrem Dominum Trezolani, Liber Unus* (Geneva, 1667) and bears a close comparison. See Stolleis, *Geschichte des öffentlichen Rechts*, 209–12; and "Textor und Pufendorf über die Ratio Status Imperii im Jahr 1667," in Roman Schnur, ed., *Staatsräson: Studien zur Geschichte eines politischen Begriffs* (Berlin: Duncker & Humblot, 1975), 441–63.

31. Will, "Textor," p. 18. Textor would leave Altdorf in 1673 for a the position of judge and assessor at the court of the Elector of the Palatinate in Heidelberg. He would publish many other treatises, including his most famous work, *Synopsis Juris Gentium* (1680). For an English translation of this classic work in international law, see Johann Wolfgang von Textor, *Synopsis Juris Gentium*, ed. Ludwig Bar, trans. John Pawley (New York: Oceana, 1964). Today, Textor is best known as the grandfather of Germany's greatest poet, Johann Wolfgang von Goethe.

32. Johann Wolfgang Textor and Mauritius Hieronymus de Venne, *Disputatio Juridica de Corpore Delicti in Homicidio* (disputation, Altdorf University, 1672). Hereafter cited as Textor, *Disputatio Juridica*. While de Venne's name appears as coauthor on this significant little treatise, the startling originality of arguments points to Textor as the author.

33. Like other professors of law, Textor held disputations as a routine matter of course when thinking through questions of importance. Contemporary critics of universities missed the fact that disputations were actually signs of intellectual vitality and a practical forum for engaging issues of the day. It was through the jurisconsult system and university disputations that the turning point came in legal approaches to witchcraft in the 1690s. On German universities as lively centers of intellectual activity, see R. J. W. Evans, "German Universities After the Thirty Years War," *History of Universities* 1 (1981), 169–90.

34. Hans Recknagel, *Die Nürnbergische Universität Altdorf* (Altdorf: Nürnberger Versicherungsgruppe, 1993), 21–22.

35. Will's biographical accounts in his *Nürnbergisches Gelehrten-Lexicon* make it plain how important disputations were to the intellectual life of Altdorf and Nuremberg. See also Recknagel, *Die Nürnbergische Universität Altdorf*.

36. Textor, *Disputatio Juridica*, Thesis II, 1–2.

37. Textor, *Disputatio Juridica*, Thesis IV, 3.

38. Textor, *Disputatio Juridica*, Theses VI–XI, 4–6.

39. Textor, *Disputatio Juridica*, Thesis IX, 5.

40. *Dicimus corpus delicti in homicidio nihil esse aliud, quam occionem hominis dolosam ex relicti cadaveris vulneribus, vel aliis legitimis indiciis praesumtive apparentem.* Textor, *Disputatio Juridica*, Thesis V, 3–4.

41. In discussing the "lethality of wounds" Textor furthered the trend toward engaging forensic medical experts. especially anatomically trained physicians, in the legal process. The concept evolved out of Articles 147 and 149 of *Carolina*, which calls for a judge to consult a surgeon or other experts to determine the specific wounds that killed a victim and required a judge "along with two legal assessors (*Schöffen*), a court scribe and one or more surgeons (if they are available and can appear)" to inspect the corpse and all of the wounds on it.

42. Textor, *Disputatio Juridica*, Theses XXXI–XXXIX, 16–20.

43. Textor, *Disputatio Juridica*, Theses XLI–L, 20–25.

44. Textor, *Disputatio Juridica*, Thesis XL, 20.

45. Textor recognized the potential for controversy that this procedure could engender, but believed so profoundly in the power of legal procedure that he thought these difficult issues could be mastered.

46. Textor, *Disputatio Juridica*, Theses LI–LXV, 25–33.

47. Textor, *Disputatio Juridica*, Theses LXXVI–LXXVII, 33–39.

48. Textor, *Disputatio Juridica*, Thesis LXXIX, 39–40.

49. In developing this line of reasoning Textor went beyond the Italian jurists who had shaped the legal concepts regarding evidence up to that time. Already Carpzov had argued for including more of the subjective circumstances, not just the body itself, in determining whether a crime had taken place or not. Textor went one step further: He defined evidence in a more comprehensively material fashion. His concept of "presumptive malice" or "presumptive intent to kill" (*dolus sive animus occidendi*) also threatened conventional legal thought on how to determine the facts in a case. Whereas in conventional thinking a General Inquisition established the facts of a crime, Textor's concept of "presumptive malice" effectively enabled a judge to rule on his own on the fact of a crime. In collapsing the subjective circumstances of a case—a suspect's intentions to kill, for example—into the material evidence, Textor anticipated the reforms of Enlightenment jurists like Johann Samuel Friedrich Boehmer. For a general discussion of this problem, see Hall, *Die Lehre vom Corpus Delicti*; Marianne Hornung-Grove, *Beweisregeln im Inquisitionsprozess Johann Brunnemanns, Johann Paul Kress' und Johann Samuel Friedrich Boehmers* (diss., Erlangen, 1974); and Gottfried Boldt, *Johann Samuel Friedrich von Böhmer und die gemeinrechtliche Strafrechtswisseschaft* (Goldbach: Keip, 1997).

CHAPTER XIII *A Question of Poison*

1. Cited in Silvia de Renzi, "Witnesses of the Body: Medico-Legal Cases in Seventeenth-Century Rome," *Studies in History and Philosophy of Science* 33 (2002), 222.

2. Endres, "Nürnbergs Stellung im Reich," 38–39.

3. On this wider cultural milieu, see Endres, "Nürnbergs Stellung im Reich." For one splendid example of the effect this stimulating scientific and artistic milieu had on contemporaries, see Natalie Davis's study of the artist and naturalist Maria Sybilla Merian (1647–1717) in her *Women on the Margins: Three Seventeenth-Century Lives* (Cambridge: Harvard University Press, 1995), 140–202.

4. Georg Will, "Hofmann, Moritz," in his *Nürnbergisches Gelehrten-Lexicon . . .* (Nuremberg: Lorenz Schüpfel, 1756), pt. 2, 171.

5. For one view on how Renaissance anatomy shaped public culture, see Jonathan Saw-day, *The Body Emblazoned: Dissection and the Human Body in Renaissance Culture* (London: Routledge, 1996). On the beginnings of human dissection, see also Katherine Park, *Secrets of Women: Gender, Generation, and the Origins of Human Dissection* (New York: Zone Books, 2006).

6. Olaf Pedersen, "Tradition and Innovation," in Walter Rüegg, gen. ed., *A History of the University in Europe*, vol. 2: *Universities in Early Modern Europe (1500–1800)* (Cambridge: Cambridge University Press, 1996), 473.

7. For a sketch of Hofmann's life, see Georg Will, "Hofmann, Moritz," in his *Nürnbergisches Gelehrten-Lexicon*, pt. 2, 170–74.

8. For an overview of the development of anatomy, see Nancy G. Siraisi, *Medieval and Early Renaissance Medicine: An Introduction to Knowledge and Practice* (Chicago: University of Chicago Press, 1990), 78–114; and Wear, "Medicine in Early Modern Europe," 264–92.

9. Will, "Hofmann, Moritz," 170.

10. Will, "Hofmann, Moritz," 171.

11. Will, "Hofmann, Moritz," 171.

12. Hofmann's modernizing leadership at Altdorf can be seen in his championing William Harvey's theory on the circulation of the blood in opposition to his old teacher, Kaspar Hofmann. Whereas his mentor had led a public, and losing, campaign against Harvey's theory, the young Moritz championed Harvey and his anatomical methods, proving the English physician's findings through his own public anatomical demonstrations. See Moritz Hofmann, *De Motu Cordis et Cerebri, Sanguinis Que ac Spiri-tivum Animalium pro Vitae Continuatione per Corpus Commeatu* (diss., Altdorf University, 1653); and *De Transitu Sanguinis per Medios Pulmones Facili* (diss., Altdorf University, 1650).

13. Under Hofmann's supervision Bruno carried out disputations on tumors (*De Tumoribus*, 1649) and purging (*De Purgationis Modo,* 1652). Georg Will, "Bruno, Jacob Pan-cratius," in his *Nürnbergisches Gelehrten-Lexicon,* pt. 1, 145–47.

14. For an overview of Galenic physiology and anatomy, see Siraisi, *Medieval and Early Renaissance Medicine,* 78–114. On the evolution of new concepts in Galenic medicine by the seventeenth century, see Wear, "Medicine in Early Modern Europe," 260–64.

15. Jacob Pancratius Bruno, *De Natura Purgantium Nochua* (disputation, Altdorf University, 1672); and *De Sanitate Purgationis non Indiga* (disputation, Altdorf University, 1672).

16. In his treatment of sweating and the sweat glands, Bruno blended firsthand observa-tions (taken from Hofmann) with Aristotelian and Galenic concepts. See Jacob Pancratius Bruno, *De Sudore Secundum Naturam* (disputation, Altdorf University, 1669).

17. Daniel Sennert was a prime example of the medical syncretism of the seventeenth century.

18. *Erlangen-Universtitätsbibliothek Handschriftenabteiling* AUA 21.

19. See the astute observations by Wear, "Medicine in Early Modern Europe," 292.

20. ALGAL 529/44, July 2, 1672.

21. ALGAL 529/44, July 2, 1672.

22. ALGAL 529/44, July 2, 1672.

23. ALGAL 529/44, July 2, 1672.

24. ALGAL 529/44, July 2, 1672.

25. On this point I have been influenced by the analysis of de Renzi, "Witnesses of the Body."

26. Paolo Zacchia (1584–1659) served as the personal physician to Popes Innocent X and Alexander VII. In addition, he became a respected authority on forensic medicine. His major work, the *Quaestiones Medico-Legales,* went through a number of editions in the seventeenth century and became the standard manual in forensic medicine until late in the seventeenth century. He argued that physicians' opinions should have full binding legal power when properly presented before a court. Moritz Hofmann knew Zacchia's manual, having borrowed the *Quaestiones Medico-Legales* from the Altdorf University Library in 1654. His and Bruno's analysis of poisoning in the Schmieg case followed Zacchia's in bk. 2 almost exactly. See Paulus Zacchia, *Quaestiones Medico-Legales, in Quibus Omnes ex Materiae Medicae, Quae ad Legales Facultates Videntur Pertinere, Proponuntur, Pertractantur, Resoluuntur* (Leipzig: Fredericus Lanckisch, 1630), 4 vols., especially the section on poisonings in vol. 2, "*Titulus Secundus, De Venenis & Veneficiis*," 191–310. On the library borrowings of Hofmann and Bruno, see *Erlangen-Universtitätsbibliothek Handschriftenabteiling* AUA 21. On the development of forensic medicine, see Fischer-Homberger, *Medizin vor Gericht*, 293–321.

27. Zacchia, *Quaestiones Medico-Legales*, vol. 2, Qu. 7, 252–60.

28. Zacchia acknowledged the novel sixteenth-century theory that certain poisons might mysteriously attack the "entire substance of the body" (*in tota substantia*), but spent little time discussing this mystical view of poisons and focused instead on the material signs of natural poisons. Zacchia, *Quaestiones Medico-Legales,* vol. 2, Qu. 7, 260. See also Wear, "Medicine in Early Modern Europe," 261–64.

29. Zacchia, *Quaestiones Medico-Legales*, vol. 2, Qu. 7, 265.

30. The roots of the interest in arsenic went back to the Arab commentators on Galen and Hippocrates, but it had been furthered by sixteenth-century discussions of the poison by Girolamo Cardano, Geronimo Mercurialis, Ambrosius Paré, Johann Weyer, and Giovanni Battista Codronchi. See Fischer-Homberger, *Medizin vor Gericht*, 353–406.

31. Fischer-Homberger, *Medizin vor Gericht*, 379–85.

32. Zacchia described arsenic's terrible powers of corruption and distinguished it as a "natural poison" that had only harmful effects on the human body. "*Alterum eorum, quae & natura mala sunt, & talia semper permanent, quae nos proprie venena naturalia appellamus, quod a Natura venenosam contrarieratem humano generi inimicam fortiantur, quale est Arsenicum.*" "There is the other class of poisons which are naturally and permanently evil which we properly call natural poisons which by Nature are made extremely poisonous and inimical to human beings, among them being Arsenic." Zacchia, *Quaestiones Medico-Legales*, vol. 2, Qu. 3, 213.

CHAPTER XIV *Impasse*

1. Many German princes, especially the vulnerable ones close to France and the western borders with France, feared an outbreak of chaos reminiscent of the Thirty Years' War. On

the outbreak of the French war and the resulting political crisis, see von Aretin, *Das alte Reich 1648–1806,* 237–52.

2. ALGAL 527/13, June 5, 1672.

3. ALGAL 527/16, June 15, 1672.

4. Article 37 of the *Carolina* identified the purchase and possession of poison, especially from someone already under suspicion for a crime, as a "specific indication" of poisoning. *PGO* Article 37, 47.

5. Grieve, *A Modern Herbal,* vol. 1, 265–76.

6. Grieve, *A Modern Herbal,* vol. 1, 76–77.

7. "Eisenkraut," in *HDA,* vol. 2, cols. 733–41.

8. Schleicher's pharmacy also included *Nieswurz* or hellebore, sometimes called Christ's herb, and tormentil. Legend had it that Christ's herb bloomed on Christmas at night. To ward off disease from their cows, peasants bored a hole through the ear of a cow and stuck a piece of hellebore through it. "Nieswurz," in *HDA,* vol. 6, cols. 1083–85. Villagers gave their cows tormentil against pains, or "*die tormenta.*" Jacob and Wilhelm Grimm, *Deutsches Wörterbuch* (Leipzig: Hirzel, 1935), v. 21, col. 895.

9. ALGAL 527/17, June 20–22, 1672.

10. ALGAL 527/17, June 20–22, 1672.

11. ALGAL 529/62, July 28, 1672.

12. ALGAL 529/64, August 14, 1672.

13. Mandrake root is largely found in countries of the Mediterranean. It contains alcoloids that affect the nervous system, triggering tremors, paralysis, and drowsiness. The mandrakes sold in the German lands were most likely made out of the roots of native plants, however. "Alraun," in *HDA,* vol. 1 (1927), cols. 312–24.

14. "Alraun," cols. 319–20.

15. In old German the word *Katzenkopf,* "cat's head," referred to a variety of different things. In addition to the head of a cat, it also referred to a specialized hammer used by millers as well as a metal fitting that secured bolts or crossbars in place. It is possible that Hans and his mill hand were actually thinking about different kinds of *Katzenkopf* when they discussed keeping the gear wheels from popping out of their fittings. Grimm, *Deutsches Wörterbuch,* vol. 11, col. 297.

16. ALGAL 529/64 & 67, August 14, 1672.

17. ALGAL 529/68, August 19, 1672.

18. ALGAL 529/64, August 14, 1672.

19. ALGAL 529/68, August 19, 1672.

20. On the psychological and spiritual processes involved in the confession, I disagree with the argument that witchcraft accounts elicited under torture were the collective "fantasies" of the inquisitor and the accused. Such arguments rest on a modern distinction between "fantasy" and "reality" and run the risk of distorting contemporary views of the evidence, thereby reinforcing stereotypes about witchcraft and witch trials as "irrational." But the approach can yield intriguing perspectives, as in Lyndal Roper, *Oedipus*

and the Devil: Witchcraft, Sexuality, and Religion in Early Modern Europe (London: Routledge, 1994), and *Witch Craze*.

21. ALGAL 529/45, July 26, 1672.

22. ALGAL 529/45, July 26, 1672.

23. ALGAL 529/46, July 26, 1672.

24. ALGAL 529/46, July 26, 1672.

25. ALGAL 529/46, July 26, 1672.

26. ALGAL 529/46, July 26, 1672.

27. ALGAL 529/46, July 26, 1672.

28. Evans, *Rituals of Retribution*, 84.

29. ALGAL 529/46, July 26, 1672.

30. ALGAL 529/47, July 26, 1672.

31. ALGAL 529/49, August 14, 1672.

32. ALGAL 529/88, September 4, 1672.

33. ALGAL 529/89, September 4, 1672.

34. ALGAL 529/89, September 4, 1672.

35. ALGAL 529/89, September 4, 1672.

36. ALGAL 529/89, September 4, 1672.

37. On judicial skepticism and the decline of witch trials, see Levack, "Decline and End of Witchcraft Prosecutions." Christian Thomasius, the first prominent jurist to call for ending witchcraft prosecutions, developed his arguments out of the critical discussions about evidence going back to the 1630s. His famous legal treatise against witchcraft, *De Crimine Magiae* (1701), set the tone for the skeptical Enlightenment attitude toward witchcraft. See the modern edition translated and edited by Rolf Lieberwirth, *Vom Laster der Zauberei-De Crimie Magiae; Über die Hexenprozesse-Processus Inquisitorii Contra Sagas*, 2nd ed. (Munich: Deutscher Taschenbuch, 1987). On the wider legal context, see Winfried Trusen, "Rechtliche Grundlagen der Hexenprozesse und ihrer Beendigung," in Sönke Lorenz and Dieter R. Bauer, eds., *Das Ende der Hexenverfolgung, Hexenforschung*, vol. 1 (Stuttgart: Franz Steiner, 1995), 203–26.

CHAPTER XV *Politics*

1. ALGAL 529/90, September 7–8, 1672.

2. ALGAL 529/90, September 7–8, 1672.

3. ALGAL 529/90, September 7–8, 1672.

4. ALGAL 529/55, September 12, 1672.

5. ALGAL 529/55, September 12, 1672.

6. ALGAL 529/55, September 12, 1672.

7. ALGAL 529/56, September 12, 1672.

8. ALGAL 529/55, September 12–14, 1672.

9. ALGAL 529/55, September 12–14, 1672.

10. ALGAL 529/55, September 12–14, 1672.

11. ALGAL 529/91, September 19, 1672.

12. On Strasbourg in the late seventeenth century, see Franklin Ford, *Strasbourg in Transition, 1648–1789* (Cambridge, Mass.: Harvard University Press, 1958); and, more generally, Philippe Dollinger, *Histoire de l'Alsace* (Toulouse: Édouard Privat, 1970), 259–303; also Wallmann, *Philipp Jakob Spener*, 1–34.

13. Peter Oestmann, *Rechtsvielfalt vor Gericht: Rechtsanwendung und Partikularrecht im Alten Reich, Rechtsprechung: Materialien und Studien*, Veröffentlichungen des Max-Planck-Instituts für Europäische Rechtsgeschichte Frankfurt am Main, vol. 18 (Frankfurt a.M.: Vittorio Klostermann, 2002), 683–85.

14. On Strasbourg's university culture after the Thirty Years' War, see especially Wallmann, *Philipp Jakob Spener*, 62–123.

15. On the close association of the political theory of divine-right monarchy and absolutism with witch beliefs, see Clark, *Thinking with Demons*, 602–18.

16. See Stuart Clark's brilliant discussion of Bodin's political thought and its connections to witch theory in *Thinking with Demons*, 668–82.

17. On the reception of Bodin's ideas about witchcraft among German thinkers, see Gerhild Scholz Williams, *Defining Dominion: The Discourses of Magic and Witchcraft in Early Modern France and Germany* (Ann Arbor: University of Michigan Press, 1995).

18. A Strasbourg humanist, Johann Fischart, translated Bodin's work into German in 1591 as *De Magorum Daemonomania: vom aussgelasnen wütigen Teuffelssheer allerhand Zauberern, Hexen unnd Hexenmeistern* . . . (Strasbourg: Bernhart Jodin, 1591). Written at the time when witch trials surged alarmingly and unexpectedly, Fischart's introduction helped make Bodin's arguments about witches appealing to a German audience. By the 1630s and 1640s Bodin's thinking about divine-right sovereignty and the state found echoes in the political thought of Benedict Carpzov and Theodor Reinkingk, both of whom applied their ideas explicitly to the Holy Roman Empire, its institutions and territories. Among others, Johann Heinrich Boecler kept the interest in Bodin alive in Strasbourg in the 1660s. See Dietmar Willoweit, *Rechtsgrundlagen der Territorialgewalt: Landesobrigkeit, Herrschaftsrechte und Territorium in der Rechtswissenschaft der Neuzeit* (Cologne: Böhlau, 1975), 138–72; and Stolleis, *Geschichte des öffentlichen Rechts*, 170–86. For one view about the long-term significance of these political debates, see Ian Hunter, *Rival Enlightenments: Civil and Metaphysical Philosophy in Early Modern Germany* (Cambridge: Cambridge University Press, 2001).

19. Wallman, *Philipp Jakob Spener*, pp. 69–70.

20. In the 1630s and 1640s Matthias Bernegger, a popular jurist and historian at the university, became a vocal advocate for Hugo Grotius and his arguments for natural law and the state. When Johann Textor studied at Strasbourg in the 1660s, he came into contact with law professors who saw the state and society in these terms. See Wallmann, *Philipp Jakob Spener*, 78.

21. For an argument about the disinclination of natural-law proponents to make witchcraft integral to their views on civil society, see Clark, *Thinking with Demons*, 602–18.

22. The spiritualizing tradition about witchcraft, sometimes called the Providential tradition, went back to the *Canon Episcopi* in the Middle Ages. See Midelfort, *Witch Hunting in Southwestern Germany*, 15–19, 42–51, 63–66, 193–94. During the notorious Esslingen trials of 1662–63, Strasbourg jurists had initially supported repressive legal methods, but had then later insisted that the courts rely only on credible witnesses, that they prove material harm through sorcery or witchcraft, and that they question a suspect under torture only after the testimonies of two eyewitnesses. See Jerouschek, *Die Hexen und ihr Prozess*, 219–21.

23. Reflecting a growing caution about criminal prosecutions and legal procedures, the Strasbourg law faculty had debated a host of the legal issues reflected in the Schmieg affair, including unjust prosecutors, controversial eyewitness confrontations, false testimonies, the rules of evidence, judicial caution, and unjust prosecutions of the innocent. See the following disputations: Gerhard von Stökken, *Disputatio Solemnis de Jure Odioso* (disputation, Strasbourg University, 1668); and *Disputatio Juridica de Arbitris* (disputation: Strasbourg University, 1672); and Johann Tabor, *De Confrontatione, Difficili et Inexplorato Juris Articulo, Disputationes Quinque* (disputation, Strasbourg University, 1663); Johann Rebhan, *Tractatus de Erroribus Testamenorum* (Strasbourg: Dolhoff & Zetzner, 1669); and Johann Rebhan, *Disputatio Juridica de Indiciis Delictorum in Genere* (disputation: Strasbourg University, 1668).

24. Jacob Schaller, *Paradoxon de Tortura in Christiana Repvblica non Exercenda* . . . (diss., Strasbourg University, 1658). I have consulted the edition published together with Augustin Nicolas, *Quaestione per Tormenta Criminum Veritas Elucescat, Dissertation Moralis et Juridica* . . . (Strasbourg: Spoor, 1697). In many universities opinion shifted against torture in the late seventeenth century. See also Trusen, "Rechtliche Grundlagen der Hexenprozesse und ihrer Beendigung," 220–24.

25. Spee's incisive critique of torture anticipated the scathing denunciations of the Enlightenment and still resonate with modern readers. For a modern English translation of his *De Cautio Criminalis*, see Friedrich Spee von Langenfeld, *Cautio Criminalis, or a Book on Witch Trials*, trans. Marcus Hellyer (Charlottesville: University of Virginia Press, 2003). For a brief introduction to Spee and his influence, see Theo G. M. van Oorschot, "Ihrer Zeit voraus: Das Ende der Hexenverfolgung in der *Cautio Criminalis*," in Lorenz and Bauer, eds., *Das Ende der Hexenverfolgung*, pp. 1–18.

26. ALGAL 529/94, October 8, 1672.

27. ALGAL 529/94, October 8, 1672.

28. ALGAL 529/94, October 8, 1672.

29. To use the terms of Jean Bodin or Benedict Carpzov, Schmieg offended against the sovereign majesty of God. Of all crimes, the crime of *lèse-majesté* against God was the most abominable of all. Carpzov, *Practicae Novae Imperialis*, Pars I, Qu. 41, 245–58; Qu. 44, 277–84; and especially Qu. 48 (*De Crimine Sortilegii: et Num Recte Magistratq in Sortilegos & Maleficos Poena Mortis Animadvertat?*), 307–17.

30. ALGAL 529/94, October 8, 1672.

31. ALGAL 529/94, October 8, 1672.

32. ALGAL 529/94, October 8, 1672.

33. ALGAL 529/94, October 8, 1672.

34. ALGAL 529/94, October 8, 1672.

35. ALGAL 529/94, October 8, 1672.

36. ALGAL 529/94, October 8, 1672.

37. Textor pulled together his thinking about the nature of the state in his *Synopsis Juris Gentium* (Basel, 1680). I have consulted a modern reproduction and translation: Johann Wolfgang Textor, *Synopsis of the Law of Nations*, trans. John Pawley Bate (New York: Oceana, 1964), vol. 2, 1–7.

38. Stolleis, "Textor and Pufendorf," 461–62.

39. Textor, *Law of Nations*, vol. 2, 47–56.

40. Stolleis, "Textor and Pufendorf," 450–53.

41. Textor, *Law of Nations*, vol. 2, 92–101.

42. Textor, *Laws of Nations*, vol. 2, 102–17.

43. In 1681, Samuel Stryk, a well known late-seventeenth-century jurist associated with the *usus modernus* school of law, called attention to the rancor at Strasbourg directed at jurists supporting natural-law views of the state, one of whom was Textor. So disturbing was their thinking to Johann Rebhan that he denounced them publicly in disputations as "religious sectarians." See Stolleis, "Textor and Pufendorf," 461–62; and Rebhan's own polemic against them, *De Sectis, seu Diversis Veterum Jurisconsultum Familiis* (Strasbourg: Paulli, 1666).

44. ALGAL 529/93, October 8, 1672.

CHAPTER XVI *A Vengeful Heart*

1. Johann Arndt, *Sechs Bücher vom wahren Christentum* (Stuttgart: J. F. Steinkopf, 1919), bk. 1, 60. Originally published as *Vier Bücher vom wahren Christentum* (1606).

2. Arndt, *Sechs Bücher vom wahren Christentum,* bk. 1, 11–12.

3. Arndt, *Sechs Bücher vom wahren Christentum,* bk. 1, 21.

4. Franz, ed., *Grafschaft Hohenlohe*, 290.

5. The quote is from Hartmann, *Hand-Buch für Seelsorger*, 776. See also Hartmann's *Absolution-Buch.*

6. Rublack, "Lutherische Beichte."

7. ALGAL 529/104, October 21 and 23, 1672.

8. ALGAL 529/104, October 21 and 23, 1672.

9. ALGAL 529/104, October 21 and 23, 1672.

10. ALGAL 529/101, October 22, 1672.

11. ALGAL 529/101, October 22, 1672.

12. ALGAL 529/102, October 22, 1672.

13. ALGAL 529/104, October 23, 1672.

14. ALGAL 529/98, October 24, 1672.

15. Arndt, *Sechs Bücher vom wahren Christentum*, bk. 1, 60.

16. ALGAL 529/100, October 24–25, 1672.

17. ALGAL 529/97, October 25, 1672.

18. ALGAL 529/97, October 25, 1672.

19. ALGAL 529/100. October 24–25, 1672.

20. ALGAL 529/97, October 25, 1672.

21. Learned witch theory worked through contrarieties and inversions; the magistrate took down a statement and, instead of interpreting it at face value, ascribed to it an inverse or contrary meaning. It was like looking at the world upside down or inside out. Schooled in Johann Arndt's devotional language, the Langenburg magistrates also filtered Anna's words through Arndt's notions of the self and the heart. By confronting her, the sinner, with the fact that her language actually meant its perverse opposite, they aimed to unmask her as a "false Christian" and jolt her into converting to Christ. On the logic of this language, see Stuart Clark, "Inversion, Misrule, and the Meaning of Witchcraft," *Past and Present*, no. 87 (1980), 98–127; and more fully in Clark, *Thinking with Demons*, 9ff.

22. ALGAL 529/97, October 25, 1672.

23. ALGAL 529/97, October 25, 1672.

24. ALGAL 529/97, October 25, 1672.

25. Arndt, *Sechs Bücher vom wahren Christentum*, bk. 1, 21.

26. ALGAL 529/105, October 26, 1672.

27. ALGAL 529/109, October 29, 1672.

28. ALGAL 529/105, October 26, 1672.

29. ALGAL 529/108, October 29, 1672.

30. In calling her demon lover "Heinrich Zacharias," Anna invoked the name of a common Catholic blessing against the plague, the Zacharias blessing. Here Zacharias was taken to refer not to St. Zacharias, a medieval bishop, but to a demon. Perhaps hearing the strange name when Catholics aggressively advanced their faith in the region during the Thirty Years' War—also a time of plague—Anna inverted its meaning, as Protestants often did with Catholic blessings, and associated it with diabolism. See *HDA*, vol. 9, cols. 875–77.

31. ALGAL 529/108, October 29, 1672.

32. ALGAL 529/108, October 29, 1672.

33. ALGAL 529/109, October 29, 1672.

34. ALGAL 529/117, November 2, 1672.

35. ALGAL 529/117, November 2, 1672.

36. ALGAL 529/117, November 2, 1672.

37. ALGAL 529/117, November 2, 1672.

38. ALGAL 529/117, November 2, 1672.

39. ALGAL 529/118, November 2, 1672.

40. ALGAL 529/121, November 4, 1672.

41. Robisheaux, " 'The Queen of Evidence.' "

42. ALGAL 527/62, November 4, 1672.

CHAPTER XVII *Poor Sinner*

1. ALAL 529/123, November 7, 1672.

2. Because no eyewitness accounts of the execution day have survived, I have reconstructed the events from the instructions for the court that were drawn up and other studies on executions. ALAL 144/11, November 8, 1672. The two best sources on executions are van Dülmen, *Theatre of Horror*, and Evans, *Rituals of Retribution*.

3. Van Dülmen, *Theatre of Horror*, 53–61.

4. ALAL 144/11, December 10, 1673 [*sic*].

5. ALAL 144/11, [November or December 1672].

6. ALAL 144/11, November 8, 1672.

7. ALGAL 527/63, November 8, 1672.

8. ALGAL 525/64, November 5, 1672.

9. The quote comes from Johann Ludwig Hartmann's manual of advice for Lutheran confessors, *Hand-Buch für Seelsorger*, 824–25. Hartmann describes the confessing and consoling of "poor sinners" about to be executed in his *Absolution-Buch*, 132–42, and in greater detail in *Hand-Buch für Seelsorger*, 773–828.

10. Hartmann, *Absolution-Buch*, 141–42.

11. Evans, *Rituals of Retribution*, 65–67.

12. ALAL 529/123, November 7, 1672.

13. Siegfried Hardung, *Die Vorladung vor Gottes Gericht: Ein Beitrag zur rechtlichen und religiösen Volkskunde*, Bausteine zur Volkskunde und Religionswissenschaft, no. 9 (Bühl-Baden: Konkordia A.G., 1934), 33–34.

14. ALAL 144/11, November 8, 1672.

15. ALAL 144/11, November 8, 1672.

16. ALGAL 529/125, November 8, 1672.

17. Grimm, *Deutsches Wörterbuch*, vol. 2., col. 183.

18. ALAL 144/11, November 8, 1672.

19. KB 1276.

CHAPTER XVIII *Ruin*

1. ALGAL 530/15, November 22, 1672.

2. ALGAL 530/11, November 22, 1672.

3. ALGAL 530/13, November 22, 1672.

4. ALGAL 530/20, November 28, 1672.

5. ALGAL 530/20, November 28, 1672.

6. ALGAL 530/20, November 28, 1672.

7. ALGAL 530/29, December 4, 1672.

8. ALGAL 530/39, December 17, 1672.

9. ALGAL 530/66, January 12, 1673.

10. ALGAL 529/62, July 28, 1672; and ALGAL 529/88, September 4, 1672.

11. On the differences between men and women in witchcraft, see Eva Labouvie, "Männer in Hexenprozess: Zur Sozialanthropologie eines 'männlichen' Verständnisses von Hexerei," in Claudia Opitz, ed., *Der Hexenstreit: Frauen in der frühneuzeitlichen Hexenverfolung* (Freiburg: Herder, 1995), 211–45.

12. ALGAL 530/4, November 12, 1672. For an explanation of this practice, see "Zwiesel," in *HDA*, vol. 9, cols. 971–78.

13. ALGAL 530/136, January 12, 1673.

14. ALGAL 530/4, November 12, 1672.

15. ALGAL 530/87, February 13, 1673.

16. ALGAL 530/91, February 18, 1673. The evidence comes from the watchman who overheard this conversation. Given what then happened, the report seems credible.

17. ALGAL 530/90, February 17, 1673.

18. One other possibility is that Count Heinrich Friedrich secretly ordered that Hans and Michel be allowed to escape. Heinrich Friedrich had long had a special tie of patronage to his old miller and repeatedly intervened on Hans's behalf. Unfortunately the mystery of the Schmiegs' escape is unlikely to be solved.

19. ALGAL 530/146, December 13, 1673.

20. ALGAL 530/122, July 19, 1673.

21. ALGAL 530/124, July 19, 1673.

22. Eva was questioned on July 31 about her father's whereabouts and the rumor that she was sending clothes secretly to him. ALGAL 530/132, July 31, 1672.

23. ALGAL 530/120, July 19, 1673.

24. No documents record Langenburg enlisting the aid of the Heidelberg government in looking for the Schmiegs.

25. ALGAL 709/17, November 4, 1693.

26. ALGAL 530/107, May 23, 1673.

27. ALGAL 530/111, June 11, 1673.

28. ALGAL 530/118, July 18, 1673.

29. ALGAL 530/132, July 31, 1673.

30. KB 1276. The parish register records the baptism of Barbara Küstner on February 22, 1674. While noting Hans Jörg's name, the register does not record the date of his baptism.

31. ALGAL 709/2, January 16, 1673.

32. ALGAL 709/3, February 26, 1673.

33. ALGAL 709/3, February 26, 1673.

34. ALGAL 709/3, February 26, 1673.

35. ALGAL 709/16, March 20, 1673.

36. ALGAL 709/13, March 22, 1673.

37. ALGAL 709/17, November 4, 1693.

38. ALGAL 709/17, November 4, 1693.

39. ALGAL 701/15, March 30, 1676; ALGAL 701/16, June 15, 1676; ALGAL 701/17, June 15, 1676; ALGAL 701/18, June 26, 1676; ALGAL 701/19, August 19, 1676; ALGAL 701/9, February 13, 1680.

40. ALGAL 709/20, November 9, 1693.

CHAPTER XIX *Stories*

1. ALGAL 554/19, 1675.

2. ALGAL 542/1677–78.

3. On the crafting of official narratives about social dramas, see Victor Turner, "Social Dramas and Stories About Them," in W. J. T. Mitchell, ed., *On Narrative* (Chicago: University of Chicago Press, 1981), 137–64. About disorderly women and witches in German broadsides and pamphlets, see Joy Wiltenburg, *Disorderly Women and Female Power in the Street Literature of Early Modern England and Germany* (Charlottesville: University of Virginia Press, 1992).

4. The Gemeinschaftliches Archiv Langenburg, or Common Archive of Langenburg.

5. The documents of Anna Schmieg's trial were filed in the Common Archive of Langenburg as LVIII no. 3. ALGAL 529, 1672.

6. ALGAL 529, 1672.

7. Johann Christian Wibel, *Hohenlohische Kyrchen- und Reformations-Historie, aus bewährten Urkunden und Schriften verfasset* . . . (Onolzbach: Jacob Christoph Poschens, 1752–53), 3 vols.

8. Johann Christoph Wibel, "Langenburgische Acta Ecclesiastica" (unpublished ms., Pfarramt Langenburg, ca. 1750).

9. Wibel, *Hohenlohische Kyrchen- und Reformations-Historie*, vol. 1, 779.

10 Wibel, *Hohenlohische Kyrchen- und Reformations-Historie*, vol. 1, 779–80.

11. Wibel, *Hohenlohische Kyrchen- und Reformations-Historie*, vol. 1, 784.

12 There is no evidence that Wibel or other Lutheran church leaders in Hohenlohe wrestled with the early Enlightenment controversies over witchcraft.

13 There are numerous accounts of Günther's life. The most detailed accounts were provided first by her husband, Rudolf, in his *Unter dem Schleier der Gisela: Aus Agnes Günthers Leben und Schaffen* (Stuttgart: J. F. Steinkopf, 1936) and then later by her son, Gerhard Günther, in *Ich denke der alten Zeit, der vorigen Jahre: Agnes Günther in Briefen, Erinnerungen, Berichten* (Stuttgart: J. F. Steinkopf, 1972).

14. Günther, *Ich denke der alten Zeit*, 547–48.

15. Rudolf Günther, *Bilder aus dem kirchlichen Leben Langenburgs: Vortrag anlässlich des 400 jährigen Bestehens der Stadtkirche bei eine Gemeindefeier am 26. Januar 1903* (Langenburg: [Pfarramt Langenburg], 1903).

16. Günther, *Unter dem Schleier der Gisela*, 73.

17. Agnes Günther, *Von der Hexe, die eine Heilige war* (Marburg: Verlag der Christlichen Welt, 1913), 8.

18. Günther, *Unter dem Schleier der Gisela*, 73.

19. For a complete text of the play, see Günther, *Unter der Schleier der Gisela*, 111–208. Her son argues that this printed version does not correspond precisely with the script and the production of the 1906 play, however. For a summary of the play's plot, see Günther, *Ich denke der alten Zeit*, 364–65.

20. Agnes Günther, *Von der Hexe, die eine Heilige war*, 26.

21. Agnes Günther, *Von der Hexe, die eine Heilige war*, 55.

22. Agnes Günther, *Die Heilige und ihr Narr,* 142nd ed. (Kiel: Steinkopf, 1996). This edition is a reproduction of the 1913 edition.

23. For a recent analysis of the novel, see Elke Bauernfeind, *Agnes Günther: Die Heilige und ihr Narr: Leserlenkung und Rezeption*, Stuttgarter Arbeiten zur Germanistik, no. 269 (Stuttgart: Hans-Dieter Heinz, 1993). On the popular reception, 147–55.

24. Bauernfeind, *Agnes Günther*, 112–17.

25. See Gisela Brinker-Gabler, "Perspektiven des Übergangs: Weibliches Bewusstsein und frühe Moderne," in Gisela Brinker-Gabler, ed., *Deutsche Literatur von Frauen*, vol. 2: *19. und 20. Jahrhundert* (Munich: C. H. Beck, 1988), 169–204.

26. Bauernfeind, *Agnes Günther*, 59–69.

27. On the burgeoning Heimat literature of the early twentieth century, see Sigrid Schmid-Bortenschlager, "Besinnung auf Traditionen: Heimat und Geschichte im Roman des frühen 20. Jahrhunderts," in Gisela Brinker-Gabler, ed, *Deutsche Literatur von Frauen*, vol. 2: *19. und 20. Jahrhundert* (Munich: C. H. Beck, 1988), 235–48.

28. See especially Gudrun Gersmann, "Die Hexe als Heimatheldin: Die Hexenverfolgungen der Frühen Neuzeit im Visier der Heimathistoriker," *Westfälische Forschungen* 45 (1995), 102–33.

29. See the case of the Ruhr historian Wilhelm Schmitt, who created the witch as a mythical heroine in the 1920s in Gersmann, "Die Hexe als Heimatheldin," 118–24. While nineteenth-century scholars like Wilhelm Gottlieb Soldan established a popular and compelling modern "rationalist paradigm" about witchcraft and witch trials, treating witchcraft as an imaginary crime and the accused as victims of zealous persecution, regional historians provided the local accounts and archival records that supported this view. By the 1880s historians were publishing rich material about Franconia's witches and witch trials. On the creation of the modern "rationalist" paradigm, see Wolfgang Behringer, "Zur Geschichte der Hexenforschung," in Lorenz, ed., *Hexen und Hexenverfolgung im deutschen Südwesten*, vol. 2, 105–7. Examples of the new regional literature for Franconia included Paul Beck, "Hexenprozesse aus dem Fränkischen," *Württembergische Vierteljahrshefte für Landesgeschichte* 7 (1884), 76–80, 157–60, 297–302; and Adolf Bacmeis-

ter, "Zur Geschichte der Hexenprozesse," *Württembergische Vierteljahrshefte für Landes-geschichte* 9 (1886), 282–92.

30. Ingaruth Schlauch,"Die Hexe von Hürden: Ein Heimatspiel" (Unpublished ms., ca. 1957).Typescript manuscript made available by the author.

31.Author's personal communication,June 1998.

32.Author's personal communication,June 1998.

33.Rudolf Schlauch, *Hohenlohe Franken: Landschaft, Geschichte, Kultur, Kunst* (Nuremberg: Glock & Lutz, 1964).

34. Schlauch, *Hohenlohe Franken*, 75.

35. *Hexen: Hexenwahn und Hexenverfolgung in und um Schwäbisch Hall: Hällisch-Fränkisches Museum Schwäbisch Hall 18. Juni–7. August 1988* (Schwäbisch Hall: Hällisch-Fränkisches Museum, 1988). I am grateful to Winfried Beuter, archivist at Neuenstein, and Herta Beuter, archivist at the municipal archives in Schwäbisch Hall, for a copy of the exhibition catalogue.

36. *Hexen: Hexenwahn und Hexenverfolgung in und um Schwäbisch Hall*, 84–88.

37. *Hexen: Hexenwahn und Hexenverfolgung in und um Schwäbisch Hall*, 56.

38.For a discussion of continued fascination with witches and witchcraft, see Purkiss, *The Witch in History*, 7–58; Marion Gibson, *Witchcraft Myths in American Culture* (New York: Routledge, 2007); and especially Tanya Luhrmann, *Persuasions of the Witch's Craft: Ritual Magic in Contemporary England* (Cambridge, Mass.: Harvard University Press, 1989).

39. Gottlob Haag,"Maientanz und Hexentanz," in his *Und manchmal krähte der Wetterhahn: Ein hohenlohisches Tagebuch* (Bergatreue:Wilfried Eppe, 1992), 15.

40 Author's memory.

Bibliography

MANUSCRIPT SOURCES

HOHENLOHE-ZENTRALARCHIV (NEUENSTEIN):

GA Series: Gemeinschaftliche Archive des Gesamthauses Hohenlohe (GA)

GA 05: Gemeinschaftliches Hausarchiv, Abteilung I/II: Grunddokumente der hohenlohischen Geschichte

GA 10: Gemeinschaftliches Hausarchiv, Abteilung III: Kirchliche und Geistliche Stiftungen in der Grafschaft Hohenlohe

GA 75: Hohenlohe-Bibliothek: Handschriften

GA 85: Religionsdrucksachen

GA 90: Leichenpredigten

GA 100: Archiv Kooperation Hohenlohe: Handgezeichnete Karten

GA 105: Gedrukte Karten

GL Series: Gemeinschaftliche Archive der Neuensteiner Linie (GAN)

La Series: Archiv Langenburg

La 5: Gemeinschaftliches Archiv (ALGAL)

La 15: Kanzlei I (ALKI)

La 35: Regierung I (ALRI)

La 40: Kammer I (ALKaI)

La 75: Amt Langenburg (ALAL)

La 135: Nachlässe (ALN)

La 155: Sonstige Bestände, Lager- Gült- und Schatzungsbücher (ALSBLGS)

La 160: Sonstige Bestände, Rechnungen (ALSBR)

Ki Series: Archiv Kirchberg (AK)

Oe Series: Archiv Öhringen (AÖ)

Oe 10: Partikulararchiv Öhringen (AÖPaÖ)

LANGENBURG HOF-PRÄDIKATUR BIBLIOTHEK (LANGENBURG)

UNIVERSITÄTSBIBLIOTHEK ERLANGEN, HANDSCHRIFTENABTEILUNG

STADTSARCHIV HALL (SCHWÄBISCH HALL)

EVANGELISCHES LANDESKIRCHLICHES ARCHIV (STUTTGART)

PRINTED PRIMARY SOURCES

Alber, Mathäus, and Wilhelm Bidenbach. *Ein Suma etlicher Predigen vom Hagel und Unholden gethon in der Pfarkirch zu Stuttgarten im Monat Augusto Anno M.D.LXII.* Tübingen: Ulrich Norhart's Widow, 1562.

Albrecht, Georg. *Beicht-Spiegel darinnen eine sonderbare Beichtform (so meistentheills in den Evangelischen Hällischen und Lympurgischen Kirchen gebäuchlish ist* . . . Nuremberg: Christoph Endter, 1671.

Arndt, Johann. *Sechs Bücher vom wahren Christentum.* Stuttgart: J. F. Steinkopf, 1919.

———. *Vier Bücher Von wahrem Christenthumb Heilsamer Busse: Hertzlicher Rewe unnd Leid uber die Sünde warem Glauben heiligem Leben und Wandel der rechten wahren Christen . . . Auffs newe ubersehen und gebessert.* Brunswick: Andreas Duncker, 1606.

Binsfeld, Peter. *Tractat ob der Zauberer Aussag oder Bekantnuss Glauben zu geben.* Munich: A. Berg, 1591.

Bodin, Jean. *De Magorum Daemonomania: vom aussgelasnen wütigen Teuffelssheer allerhand Zauberern, Hexen unnd Hexenmeistern* . . . Strasbourg: Bernhart Jodin, 1591.

Bohn, Johannes Bohn. *De Renunciatione Vulnerum, seu Vulnerum Lethalium Examen* . . . Leipzig: Thomas Fritsch, 1711.

Brenz, Johann. *Von Zauberey und ihrer Straffe: Ein Predig Gehalten uber das Evangelium Matth. 8. Wie ein Ungestimme sich im Mer Erhebt* . . . Frankfurt: Johann Saur, 1612.

Brunnemann, Johannes. *Tractatus Juridicus de Inquisitionis Processu, Ingratiam Illorum, Qui Causas Criminales Tractant Olim Conscriptus* . . . Wittenberg: Samuelis Krebsii, 1672.

Bruno, Jacob Pancratius. *De Natura Purgantium Nochua.* Disputation, Altdorf University, 1672.

————. *De Sanitate Purgationis Non Indiga*. Disputation, Altdorf University, 1672.

————. *De Sudore Secundum Naturam*. Disputation, Altdorf University, 1669.

————. *Disputatio Physiologico-Medica de Circuitus Sanguinis in Homine ad Vitam et Valetudinem Necessitate* . . . Disputation, Altdorf University, 1690.

————. *Disquisitionem Medicam de Medicamento sum Facultatibus ad Mentem* . . . Disputation, Altdorf University, 1670.

Carpzov, Benedict. *Practicae Novae Imperialis Saxonicae Rerum Criminalium*. 3 vols. Wittenberg: Mevius & Schumacher, 1670.

Codronchius, Baptista. *De Morbis Veneficis, ac Veneficiis, Libri Quattuor*. Milan, 1618.

Dietzel, Ludwig Casimir. *Leichenpredigt Herrn Tobiae Ulrichi von Gülchen*. Schwäbisch Hall: Hans-Reinhard Läidogen, 1675.

Dilherr, Johann Michael. *Augen- und Hertzens-Lust, das ist emblematische Fürstellung der Sonn- und Festäglichen Evangelien* . . . Nuremberg: Wolfgang Endter, 1661.

————. *Heilig-epistolischer Bericht, Licht, Geleit, und Freud, das ist: emblematische Fürstellung der heilgen Sonn- und festtäglichen Episteln: in welcher gründlicher Bericht von den rechten Wort-Verstand ertheilet, dem wahren Christentum ein helles Licht fürgetragen* . . . Nuremberg: Wolfgang Endter, 1663.

————. *Weg zu der Seligkeit*. Nuremberg: Wolfgang Endter, 1646.

Feltman, Gerhard. *Tractatus de Cadavere Inspiciendo, in Cujus Recessu, Praeter ea Quae in Fronte Promittuntur, Varia de Funeribus, Sepulturis, Medicis, Vulneribus, Venenis, Cruentationibus, Similisque Argumenti Rebus Edissertantur*. Gröningen: Remberti Huzsman, 1673.

Fidelis, Fortunatus. *De Relationionibus Medicorum, Libri Quatuor*. Panormi: De Franciscis, 1602.

Franz, Gunther, ed. *Die evangelischen Kirchenordnungen des XVI. Jahrhunderts*, vol. 15: *Württemberg, pt. 1, Grafschaft Hohenlohe*. Gen. ed. Emil Sehling. Tübingen: J. C. B. Mohr, 1977.

Freudius, Michael. *Gewissens-Fragen von Processen wieder die hexen, insonderheit denen Richtern hochnötig zuwissen* . . . Güstrow: Christian Scheippeln, 1667.

Gödelmann, Johann Georg. *Von Zäuberern, Hexen und Unholden: warhafftiger vnd wolgegründter Bericht Herrn Georgji Gödelmann, beyder Rechten Doctor und Professorn in der Hohen Schbul zu Rostock, wie dieselbigen zuerkennen und zu straffen* . . . Translated by Georg Nigrinus. Frankfurt a.M.: Nicolaus Basse, 1592.

Guldenklee, Baldassar Timaeus von. *Casus Medicinales Praxi Triginta Sex Annorum Observati, Accessere et Medicamentorum Singularium Quae in Casibus Proponuntur Descriptiones*. Leipzig: Christian Kirchner, 1662.

Günther, Agnes. *Die Heilige und ihr Narr*. 142nd ed. Kiel: Steinkopf, 1996.

————. *Von der Hexe, die eine Heilige war*. Marburg: Verlag der Christlichen Welt, 1913.

Hartmann, Johann Ludwig. *Absolution-Buch nechst Nothwendigem Bericht /wie ein Seelsorger bey so vielerley Fällen nach den Zeiten und Leuten im Beicht-Stuhl sich zu verhalten*. Rothenburg: Noah von Millenan, 1679.

————. *Hand-Buch für Seelsorger* . . . Nuremberg: Wolfgang-Moritz Endter, 1699.

Heerbrand, Jacob. *Ein Predig von dem erschrocklichen Wunderzeichen am Himmel dem newen cometen oder Pfawenschwantz*. Tübingen: Gruppenbach, 1577.

Hoffmann, Moritz. *Ad Demonstrationes Partium Corporis Humani Curiose Dissecti in Theatro Anatomico* . . . Altdorf: Henricius Meyer, 1672.

————. *De Motu Cordis et cerebri, Sanguinis que ac Spirtiuum Animalium pro Vitae Continuatione per Corpus Commeatu.* Diss., Altdorf University, 1653.

————. *De Partibus Similaribus Humani Corporis.* Diss., Altdorf University, 1675.

————. *De Purgationis Modo.* Diss., Altdorf University, 1652.

————. *De Transitu Sanguinis per Medios Pulmones Facili.* Diss., Altdorf University, 1650.

————. *De Tumoribus.* Disputation, Altdorf University, 1649.

————. *Die wandrende Zerglieder-Kunst dem Hoch-Edlen und hochgelehrten Herrn Joh. Mavricio Hoffmann . . . in der Leopoldinischen Reichs-Academie der Naturae Curiosorum hochansehnlichen Mitgleide Heliodoro genannt etc. für seine Lehr- und sinnreiche Anweisung und Auslegung des menschlichen Kunst-Gebäues an einer enthaubteten Kinder-Mörderin auf der altdorfischen Schneid- und Schaubühne im Wintermonat des 1700 Heil Jahrs* . . . Altdorf: Heinrich Meyer, 1700.

————. *Florae Altdorffinae Deliciae Hortenses, sive Catalogus Plantarum Horti Medici, Quibus Post Felicium Temporum Reparationem* . . . Altdorf: Henrici Meyeri, 1677.

————. *Florae Altdorffinae Deliciae Sylvestres sive Catalogus Plantarum in Agro Altdorffino, Locisque Vicinis Sponte Nascentium, cum Synonymis Auctorum, Designatione Locorum Atq; Mensium, Quibus Vegent* . . . Altdorf: Heinrici Meyeri, 1672.

————. *Medicinae atq. Sapientiae Studiosis Anatomen Corporis Foeminini in Theatro Anatomico Publice Celebrandam Intimat eosdemque Frequentes Spectatores Adesse Iubet.* Altdorf: Georgi Hagen, 1662.

————. *Prudentiae Medicae ex Sanguine pro Saluti Mortalium Agen Dorum Rationes Exponentis: Fundamenta in Incluta Norimbergensium Universitate Altdorfina.* Altdorf: Henricius Meyer, 1672.

————. *Theses Medicae de Motu Cordis et Cerebri Sanguinisque ac Spirituum Animalium pro Vitae Continuatione per Corpus Commeatu* . . . Disputation, Altdorf University, 1653.

Institoris, Heinrich. *Nürnberger Hexenhammer 1491: Faksimile der Handschrift von 1491 aus dem Staatsarchiv Nürnberg, Nr. D 251.* Edited by Günter Jerouschek. Hildesheim: G. Olms, 1992.

Lang, Abraham. *Zwo Wetterpredigten aus dem 18. Psalm des Königlichen Propheten Davids* . . . Jena: Mattaeus Pfeilschmidt, 1613.

Leib, Johann. *Consilia, Responsa ac Deductiones Juris Variae* . . . Frankfurt: Hermannum Sande, 1666.

Leuchtius, Christian Leonhard. *Consilia sive Responsa Juris Altdorfina* . . . Nuremberg: Wolfgang Michaellis & Johannis Adolphi, 1702.

Linck, Henricus. *Consilia sive Responsa, a Facultate Juridica approbata* . . . Nuremberg: Wolfgang Michaelis & Johannes Adolphus, 1704.

————. *De Advocatus.* Diss, Altdorf University, 1668.

Ludwell, Wilhelm. *Commentarii in Imperatoris Justiniani Institutionum Libros Quatuor* . . . Nuremberg: Johann Andreae & Wolgang Endteri, 1671.

————. *Decadem Thematum Principalirorum in Frequentissima & in Foro Utillissima Materia Homicidii.* Disputation, Altdorf University, 1640.

————. *De Aristocratia.* Disputation, Altdorf University, 1646.

————. *De Fide Civili Jurisconsultorum.* Disputation, Altdorf University, 1646.

————. *De Jurisdictione et Imperio de qua Publice.* Disputation, Altdorf University, 1641.

————. *De Publicis Judicis.* Disputation, Altdorf University, 1654.

————. *Exercitationes XVIII. ad IV. Libros Institutionum Imperialim in Universitate Altdorffina.* Altdorf: Georg Hagen, 1663.

————, and Georg von Gülchen. *De Foro Competente quam Divina Favente Clementia.* Diss., Altdorf University, 1639.

Meder, David. *Acht Hexenpredigten darinnen Von des Teuffels Mordkindern der Hexen Unholden Zauberischen Drachenleuten Milchdieben, etc. erschrecklichem Abfalle Lastern und Ubelthaten dadurch die Göttliche Maiestät gelestert und Menschen und Viehe [et]c verderblicher Schaden zugefüget.* Leipzig: Jacob Apels, 1605.

Merian, Matthaeus, and Martin Zeiller. *Topographia Germania,* vol. 8: *Topographia Franconiae, Das ist Beschreibung und Eÿgentliche Contrafactur der Vornembsten Stätte und Plätze des Frankenlandes . . .* Basel: Bärenreiter, 1962. (First published in Frankfurt, 1654.)

Meyfart, Johann Mattäus. *Christliche Erinnerung an gewaltige Regenten und gewissenhaffte Praedicanten wie das abscheuliche Laster der Hexerey mit Ernst ausszurotten . . .* Schleusingen, Peter Schmid, 1636.

Oldekop, Justus. *Contra Dn. Benedictum Carpzovium . . .* Bremen: Jacobus Könlerius, 1664.

————. *Obervationes Criminales Practicae Congestae . . .* 2nd ed. Frankfurt a.O.: Jeremias Schrey & Heinricus Johann Meyer, 1685.

Paré, Ambroise. *Wund Artzney oder Artzney Spiegell.* Frankfurt a.M.: Caspar Tötell, 1635.

Pfizer, Johann Nicolas. *Vernünfftiges Wunden-Urtheil, Wie man nemlich Von allen Wunden dess menschlichen Leibs gründlichen Bericht . . .* Nuremberg: Johann Andreae and Wolfgang Endter d.J., 1674.

Puschner, J. G. *Amoenitates Altdorfinae oder Eigenliche nach dem Leben gezeichnete Prospecten der Löblichen Nürnbergischen Universität Altdorf . . .* Nürnberg: Wolfgang Michahelles, [1710].

Radbruch, Gustav, ed. *Die Peinliche Gerichtsordnung Kaiser Karls V. von 1532 (Carolina).* Stuttgart: Philipp Reclam, 1962.

Reinkingk, Theodor von. *Tractatus de Regimine Saeculari et Ecclesiastico.* 5th ed. Frankfurt: Hampelius, 1651.

Rem, Georg Rem. *Nemesis Karulina: Divi Karuli V. Imp. Caes. PP. Augusti, Invictiss. & Gloriosiss. Principis, Sacriq. Rom. Imperii Ordinum, Leges Rerum Capitalium.* Frankfurt a.M., 1618.

Remy, Nicolas. *Daemonolatria, Das ist von Unholden und Zauber Geistern . . .* Frankfurt a.M., 1598.

Ritterhausen, Conrad. *Consilia sive Responsa Altorfina de Ivre . . .* Hannover: Claudis Marnium & Haeredes Ioannis Aubrii, 1603.

Rüff, Jakob. *De Conceptu, et Generatione Hominis: de Matrice et Eius Partibus, Nec Non de Conditione Infantis in Utero* . . . Frankfurt a.M.: P. Faricium, 1587.

Sawr, Abraham, ed. *Theatrum de Veneficiis: Das ist von Teuffelsgespenst, Zauberrn und Gifftbereitern, Schwarzkünstlern, Hexen Und Urholden vieler fürnemmen Historien und Exempel bewärten.* Frankfurt a.M.: Ö Basseus, 1586.

Schaller, Daniel. *Zauber Handel: Acht Predigten über das Acht und Zwanzigste Capittel des Ersten Buchs Samuelis* . . . Magdeburg: Johan Francken, 1611.

Schaller, Jacob. *Paradoxon de Tortura in Christiana Republica non Exercenda* . . . Diss., Strasbourg University, 1658.

Schlauch, Ingaruth. "Die Hexe von Hürden: Ein Heimatspiel." Unpublished mss., ca. 1957.

Scriver, Christian. *Gotthold's Zufälliger Andachten: Vier Hundert, bey Betrachtung, mancherley Dinge, der Kunst und Natur, in unterschiedenen Veranlassungen, zu Ehre Gottes, Besserung des Gemüths und Übung zur Gottseligkeit, ausgefasset und entworfen* . . . Leipzig: J. M. Süstermann, 1706.

———. *Herrn M. Christian Scrivers . . . Seelen-Schatzes Kern und Stern, oder, dessen nochmals übersehene, vermehrte und vollkommene Register* . . . Leipzig: Christoph Seidel, 1717.

Scultetum, Abraham. *Warnung für der Warsagerey der Zäuberer und Sterngücker* . . . Amberg: Michael Forster, 1609.

Seckendorf, Veit Ludwig von. *Teutscher Fürsten-Stat, oder Gründliche und kurtze Beschreibung, welcher gestalt Fürstenthümer, Graff- und Herrschafften im H. Römischen Reich teutscher Nation . . . beschaffen zu seyn, regieret zu werden pflegen.* Frankfurt: Th. M. Goetzen, 1656.

Seiler, Tobias. *Daemonomania: Oberaus schreckliche Historia von einem besessenen zwelffjährigen Jungfräulein zu Lewenbert in Schlesien* . . . Wittenberg: Georg Müllern, 1605.

Sennert, Daniel. *Operum Omnia.* 3 vols. Lyon: Ioanni Antonii Huguetan & Marci Antonii Ravavd, 1650.

Sigwart, Johann Georg. *Ein Predig von Hagel und Ungewitter* . . . Tübingen: Johann Allexandro Cellio, 1613.

Spee, Friedrich von. *Cautio Criminalis, seu, De processibus Contra Sagas Liber* . . . 2nd ed. Frankfurt: Ioannis Gronaei Austrij, 1632.

Stökken, Gerhard von. *De Jurisdictione* Diss., Strasbourg University, 1671.

———. *De Jure Odioso.* Diss., Strasbourg University, 1668.

Stösser, Gottfried. *De Appellatione, in Criminalibus* . . . Diss., Strasbourg University, 1671.

Struve, Georg Adam. *Jurisprudentia Romano-Germanica Forensis.* 7th ed. Jena, 1697.

———. *Juris-Prudenz, oder Verfassung der Landüblichen Rechte* . . . Merseburg: Forberger, 1696.

Suewus, Bernadus. *Tractatus de Inspectione Vulnerum Lethalium et Sanabilium Praecipuarum Partium Corporis Humani.* Marburg: Caspar Chemlini, 1629.

Tabor, Johann Otto. *De Advocatis.* Diss., Strasbourg University, 1654.

———. *De Confrontatione, Difficili et Inexplorato Juris Articulo, Disputationes Quinque.* Diss., Strasbourg University, 1663.

————. *De Executione Rei Judicatae.* Diss., Strasbourg University, 1661.

————. *Dissertationes Nonnullae de Tortura et Indiciis Delictorum, &c . . .* Giessen: Friderici Kargeri, 1668.

Textor, Johann Wolfgang. *Synopsis Juris Gentium.* Edited by Ludwig von Bar and translated by John Pawley Bate. New York: Oceana, 1964. 2 vols. (First published in Frankfurt, 1680.)

————. *Tractatus Juris Publici de Vera et Varia Ratione Status Germaniae Modernae.* Altdorf: Johann Heinrich Schönnerstaede, 1667.

————. *De Auctoritte Interpretum Juris.* Disputation, Altdorf University, 1670.

————. *De Judicibus Delegatis vel Commissariis, Quos Vocant, et Assessoribus.* Disputation, Altdorf University, 1673.

————. *De Judiciis Imperiii Caesareis, ac in Specie de Consilio Imperiali Aulico et Dicasterio Rotwilensi.* Disputation, Altdorf University, 1668.

————. *De Jure Episcopali in Terris Statuum Protestantium.* Disputation, Altdorf University, 1671.

————. *De Plenitudine Potestatis.* Disputation, Altdorf University, 1672.

————, and Mauritius Hieronymus de Venne. *Disputatio Juridica de Corpore Delicti in Homicidio.* Disputation, Altdorf University, 1672.

Thomasius, Christian. *Vom Laster der Zauberei—De Crimie Magiae: Über die Hexenprozesse— Processus Inquisitorii Contra Sagas.* Translated and edited by Rolf Lieberwirth. 2nd ed. Munich: Deutscher Taschenbuch, 1987.

Der Weiland Hoch-Ehrwürdig-Hoch-Achbar und Hochgelehrte Herr Ludwig Casimir Dietzel / Hoch-Gräfl: Hohenloh:: Langenburg: 43 jähriger wohl—verdienter Statt-Pfarrer / Hof-Prediger und Superintenddent derselbsten. Rothenburg: Noah von Millenau, 1686.

Welsch, Gottfried. *Rationale Vulnerum Lethalium Judicium, Inquo de Vulnerum Lethalium Natura, & Causis; Legitima Item Eorundem Inspectione, ac Aliis Circa Hanc Materiam Scitu Dignis Juxta, Quam Necessariis, Agitur.* Leipzig: Ritzsch, 1662.

Wepferus, Johann Jacob. *Historia Cicutae Aquaticae, Qua Non Solum Plantae Hujus Venenatae Structura Naturalis, Vires & Operationes deletterae in Hominibus ac Brutis . . .* Leiden: Gerardus Potvliet, 1733. (First edition, 1679.)

Weyer, Johann. *Witches, Devils, and Doctors in the Renaissance: Johann Weyer, De Praestigiis Daemonum.* Edited by George Mora. Translated by John Shea. Medieval and Renaissance Studies Texts and Studies, v. 73. Binghamton: State University of New York, 1991.

Wibel, Johann Christian. *Hohenlohische Kyrchen- und Reformations-Historie, aus bewährten Urkunden und Schriften verfasset . . .* 4 vols. Onzbach: Jacob Chrisoph Poschens, 1752–55.

————. "Langenburgische Acta Ecclesiastica." Unpublished mss., Pfarramt Langenburg, ca. 1750.

Wibel, Johann David. *Trauer-Sermon und Leichen-Predigten welche der Naechtlichen Beysess- und Beerdigung des verblichenen Leichnambs des Weiland Hochgebohrnen Grafen und Herrn / Herrn Heinrich Friderichen Fragen von Hohenlohe und Gleichen / Herrn zu Langenburg und Cranichfeld . . .* Öhringen: Johann Fuchs, 1699.

Will, Georg. *Nürnbergisches Gelehrten-Lexicon oder Beschreibung aller Nürnbergischen Gelehrten beyderley Geschlechtes nach Ihrem Leben, Verdiensten und Schrifften* . . . Nuremberg: Lorenz Schüpfel, 1755.

Zacchia, Paulus. *Quaestiones Medico-Legales, in Quibus Omnes ex Materiae Medicae, Quae ad Legales Facultates Videntur Pertinere, Proponuntur, Pertractantur, Resoluuntur.* 4 vols. Leipzig: Fredericus Lanckisch, 1630.

Zehner, Joachim. *Fünff Predigten von den Hexen, ihren anfang, Mittel und End in sich haltend und erklärend* . . . Leipzig: Thomas Schürer, 1613.

SECONDARY SOURCES

Ackerknecht, Erin H. "Early History of Legal Medicine." In Chester R. Burns, ed. *Legacies in Law and Medicine*, 249–71. New York: Science History Publications, 1977.

Adam, Johann. *Evangelische Kirchengeschichte der Stadt Strassburg biz zur französischen Revolution.* Strasbourg: J. H. Ed. Heitz, 1922.

Adam, Wolfgang. "*Der Ablenkende*: Ein Mitglied der Fruchtbringenden Gesellschaft und seine Bibliothek in Langenburg." In Paul Raabe, ed., *Bücher und Bibliotheken im 17. Jahrhundert in Deutschland: Vorträge des vierten Jahrestreffens des Wolfenbütteler Arbeitskreises für Geschichte des Buchwesens in der Herzog August Bibliothek Wolfenbüttel 22. bis 24. Mai 1979.* Wolfenbütteler Schriften zur Geschichte des Buchwesens, vol. 6, 186–207. Hamburg: Dr. Ernst Hauswedell & Co., 1980.

———. "Kataloge und Bücherverzeichnisse der Schlossbibliothek Langenburg." In Reinhard Wittmann, ed., *Bücherkataloge als buchgeschichtliche Quellen in der frühen Neuzeit.* Wolfenbütteler Schriften zur Geschichte des Buchwesens, vol. 10, 259–73. Wiesbaden: Otto Harrassowitz, 1984.

———. "Lesen und Vorlesen am Langenburger Hof: Zur Lesefähigkeit und zum Buchbesitz der Diener und Beamten." In Wolfgang Brückner, Peter Blickle, and Dieter Breuer, eds., *Literatur und Volk im 17. Jahrhundert: Probleme populärer Kultur in Deutschland.* Wolfenbütteler Arbeiten zur Barockforschung, vol. 13, pt. 2, 475–88. Wiesbaden: Otto Harrassowitz, 1985.

Ahrendt-Schulte, Ingrid, et al., eds. *Geschlecht, Magie und Hexenverfolgung.* Institut für Geschichtliche Landeskunde und Historische Hilfswissenschaften der Universität Tübingen: Hexenforschung. Bielefeld: Verlag für Regionalgeschichte, 2002.

———. *Weise Frauen, Böse Weiber: die Geschichte der Hexen in der Frühen Neuzeit.* Freiburg: Herder, 1994.

———. *Zauberinnen in Der Stadt Horn (1554–1603): Magische Kultur und Hexenverfolgung in der Frühen Neuzeit.* Geschichte und Geschlechter, vol. 21. Frankfurt a.M.: Campus, 1997.

———. "Schadenzauber und Konflikte: Sozialgeschichte von Frauen im Spiegel der Hexenprozesse des 16. Jahrhunderts in der Grafschaft Lippe." In Heide Wunder and Christina Vanja, eds., *Wandel der Geschlechterbeziehungen zu Beginn der Neuzeit*, 198–228. Frankfurt: Suhrkamp, 1991.

Ankarloo, Bengt, and Stuart Clark, eds. *Witchcraft and Magic in Europe: The Eighteenth and Nineteenth Centuries.* Philadelphia: University of Pennsylvania Press, 1999.

Anrich, Ernst. *Zur Geschichte der deutschen Universität Strassburg.* Strasbourg: Hünenburg, 1941.

Apps, Lara, and Andrew Gow. *Male Witches in Early Modern Europe.* New York: Manchester University Press, 2003.

Aretin, Karl Otmar von. *Das alte Reich 1648–1806,* vol. 1: *Föderalistische oder hierarchische Ordnung (1648–1684).* Stuttgart: Klett-Cotta, 1993.

———. *Das Reich: Friedensgarantie und europäisches Gleichgewicht 1648–1806.* Stuttgart: Klett-Cotta, 1986.

Bächtold-Stäubli, Hanns, gen. ed. *Handwörterbuch des deutschen Aberglaubens.* 10 vols. Berlin: Walther de Gruyter, 1987.

Bacmeister, Adolf. "Zur Geschichte der Hexenprozesse." *Württembergische Vierteljahrshefte für Landesgeshichte* 9 (1886), 282–92.

Baier, Johann Jakob. *Biographiae Professorum Medicinae Qui in Academia Altorfina Unqvam Vixerunt.* Nuremberg: Haeredes Johann Daniel Tauber, 1728.

Baroja, Julio Caro. *The World of the Witches.* Translated by O. N. V. Glendinning. Chicago: University of Chicago Press, 1964.

Barry, Jonathan, Marianne Hester, and Gareth Roberts, eds. *Witchcraft in Early Modern Europe: Studies in Culture and Belief.* Cambridge: Cambridge University Press, 1998.

Bauernfeind, Elke. *Agnes Günther: Die Heilige und ihr Narr: Leserlenkung und Rezeption.* Stuttgarter Arbeiten zur Germanistik, no. 269. Stuttgart: Hans-Dieter Heinz, 1993.

Beck, Paul. "Hexenprozesse aus dem Fränkischen." *Württembergische Vierteljahrshefte für Landesgeschichte* 7 (1884), 76–80, 157–60, 297–302.

Bedal, Konrad ed. *Mühlen und Müller in Franken.* 2nd ed. Bad Windsheim: Fränkisches Freilandmuseum, 1992.

Behringer, Wolfgang. *Shaman of Oberstdorf: Chonrad Stoeckhlin and the Phantoms of the Night.* Charlottesville: University of Virginia Press, 1998.

———. *Witchcraft Persecutions in Bavaria: Popular Magic, Religious Zealotry, and Reason of State in Early Modern Europe.* Translated by J. C. Grayson and David Lederer. Cambridge: Cambridge University Press, 1997.

———. *Witches and Witch-Hunts: A Global History.* Cambridge, Mass.: Polity Press, 2004.

———. "Erträge und Perspektiven der Hexenforschung." *Historische Zeitschrift* 249, no. 3 (1989), 619–40.

———. "Geschichte der Hexenforschung." In Sönke Lorenz and Jürgen Michael Schmidt, eds., *Wider alle Hexerei und Teufelswerk: Die europäische Hexenverfolgung und ihre Auswirkungen auf Südwestdeutschland,* 485–668. Ostfildern: Jan Thorbeck, 2004.

———. "Weather, Hunger and Fear: The Origins of the European Witch Persecution in Climate, Society and Mentality." *German History* 13 (1995), 1–27.

————. "Witchcraft Studies in Austria, Germany and Switzerland." In Jonathan Barry, Marianne Hester, and Gareth Roberts, eds., *Witchcraft in Early Modern Europe: Studies in Culture and Belief*, 64–95. Cambridge: Cambridge University Press, 1996.

Bever, Edward. "Witchcraft Fears and Psychosocial Factors in Disease." *Journal of Interdisciplinary History* 30, no. 4 (2000), 573–90.

————. "Witchcraft, Female Aggression, and Power in the Early Modern Community." *Journal of Social History* 35, no. 4 (2002), 955–88.

Blécourt, Willem de. "The Making of the Female Witch: Reflections on Witchcraft and Gender in the Early Modern Period." *Gender and History* 12, no. 2 (2000), 287–309.

Blickle, Peter. *Deutsche Untertanen: Ein Widerspruch*. Munich: C. H. Beck, 1980.

————, ed. *Der Fluch und der Eid: Die metaphysische Begründung gesellschaftlichen Zusammenlebens und politischer Ordnung in der ständischen Gesellschaft*. Zeitschrift für historische Forschung, Beiheft no. 15. Berlin: Duncker & Humblot, 1993.

Blickle, Renate. "Nahrung und Eigentum als Kategorien in der ständischen Gesellschaft." In Winfried Schulze, ed., *Ständische Gesellschaft und soziale Mobilität*, 73–93. Schriften des Historischen Kollegs, Kolloquien no. 12. Munich: R. Oldenbourg, 1988.

Blumenberg, Hans. *Die Lesbarkeit der Welt*. Frankfurt a.M., 1989.

Bossert, Gustav. *Bächlinger Ortschronik*. HZAN Sammlung von Manuskripten 36. N.d., ca. 1870.

Bostridge, Ian. *Witchcraft and Its Transformations c. 1650–c. 1750*. Oxford: Clarendon Press, 1997.

Breuer, Dieter. "Absolutische Staatsreform und neue Frömmigkeitsformen: Vorüberlegungen zu einer Frömmigkeitsgeschichte der frühen Neuzeit aus literarhistorischer Sicht." In Dieter Breuer, ed., *Frömmigkeit in der Frühen Neuzeit: Studien zur religiösen Literatur des 17. Jahrhunderts in Deutschland*, 5–26. Chloe, Beihefte zum Daphnis, vol. 2. Amsterdam: Rodopi, 1984.

Briggs, Charles L., ed. *Disorderly Discourse: Narrative, Conflict, and Inequality*. New York: Oxford University Press, 1996.

Briggs, Robin. *Witches and Neighbors: The Social and Cultural Context of European Witchcraft*. New York: Viking, 1996.

Brinker-Gabler, Gisela. "Perspektiven des Übergangs: Weibliches Bewusstsein und frühe Moderne." In Gisela Brinker-Gabler, ed., *Deutsche Literatur von Frauen*, vol. 2: *19. und 20. Jahrhundert*, 169–204. Munich: C. H. Beck, 1988.

Brückner, Wolfgang, Peter Blickle, and Dieter Bauer, eds. *Literatur und Volk im 17ten Jahrhundert: Probleme populärer Kultur in Deutschland*. Wolfenbütteler Arbeiten zur Barockforschung, vol. 13. Wiesbaden: Harrassowitz, 1985.

Burghartz, Susanna. "Hexenverfolgung als Frauenverfolgung? Zur Gleichsetzung von Hexen und Frauen am Beispiel der Luzerner und Lausanner Hexenprozesse des 15. und 16. Jahrhunderts." In Claudia Opitz, ed., *Der Hexenstreit: Frauen in der frühneuzeitlichen Hexenverfolung*, 147–73. Freiburg: Herder, 1995.

Bussmann, Klaus, and Heinz Schilling, eds. *1648: War and Peace in Europe*. 3 vols. Münster: Veranstaltungsgesellschaft 350 Jahre Westfälischer Frieden, 1998.

Campbell, Ted. *The Religion of the Heart: A Study of European Religious Life in the Seventeenth and Eighteenth Centuries.* Columbia: University of South Carolina Press, 1991.

Clark, Michael, and Catherine Crawford, eds. *Legal Medicine in History.* Cambridge: Cambridge University Press, 1994.

Clark, Stuart. *Thinking with Demons: The Idea of Witchcraft in Early Modern Europe.* Oxford: Oxford University Press, 1997.

————, ed. *Languages of Witchcraft: Narrative, Ideology, and Meaning in Early Modern Culture.* New York: St. Martin's Press, 2001.

————. "Glaube und Skepsis in der deutschen Hexenliteratur von Johann Weyer bis Friedrich von Spee." In Hartmut Lehmann and Otto Ulbricht, eds., *Vom Unfug des Hexen-Prozesses: Gegner der Hexenverfolgungen von Johann Weyer bis Friedrich von Spee,* 15–34. Wolfenbütteler Forschungen, vol. 55. Wiesbaden: Otto Harrassowitz, 1992.

————. "Inversion, Misrule, and the Meaning of Witchcraft." *Past and Present,* no. 87 (1980), 98–127.

Cohn, Norman. *Europe's Inner Demons: An Enquiry Inspired by the Great Witch-Hunt.* New York: Basic Books, 1975.

Conrad, Lawrence I., et al, eds. *The Western Medical Tradition, 800 B.C. to 1800 A.D.* Cambridge: Cambridge University Press, 1995.

Crawford, Catherine. "Legalizing Medicine: Early Modern Legal Systems and the Growth of Medico-Legal Knowledge." In Michael Clark and Catherine Crawford, eds., *Legal Medicine in History,* 89–116. Cambridge: Cambridge University Press, 1994.

Danckert, Werner. *Unehrliche Leute: Die verfremten Berufe.* Bern: Francke, 1963.

Daston, Lorraine. "Marvelous Facts and Miraculous Evidence in Early Modern Europe." *Critical Inquiry* 18 (1991), 93–124.

————. "Objectivity and the Escape from Perspective." *Social Studies of Science* 22, 4 (1992), 597–618.

————, and Katherine Park. *Wonders and the Order of Nature, 1150–1750.* New York: Zone Books, 1998.

Davies, Owen. *Cunning-Folk: Popular Magic in English History.* London: Hambledon & London, 2003.

Dear, Peter. *Revolutionizing the Sciences: European Knowledge and its Ambitions, 1500–1700.* Princeton, N.J.: Princeton University Press, 2001.

Debus, Allen. *Man and Nature in the Renaissance.* Cambridge: Cambridge University Press, 1978.

————. "Chemistry and the Universities in the Seventeenth Century." *Estudos Avançados* 4, no. 10 (1990), 173–96.

Dillinger, Johannes. *"Böse Leute": Hexenverfolgungen in Schwäbisch-Österreich und Kurtrier im Vergleich.* Trierer Hexenprozesse, Quellen und Darstellungen, vol. 5. Trier: Spee, 1999.

————. "Terrorists and Witches: Popular Ideas of Evil in the Early Modern Period." *History of European Ideas* 30, no. 2 (2004), 167–82.

————, Thomas Fritz, and Wolfgang Mährle, eds. *Zum Feuer Verdammt: Die Hexenverfol-zungen in der Grafschaft Hohenberg, der Reichstadt Reutlingen und der Fürstpropstei Ellwan-gen.* Hexenforschung, vol. 2. Stuttgart: Franz Steiner, 1998.

Duden, Barbara. *The Woman Beneath the Skin: A Doctor's Patients in Eighteenth-Century Ger-many.* Translated by Thomas Dunlap. Cambridge, Mass.: Harvard University Press, 1991.

Duerr, Hans Peter. *Dreamtime: Concerning the Boundary Between Wilderness and Civilization.* Translated by Felicitas Goodman. New York: Basil Blackwell, 1985.

Dülmen, Richard van. *Frauen vor Gericht: Kindsmord in der frühen Neuzeit.* Frankfurt a.M.: Fischer, 1991.

————. *Kultur und Alltag in der Frühen Neuzeit.* 3 vols. Munich: C. H. Beck, 1990–94.

————. *The Theatre of Horror: Crime and Punishment in Early Modern Germany.* Translated by Elisabeth Neu. Cambrige, Mass.: Basil Blackwell, 1991.

————. "Der infame Mensch: Unehrliche Arbeit und soziale Ausgrenzung in der Frühen Neuzeit." In Richard van Dülmen, ed., *Arbeit, Frömmigkeit und Eigensinn: Studien zur historischen Kulturforschung,* 106–40. Frankfurt a.M.: Fischer, 1990.

————, ed. *Entdeckung des Ich: Die Geschichte der Individualisierung vom Mittelater bis zur Gegenwart.* Cologne: Böhlau, 2001.

Dürr, Renate. *Mägde in der Stadt: Das Beispiel Schwäbisch Hall in der Frühen Neuzeit.* Geschichte und Geschlechter, vol. 13. Frankfurt: Campus, 1995.

Erler, Adalbert, gen. ed. *Handwörterbuch zur deutschen Rechtsgeschichte.* 5 vols. Berlin: Erich Schmidt, 1998.

Evans, R. J. W. "German Universities After the Thirty Years War." *History of Universities* 1 (1981), 169–90.

Evans, Richard J. *Rituals of Retribution: Capital Punishment in Germany, 1600–1987.* Oxford: Oxford University Press, 1996.

Fasolt, Constantin. *The Limits of History.* Chicago: University of Chicago Press, 2004.

Favret-Saada, Jeanne. *Deadly Words: Witchcraft in the Bocage.* Cambridge: Cambridge Uni-versity Press, 1980.

Fischer, Adolf. *Geschichte des Hause Hohenlohe.* 2 vols. Stuttgart: W. Kohlhammer, 1866–71.

Fischer-Homberger, Esther. *Medizin vor Gericht: Gerichtsmedizin von der Renaissance bis zur Aufklärung.* Bern: Hans Huber, 1983.

Flessa, Dorothee. *Die Professoren der Medizin zu Altdorf von 1580–1809.* Diss., Erlangen University, 1979.

Franklin, James. *The Science of Conjecture: Evidence and Probability Before Pascal.* Baltimore, Md.: Johns Hopkins University Press, 2001.

Franz, Gunther. *Der Dreissigjährige Krieg und das deutsche Volk: Untersuchung zur Bevölkerungs- und Agrargeschichte.* 4th ed. Stuttgart: Fischer, 1979.

————, ed. *Friedrich Spee zum 400. Geburtstag: Kolloquium der Friedrich-Spee-Gesellschaft Trier.* Paderborn: Bonifatius, 1995.

————, and Franz Irsigler, eds. *Methoden und Konzepte der historischen Hexenforschung.* Trierer Hexenprozesse, Quellen und Darstellungen, vol. 4. Trier: Spee, 1998.

French, Roger. *Dissection and Vivisection in the European Renaissance*. Aldershot: Ashgate, 1999.

———, and Andrew Wear, eds. *The Medical Revolution of the Seventeenth Century*. Cambridge: Cambridge University Press, 1989.

Gaskill, Malcolm. *Crime and Mentalities in Early Modern England*. Cambridge: Cambridge University Press, 2000.

Geis, Gilbert, and Ivan Bunn. *A Trial of Witches: A Seventeenth-Century Witchcraft Prosecution*. London: Routledge, 1997.

Gentilcore, David. *From Bishop to Witch: The System of the Sacred in Early Modern Terra d'Otranto*. Manchester: Manchester University Press, 1992.

Gersmann, Gudrun. "Die Hexe als Heimatheldin: Die Hexenverfolgungen der Frühen Neuzeit im Visier der Heimathistoriker." *Westfälische Forschungen* 45 (1995), 102–33.

———. "Der Kampf um die Gerichtsbarkeit: Adlige Hexenpolitik im Frühneuzeitlichen Fürstbistum Münster." *Historische Zeitschrift* (2001), 369–76.

Giese, Ernst, and Benno von Hagen. *Geschichte der medizinischen Fakultät der Friedrich-Schiller-Universität Jena*. Jena: VEB Gustav Fischer Verlag, 1958.

Ginzburg, Carlo. *The Cheese and the Worms: The Cosmos of a Sixteenth-Century Miller*. Translated by John and Anne Tedeschi. Baltimore: Johns Hopkins University Press, 1992.

———. *Clues, Myths, and the Historical Method*. Translated by John and Anne Tedeschi. Baltimore: Johns Hopkins University Press, 1989.

———. *Ecstasies: Deciphering the Witches' Sabbath*. Translated by Raymond Rosenthal. New York: Pantheon, 1991.

———. *The Night Battles: Witchcraft and Agrarian Cults in the Sixteenth and Seventeenth Centuries*. Translated by John and Anne Tedeschi. Baltimore: Johns Hopkins University Press, 1983.

Grieve, Maud. *A Modern Herbal*. 2 vols. New York: Dover, 1931.

Günther, Gerhard. *Ich denke der alten Zeit, der vorigen Jahre: Agnes Günther in Briefen, Erinnerungen, Berichten*. Stuttgart: J. F. Steinkopf, 1972.

Günther, Rudolf. *Bilder aus dem kirchlichen Leben Langenburgs: Vortrag anlässlich des 400 jährigen Bestehens der Stadtkirche bei eine Gemeindefeier am 26. Januar 1903*. Langenburg: [Pfarramt Langenburg], 1903.

———. *Unter dem Schleier der Gisela: Aus Agnes Günthers Leben und Schaffen*. Stuttgart: J. F. Steinkopf, 1936.

Haag, Gottlob. *Und manchmal krähte der Wetterhahn: Ein hohenloisches Tagebuch*. Bergatreue: Wilfried Eppe, 1992.

Hall, Karl Alfred. *Die Lehre vom Corpus Delicti: Eine dogmatische Quellenexegese zur Theorie des gemeinen deutschen Inquisitionsprozesses*. Stuttgart: W. Kohlhammer, 1933.

Hällisch-Fränkisches Museum. *Hexen: Hexenwahn und Hexenverfolgung in und um Schwäbisch Hall: Hällisch-Fränkisches Museum Schwäbisch Hall 18. Juni–7. August 1988*. Schwäbisch Hall: Hällisch-Fränkisches Museum, 1988.

Hammerstein, Notker. *Jus und Historie: Ein Beitrag zur Geschichte des historischen Denkens an deutschen Universitäten im späten 17. und im 18. Jahrhundert.* Göttingen: Vandenhoeck & Ruprecht, 1972.

———. "Universitäten—Territorialstaaten—Gelehrte Räte." In Roman Schnur, ed., *Die Rolle der Juristen bei der Entstehung des modernen Staates*, 687–735. Berlin: Duncker & Humblot, 1986.

Hardung, Siegfried. *Die Vorladung vor Gottes Gericht: Ein Beitrag zur rechtlichen und religiösen Volkskunde.* Bausteine zur Volkskunde und Religionswissenschaft, no. 9. Bühl-Baden: Konkordia A.G., 1934.

Heitsch, Bernhard. "Beweis und Verurteilung im Inquisitionsprozess Benedict Carpzov's: Zur Geschichte des Inquisitionsprozesses von der Constitutio Criminalis Carolina bis zu Benedict Carpzov's *Practica nova imperialis Saxonica rerum criminalium*." Diss., Göttingen University, 1964.

Holl, Karl. "Die Bedeutung der grossen Kriege für das religiöse und kirchliche Leben innerhalb des deutschen Protestantismus." In his *Gesammelte Aufsätze zur Kirchengeschichte*, vol. III: *Der Westen*, 302–84. Tübingen: J. C. B. Mohr, 1929.

Holmes, Clive. "Women: Witnesses and Witches." *Past and Present*, no. 140 (1993), 45–78.

Hornung-Grove, Marianne. *Beweisregeln im Inquisitionsprozess Johann Brunnemanns, Johann Paul Kress' und Johann Samuel Friedrich Boehmers.* Diss., Erlangen University, 1974.

Hsia, R. Po-Chia. *Social Discipline in the Reformation: Central Europe, 1550–1750.* London: Routledge, 1989.

Hunter, Ian. *Rival Enlightenments: Civil and Metaphysical Philosophy in Early Modern Germany.* Cambridge: Cambridge University Press, 2001.

Hutton, Ronald. "Anthropological and Historical Approaches to Witchcraft: Potential for New Collaboration?" *Historical Journal* 47, no. 2 (2004), 413–34.

Jerouschek, Günter, Wolfgang Schild, and Walter Gropp, eds. *Benedict Carpzov: Neue Perspektiven zu einem umstrittenen sächsischen Juristen.* Rothenburger Gespräche zur Strafrechtsgeschichte, vol. 2 Tübingen: diskord, 2000.

———. *Die Hexen und ihr Prozess: Die Hexenverfolgung in der Reichstadt Esslingen.* Esslinger Studien, Shriftenreihe, vol. 11. Sigmaringen: Jan Thorbecke, 1992.

———. "Friedrich Spee als Justizkritiker: Die *Cautio Criminalis* im Lichte des gemeinen Strafrechts der frühen Neuzeit." In Gunther Franz, ed., *Friedrich Spee zum 400. Geburtstag: Kolloquium der Friedrich-Spee-Gesellschaft Trier*, 115–36. Paderborn: Bonifatius, 1995.

Jütte, Robert. *Ärzte, Heiler und Patienten: Medizinischer Alltag in der frühen Neuzeit.* Munich: Artemis & Winkler, 1991.

Kalb, Friedrich. *Die Lehre vom Kultus der lutherischen Kirche zur Zeit der Orthodoxie.* Berlin: Lutherisches Verlagshaus, 1959.

Kaufmann, Thomas. *Dreissigjähriger Krieg und Westfälischer Friede: Kirchengeschichtliche Studien zur lutherischen Konfessionskultur.* Tübingen: Mohr Siebeck, 1998.

King, Lester S. *The Road to Medical Enlightenment, 1650–1695.* London: MacDonald, 1970.

Klaits, Joseph. *Servants of Satan: The Age of the Witch Hunts.* Bloomington: Indiana University Press, 1985.

Kleefeld, Traudl, Hans Gräser, and Gernot Stepper. *Hexenverfolgung im Markgraftum Brandenburg-Ansbach und in der Herrschaft Sugenheim.* Mittelfränkische Studien, vol. 15. Ansbach: Historischer Verein für Mittelfranken, 2001.

Kleinehagenbrock, Frank. *Die Grafschaft Hohenlohe im Dreissigjährigen Krieg: Eine erfahrungsgeschichtliche Untersuchung zu Herrschaft und Untertanen.* Veröffentlichungen der Kommission für geschichtliche Landeskunde in Baden-Württemberg, Reihe B, vol. 153. Stuttgart: W. Kohlhammer, 2003.

———. "'Nun müsst ihr doch wieder alle Katholisch werden': Der Dreissigjährige Krieg als Bedrohung der Konfession in der Grafschaft Hohenlohe." In Matthias Asche and Anton Schindling, eds., *Das Strafgericht Gottes: Kriegserfahrungen und Religion im Heiligen Römischen Reich Deutscher Nation im Zeitalter des Dreissigjährigen Krieges,* 59–122. 2nd ed. Münster: Aschendorff, 2002.

Kleinheyer, Gerd. "Zur Rolle des Geständnisses im Strafverfahren des späten Mittelalters und der frühen Neuzeit." In Gerd Kleinheyer and Paul Mikat, eds., *Beiträge zur Rechtsgeschichte: Gedächnisschrift für Hermann Conrad,* 367–84. Rechts- und Staatswissenschaftlich Veröffentlichungen der Görres-Gesellschaft, N.F., no. 34. Paderborn: Ferdinand Schöningh, 1979.

Knod, Gustav C. *Die alten Matrikel der Universität Strassburg, 1621–1793,* 3 vols. Strasbourg: Karl J. Trübner, 1897.

Koepp, Werner. *Johann Arndt: Eine Untersuchung über die Mystik in Lutherthum.* Aalen: Scientia Verlag, 1973.

Kramer, Karl-Sigismund. *Bauern und Burger im Nachmittelalterlichen Unterfranken: Eine Volkskunde auf Grund archivalischer Quellen.* Veröffentlichungen der Gesellschaft für fränkische Geschichte, Reihe IX, vol 12. Würzburg: Ferdinand Schöningh, 1957.

———. *Grundriss einer rechtlichen Volkskunde.* Göttingen: Otto Schwartz, 1974.

———. *Volksleben im Fürstentum Ansbach und seinen Nachbargebieten (1500–1800): Eine Volkskunde auf Grund archivalischer Quellen.* Beiträge zur Volkstumsforschung herausgegeben von der bayerischen Landesstelle für Volkskunde, vol. 13. Würzburg: Ferdinand Schöningh, 1961.

———. *Volksleben im Hochstift Bamberg und im Fürstentum Coburg (1500–1800).* Veröffentlichungen der Gesellschaft für Fränkische Geschichte, Reihe IX, vol. 24. Würzburg: Ferdinand Schöningh, 1967.

Kroeschell, Karl. *Deutsche Rechtsgeschichte.* 3 vols. Opladen: Westdeusche Verlag, 1992–93.

Kunstmann, Hartmut H. *Zauberwahn und Hexenprozess in der Reichstadt Nürnberg.* Nürnberg: Shriftenreihe des Stadtarchivs Nürnberg, 1970.

Labouvie, Eva. *Andere Umstände: Eine Kulturgeschichte der Geburt.* Cologne: Böhlau, 1998.

———. *Zauberei und Hexenwerk: Ländliche Hexenglaube in der Frühen Neuzeit.* Frankfurt a.M.: Fischer, 1993.

———. "Männer in Hexenprozess Zur Sozialanthropologie eines 'männlichen' Verständnisses von Hexerei." In Claudia Opitz, ed., *Der Hexenstreit: Frauen in der frühneuzeitlichen Hexenverfolung,* 211–45. Freiburg: Herder, 1995.

———. "Verwünschen und Verfluchen: Formen der verbalen Konfliktregelung in der ländlichen Gesellschaft der Frühen Neuzeit." In Peter Blickle, ed., *Der Fluch und der*

Eid: Die metaphysische Begründung gesellschaftlichen Zusammenlebens und politischer Ord-nung in der ständischen Gesellschaft, 121–45. Zeitschrift für historische Forschung, Beiheft no. 15. Berlin: Duncker & Humblot, 1993.

Landau, Peter, and Friedrich-Christian Schroeder, eds. *Strafrecht, Strafprozess und Rezep-tion: Grundlagen, Entwicklung und Wirkung der Constitutio Criminalis Carolina.* Juristische Abhandlungen, vol. 19. Frankfurt a.M.: Vittorio Klostermann, 1984.

Langbein, John H. *Prosecuting Crime in the Renaissance: England, Germany, France.* Cam-bridge, Mass.: Harvard University Press, 1974.

Larner, Christina. *Enemies of God: The Witch-Hunt in Scotland.* Baltimore: Johns Hopkins University Press, 1981.

Lehmann, Hartmut. *Das Zeitalter des Absolutismus: Gottesgnadentum und Kriegsnot.* Stuttgart: Kohlhammer, 1980.

———. "Johann Matthäus Meyfart warnt hexenverfolgende Obrigkeiten vor dem Jüng-sten Gericht." In Hartmut Lehmann and Otto Ulbricht, eds., *Vom Unfug des Hexen-Prozesses: Gegner der Hexenverfolgungen von Johann Weyer bis Friedrich von Spee,* 323–29. Wolfenbütteler Forschungen, vol. 55. Wiesbaden: Otto Harrassowitz, 1992.

———, and Anne-Charlott Trepp, eds. *Im Zeichen der Krise: Religiosität im Europa des 17ten Jahrhundert.* Veröfftentlichungen des Max-Planck-Instituts für Geschichte, vol. 152. Göttingen: Vandenhoeck & Ruprecht, 1999.

———, and O. Ulbrich, eds. *Von Unfug des Hexen-Prozesses: Gegner der Hexenverfolgungen von Johann Weyer bis Friedrich Spee.* Wiesbaden: Harrassowitz, 1992.

Lepsius, Susanne. *Der Richter und die Zeugen: Eine Untersuchung anhand des Tractatus testimo-niorum des Bartolus von Sassoferrato.* Studien zur Europäischen Rechtsgeschichte, Veröff-tentlichungen des Max-Planck-Instituts für europäische Rechtsgeschichte Frankfurt am Main, vol. 158. Frankfurt a.M.: Vittorio Klostermann, 2003.

———. *Von Zweifeln zur Überzeugung: Der Zeugenbeweis im gelehrten Recht ausgehend von der Abhandlung des Bartolus von Sassoferrato.* Studien zur Europäischen Rechts-geschichte, Veröfftentlichungen des Max-Planck-Instituts für europäische Rechts-geschichte Frankfurt am Main, vol. 160. Frankfurt a.M.: Vittorio Klostermann, 2003.

Levack, Brian P. *The Witch-Hunt in Early Modern Europe.* 3rd ed. Harlow: Pearson Long-man, 2006.

———. "The Decline and End of Witchcraft Prosecutions." In Bengt Ankarloo and Stu-art Clark, eds. *Witchcraft and Magic in Europe: The Eighteenth and Nineteenth Centuries,* 1–93. Philadelphia: University of Pennsylvania Press, 1999.

Lévy, Jean-Philippe. *La hiérarchie des preuves dans le droit savant du Moyen-Age depuis la Renaissance du Droit Romain jusqu'à la fin du XIV siècle.* Annales de l'université de Lyon, 3rd ser., Law, no. 5. Paris: Librairie du Recueil Sirey, 1939.

———. "L'evolution de la preuve, des origins a nos jours: Synthèse générale." *Recueils de la Société Jean Bodin pour l'histoire comparative des institutions* XVII (1965), 9–70.

———. "Le problème de la preuve dans les droites savantes du Moyen Age." *Recueils de la Société Jean Bodin pour l'histoire comparative des institutions* XVII (1965), 137–67.

Lloyd, G. E. R. *Demystifying Mentalities.* Cambridge: Cambridge University Press, 1990.

Lorenz, Sönke. *Aktenversendung und Hexenprozess dargestellt am Beispiel der Juristenfakultäten Rostock und Greifswald (1570/82–1630).* 2 vols. Studia Philosophica et Historica, vol. 1. Frankfurt a.M.: Peter Lang, 1982.

———. "David Mevius (1609–1670) und der Hexenprozess: Zur Problematik der Diskussion, wer als Gegner der Hexenverfolgung bezeichnet werden kann." In Hartmut Lehmann and Otto Ulbricht, eds., *Vom Unfug des Hexen-Prozesses: Gegner der Hexenverfolgungen von Johann Weyer bis Friedrich von Spee*, 305–24. Wolfenbütteler Forschungen, vol. 55. Wiesbaden: Otto Harrassowitz, 1992.

———. "Der Hexenprozess." In Sönke Lorenz, ed. *Hexen und Hexenverfolgung im deutschen Südwesten: Aufsatzband*, 67–84. Karlsruhe: Badisches Landesmuseum, 1995.

———. "Die letzten Hexenprozesse in den Spruchakten der Juristenfakultäten: Versuch einer Beschreibung." In Sönke Lorenz and Dieter R. Bauer, eds., *Das Ende der Hexenverfolgung*, 226–47. Hexenforschung, vol. 1. Stuttgart: Franz Steiner, 1995.

———, ed. *Hexen und Hexenverfolgung im deutschen Südwesten.* 2 vols. Volkskundliche Veröffentlichungen des Badischen Landesmuseums Karlsruhe, 2/2. Karlsruhe: Badisches Landesmuseum Karlsruhe, 1994.

———, and Dieter R. Bauer, eds. *Das Ende der Hexenverfolgung.* Hexenforschung. Vol. 1. Stuttgart: Franz Steiner, 1995.

Lüdtke, Alf, ed. *The History of Everyday Life: Reconstructing Historical Experience and Ways of Life.* Translated by William Templer. Princeton, N.J.: Princeton University Press, 1995.

Lund, Eric. "Johann Arndt and the Development of a Lutheran Spiritual Tradition." Ph.D. diss, Yale University, 1979.

MacDonald, Michael, ed. *Witchcraft and Hysteria in Elizabethan London: Edward Jordan and the Mary Glover Case.* London: Tavistock/Routledge, 1991.

Maclean, Ian. *Interpretation and Meaning in the Renaissance: The Case of Law.* Cambridge: Cambridge University Press, 1992.

———. "Evidence, Logic, the Rule, and the Exception in Renaissance Law and Medicine." *Early Science and Medicine* 5 (2000), 227–57.

Mager, Johannes, Günter Meissner, and Wolfgang Orf. *Die Kulturgeschichte der Mühlen.* Leipzig: Edition Leipzig, 1988.

Mährle, Wolfgang. *Academia Norica: Wissenschaft und Bildung an der Nürnberger Hohen Schule in Altdorf (1575–1623).* Contubernium: Tübinger Beiträge zur Universitäts- und Wissenschaftsgeschichte, vol. 54. Stuttgart: Franz Steiner, 2000.

Maleissye, Jean de. *Histoire du poison.* Paris: Éditions François Bourin, 1991.

Mallach, Hans Joachim. *Geschichte der gerichtlichen Medizin im deutschsprachigen Raum.* Lübeck: Schmidt-Römhild, 1996.

Marchand, Suzanne L., Elizabeth Lunbeck, and Josine Blok, eds. *Proof and Persuasion: Essays on Authority, Objectivity, and Evidence.* Turnhout, Belgium: Brepols, 1996.

Martin, John Jeffries. *Myths of Renaissance Individualism.* Houndmills: Palgrave Macmillan, 2004.

Martintz, Dieter, and Karlheinz Lohs. *Poison: Sorcery and Science, Friend and Foe.* Translated by Alistair and Alison Wightman. Leipzig: Edition Leipzig, 1987.

McIntosh, Terence. *Urban Decline in Early Modern Germany: Schwäbisch Hall and Its Region, 1650–1750.* Chapel Hill: University of North Carolina Press, 1997.

Medick, Hans. *Weben und Überleben in Laichingen 1650–1900: Lokalgeschichte als Allgemeine Geschichte.* Veröffentlichungen des Max-Planck-Instituts für Geschichte, vol. 126. Göttingen: Vandenhoeck & Ruprecht, 1996.

Midelfort, H. C. Erik. *Witch Hunting in Southwestern Germany, 1562–1684: The Social and Intellectual Foundations.* Stanford, Calif.: Stanford University Press, 1972.

Mollenauer, Lynn Wood. *Strange Revelations: Magic, Poison, and Sacrilege in Louis XIV's France.* University Park: Pennsylvania State University Press, 2007.

Muchembled, Robert. *Les derniers bûchers: Un village de Flandre et ses sorcières sous Louis XIV.* Paris: Éditions Ramsay, 1981.

———. *Le roi et la sorcière: L'Europe des bûchers (XVe–XVIIIe siècle).* Paris: Desclée, 1993.

———. "The Witches of the Cambresis: The Acculturation of the Rural World in the Sixteenth and Seventeenth Centuries." In James Obelkevich, ed., *Religion and the People, 800–1700,* 221–76. Chapel Hill: University of North Carolina Press, 1979.

Muir, Edward. *Ritual in Early Modern Europe.* 2nd ed. Cambridge: Cambridge University Press, 2005.

Münch, Paul. *Lebensformen in der frühen Neuzeit.* Frankfurt a.M.: Propyläen, 1992.

Neuberger, Max, and Julius Pagel, eds. *Handbuch der Geschichte der Medizin.* 2 vols. Hildesheim: Georg Olms, 1971.

Nowosadtko, Jutta. *Scharfrichter und Abdecker: Der Alltag zweier "unehrlicher Berufe" in der Frühen Neuzeit.* Paderborn: Ferdinand Schöningh, 1994.

———. "Die Ehre, die Unehre und das Staatsinteresse." *Geschichte in Wissenschaft und Unterricht* 44, 6 (1993), 362–81.

Oestmann, Peter. *Rechtsvielfalt vor Gericht: Rechtsanwendung und Partikularrecht im Alten Reich.* Veröffentlichungen des Max-Planck-Instituts für Europäische Rechtsgeschichte Frankfurt am Main, vol. 18. Frankfurt a.M.: Vittorio Klostermann, 2002.

———. "Böse Nachbarn—gute Juristen? Rechtshistorische Anmerkungen zur neueren Hexenforschung." *Zeitschrift für Neuere Rechtsgeschichte* 23 (2001), 254–84.

Ogilvie, Sheilagh, ed. *Germany: A New Social and Economic History,* vol. 2: *1630–1800.* London: Arnold, 1996.

Opitz, Claudia, ed. *Der Hexenstreit: Frauen in der frühneuzeitlichen Hexenverfolung.* Freiburg: Herder, 1995.

Paas, John Roger, ed. *Der Franken Rom: Nürnbergs Blütezeit in der zweiten Hälfte des 17. Jahrhunderts.* Wiesbaden: Otto Harrassowitz, 1995.

Park, Katherine. "The Criminal and the Saintly Body: Autopsy and Dissection in Renaissance Italy." *Renaissance Quarterly* 47, 1 (1994), 1–33.

Parker, Geoffrey. *The Thirty Years' War.* London: Routledge & Kegan Paul, 1984.

Peters, Edward. *Torture.* Expanded ed. Philadelphia: University of Pennsylvania Press, 1996.

Pohl, Herbert. *Hexenglaube und Hexenverfolgung im Kurfürstentum Mainz: Ein Beitrag zur Hexenfrage im 16. und beginnenden 17. Jahrhundert.* Geschichtliche Landeskunde, Veröffentlichungen des Instituts für geschichtliche Landeskunde an der Universität Mainz, vol. 32. Stuttgart: Franz Steiner, 1988.

Pomata, Gianna. *Contracting a Cure: Patients, Healers, and the Law in Early Modern Bologna.* Baltimore: Johns Hopkins University Press, 1998.

Poppen, Enno. *Die Geschichte des Sachverständigenbeweises im Strafprozess des deutschsprachigen Raumes.* Göttinger Studien zur Rechtsgeschichte, vol. 16. Göttingen: Musterschmidt, 1984.

Press, Volker. "Das Haus Hohenlohe in der frühen Neuzeit." In his *Adel im Alten Reich: Gesammelte Vorträge und Aufsätze.* Edited by Franz Brendle and Anton Schindling, 167–88. Tübingen: Bibliotheca Academica, 1998.

———. "Soziale Folgen des Dreissigjährigen Krieges." In Winfried Schulze, ed., *Ständische Gesellschaft und soziale Mobilität.* Schriften des Historischen Kollegs, Kolloquien 12, 239–68. Munich: R. Oldenbourg, 1988.

Purkiss, Diane. *The Witch in History: Early Modern and Twentieth-Century Representations.* London & New York: Routledge, 1996.

Recknagel, Hans. *Die Nürnbergische Universität Altdorf.* Altdorf: Nürnberger Versicherungsgruppe, 1993.

Recktenwald, Horst Claus, ed. *Gelehrte der Universität Altdorf.* Nuremberg: Lorenz Spindler, 1966.

Reddy, William M. "The Logic of Action: Indeterminancy, Emotion, and Historical Narrative." *History and Theory* 40, no. 4 (2001), 10–33.

Renzi, Silvia de. "Witnesses of the Body: Medico-Legal Cases in Seventeenth-Century Rome." *Studies in History and Philosophy of Science* 33 (2002), 219–42.

Richardson, L. Deer. "The Generation of Disease: Occult Causes and Diseases of the Total Substance." In A. Wear, R. K. French, and I. M. Lonie, eds., *The Medical Renaissance of the Sixteenth Century,* 175–94. Cambridge: Cambridge University Press, 1985.

Ridder-Symoens, Hilde de, ed. *Universities in Early Modern Europe, 1500–1800.* A History of the University in Europe, vol. 2. Cambridge: Cambridge University Press, 1996.

Robisheaux, Thomas. *Rural Society and the Search for Order in Early Modern Germany.* Cambridge: Cambridge University Press, 1989.

———. "Peasant Unrest and the Moral Economy in the German Southwest, 1560–1620." *Archiv für Reformationsgeschichte* 77 (1987), 174–86.

———. "'The Queen of Evidence': The Witchcraft Confession in the Age of Confessionalism." In John Headley and Hans Hillerbrand, eds., *Confessionalization in Europe, 1550–1700: Essays in Honor and Memory of Bodo Nischan,* 175–206. Aldershot: Ashgate, 2004.

Roeck, Bernd. "Christlicher Idealstaat und Hexenwahn: Zum Ende der europäischen Hexenverfolgung." *Historisches Jahrbuch* 108 (1988), 379–405.

———. "Wahrnehmungsgeschichtliche Aspekte des Hexenwahns—Ein Versuch." *Historisches Jahrbuch* 112 (1992), 72–103.

Roper, Lyndal. *Oedipus and the Devil: Witchcraft, Sexuality, and Religion in Early Modern Europe.* London: Routledge, 1994.

———. *Witch Craze: Terror and Fantasy in Baroque Germany.* New Haven, Conn.: Yale University Press, 2004.

———. " 'Evil Imaginings and Fantasies': Child-Witches and the End of the Witch Craze." *Past and Present,* no. 167 (2000), 107–39.

Rowlands, Alison. *Witchcraft Narratives in Germany: Rothenburg, 1561–1652.* Manchester and New York: Manchester University Press, 2003.

———. "Witchcraft and Old Women in Early Modern Germany." *Past and Present,* no. 173 (2001), 50–89.

———, and Rita Voltmer. "The Persecution of Witches and the Practice of Lordship. ('Hexenverfolgung und Herrschaftspraxis'): Wittlich, Germany, 11–13 October 2001." *German History* 20, no. 2 (2002): 221–24.

Rublack, Hans-Christoph. "Lutherische Beichte und Sozialdisziplinierung." *Archiv für Reformationsgeschichte* 84 (1993), 127–55.

———. " 'Der wohlgeplagte Priester': Vom Selbstverständnis lutherischer Geistlichkeit im Zeitalter der Orthodoxie." *Zeitschrift für historische Forschung* 16, no. 1 (1989), 1–30.

———. "Zur Problemlage der Forschung zur lutherischen Orthodoxie in Deutschland." In Hans-Christoph Rublack, ed., *Die lutherische Konfessionalisierung in Deutschland: Wissenschaftliches Symposium des Vereins für Reformationsgeschichte,* 13–32. Schriften des Vereins für Reformationsgeschichte, vol. 197. Bonn: Gerd Mohn, 1992.

Rublack, Ulinka. *The Crimes of Women in Early Modern Germany.* Oxford: Oxford University Press, 1999.

———, ed. *Gender in Early Modern Germany.* New York: Cambridge University Press, 2002.

———. "Körper, Geschlecht und Gefühl in der Frühen Neuzeit." *Historische Zeitschrift* (2001), 99–105.

———. "Pregnancy, Childbirth, and the Female Body in Early Modern Germany." *Past and Present,* no. 150 (1996), 84–110.

Ruggiero, Guido. *Binding Passions: Tales of Magic, Marriage, and Power at the End of the Renaissance.* New York: Oxford University Press, 1993.

———. "The Strange Death of Margarita Marcellini: Male, Signs, and the Everyday World of Pre-Modern Medicine." *American Historical Review* 106, no. 4 (2001), 1141–58.

Rummel, Walter. *Bauern, Herren und Hexen: Studien zur Sozialgeschichtliche sponheimischer und kurtrierischer Hexenprozesse, 1574–1664.* Kritische Studien zur Geschichtswissenschaft, vol. 94. Göttingen: Vandenhoeck & Ruprecht, 1991.

———. " 'Der Krieg Gegen Die Hexen'—Ein Krieg fanatischer Kirchenfürsten oder ein Angebot zur Realisierung Sozialer Chancen? Sozialgeschichtliche Anmerkungen zu zwei neuen Büchern." *Rheinische Vierteljahresblätter* 56 (1992), 311–24.

———. "Das 'Ungestüme Umherlaufen' der Untertanen: Zum Verhältnis von Religiöser Ideologie, Sozialem Interesse und Staatsräson in den Hexenverfolgungen im Rheinland." *Rheinische Vierteljahresblätter* 67 (2003), 121–61.

Sabean, David. *Power in the Blood: Popular Culture and Village Discourse in Early Modern Germany*. Cambridge: Cambridge University Press, 1984.

———. "Peasant Voices and Bureaucratic Texts: Narrative Structure in Early Modern Protocols." In Peter Becker and William Clark, *Little Tools of Knowledge: Historical Essays on Academic and Bureaucratic Practices*, 67–93. Ann Arbor: University of Michigan Press, 2001.

———. "The Production of Self During the Age of Confessionalism." *Central European History* 29 (1998), 1–18.

———. "Selbsterkundung: Beichte und Abendmahl." In Richard van Dülmen, ed., *Entdeckung des Ich: Die Geschichte der Individualisierung vom Mittelalter bis zur Gegenwart*, 148–62. Cologne: Böhlau, 2001.

Sander, Sabine. *Handwerkschirurgen: Sozialgeschichte einer verdrängten Berufsgruppe*. Kritische Studien zur Geschichtswissenschaft, vol. 83. Göttingen: Vandenoeck & Ruprecht, 1989.

Sawday, Jonathan. *The Body Emblazoned: Dissection and the Human Body in Renaissance Culture*. London: Routledge, 1995.

Schilling, Heinz. *Religion, Political Culture, and the Emergence of Early Modern Society*. Studies in Medieval and Reformation Thought, vol. 50. Leiden: E. J. Brill, 1992.

———. " 'History of Crime' or 'History of Sin'? Some Reflections on the Social History of Early Modern Church Discipline." In E. I. Kouri and Tom Scott, eds., *Politics and Society in Reformation Europe: Essays for Sir Geoffrey Elton on his Sixty-Fifth Birthday*, 289–311. Houndmills: Macmillan, 1987.

Schindler, Norbert. *Rebellion, Community, and Custom in Early Modern Germany*. Translated by Pamela E. Selwyn. Cambridge: Cambridge University Press, 2002.

Schindling, Anton. *Bildung und Wissenschaft in der frühen Neuzeit, 1650–1800*. Enzyklopädie deutscher Geschichte, vol. 30. Munich: R. Oldenbourg, 1994.

Schlauch, Rudolf. *Hohenlohe Franken: Landschaft, Geschichte, Kultur, Kunst*. Nuremberg: Glock & Lutz, 1964.

Schlögl, Rudolf. *Bauern, Krieg und Staat: Oberbayerische Bauernwirtschaft und frühmoderner Staat im 17. Jahrhundert*. Veröffentlichungen des Max-Planck-Instituts für Geschichte, vol. 89. Göttingen: Vandenhoeck & Ruprecht, 1988.

Schlosser, Hans, Rolf Sprandel, and Dieter Willoweit, eds. *Herrschaftliches Strafen seit dem Hochmittelalter: Formen und Entwicklungsstufen*. Konflikt, Verbrechen und Sanktion in der Gesellschaft Alteuropas Symposien und Synthese, vol. 5. Vienna: Böhlau, 2002.

Schlumbohm, Jürgen et al., eds. *Mikrogeschichte, Makrogeschichte: komplementär oder inkommensurabel?* Göttingen: Wallstein Verlag, 1998.

Schmale, Wolfgang. "Das 17. Jahrhundert und die neuere europäische Geschichte." *Historische Zeitschrift* 264, no. 3 (1997), 587–612.

Schmidt, Burghart, and Katrin Moeller, eds. *Realität und Mythos: Hexenverfolgung und Rezeptionsgeschichte*. Veröffentlichungen des Arbeitskreises für historische Hexen- und Kriminalitätsforschung in Norddeutschland, vol. 1. Hamburg: DOBU, 2003.

Schmidt, Jürgen Michael. *Glaube und Skepsis: Die Kurpfalz und die abendländische Hexenverfolgung 1446–1685*. Hexenforschung, vol. 5. Bielefeld: Verlag für Regionalgeschichte, 2000.

Schoch, Norbert. *Die Wiedereinführung und Ausübung des öffentlichen römisch-katholischen Gottesdienstes in der Grafschaft Hohenlohe-Waldenburg im 17. und 18. Jahrhundert verglichen mit den Bestimmungen des Westfälischen Friedens und der hohenlohischen Hausverträge.* Diss., Tübingen University, 1958.

———. "Eine Gegenreformation in Hohenlohe." *Württembergisch Franken* 50, N.F. 40 (1966), 304–33.

Scholtz Williams, Gerhild. *Defining Dominion: The Discourses of Magic and Witchcraft in Early Modern France and Germany.* Ann Arbor: University of Michigan Press, 1995.

———. *Ways of Knowing in Early Modern Germany: Johannes Praetorius as a Witness to His Time.* Aldershot: Ashgate, 2006.

Schorn-Schütte, Luise. *Evangelische Geistlichkeit in der Frühneuzeit: Deren Anteil an der Entfaltung frühmoderner Staatlichkeit und Gesellschaft dargestellt am Beispiel des Fürstentums Braunschweig-Wolfenbüttel, der Landschaft Hessen-Kassel und der Stadt Braunschweig.* Quellen und Forschungen zur Reformationsgeschichte, vol. 62. Gütersloh: Gütersloher Hausverlag, 1996.

———. "Prediger an Protestantischen Höfen der Frühneuzeit: Zur politischen und sozialen Stellung einer neuen bürgerlichen Führungsgruppe in der höfischen Gesellschaft des 17. Jahrhunderts, dargestellt am Beispiel von Hessen-Kassel, Hessen-Darmstadt und Braunschweig-Wolfenbüttel." In Heinz Schilling and Herman Diederiks, eds., *Bürgerliche Eliten in den Niederlanden und in Nordwestdeutschland: Studien zur Sozialgeschichte des europäischen Bürgertums im Mittelalter und in der Neuzeit,* 275–336. Städteforschung, Reihe A, Darstellungen, vol. 23. Cologne: Böhlau, 1985.

Schraut, Elisabeth. "Fürstentum Hohenlohe." In Sönke Lorenz, ed. *Hexen und Hexenverfolgung im deutschen Südwesten,* 275–80. Volkskundliche Veröffentlichungen des Badischen Landesmuseums Karlsruhe, vol. 2/2. Karlsruhe: Badisches Landesmuseum Karlsruhe, 1994.

Schröder, Richard, and Eberhard Frieherr von Kunssberg. *Deutsches Rechtswörterbuch.* Weimar: Herman Böhlaus Nachfolger, 1914–32.

Schulte, Rolf. *Hexenmeister: Die Verfolgung von Männern im Rahmen der Hexenverfolgung von 1530–1730 im Alten Reich.* Kieler Werkstücke, Reihe G: Beiträge zur Frühen Neuzeit, vol. 1. Frankfurt a.M.: Peter Lang, 2000.

Schulze, Winfried. "Herrschaft und Widerstand in der Sicht des 'gemeinen Mannes' im 16./17. Jahrhundert." In Hans Mommsen and Winfried Schulze, eds. *Vom Elend der Handarbeit,* 182–98. Stuttgart: Klett-Cotta, 1981.

———. "Vom Gemeinnutz zum Eigennutz: Über den Normenwandel in der ständischen Gesellschaft der frühen Neuzeit." *Historische Zeitschrift* 243 (1986), 591–622.

Schwerhoff, Gerd. "Justiz-Erfahrungen: Einige Einleitende Gedanken." *Historische Zeitschrift* (2001), 341–48.

———. "Rationalität in Wahn: Zum Gelehrten Diskurs über die Hexen der frühen Neuzeit." *Saeculum* 37 (1986), 45–82.

———. "Vom Alltagsverdacht zur Massenverfolgung: Neuere deutsche Forschungen zum frühneuzeitlichen Hexenwesen." *Geschichte in Wissenschaft und Unterricht* 46 (1995), 359–80.

Scribner, Robert. "Cosmic Order and Daily Life: Sacred and Secular in Pre-Industrial German Society." In Kaspar von Greyerz, ed., *Religion and Society in Early Modern Europe, 1500–1800*, 17–33. London: George Allen & Unwin, 1984.

———, ed. *Germany: A New Social and Economic History, 1450–1630*. London: Arnold, 1996.

Shapin, Steven. *A Social History of Truth: Civility and Science in Seventeenth-Century England.* Chicago: University of Chicago Press, 1994.

Sharpe, James. *Instruments of Darkness: Witchcraft in England, 1550–1750.* London: Hamish Hamilton, 1996.

Sillert, Wolfgang. "Benedict Carpzov—Ein fanatischer Strafjurist und Hexenverfolger?" In Hartmut Lehmann and Otto Ulbricht, eds., *Vom Unfug des Hexen-Prozesses: Gegner der Hexenverfolgungen von Johann Weyer bis Friedrich von Spee*, 325–40. Wolfenbütteler Forschungen, vol. 55, Wiesbaden: Otto Harrassowitz, 1992.

Siraisi, Nancy G. *Medieval and Early Renaissance Medicine: An Introduction to Knowledge and Practice.* Chicago: University of Chicago Press, 1990.

Smith, William Bradford. "Friedrich Förner, the Catholic Reformation, and Witch-Hunting in Bamberg" *Sixteenth Century Journal* 36, 1 (2005), 115–28.

Stephens, Walter. *Demon Lovers: Witchcraft, Sex, and the Crisis of Belief.* Chicago: University of Chicago Press, 2002.

Stewart, Pamela J., and Andrew Strathern, eds. *Witchcraft, Sorcery, Rumors, and Gossip.* Cambridge: Cambridge University Press, 2004.

Stintzing, Rudolf. *Geschichte der deutschen Rechtswissenschaft.* 2 vols. Munich: R. Oldenbourg, 1880–84.

Stolleis, Michael. *Geschichte des öffentlichen Rechts in Deutschland*, vol. 1: *Reichspublizistik und Policeywissenschaft 1600–1800.* Munich: C. H. Beck, 1988.

———. "*Condere leges et interpretari*: Gesetzgebungsmacht und Staatsbildung im 17. Jahrhundert." *Zeitschrift der Savigny-Stiftung für Rechtsgeschichte, Kanonische Abteilung* 101 (1984), 89–116.

———. "Grundzüge der Beamtenethik (1550–1650)." In Roman Schnur, ed., *Die Rolle der Juristen bei der Entstehung des modernen Staates*, 273–302. Berlin: Duncker & Humblot, 1986.

———. "Textor und Pufendorf über die Ratio Status Imperii im Jahr 1667." In Roman Schnur, ed. *Staatsräson: Studien zur Geschichte eines politischen Begriffs*, 441–63. Berlin: Duncker & Humblot, 1975.

Strauss, Gerald. *Law, Resistance, and the State: The Opposition to Roman Law in Reformation Germany.* Princeton, N.J.: Princeton University Press, 1986.

Ströhmer, Michael. *Von Hexen, Ratsherren und Juristen: Die Rezeption der peinlichen Halsgerichtsordnung Kaiser Karls V. in den frühen Hexenprozessen der Hansestadt Lemgo, 1583–1621.* Studien und Quellen zur Westfälischen Geschichte, vol. 43. Paderborn: Bonifatius, 2002.

Stuart, Kathy Stuart. *Defiled Trades and Social Outcasts: Honor and Ritual Pollution in Early Modern Germany.* Cambridge: Cambridge University Press, 1999.

Taddey, Gerhard. "Neue Forschungen zur Baugeschichte von Schloss Langenburg." *Württembergisch Franken* (1979), 13–46.

Telle, Joachim, ed. *Pharmazie und der gemeine Mann: Hausarznei und Apotheke in deutschen Schriften der frühen Neuzeit: Ausstellung der Herzog August Bibliothek Wolfenbüttel in der Halle des Zeughauses vom 23. August 1982 bis März 1983.* Wolfenbüttel: Herzog August Bibliothek, 1982.

Theibault, John. *German Villages in Crisis: Rural Life in Hesse-Kassel and the Thirty Years War, 1580–1720.* Atlantic Highlands, N.J.: Humanities Press, 1995.

Thumm, Gustav Adolf. *Die bäuerlichen und dörflichen Rechtsverhältnisse des Fürstentums Hohenlohe im 17. und 18. Jahrhundert.* Forschungen aus Württembergisch Franken, vol. 6. Benningen/N.: Neckar Druck & Verlagsgesellschaft, 1970.

Tlusty, Ann. *Bacchus and the Civic Order: The Culture of Drink in Early Modern Germany.* Charlottesville: University of Virginia Press, 2001.

Trunz, Erich. *Johann Mattäus Meyfart: Theologe und Schriftsteller in der Zeit des Dreissigjährigen Krieges.* Munich: C. H. Beck, 1987.

Trusen, Winfried. "Rechtliche Grundlagen der Hexenprozesse und ihrer Beendigung." In Sönke Lorenz and Dieter R. Bauer, eds., *Das Ende der Hexenverfolgung, Hexenforschung,* vol. 1, 203–26. Stuttgart: Franz Steiner, 1995.

———. "Strafprozess und Rezeption: Zu den Entwicklungen im Spätmittelalter und den Grundlagen der Carolina." In Peter Landau and Friedrich-Christian Schroeder, eds., *Strafrecht, Strafprozess und Rezeption: Grundlagen, Entwicklung und Wirkung der Constitutio Criminalis Carolina,* 29–118. Juristische Abhandlungen, vol. 19. Frankfurt a.M.: Vittorio Klostermann, 1984.

Tschaikner, Manfred. *Damit das Böse Ausgerottet Werde: Hexenverfolgungen in Vorarlberg im 16. und 17. Jahrhundert.* Studien zur Geschichte und Gesellschaft Vorarlberg, vol. 11. Bregenz: Vorarlberger Autoren Gesellschaft, 1992.

———. *Hexenverfolgungen in Hohenems: Einschliesslich des Reichshofs Lustenau, sowie der Österreichischen Herrschaften Feldkirch und Neuburg unter Hohenemsischen Pfandherren und Vögten.* Forschungen Zur Geschichte Vorarlbergs, Bd. 5 (N.F.). Constance: UVK Verlagsgesellschaft, 2004.

———. *Magie und Hexerei im südlichen Vorarlberg zu Beginn der Neuzeit.* Constance: UVK, Universitätsverlag Konstanz, 1997.

Turner, Victor. "Social Dramas and Ritual Metaphors." In Victor Turner, *Dramas, Fields, and Metaphors: Symbolic Action in Human Society,* 23–59. Ithaca, N.Y.: Cornell University Press, 1974.

———. "Social Dramas and Stories About Them." In W. J. T. Mitchell, ed. *On Narrative,* 137–64. Chicago: University of Chicago Press, 1981.

Ulbrich, Claudia. *Shulamit und Margarete: Macht, Geschlecht und Religion in einer ländlichen Gesellschaft des 18ten Jahrhunderts.* Vienna: Böhlau, 1999.

Ulbricht, Otto, ed. *Von Huren und Rabenmütter: Weibliche Kriminalität in der frühen Neuzeit.* Cologne: Böhlau, 1995.

Valletta, Frederick. *Witchcraft, Magic, and Superstition in England, 1640–70.* Aldershot: Ashgate, 2000.

Vierhaus, Rudolf. *Germany in the Age of Absolutism, 1648–1743*. Translated by Jonathan B. Knudsen. Cambridge: Cambridge University Press, 1988.

———. *Staaten und Stände: Vom Westfälischen bis zum Hubertusburger Frieden 1648 bis 1763*. Propyläen Geschichte Deutschlands, vol. 5. Berlin: Propyläen, 1984.

Wallmann, Johannes. *Philipp Jakob Spener und die Anfänge des Pietismus*. Tübingen: J. C. B. Mohr, 1970.

———. "Reflexionen und Bemerkungen zur Frömmigkeitskrise des 17. Jahrhunderts." In Manfred Jakubowski-Tiessen, ed., *Krisen des 17. Jahrhunderts: Interdisziplinäre Perspektiven*, 25–42. Göttingen: Vandenhoeck & Ruprecht, 1999.

Walz, Rainer. *Hexenglaube und magische Kommunkation im Dorf der Frühen Neuzeit: Die Verfolgungen in der Grafschaft Lippe*. Westfälisches Institut für Regionalgeschichte, Landschaftsverband Westfalen-Lippe, Forschungen zur Regionalgeschichte, vol. 9. Paderborn: Ferdinand Schöningh, 1993.

———. "Schimpfende Weiber: Frauen in lippischen Beleidigungsprozessen des 17. Jahrhunderts." In Heide Wunder and Christina Vanja, eds., *Weiber, Menscher, Frauenzimmer: Frauen in der ländlichen Gesellschaft 1500–1800*, 175–98. Göttingen: Vandenhoeck & Ruprecht, 1996.

Wear, Andrew. "Medicine in Early Modern Europe." In Lawrence I. Conrad et al., eds., *The Western Medical Tradition, 800 B.C. to 1800 A.D.*, 215–361. Cambridge: Cambridge University Press, 1995.

Weber-Kellermann, Ingeborg. *Saure Wochen, Frohe Feste: Fest und Alltag in der Sprache der Bräuche*. Munich: C. J. Bucher, 1985.

Wieacker, Franz. *A History of Private Law in Europe with Particular Reference to Germany*. Translated by Tony Weir. Oxford: Oxford University Press, 1995.

Wiesner, Merry. *Working Women in Renaissance Germany*. New Brunswick, N.J.: Rutgers University Press, 1986.

Wilbertz, Gisela, Gerd Schwerhoff, and Jürgen Scheffler, eds. *Hexenverfolgung und Regionalgeschichte: Die Grafschaft Lippe im Vergleich*. Studien zur Regionalgeshichte, vol. 4. Beiträge zur Geschichte der Stadt Lemgo, vol. 4. Bielefeld: Verlag für Regionalgeschichte, 1994.

Willis, Deborah. *Malevolent Nurture: Witch-Hunting and Maternal Power in Early Modern England*. Ithaca, N.Y.: Cornell University Press, 1995.

Willoweit, Dieter. *Rechtsgrundlagen der Territorialgewalt: Landesobrigkeit und Territorium in der Rechtswissenschaft der Neuzeit*. Cologne: Böhlau, 1975.

Wiltenburg, Joy. *Disorderly Women and Female Power in the Street Literature of Early Modern England and Germany*. Charlottesville: University of Virginia Press, 1992.

———. "The Carolina and the Culture of the Common Man: Revisiting the Imperial Penal Code of 1532." *Renaissance Quarterly* 53, no. 3 (2000), 713–34.

Wunder, Bernd. "Die Sozialstruktur der Geheimratskollegien in den süddeutschen protestantischen Fürstentümern (1660–1720): Zum Verhältnis von sozialer Mobilität und Briefadel im Absolutismus." *Vierteljahrschrift für Sozial- und Wirtschaftsgeschichte* 58 (1971), 145–220.

Wunder, Heide. *"Er ist die Sonn', sie ist der Mond": Frauen in der Frühen Neuzeit.* Munich: C. H. Beck, 1992.

————, and Christina Vanja, eds. *Weiber, Menscher, Frauenzimmer: Frauen in der ländlichen Gesellschaft 1500–1800.* Göttingen: Vandenhoeck & Ruprecht, 1996.

Zeller, Winfried. *Der Protestantismus des 17. Jahrhunderts.* Klassiker des Protestantismus, vol. 5. Bremen: Carl Schünemann, 1962.

Zunkel, Friedrich. "Ehre, Reputation." In Otto Brunner, Werner Conze, and Reinhart Koselleck, eds., *Geschichtliche Grundbegriffe: Historisches Lexikon zur politisch-sozialen Sprache in Deutschland,* vol. 2, 1–65. Stuttgart: Ernst Klett, 1975.

Illustration Credits

page 114

Enlargement of an eighteenth-century sketch of Langenburg and its environs by an unknown artist. Reproduced with permission of Hohenlohe-Zentralarchiv Neuenstein.

page 123

Illustration to a seventeenth-century German broadsheet.

page 138

Matthias Merian the Elder (1622).

page 144

Illustration to a seventeenth-century German broadsheet (1634).

page 176

Illustration to a seventeenth-century German broadsheet.

page 189

Illustration to Johann Dilherr, *Augen- und Herzens-Lust* (Nuremberg: Johann Endter, 1661). Reproduced with permission of Rare Book, Manuscript, and Special Collections Library, Duke University, Durham, North Carolina.

page 236

Woodcut illustration to Matthias Merian and Martin Zeiller, *Topographia Germaniae*, vol. 8: *Franken* (Frankfurt a.M., 1656).

page 238

Illustration reproduced with permission of the Herzog August Bibliothek Wolfenbüttel.

page 239

Illustration to J. G. Puschner, *Amoenitates Altdorfinae oder Eigenliche nach dem Leben gezeichnete Prospecten der Löblichen Nürnbergischen Universität Altdorf* (Nürnberg: Wolfgang Michahelles, 1710). Reproduced with permission of the Universitätsbibliothek Erlangen, Handschriftenabteilung.

page 247

Illustration to J. G. Puschner, *Amoenitates Altdorfinae oder Eigenliche nach dem Leben gezeichnete Prospecten der Löblichen Nürnbergischen Universität Altdorf* (Nürnberg: Wolfgang Michahelles, 1710). Reproduced with permission of the Universitätsbibliothek Erlangen, Handschriftenabteilung.

page 249

Illustration reproduced with permission of the Herzog August Bibliothek Wolfenbüttel.

page 256

Hohenlohe-Zentralarchiv Neuenstein, ALGAL 529/85, September 2, 1672. Copy of original Altdorf medical opinion issued July 2, 1672. Reproduced with permission of the Hohenlohe-Zentralarchiv Neuenstein.

page 280

Jacques de Geyn II, *Study of Three Hags.*

page 296

Illustration to Johann Praetorius, *Blockes-Berges Verrichtung* (Leipzig: Johann Scheiben, 1668). Reproduced with permission of Rare Book, Manuscript, and Special Collections Library, Duke University, Durham, North Carolina.

page 300

Hohenlohe-Zentralarchiv Neuenstein, ALGAL 529/122, November 4, 1672. Reproduced with permission of the Hohenlohe-Zentralarchiv Neuenstein.

Index

Italicized numbers refer to illustrations and maps.
Page numbers beginning with 339 refer to notes.